MODERN BUFFET PRESENTATION

MODERN BUFFET PRESENTATION

Carol Murphy Clyne & Vincent Clyne

Photography by Francesco Tonelli

THE CULINARY INSTITUTE OF AMERICA®

WILEY

The Culinary Institute of America

President	Dr. Tim Ryan '77, CMC
Provost	Mark Erickson '77, CMC
Director of Publishing	Nathalie Fischer
Senior Editorial Project Manager	Margaret Wheeler '00
Editorial Assistants	Erin Jeanne McDowell '08
	Laura Monroe '12

Published by John Wiley & Sons, Inc., Hoboken, New Jersey
Published simultaneously in Canada

LIBRARY OF CONGRESS CATALOGING-IN-PUBLICATION DATA:

Clyne, Carol Murphy.
  Modern buffet presentation / Carol Murphy Clyne and Vincent Clyne ; photography by Francesco Tonelli.
    p. cm.
  Includes index.
  ISBN 978-0-470-58784-3 (cloth)
  1. Buffets (Cooking) 2. Food presentation. I. Clyne, Vincent. II. Title. III. Culinary Institute of America
  TX738.5.C56 2014
  642--dc23
                    2012017361
Printed in the United States of America
10 9 8 7 6 5 4 3 2 1

Food styling by Janet Denson and Robin Early
Cover design by Wendy Lai
Interior design by Vertigo Design NYC

CONTENTS

RECIPE CONTENTS

CHAPTER 9 BREAD, BRUNCH, AND DESSERT   258

CHAPTER 10 SAUCES, DRESSINGS, AND CONDIMENTS   310

PREFACE

The Line on Buffets

What we know, or rather think we know, about the buffet line is wrong. That's right, wrong. We're all familiar with the come-ons that lure us to the casino banquet, the barbecue or chili cook-off, or the cruise's midnight buffet. The spectacular show off with linens and fine china, while others offer only paper and plastic, but all offer huge quantities of food, platters heaped high with choice after choice after choice. There's something for everyone. Ultimately, however, they all present the same one-dimensional view of plenty, the perception of lackluster and lesser-quality food despite the glitz of ice carvings or lavish floral arrangements or limitless platefuls of more. The quality-versus-quantity dilemma leads us to perceive this as less than fair fare.

So how willing are we to be satisfied by "more" of "less"? Actually, we aren't, and that's why the very notion of the buffet has changed so greatly over the past decade. Where there was once only the inexpensive all-you-can-eat buffet, we now find originality and creativity directly stemming from the fact that our world of food is an increasingly smaller place. Cutting-edge techniques and ingredients formerly considered exotic, from Spain and Japan, Asia, Africa, and South America, are found now not only on buffets at hotels and casinos but also at mom-and-pop caterers on Main Street and at church socials and corporate cafeterias.

Once this trickle-down influence has hit the hometown heart of America, it's safe to say that the age-old and tired buffet line is history. In its stead, we find the contemporary buffet illustrative of ethnic ingredients and old-world ways made new. Such an au courant approach highlights not only special ingredients and methods but also up-to-date presentation principles reflective of recent advances in equipment and technology.

Modern Buffet Presentation presents a complete business plan built around the modern buffet for chefs, caterers, and event planners. From planning to execution, from prep to production, from setup to cleanup, methods are thoroughly explained and readily tailored to any event according to size, site, and season. **Chapter 1: Mise en Place** outlines all of the details you need to know to prepare for the execution of the buffet, from the client meeting to developing the concept and theme to making the production plan. **Chapter 2: Designing the Buffet** provides thorough instructions and illustrations for designing the buffet in a way that will exceed the customers' expectations every time. **Chapter 3: Buffet Stations: Equipment, Service, and Setup** describes the different types of stations that can be incorporated into the buffet, including a comprehensive section on action stations with instructions for physically setting up the buffet. **Chapter 4: Executing the Buffet** is full of practical information about executing all different types of buffets, including portioning information and examples of platter arrangement. **Chapters 5 through 10** provide recipes for dishes that can be held at temperature and that are suitable for intimate dinners or large parties while being budget sensitive. Skills and techniques are described in detail, with attention given to the safe handling and holding of foods; the balancing of flavors, colors, and textures; and the designing of displays that excite and entice. **Chapters 1 through 4** illuminate the actual steps in planning an event: the initial meeting with the client, menu development and ingredient selection, budgeting and staffing, designing and displaying, and the "how to wow."

Background Check

Here's an amuse-gueule, if you will, a little history to ponder. First, let's agree that "banquet" and "buffet" are nearly synonymous for our application here, and realize that the manner of presentation and the goods presented obviously vary according to price. And price point, per-person cost, and profitability are the underlying factors to consider.

Before all this gives you that glazed-over look, think about this: The buffet has been around for a long time. It's often mentioned that it originated in Las Vegas after World War II, when hotels and casinos were under construction. They needed to lure customers to the gaming tables, and by luring them with all-you-can-eat buffets, a trend was started. While this bit of lore is true enough, the buffet as we know it began long before, in late sixteenth-century France, where serving yourself from an elaborate sideboard was popular. The French word *buffet* refers not only to the presentation of food but also to the actual piece of furniture upon which it is presented. Many of us have learned from Grandma about sideboards and buffets and servers and how to lay out the foods for holidays and family get-togethers. While not as grandiose as those French country manors or contemporary casino-hotels, the home buffet offers a complete micro-view, our first encounter with the buffet.

The view that remains peculiarly American, though, is the one of repeated trips to the land of bountiful. Unlimited choices with unlimited amounts is still an all-American institution, but with a broadened appeal. By incorporating international influences once found only in ethnic enclaves, the foods featured on buffets are a tribute to the melting pot that is America, spanning the world of flavor from sushi to spaghetti, from vindaloo to vol-au-vent, from *jiaozi* to Jamaican jerk, and from tacos and tapas to turkey and trimmings. What remains clear, then, is that we must fully comprehend the fundamentals in order to keep the consumers coming and to ensure the viability of the bottom line.

Perception Is Paramount

The contemporary buffet is something to be proud of and to be involved with. It is interactive and all-encompassing, inclusive of you and your guest, the chef and the client, the server and the diner. In an age of interactive technology, feeding large groups of people while considering time constraints and budgetary concerns remains a primary duty of the new culinary professional. When we, as leaders in the culinary field, maintain a fresh approach to these concepts, we will certainly find ample room for our own creativity to shine through. After all, isn't that what draws us into the kitchen to begin with?

We will outline in the following chapters a systematic method of exploration: the who, what, when, where, how, and why. This information will become the cornerstone of successful banquet presentation and will carry over into other kitchen and managerial duties.

THE WHO: Chef and client. The chef must meld what is expected by the client and what is possible from the kitchen. The chef must formulate a menu offering the client's choices while maintaining the budget. Miscommunication is the enemy here, as clarity simplifies the task at hand.

THE WHAT: Concept and theme. This foundation must be identified in order for all menu development to proceed. The menu should reflect the theme in every aspect.

THE WHEN: Scheduling. This refers not just to the actual date and time of the event but also to the months and weeks of planning that will make the affair run seamlessly. Here the chef's duties include all food ordering, with attention to timely receiving and inventory of raw materials, estimates of food preparation times and staff requirements, scheduling of kitchen and wait staff, and probable layouts and displays.

THE WHERE: Location. It is obvious that the chef knows where the buffet is to be held and understands the limits of the kitchen and facility. But there are occasions when off-site galas are expected, and the chef must be prepared for the unexpected. The sign of a truly knowledgeable chef is the manner in which disaster is averted and success achieved.

THE HOW: Quality. In the hands of a skilled chef, every event appears to go off without a hitch; what happens behind the scenes ensures this. These essential steps of complete planning allow every banquet to reflect the needs of all guests while maintaining a high standard of quality, regardless of budget.

THE WHY: Success. Meeting and exceeding the expectations of the client is the ultimate measure. This, coupled with the bottom line, signifies success for the chef. As we all understand, profitability is the goal, and in each aspect of the chef's craft, cost of production is the key factor. When a balance is reached, costs are minimized and profitability is maximized.

By being creative, staying current with trends, and implementing service and foods accordingly, the chef will meet and exceed the client's expectations. Since the customer's experience is only as good as the last meal served, only as good as the wait staff serving, and only as good as the taste left in guests' mouths at the end of the event, it's imperative that we offer only our best.

In so doing, the customer leaves elated, repeat business is encouraged, and profitability is promoted. In all these respects, the buffet is a model representing all the training, all the learning, all the performing, all the planning that a chef's career entails. The buffet, then, carries a lot more weight than we might previously have thought.

Resources

Modern Buffet Presentation offers an *Instructor's Manual,* including a Test Bank to help instructors who are designing courses based around healthy menu items.

A password-protected Wiley Instructor Book Companion Web site (www.wiley. com/college/CIA) provides access to the online *Instructor's Manual* and the text-specific teaching resources. The PowerPoint lecture slides are also available for download on the Web site.

ACKNOWLEDGMENTS

How do we thank people who have been such a large part of our journey to get this project finished? We need to express our gratitude and heartfelt appreciation to all of you who have stuck by us while we have tested recipes and tasted too much. You have provided more support than you realize, and we feel forever indebted to you for this generosity of spirit and concern for our well-being. So to family and friends, we say from the bottom of our hearts and the tips of our taste buds, thank you, *gracias, xie xie.*

The first thank-you goes to our daughters, Carrie and Emily, who make us especially proud to be parents. You have supported us even when you knew we were not cooking anything special for you, because it was always the catering business or the classes we were teaching or the buffet book or PAIRINGS that came first. Well, truth be told, you are first in our hearts and minds, always. To our sister Janice Murphy Warner—friend, mentor, travel companion, and confidante—we could not have done it without your generous and loving support. To our parents, Marie and Jack Clyne and Esther Murphy, and Grandma Dorothea Sanguiliano, a love-filled thank-you for getting us started and helping us carry on, and for all those unwritten recipes and for watching over all of us always as true guardian angels. Thank you to Aunts Rita Freer and Flo Root for your love and support, to Mary Ellen Clyne for your inspiration, to Nigel Fung-A-Fat for working side by side with us to get a new catering business off the ground all those years ago, and to our other brothers and sisters, nieces and nephews.

To Nathalie Fischer of The Culinary Institute of America, thank you for this opportunity. And thank you to our CIA editorial project manager, Maggie Wheeler, for your constant professional advice, solid guidance, and diligent work with the photos and manuscript, and also to Erin McDowell and Laura Monroe. Thank you to John Wiley & Sons, especially JoAnna Turtletaub, Pam Chirls, Julie Kerr, and Valerie Cimino. Thank you, Francesco Tonelli; we are honored to have worked with such a brilliant food photographer.

To the chefs of The Culinary Institute of America, who reinvigorated in us a drive and determination to see things done right, thank you. The ProChef Certification and the Certified Wine Professional expanded our horizons after we sold our catering company, Clyne & Murphy. Thank you especially to chefs Mark Ainsworth and David Kamen—you define what it is to be great teachers and chefs, and you inspire, encourage, critique, and push us all to our fullest potential. Thank you, Tama Murphy, for your guidance. Thank you, Bruce Mattel and Ezra Eichelberger, for unconditionally sharing your wealth of knowledge. Words don't convey the intense respect we feel for all of you and for the school.

A special heartfelt thank-you from Carol to Chef Robert Briggs for believing in me on April 25, 2006, when you hired me to teach in the Food Enthusiast Program at The Culinary Institute of America, my proudest professional achievement. Not a day goes by that I don't discuss the opportunity you gave me. Thank you, Bob; you truly changed my life and opened doors I dared not dream I could step through. I promise I will pay your generosity forward and help others open their doors like you helped me open mine.

To all who have helped with testing and tasting and from whom we have begged and borrowed recipe ideas: thank you, Barbara Vass, Ginny McGeary, Lynda Stauderman, Carolynn and Mike Kalellis, Marion and Michael Sansone, and Marilyn and Joe Vidovich. Thank you, Mark Bauman and Sheila Crye, for your gracious support. And thank you Ken Esposito, Ken-Rent, Bernardsville, NJ, for your invaluable advice.

Thank you to the PAIRINGS team: chefs Norma Ochoa, Louise Ayd, Janet Denson, and Robin Early, who worked tirelessly to create photo-ready food à la minute and to style every photo; and to pastry chefs Hayley Baker and Vanessa Aronson Kenney and chefs Karen Randazzo and Andrew Valentino-Davison and to Brian Warner. And thank you to the PAIRINGS team that came on board after the first draft: chefs Brian Bouchard, Naved Ferdinands, Josie Grant, Chloe Dagress, Gerardo Santiago, and Janet Deiner for your enthusiasm and patience in helping retest and re-edit.

Thank you, Angela Bancalari, Vice President, Catering and Sales, Restaurant Associates, NYC, for sharing so much about your company so willingly: *food philosophy is a commitment to quality that encompasses simplicity, style, and passion.*

And to the companies that generously gave or lent equipment for the photo shoots for this project: Your representatives really rock. They know your products and offered their time and advice freely. Special thanks to:

Gary Harris from Willow Group, Ltd., for an extremely generous amount of platters, baskets, displays, risers, and elegant centerpieces, and for all the time and energy, advice, and phone calls.

Stephanie Fields from Le Creuset and Chicago Metallic Bakeware for all the stunning pots, pans, enamelware, and baking sheets.

Lee Ann Kelly from American Metalcraft for the striking displays, risers, chafing dishes, and serving pieces.

Amanda Blanchard from Southern Aluminum for the fabulous linen-less tables and riser sets—the strong, lightweight foundation for most of the buffet shots.

Laura Bolser from Front of the House for the sophisticated risers, utensils, displays, glassware, unique grab-and-go vessels, and all the time and advice.

Karyn Millman from CAL-MIL for the dynamic chafing dish alternatives, displays, risers, and drink towers.

David Wrightman from Fortessa for the cases of elegant china, glassware, and flatware and the spectacular spoon wall.

Karin Brewer from Vidacasa for the cool keep-it-cold display systems.

Brande Fanara from Riegel Linens for the chic tablecloths and napkins.

Mike Halles from Mikon International Inc. (AKA Culinaire) for the Hot Rocks.

Adam Loffredo from Top Line Appliance for the Summit induction burner.

ABOUT THE AUTHORS

CAROL MURPHY CLYNE and VINCENT CLYNE built PAIRINGS palate + plate in 2010, a restaurant concept based on constantly evolving seasonal recipes featured in its globally inspired contemporary American dinner menu, on-site buffet menu, and cooking classes. They also owned one of the largest and most successful catering companies in the highly competitive New Jersey market for 20 years. Carol obtained a ProChef Level II Certification at The Culinary Institute of America in Hyde Park, while Vincent embarked on the Professional Wine Studies Certification at the CIA in Napa Valley. Vince was awarded the Signorello Vineyards Food Writing Scholarship to the Symposium for Professional Food Writers at The Greenbrier. Carol has been a Visiting Instructor at the CIA in the Food Enthusiasts Program for 7 years.

ABOUT THE CULINARY INSTITUTE OF AMERICA

Founded in 1946, THE CULINARY INSTITUTE OF AMERICA is an independent, not-for-profit college offering associate and bachelor's degrees with majors in culinary arts, baking and pastry arts, and culinary science, as well as certificate programs in culinary arts and wine and beverage studies. As the world's premier culinary college, the CIA provides thought leadership in the areas of health and wellness, sustainability, and world cuisines and cultures through research and conferences. The CIA has a network of 45,000 alumni that includes industry leaders such as Grant Achatz, Anthony Bourdain, Roy Choi, Cat Cora, Dan Coudreaut, Steve Ells, Johnny Iuzzini, Charlie Palmer, and Roy Yamaguchi. The CIA also offers courses for professionals and enthusiasts, as well as consulting services in support of innovation for the foodservice and hospitality industry. The college has campuses in Hyde Park, NY; St. Helena, CA; San Antonio, TX; and Singapore.

The modern buffet is here to stay. Why? Well, the answer is simple enough; there is just no other way to feed large numbers of people so efficiently. In order to continuously engage the senses and attract clientele, however, the modern buffet must represent both the scope of the hospitality industry as a whole and the creative side of our imaginations as chefs. No longer humdrum, no longer stale and tired, no longer high on the list of unexciting dining options, it has progressed far beyond the realm of lowered expectations. Though often considered on par with a jug wine, the modern buffet is truly a proprietary blend of techniques, styles, and cuisines, a showcase for creativity and profitability.

MISE *en* PLACE

PREPARATION IS EVERYTHING

To be successful, the modern buffet must excite interest and entice attendance while demonstrating culinary acuity not only in menu development and execution, but also in adherence to budgetary and time constraints. This definition of success implies that the effort to work hard must at the same time include the ability to work smart. With so many components contributing to its overall success, it is no surprise that the modern buffet must be smartly planned with a keen eye to details. From barrel to bottle, from kitchen to table, from plate to palate, from idea to execution, preparation is all.

Preparation is, in fact, everything, and nowhere more so than for the modern buffet. It is anticipating. It is prepping. It is preparing. It is attention to detail. It is putting in place all that is needed. But before gathering all the pots, pans, and utensils, before ordering a single ingredient, before entering the kitchen, the buffet must be planned. Think of a blueprint, or a map, or a recipe, and see the process at work: detail by detail, turn by turn, ingredient by ingredient, the plan comes into view. Whether it is a buffet open to the public or a private catered affair, the planning process remains the same. As bits of pertinent information are gathered, a clear vision of the event emerges. This is the foundation upon which the buffet is planned, the menu is developed, and the client base is built.

The goal, though, is to surpass, not merely meet, the client's expectations. To do so, the gap between the client's wants and the kitchen's abilities must be bridged with a detailed plan that leaves nothing to chance, nothing to misunderstanding, nothing to miscommunication. This means steering toward menu choices that work for the client and for the kitchen, so that ultimately what is created in the kitchen translates successfully onto the buffet table.

PERSONALITY AND PROFESSIONALISM

Hospitality is our business. In the first few moments, a client notes our honesty and integrity, composure and comportment, politeness and polish. Based on sights and sounds and smells, cleanliness and clutter, personality and professionalism, a client decides to do business here or to go elsewhere. First impressions count.

The initial meeting with a client, therefore, is the first opportunity to showcase our hospitality. It is through this meeting that the client is convinced that what we offer is better than that of the competition. This means silencing the smartphone and putting all else on hold because this client comes first. Texts and tweets scream that our attention is divided, that this client is not important enough to warrant our full attention. Focus only on this client here and now; otherwise, not only do we risk the business at hand, but we also jeopardize future opportunities. Our hospitality now allows the client to anticipate a great event. These first impressions help ensure that we capture the sale, sign the contract, and collect the deposit. There is never a second first impression.

CONCEPTS AND THEMES

ALL BUFFET PLANNING STARTS BY ESTABLISHING FIRST THE CONCEPT AND THEN THE THEME. The concept is the big picture of the event painted in broad strokes, while the theme fills in the event's details by adding color and depth. The concept is an overall view that could be as simple as breakfast, lunch, or dinner. It could be an all-you-can-eat buffet or a continental breakfast. It could be a birthday, a wedding, or an anniversary. It could be a conference, convention, or reunion. Each of these concepts comes with a specific set of expectations. Further refinement of the concept leads to a unifying theme that brings focus to the menu: French or Italian, Mexican or Asian; pig roast or luau or barbecue; lobster fest or clambake; holiday or holy day. The theme could be a cartoon, character, color, or car. It could also be traditional or regional. It takes both the concept and theme to define the event's vision.

While the concept—a 60th birthday brunch, for example—is broad in scope, the theme—France—is more focused and helps lead toward particular menu selections. But what are possible buffet options for a 60th birthday brunch with a French theme? The menu could run the gamut from eggs Benedict to toad-in-the-hole, lobster salad to pancakes, duck and smoked foie gras terrine to croque-monsieur. Certainly all are possible choices, but do they work for this application? Too many questions still remain, and only with the client's detailed answers can we plan what the event warrants food-wise, equipment-wise, staff-wise, and otherwise. Detailed answers need detailed questions.

These open-ended questions are designed to draw out more than yes or no answers. To be prepared here means that we must know what to ask and how to ask it while remaining personable and professional. This is an effective brainstorming and interviewing technique, for it is this questioning-and-answering process that uncovers the details needed to develop an interesting and diverse buffet menu.

THE QUESTIONS

These "wise" answers come from asking the familiar who, what, when, where, how, and why questions that at first appear so basic, they are often overlooked.

BY THE END OF THE MEETING WITH THE CLIENT, there should be some sense of an answer to each of the following questions. Some of the answers will come from the client, and some answers will depend on your business.

Who is the event for?

Who is giving or sponsoring the event?

Who will be in attendance?

What is the purpose of the event? Is it a surprise?

What are the priorities of the client?
What is on the client's wish list?

What are the budgetary concerns?

What are the expectations of the client and the guests?

When is the actual time of the event?

Is it a seasonal event, or an ethnic or religious holiday?

Where is the location? On-site? Off-site?

Is it in a familiar kitchen with usual staff?

Is it off-premises with temporary help?

How many guests will there be?

How much food is expected based on the time of day and type of event?

Why is the client having this event?

PAIRINGS
palate + plate

Shaved Fennel, Arugula,
Avocado + Orange Salad

This buffet line features fresh, colorful foods organized in two types of heating vessels. Two of the vegetarian dishes are placed in stainless-steel bowls that can be set over canned heat, while the two entrées are in traditional chafing dishes.

PAIRINGS

Creamy Polenta
Marbled with Taleggio

As important as these answers are, so too is the method used to compile, organize, and share them. A standardized form will ensure all details are clearly understood, easy to follow, and readily available. Suppose a client specifies "no pork" and the staff are not told. What happens? A disaster? No, because this detail is clearly documented for all to see in the notes, in the contract, and in the production plan. Recording these details guarantees that nothing is lost, missed, or forgotten; our attention to them is what enables us to stand out from the competition. There are no minor details.

The following buffet planning worksheet was completed while discussing a French-themed 60th birthday brunch with a client. See Appendix A on page 336 for a blank buffet planning worksheet.

On-site buffet planning worksheet for a 60th birthday party

PAIRINGS
palate + plate

ON-SITE BUFFET PLANNING WORKSHEET

Client Name: *Jack Sange*   Date of event: *Sunday 5-10-14*

Occasion: *SURPRISE - Wife's 60th birthday*   Time: *11:00am-3:00pm*

Venue: *Our Patio or Dining Rm (rain)* Invited: adults *75* kids *28* Guaranteed: *A60 K20*

Phone: home *555-555-5555*   c *only call 444-444-4444 SURPRISE*

email: *jsange@internet.com*

Billing address: *101 Midway Ave, Westfield, NJ 07090*

Special instructions: *IMPORTANT!! Do not call home number-surprise*
NO PORK PRODUCTS IN ANY DISH

Notes/time line: *About 8 vegetarians!! vegan!! gluten allergy - substantial food*
-self service - likes stations- casual atmosphere- many kids_- mostly family
- smoothie station?
Seating on patio if rain - dining room with patio doors open
Paris - French - scallops are wife's favorite dish (provençale?)
Brunch - Arrive 11:00 - Hors doeuvres - Beverages served entire time
Surprise 11:30 Continue with hors d' Buffet 12:30 - Dessert 2:00 Concludes 3:00
Tables seat 6 to 8 people. Have 4 more seats than confirmed # of guests.
Open seating - no place cards.
Flowers delivered 9:00 AM that morning

How many buffet lines: *1 self-serve grand buffet, 2 sides*

Stations: *5:hors doeuvres / crepe / dessert and coffee / juice and prosecco / smoothie*

Flowers: *Esther's Flowers 908-555-9999* Entertainment: *No*

Party planner: *No*   Rental Company: *No*

Today's date: *8-19-14* Initials: *VC* Contract Sent: *8-20-14*   Initials: *CAMC*

Deposit Received: *9-14-14*   Initials: *CAMC*

walnut + south · cranford, nj 07016 · 908-276-4026 · pairingscranford.com

The Focus

What do people typically remember about the last event they attended? The flowers, ice sculptures, and linens? Perhaps. The food, drinks, and service? Undoubtedly. When the event is all show and no substance, when the food is obviously not the priority, when it is served at the incorrect temperature or when the wait is long, the entire event suffers. But when the food is the focus, when it is displayed creatively, when it is served politely and professionally, when it is balanced in a variety of dishes that are pleasing to the eye, nose, and palate, then this event is elevated, setting the bar for all others.

The goal is to maximize each guest's experience by creating dishes that linger not only on the palate, but also in the memory. The senses are stimulated by sights, sounds, and smells long before anything is actually tasted. This kitchen symphony that foreshadows what's to come reaches a crescendo in the mind: searing and sizzling and sautéing, stir-fries and steam and smoke, grills and char and crosshatch marks. That all this is happening is part of the collective consciousness and should not be lost on the buffet, which deserves the same careful attention as a plated and served dinner.

As the crunch of a bite adds texture and flavor and mouthfeel, the synergy of all the senses is processed as a single entity: taste. All of these clues, working in unison to awaken the taste buds, must not be forgotten when deciding what food to present on a modern buffet. Ultimately it must offer a variety of dishes that not only stimulate the senses but satiate them as well. It must reflect the bounty of the season in a balance of shapes and textures and cooking methods. It must, through natural flavor affinities, reinforce the perception of freshness, comfort, and well-being. And above all, it must taste good. Food is the focus.

The Budget

Focusing on food remains the primary duty, but there is another key issue to address: the budget. And both the client and the kitchen have one. The budget dictates what can and cannot be done. Obviously, it determines the specific ingredients and dishes, the number of options, and the level of service. Here the client's vision is blended with what is feasible for the business, and, in a balancing act between high and low costs, the client is steered to an individualized menu that puts the best food forward. For off-site presentations, the need to pay strict attention to details affecting the budget is even more critical. If a detail is overlooked, it will be more costly to remedy, as there are only the facilities on hand to work with; there is no stockroom to run to, and no extra staff to lend a hand.

Ideally a catering menu should list prices, not just dishes. The reason is twofold: Prices on the menu steer the client to educated selections that fit the budget; and they indicate to the client a straightforward, honest, and fair approach to pricing. A customer armed with such a menu will readily point out budgetary parameters. For instance, if the client immediately opts for the all-inclusive brunch buffet, there is little need for a full discussion of the much more expensive rack of lamb menu requiring

The crispiness of the chicken, the aroma of the simmering meatballs, the melting cheese on the rigatoni and vegetable stack, the sizzle of the sausage, and the bright colors of the vegetables awaken the taste buds. Carefully prepared food, as simple as it may be, is certainly the focus of this traditional Italian buffet.

many additional charges. Leading clients to a price point higher or lower than they desire will not necessarily land the job. But understanding what the budget can accommodate steers the client to those menu items that deliver the most food, flavor, and flair for the money. This assures the clients that they are getting the best possible food and service regardless of their budget.

An event may be planned for a nonprofit, school, or church organization whose budget seems too low to be worth the effort, but we can seize this opportunity and make it work to our advantage. For instance, the local high school awards dinner has a budget of $25 per person, all-inclusive, with 300 of our target market in attendance. This is a major marketing opportunity that exceeds the price paid, and even when done at cost, the return on the initial investment continues indefinitely. In this one situation, 300 people will taste our food and experience our hospitality. This goodwill exposure garners more clients than costly advertising campaigns, and the ensuing word of mouth is the best recommendation. As our reputation is only as good as the last meal served, it is a time to excel. Only put the best food forward.

THE MENU

Now that all pertinent information has been collected, the appropriate dishes can be selected from the general catering menu according to the event's vision and budget. A well-developed catering menu facilitates this by allowing for customization to the event as well as the season. While it may not be practical to have different catering menus for each season, the general catering menu should at least be adaptable to seasonal items. See Appendix B on page 337 for a sample general catering menu.

Discussion of the menu and the budget have led to decisions that must now be finalized to show how highly this client's business is valued. By giving full attention to the client and weighing each of the menu options, everything has a custom-made and personally tailored feeling; however, the overall kitchen plan must always be kept in mind, because we should only promise what we can deliver. The customized menu should have a wide variety of options so that even the pickiest guest finds something pleasing. There should be no duplication of major ingredients, and the menu should include vegetarian and gluten-free options. A general rule is for twenty to fifty guests to be offered a minimum of two entrée/protein dishes, two pasta/potato/rice dishes, two vegetable dishes, and a green salad and bread; for every twenty-five to fifty guests thereafter, it is advisable to add at least another selection.

Follow along as we lead the client to finalize the plan for the French-themed 60th birthday brunch.

1. Select the main dishes. Keep in mind that there should be a well-balanced selection that satisfies all guests, including vegetarian, vegan, and gluten-free options. This will lay the foundation for the buffet:

The client looks over the list and opts for the pecan chicken, which both he and his wife have enjoyed here before. The Pecan-Studded Chicken is on the Sandwich and Salad Buffet list in Appendix B on page 337. Since costs are the same, it is an easy substitution and will keep the client at the same budget. His second selection is the Five-Spice Beef Satay Kebobs. Both are noted on our copy of the menu.

The next selection of the menu starts with crêpes, and here a crêpe creation station is proposed. The crêpes can be made à la minute in front of the guests, just like in the *crêperies* of Paris. The client is thrilled because it evokes memories of his last trip to France. He's had the cheese soufflé filling before and requests it along with several other fillings. We suggest cherries in blueberry sauce to pair with the cream cheese soufflé and

A self-serve brunch buffet station set up using modern alternatives to the chafing dish

a seasonal vegetable dish, ratatouille, listed as a side dish on the catering menu. Also, it is a vegan and gluten-free option and is being made for another party. The client sees Scallops Provençal, which is one of his wife's favorite dishes, listed on the catering menu. Experience has shown that scallops go a long way as a crêpe filling, and when heated and assembled à la minute, their delicate nature is not an issue. More important, this is an exciting food focal point. We note that a cook is needed here and discuss the additional manpower and food costs. The client is excited by how this will be the highlight of the party. We also note that they are a gluten-free option. It fits his vision and priorities perfectly.

The ratatouille would be the cost of an additional breakfast side. The scallops would be the cost of an additional main. Since it makes the crêpes into a more filling dish with a higher expense, we go back and eliminate the beef kebobs.

French rolled omelets are discussed next, as they are also perfect for the theme. The client is encouraged, however, to select an assortment of individual deep-dish quiches. These are signature dishes that make a spectacular display and require less manpower than an omelet station, again taking into consideration his budget but not compromising the menu. We continue making revisions based on season, theme, and dietary restrictions: Asparagus is in the peak of season and is nowhere else on the menu, and chèvre is the perfect French pairing. We eliminate vegetables that are redundant. Since no pork can be used in any application, we emphasize no bacon and no sausage for each dish. So we continue marking up the menu until this selection is done.

PAIRINGS BRUNCH BUFFET MENU

~~Chicken Milanese with Artichoke, Caper, and Lemon Sauce~~
SWITCH TO PECAN-STUDDED CHICKEN WITH
RASPBERRY COULIS AND HONEY MUSTARD

~~Five-Spice Beef Kebobs with Red Onion, Peppers, Zucchini, and Mushrooms~~
~~MAKE GLUTEN-FREE AND VEGAN KEBOBS~~

Crêpes: Cream Cheese Soufflé ~~Double Cinnamon Apples, vanilla scented pears~~
CHERRIES IN BLUEBERRY SAUCE RATATOUILLE GLUTEN-FREE AND
VEGAN SCALLOPS PROVENÇAL GLUTEN-FREE NEEDS COOK AND
CREATION STATION EQUIPMENT

INDIVIDUAL Deep-dish vegetable quiche

Broccoli Lorraine with Gruyère ~~and Applewood-Smoked Bacon~~ *NO BACON*

Leek, Yukon Gold Potato, and ~~Sweet Italian Sausage~~ Cheddar *NO SAUSAGE*

~~Spinach~~ Wild Mushroom and Monterey Jack
CHANGE TO ASPARAGUS, WILD MUSHROOM, AND ~~MONTEREY JACK~~
CHANGE TO CHÈVRE MAKE ALL VEGETARIAN

A self-serve hors d'oeuvre station with varying heights on chilled and warmed slate serves both form and function.

2. Fill in with side dishes to balance the menu.

The client selects side dishes. He decides on the first choice, Three-Cheese Baked Macaroni. We agree, especially because it is being cooked for another event and is a perfect addition for the children. Then a salad is selected from another menu page, and a vegetable salad is added to round out the menu. The client is made aware of the cost increase for another salad. We make a note that vegans and those following gluten-free diets would be satisfied.

+ TWO SIDES

Three-Cheese Baked Macaroni *KIDS TOO*

~~**Bleu Cheese, Bacon, and Toasted Walnut Caesar**~~ *SPINACH ENSALADE NO PANCETTA KEEP SOME WITHOUT CROUTONS FOR GLUTEN-FREE AND SOME WITHOUT CHEESE FOR VEGAN ADD MARINATED ROASTED RED PEPPER AND HARICOTS VERTS SALAD GLUTEN-FREE AND KEEP SOME NO CHEESE FOR VEGAN*

A bread basket placed on each table not only frees up space on the buffet line but also adds to our hospitality and makes a mouthwatering focal point.

3. Once the menu has been determined, select the hors d'oeuvre, the desserts, and the beverages. Make sure there are no redundant ingredients and that the entire menu is in balance.

The buffet menu also has several other dishes included in the price that have not been discussed yet. As the client has upgraded the menu and it seems balanced, we help him work these items into the flow of the party, maximizing their use. We suggest Cheddar-Kissed Potato Pancakes be used as an hors d'oeuvre and discuss other kid-friendly, vegetarian, and moderately priced hors d'oeuvre that would sit well on a self-serve station. We also mutually conclude that the fruit salad would be best saved for a dessert and that freshly baked breads would make more of a statement on the guests' tables.

+ INCLUDES

Cheddar-Kissed Potato Pancakes and Crème Fraîche with Chives
AS AN HORS D'OEUVRE STATION—SELF-SERVICE

Gougères

Lemony Hummus and Cashew-Studded Naan

Grilled Crudités and Red Pepper Rouille

Alsatian Pizza with Sun-Dried Tomato Pesto, Montrachet, and Fresh Mozzarella

Fruit Salad Scented with Lime and Mint
SAVE FOR DESSERT—KEBOBS WITH BITTERSWEET CHOCOLATE SAUCE

Louisiana Biscuits, Montazzoli Breakfast Buns, Montazzoli Breakfast Bread, Praline Sticky Buns, Mini Cakes and Banana Spice Cakes + Brown Sugar Glaze, Sour Cream and Walnut Muffins *ON EACH TABLE*

A well-organized beverage station requires little space and invites guests to enjoy a variety of choices.

Next is the cake. The client asks about bringing in his wife's favorite lemon cake, and we steer him to our cakes. Our policy is that we serve only our own food, but instead of stating this blatantly, he is invited to taste several of our cakes. He selects two.

What about drinks? Champagne cocktails are appropriate for the time of day. A Kir Royale is ideal for the theme, but we suggest prosecco cocktails as more affordable and offer varied versions using fruit purées. Juices, iced tea, and lemonade finalize the beverage selections.

Chiffon Cake with Lemon Curd and Toasted Coconut Whipped Cream
"HAPPY 60TH BIRTHDAY MARIE"

Chocolate Lovers' Cake with Chocolate Mocha Mousse Filling and Chocolate Whipped Cream Icing
"HAPPY MOTHER'S DAY"

Mimosa, Bellini, Rossini Cocktails with Prosecco
PEACH AND RASPBERRY PURÉE, ORANGE JUICE, GRAPEFRUIT JUICE, TOMATO JUICE, ICED TEA, LEMONADE

A cook makes customized smoothies for guests at an action station, enhancing the made-just-for-me atmosphere and providing an entertainment element.

A frozen fruity yogurt smoothie action station is suggested as a focal point. In this situation, using up leftover fruits and juices lends itself to being highly profitable because the raw food cost is exceptionally low and any labor involved is already accounted for. A high-margin item generally has a low cost while providing a high markup, thus giving a good return on the initial outlay. The profitability can offset the costs of other items. Also, this action station will engage and entertain the guests. The client is excited about this and feels additional service here would fit his vision. He agrees to the additional cost of the wait staff.

Fruity Yogurt Smoothie Station
BANANA, BLUEBERRY, MANGO, MELON, STRAWBERRY YOGURT, HONEY, VANILLA EXTRACT, MILK, ICE

The last menu item to discuss is the coffee service. We suggest café Grand Marnier with our Melitta coffee brewing station, and he is thrilled with this perfect way to end the event. It's decided to put the dessert and coffee station together, and notes are made for this.

Finally, the layout and logistics are discussed. Everything will be white except for the napkins, which will be chocolate colored. The umbrella tables will be on the patio for seating. It is safest to keep the buffet inside, where there is the most control over elements like weather, bugs, sun, and so forth. The client agrees. So the grand buffet and crêpe station will actually be inside, while the hors d'oeuvre and beverage stations will be under the awnings.

THE PLAN

THE CLIENT HAS BEEN GUIDED THROUGH ALL THE OPTIONS AND IS CONFIDENT IN HIS MENU CHOICES. Now we can prepare a detailed plan that lists the complete menu, the event timeline, and all corresponding charges.

All of this information can be compiled in one place, a spreadsheet. With a spreadsheet, a catering agreement and a production plan can be versions of the same document. On a spreadsheet, a column can list the information that everyone needs, such as the menu, with other columns dedicated to specific information for only the guest, such as the cost, and for only the kitchen, such as the food production. By hiding or revealing specific columns, relevant information can be given to the client and/or the staff without losing any information in the process. Go to www.wiley.com/college/cia for a spreadsheet based on this catering menu.

However, we don't just need the catering agreement for the client; we also need a detailed production plan and timeline for the kitchen and wait staff. Again, with this same spreadsheet, the kitchen production information and timeline can be printed by simply hiding and revealing relevant columns.

The power of the on-site production plan spreadsheet for one event is magnified when used for multiple events. On a busy weekend, party menus can be merged and the food sorted so that the kitchen production is as efficient as possible. The spreadsheet, as a production plan, lists:

- How much of each dish in total to prepare and for who

- The quantity that goes to each event

- The plating style or special instructions for the party

- The day and time each event is scheduled

- The labels for either trays of food with reheating instructions or signs for the buffet table

It can even have a column with reheating instructions for clients who are serving our food without our wait staff.

For example, a typical weekend might have four buffets scheduled. The individual spreadsheets for each buffet can be merged so that the garde manger knows to prepare 410 Cheddar-Kissed Potato Pancakes: Sange, 100 pieces, 11:00 A.M.; Freer, 100 pieces, 3:00 P.M.; Bouchard, 150 pieces, 3:00 P.M.; Sheppard, 60 pieces, 6:00 P.M.

Even more powerful, merge the parties for the entire weekend and the sauté chef knows that about 50 pounds of chicken breast are needed for the weekend and also how to prep them:

- Warner, 17.5 pounds, Buttermilk Grilled Chicken, Friday, 6:00 P.M.

- Sange, 8.4 pounds, Pecan-Studded Chicken, Saturday, 11:00 A.M.

- Ochoa, 6.6 pounds, Chicken Pecorino on a Stick, Saturday, 6:00 P.M.

- Root, 15.6 pounds, Fettuccine Marsala with Chicken, Sunday, 4:00 P.M.

Thus the entire amount of chicken breast is prepped, labeled, and stored on ice according to the day, party, and cook time.

On-site catering agreement for 60th birthday brunch for the client. This spreadsheet is printed with only the information the client needs. Rows and columns that are not relevant for the client are hidden. The sheet is printed without gridlines for a professional presentation.

PAIRINGS
palate + plate

walnut · south · cranford, nj 07016 · 908-276-4026 · pairingscranford.com

CATERING AGREEMENT

Prepared for Jack Sange	**Address** 101 Midway Ave, Westfield, NJ 07090
Date of Event Sunday, May 10, 2015	**Occasion** Marie's Surprise 60TH Birthday Party
Venue/address Pairings Patio*	**Invited** A: 75 C:28 Gauranteed: 60 A 20 C
Time of party 11:00 am to 3:00 pm - 11:30 surprise	**Phone** Only call cell 444-444-4444
* or adjacent dining room if rain	**Email** jsange@interset.com

Umbrella Tables on Patio, White Table Cloths, Chocolate Napkins
Esther's Flowers 908-555-9999 and we will confirm delivery.

tapas · mezze · antipasti · hors d'oeuvres
Hors d'oeuvre Satellite Station - Self Service - On Patio Under Awning 11:00 am to 12:00 pm

		PER 25 PIECES	TOTAL
alsatian pizza	75	$37.50	$112.50
cheddar kissed potato pancakes	75	INCLUDED IN BRUNCH	
gooey gougères	75	$25.00	$75.00
grilled vegetable crudités with (vegan and gluten free)	1	$60.00	$60.00
fire-roasted red pepper coulis (make vegan)			
lemony hummus with (vegan and gluten free)	1	$50.00	$50.00
grilled baby carrots and			
cashew-studded naan			

Surprise 11:30 am

brunch buffet
In Dining Room Next to French Doors (All Open) 12:30 pm

pecan-studded chicken
honey mustard
raspberry coulis
individual deep dish vegetable quiche
broccoli lorraine with gruyere *** NO BACON
leek, new potato and CHEDDAR *** NO SAUSAGE
ASPARAGUS, wild mushroom and CHEVRE *** NO PORK
three-cheese baked macaroni
spinach ensalada *** NO PANCETTA
*** KEEP SOME NO CHEESE AND NO CROUTONS (vegan and gluten free)
marinated roasted pepper and haricots verts salad
*** KEEP SOME NO CHEESE (vegan and gluten free)

Crêpes Creation Station - In Dining Room Next to French Doors (All Open) 12:30 pm

crêpes MADE À LA MINUTE AND FILLED WITH CHOICE OF:
day boat scallops provençal
ratatouille (vegan and gluten free)
cream cheese soufflé
cherries in blueberry sauce (vegan and gluten free)

On Individual Tables 12:30 pm

louisiana biscuits, montazzoli breakfast buns, and praline sticky buns
mini cakes: banana spice cakes and brown sugar glaze, and sour cream and walnut coffee cake

BRUNCH PLUS MAIN, PLUS SIDE	60	$46.00	$2,760.00
Children under 12 years old	20	$23.00	$460.00

beverages
Beverage Sensation Station - On Patio under Awning 11:00 am to 3:00 pm

mimosa, bellini, and rossini cocktails	60	$8.00	$480.00
peach + raspberry			
orange juice, grapefruit juice, tomato juice			
fruity yogurt smoothie sensation station	80	$8.00	$640.00
banana, blueberry, mango, melon, strawberry			

coffee + dessert
Coffee Melitta Brewing Station and Dessert Station 2:00

caffe' al grand marnier: kona french roasted coffee beans			
grand marnier, whipped cream, orange peel, sugar	60	$5.00	$300.00
coffee, tea		INCLUDED IN BRUNCH	
strawberry, pineapple, and honey dew kebobs and bittersweet chocolate sauce		INCLUDED IN BRUNCH	
chiffon cake with lemon custard and toasted coconut whipped cream			
"Happy 60th Birthday Marie"	1	$120.00	$120.00
chocolate lover's cake, mocha mousse, chocolate whipped cream			
"Happy Mother's Day"	1	$120.00	$120.00

Additional Wait Staff

For crêpe station (1) and fruity yogurt smoothie station (1)	2	$150.00	$300.00

TOTAL	$5,477.50
7% NJ SALES TAX +	$383.43
GRAND TOTAL	$5,860.93
DEPOSIT −	$500.00
BALANCE	$5,360.93

Prices are guaranteed only with a deposit on a contract specifying a menu.
CUSTOMARY 18% SERVICE CHARGE WILL BE ADDED TO FINAL BILL.
FULL PAYMENT IS APPRECIATED AND REQUIRED ON THE DAY OF PARTY.
THANK YOU!

Prepared by: CAMC On: 8/20/14
A DEPOSIT OF 500 WOULD BE APPRECIATED & IS REQUIRED TO SECURE THE DATE AND GUARANTEE THE PRICE.

PAIRINGS
palate + plate

walnut · south · · cranford, nj 07016 · 908 276 4026 · pairingscranford.com

CATERING AGREEMENT

Prepared for Jack Sange
Date of Event Sunday, May 10, 2015
Venue/address Pairings Patio*
Time of party 11:00 am to 3:00 pm - 11:30 surprise
* or adjacent dining room if rain

Umbrella Tables on Patio, White Table Cloths, Chocolate Napkins
Esther's Flowers 908-555-9999 and we will confirm delivery.

tapas · mezze · antipasti · hors d'oeuvres
Hors d'oeuvre Satellite Station - Self Service - On Patio Under Awning 11:00 am to 12:00 pm

	KITCHEN PREPARE	NO PORK	SANGE	DATE	11:00	HERE
alsatian pizza	75.0 PCS	NO PORK	SANGE	5/10	11:00	HERE
cheddar kissed potato pancakes	112.5 PCS	NO PORK	SANGE	5/10	11:00	HERE
gooey gougères	75.0 PCS	NO PORK	SANGE	5/10	11:00	HERE
grilled vegetable crudités with (vegan and gluten free)	1.0 LG	NO PORK	SANGE	5/10	11:00	HERE
fire-roasted red pepper coulis (make vegan)	0.5 QTS	NO PORK	SANGE	5/10	11:00	HERE
lemony hummus with (vegan and gluten free)	1.0 LG	NO PORK	SANGE	5/10	11:00	HERE
grilled baby carrots and	50.0 PCS	NO PORK	SANGE	5/10	11:00	HERE
cashew-studded naan	50.0 PCS	NO PORK	SANGE	5/10	11:00	HERE

Surprise 11:30 am

brunch buffet
In Dining Room Next to French Doors (All Open) 12:30 pm

	KITCHEN PREPARE	NO PORK	SANGE	DATE	11:00	HERE
pecan-studded chicken	17.5 LBS	NO PORK	SANGE	5/10	11:00	HERE
honey mustard		NO PORK	SANGE	5/10	11:00	HERE
raspberry coulis		NO PORK	SANGE	5/10	11:00	HERE
individual deep dish vegetable quiche	70.0 PCS	NO PORK	SANGE	5/10	11:00	HERE
broccoli lorraine with gruyere *** NO BACON		NO PORK	SANGE	5/10	11:00	HERE
leek, new potato and CHEDDAR *** NO SAUSAGE		NO PORK	SANGE	5/10	11:00	HERE
ASPARAGUS, wild mushroom and CHEVRE *** NO PORK		NO PORK	SANGE	5/10	11:00	HERE
three-cheese baked macaroni	17.5 LBS	NO PORK	SANGE	5/10	11:00	HERE
spinach ensalada *** NO PANCETTA	8.8 LBS	NO PORK	SANGE	5/10	11:00	HERE
*** KEEP SOME NO CHEESE AND NO CROUTONS (vegan and gluten free)		NO PORK	SANGE	5/10	11:00	HERE
marinated roasted pepper and haricots verts salad	17.5 LBS	NO PORK	SANGE	5/10	11:00	HERE
*** KEEP SOME NO CHEESE (vegan and gluten free)		NO PORK	SANGE	5/10	11:00	HERE

Crêpes Creation Station - In Dining Room Next to French Doors (All Open) 12:30 pm

	KITCHEN PREPARE	NO PORK	SANGE	DATE	11:00	HERE
crêpes MADE À LA MINUTE AND FILLED WITH CHOICE OF:	105.0 PCS	NO PORK	SANGE	5/10	11:00	HERE
day boat scallops provençal	8.8 LBS	NO PORK	SANGE	5/10	11:00	HERE
ratatouille (vegan and gluten free)	13.1 LBS	NO PORK	SANGE	5/10	11:00	HERE
cream cheese soufflé	2.2 QTS	NO PORK	SANGE	5/10	11:00	HERE
cherries in blueberry sauce (vegan and gluten free)	2.2 QTS	NO PORK	SANGE	5/10	11:00	HERE

On Individual Tables 12:30 pm

	KITCHEN PREPARE	NO PORK	SANGE	DATE	11:00	HERE
louisiana biscuits, montazzoli breakfast buns, and praline sticky buns	105.0 PCS	NO PORK	SANGE	5/10	11:00	HERE
mini cakes: banana spice cakes and brown sugar glaze, and		NO PORK	SANGE	5/10	11:00	HERE
sour cream and walnut coffee cake		NO PORK	SANGE	5/10	11:00	HERE
BRUNCH PLUS MAIN, PLUS SIDE		NO PORK	SANGE	5/10	11:00	HERE
Children under 12 years old		NO PORK	SANGE	5/10	11:00	HERE

beverages
Beverage Sensation Station - On Patio under Awning 11:00 am to 3:00 pm

	KITCHEN PREPARE	NO PORK	SANGE	DATE	11:00	HERE
mimosa, bellini, and rossini cocktails	12.0 BTL	NO PORK	SANGE	5/10	11:00	HERE
peach + raspberry	1.9 QTS	NO PORK	SANGE	5/10	11:00	HERE
orange juice, grapefruit juice, tomato juice	3.8 QTS	NO PORK	SANGE	5/10	11:00	HERE
fruity yogurt smoothie sensation station	10.0 QTS	NO PORK	SANGE	5/10	11:00	HERE
banana, blueberry, mango, melon, strawberry	10.0 QTS	NO PORK	SANGE	5/10	11:00	HERE

coffee + dessert
Coffee Melitta Brewing Station and Dessert Station 2:00

	KITCHEN PREPARE	NO PORK	SANGE	DATE	11:00	HERE
caffe' al grand marnier: kona french roasted coffee beans	7.5 QTS	NO PORK	SANGE	5/10	11:00	HERE
grand marnier, whipped cream, orange peel, sugar	7.5 QTS	NO PORK	SANGE	5/10	11:00	HERE
coffee, tea	7.5 QTS	NO PORK	SANGE	5/10	11:00	HERE
strawberry, pineapple, and honey dew kebobs and	10.0 PDS	NO PORK	SANGE	5/10	11:00	HERE
bittersweet chocolate sauce	0.8 QTS	NO PORK	SANGE	5/10	11:00	HERE
chiffon cake with lemon custard and toasted coconut whipped cream	SHEET CKE	NO PORK	SANGE	5/10	11:00	HERE
"Happy 60th Birthday Marie"						
chocolate lover's cake, mocha mousse, chocolate whipped cream	SHEET CKE	NO PORK	SANGE	5/10	11:00	HERE
"Happy Mother's Day"						

Additional Wait Staff

	KITCHEN PREPARE	NO PORK	SANGE	DATE	11:00	HERE
For crêpe station (1) and fruity yogurt smoothie station (1)		NO PORK	SANGE	5/10	11:00	HERE

Prices are guaranteed only with a deposit on a contract specifying a menu.
CUSTOMARY 18% SERVICE CHARGE WILL BE ADDED TO FINAL BILL.
FULL PAYMENT IS APPRECIATED AND REQUIRED ON THE DAY OF PARTY.
A DEPOSIT OF 500 WOULD BE APPRECIATED & IS REQUIRED TO SECURE THE DATE AND GUARANTEE THE PRICE.
All deposits are not refundable under any circumstances and constitute your acceptance of all these terms & conditions.

On-site production plan for 60th birthday brunch for the kitchen. Only the columns and rows containing the food production information are printed.

The Off-Site Plan

An away event gives rise to a series of problems not applicable to one held on the home turf; thus it requires an even more detailed game plan. Imagine arriving at the location with everything planned out, psyched to cook, only to find that the double oven you had inquired about, the one you had been assured was there and working, turns out to be a two-burner cooktop. Game changer. Since nothing comes with a guarantee, it's best to prepare for the worst, to expect the unexpected, to alleviate as many "out of our control" issues as possible, and to cover all the bases.

Whether it's a reception in an office, a museum, church hall, park, or private residence, a "walk-through" and "turn-on" inspection of the site is necessary. First assess the cooking situation. Check that the water, the burners, the oven, the exhaust fan, lights, and refrigerators are fully operational. Turn each on. Assume nothing. Look at the prep space. Then walk the line, from the kitchen to the buffet and back again, from the buffet to the farthest table and back to the buffet, and on to the kitchen. Does the layout make sense? Now determine what is visible to and within earshot of the guests and the best method of servicing the buffet discreetly. What additional equipment is needed; does anything special need to be rented? Sketch out where things go; does it all flow? Decide if streamlining the production plan by bringing everything fully prepped and/or cooked is in order. Time runs out rapidly during delivery and setup, and being fully prepared ensures that quality is maintained without having to rely on unproven equipment. Envision the cleanup both during and after the event, and structure it to be efficient, unobtrusive, and timely.

Not all facilities present such problems as inoperable ovens, limited access to water, or overloaded electrical systems, but an overlooked or unforeseen detail can wreak havoc. Our burden is to mitigate the chance of this happening with knowledge of the location. With a "just-in-case" plan in place, the snap-decision judgment call that just has to be made in the field can be made confidently and without hesitation. So think about the DJ and all those amplifiers and our coffee urns. Fuses or circuit breakers? What about permits from the fire, health, and police departments? Are there any menu restrictions when, for instance, the event is being held at a temple, shrine, cathedral, or mosque? Fretting about the latest weather forecast is useless, while anticipating the need for coatracks and umbrella stands, anti-slip mats, and a bale of hay to absorb puddles proves priceless. Whatever affects the event running smoothly, ultimately impacts the food. Our reputation is on the line. A complete game plan covers all the bases.

The following buffet planning worksheet emphasizes details needing attention when the party is off-site. Many of these details drive up the cost of off-site catering. See Appendix C on page 338 for a blank off-site buffet planning worksheet.

PAIRINGS
palate + plate

OFF-SITE BUFFET PLANNING WORKSHEET

Client name: *Jack Sange*   Date of event: *Sunday 5/10/15*

Occasion: *SURPRISE - Wife's 60th Birthday*   Time: *11:00 AM - 3:00 PM*

Venue: *His house - 101 Midway Ave. Westfield* Invited: adults *75* Kids: *28* Guaranteed: *A 60 K 20*

Phone: home *DON'T CALL 555-555-5555*   C: *ONLY CALL 444-444-4444*

Email: *jsange@internet.com*

Billing Address: *101 Midway Ave. Westfield, NJ 07090*

Special Instructions: *IMPORTANT!! Do not call home number - surprise*
NO PORK PRODUCTS IN ANY DISH

Notes/time line: *About 8 vegetarians / 1 vegan / 1 gluten allergy - substantial food - self service - likes stations - casual atmosphere - many kids - mostly family - smoothie station? Seating on patio if rain - family room with patio doors open*
Paris - French - scallops are wife's favorite dish (Provençale?)
Brunch - Arrive. 11:00 - Hors doeuvres - Beverages served entire time
Surprise 11:30 Continue with hors d' Buffet 12:30 - Dessert 2:00 Concludes 3:00
Tables seat 6 to 8 people. Have 4 more seats than confirmed number of guests. Open seating - no place cards.
Flowers delivered at 9:00 AM that morning.

How many buffet lines: *1 self-serve grand buffet on dining room table, 2 side stations—one as hors doeuvres/crepes/dessert and one as coffee/juice and prosecco/smoothie*

flowers: *Esther's Flowers 908-555-9999*   entertainment: *NO*

party planner: *NO*   rentals: *KBL Rentals 908-666-9999* Liquor/Soda/Ice (IF APPLICABLE): *NO*

Valet Parking: *NO*   Insurance Permit: *NO*   Board of Health/Fire/Police Permit: *NO*

Buffet and Equipment:

Buffet Lines: *self-serve dining rm table/2 leaves*

Stations: *2=1 hors then desserts, 1 all beverages*

Buffet Tables: *5=2 for hors/dessert + 3 for bev*

Risers: *n/a*

Tablecloths/Skirting: *7=2 for hors + 2 for dessert (need to change cloths) + 3 for beverages*

Chafers/Sterno/Electric: *need - sterno not electric*

Platters/Serving Utensils: *need*

Centerpieces: *delivered 9:00 AM Esther's*

Dinner Tables: *has no patio table - seats 8. order 8 48" umbrella tables all white - each seats 6. These will fit in family room if rains. There is also a patio set that seats 8. Does not have seating for everyone. There is other seating for people on patio furniture or in living room.*

Chairs: *need 48 white Samsonite chairs*

Tablecloths/Napkins: *9 white table cloths, 108 chocolate cloth napkins - includes bread baskets*

China/Paper Place Settings: *bamboo plates*

Glassware: *start with 2 (1 champ, 1 all purpose) per adult and then switch to plastic - all plastic for kids*

Flatware: *all heavy duty bamboo*

S&P/Coffee Service/B & B: *n/a coffee w/dessert*

Tent: *n/a*   Dance floor *n/a*   Lighting *n/a*

Bars: *using tables*

Electric: *needed for blenders - on patio working*

Other Rentals/Notes: *Electric on patio working and on kitchen island. Electric panel at bottom of basement stairs.*

Kitchen

Ovens: *36-inch double ovens both work*

Stovetop/Burners: *4 burners all work*

Grills/Propane: *N/A*

Fridge/Freezer: *Will have 2 refrigerator shelves cleared.*

Sink/Water: *good*   Dishwasher: *good*

Prep Tables: *Kitchen tables and counters - will have them cleared.*

Utensils: *bring ours.*

Trash Disposal/Recycling: *leave all separated in garage.*

Exhaust Fan: *good*

Fire Suppression/Extinguisher: *under sink.*

Electric: *Electric panel at bottom of basement stairs.*

Check List

Sterno	Extra Baking Pans
Chaffers	Ice Chest/Ice Bucket
Insert Pans/Foil Pans	Plastic Wrap/Foil
Passing Trays	Scissors
Wax Paper	Garbage Bags
Dip Cups	Gloves/Oven Mitts
Toothpicks	Hand Towels
Cocktail Napkins	Spatulas
Serving Pieces	Camera
Ice Chest /Ice Bucket	Soap
Wine Opener	Tongs
Extra Plastic Cups	Bus Tubs

Other Notes/Sketches:

Off-site buffet planning worksheet with the additional information needed to plan the menu for an off-site 60th birthday party

Off-site catering agreement for 60th birthday brunch

Again, the planning process is completed on a spreadsheet with all details spelled out. The catering agreement for an off-site event that lists a complete menu, a timeline, and all charges for the client would look like this:

PAIRINGS
palate + plate

walnut + south · cranford, nj 07016 · 908-276-4026 · pairingscranford.com

OFF-SITE CATERING AGREEMENT

Prepared for Jack Sange
Date of Event Sunday, May 10, 2015
Venue/address 101 Midway Ave, Westfield, NJ 07090
Time of party 11:00 am to 3:00 pm - 11:30 surprise

Address 101 Midway Ave, Westfield, NJ 07090
Occasion Marie's Surprise 60TH Birthday Party
Invited A: 75 C:28 Gauranteed: 60 A 20 C
Phone Only call cell 444-444-4444
Email jsange@interset.com

Changes from on site contract noted in orange.

*IF RAIN-FAMILY ROOM WITH PATIO DOORS OPEN
Umbrella Tables on Patio, White Table Cloths, Chocolate Napkins - Esther's Flowers 908-555-9999 and we will confirm delivery.
1 self-serve buffet on dining room table, 2 sides stations- one as hors d'oeuvres/crepe/dessert and one as coffed/juice and prosecco/smoothie
PLEASE HAVE ALL COUNTERS KITCHEN TABLE, AND DINING ROOM TABLE CLEARED AND 2 SHELVES IN REFRIDGERATOR CLEARED
All Rental Items will be delivered on Friday between 1 and 4 pm - Please have all outdoor preparation completed by this time (landscaping, etc.) If it rains you will have family room completely cleared out and we will set up 6 tables there - WE WILL ARRIVE AT 9:00 AM TO BEGIN SET-UP

tapas · mezze · antipasti · hors d'oeuvres
Hors d'oeuvre Satellite Station - Self Service - On Patio Under Umbrella 11:00 am to 12:00 pm IF RAINS ON KITCEN ISLAND

		PER 25 PIECES	TOTAL
alsatian pizza	75	$37.50	$112.50
cheddar kissed potato pancakes	75	INCLUDED IN BRUNCH	
gooey gougères	75	$25.00	$75.00
grilled vegetable crudités with (vegan and gluten free)	1	$60.00	$60.00
fire-roasted red pepper coulis (make vegan)			
lemony hummus with (vegan and gluten free)	1	$50.00	$50.00
grilled baby carrots and			
cashew-studded naan			

Surprise 11:30 am

brunch buffet
On Dining Room Table with 2 leaves in - 12:30 pm

pecan-studded chicken
honey mustard
raspberry coulis
individual deep dish vegetable quiche
broccoli lorraine with gruyere *** NO BACON
leek, new potato and CHEDDAR *** NO SAUSAGE
ASPARAGUS, wild mushroom and CHEVRE *** NO PORK
three-cheese baked macaroni
spinach ensalada *** NO PANCETTA
*** KEEP SOME NO CHEESE AND NO CROUTONS (vegan and gluten free)
marinated roasted pepper and haricots verts salad
*** KEEP SOME NO CHEESE (vegan and gluten free)

Crêpes Creation Station - switch hors d' station to crepes station - 12:30 pm

crepes MADE À LA MINUTE AND FILLED WITH CHOICE OF:
day boat scallops provençal
ratatouille (vegan and gluten free)
cream cheese soufflé
cherries in blueberry sauce (vegan and gluten free)

On Individual Tables 12:30 pm - IF RAINS PUT SOME ON DINING ROOM TABLE AND IN LIVING ROOM

louisiana biscuits, montazzoli breakfast buns, and praline sticky buns
mini cakes: banana spice cakes and brown sugar glaze, and sour cream and walnut coffee cake

BRUNCH PLUS MAIN, PLUS SIDE	60	$46.00	$2,760.00
Children under 12 years old	20	$23.00	$460.00

beverages
Beverage Sensation Station - On Patio under umbrella 11:00 am to 3:00 pm IF RAINS SET UP IN LIVING ROOM

walnut • south • cranford, nj 07016 • 908-276-4026 • pairingscranford.com

OFF-SITE CATERING AGREEMENT

Prepared for Jack Sange
Date of Event Sunday, May 10, 2015
Venue/address 101 Midway Ave., Westfield, NJ 07090

Address 101 Midway Ave, Westfield, NJ 07090
Occasion Marie's Surprise 60TH Birthday Party
Invited A: 75 C:28 Gauranteed: 60 A 20 C

Changes from on-site contract noted in orange. Additional notes to our off-site wait staff noted in green.

brunch buffet
On Dining Room Table with two leaves in - 12:30 pm

pecan-studded chicken	
honey mustard	Reheat uncovered at 350° until hot, about 10 to 15 min.
raspberry coulis	
individual deep dish vegetable quiche	Reheat covered at 350° until hot, about 10 to 15 min.
broccoli lorraine with gruyere *** NO BACON	
leek, new potato and CHEDDAR *** NO SAUSAGE	
ASPARAGUS, wild mushroom and CHEVRE *** NO PORK	
three-cheese baked macaroni	Reheat covered at 350° until hot, about 45 min.
spinach ensalada *** NO PANCETTA	
*** KEEP SOME NO CHEESE AND NO CROUTONS (vegan and gluten free)	
marinated roasted pepper and haricots verts salad	
*** KEEP SOME NO CHEESE (vegan and gluten free)	

Crêpes Creation Station - switch hors d' station to crêpes station - 12:30 pm

crêpes MADE À LA MINUTE AND FILLED WITH CHOICE OF:	RECHECK CREPE MISE EN PLACE, RECHECK ELECTRICITY
day boat scallops provençal	Reheat uncovered at 400° until hot, about 5 min.
ratatouille (vegan and gluten free)	Reheat in the oven or microwave in small batches until hot.
cream cheese soufflé	Reheat covered at 350° until hot, about 10 to 15 min.
cherries in blueberry sauce (vegan and gluten free)	Reheat in the oven or microwave in small batches until hot.

On Individual Tables 12:30 pm - IF RAINS PUT SOME ON DINING ROOM TABLE AND IN LIVING ROOM

louisiana biscuits, montazzoli breakfast buns, and praline sticky buns
mini cakes: banana spice cakes and brown sugar glaze, and sour cream and walnut coffee cake

BRUNCH PLUS MAIN, PLUS SIDE	**60**
Children under 12 years old	**20**

wait staff

For 6 continuous hours of service including the required set-up & clean-up. The time begins when leaving Westfield & ends when returning to Westfield. Should your party require more time the charge is $50.00 per hour per server.

7 Staff: Captain, 2 Bartenders,
2 food handlers at crepe action station
2 food handlers replenishing

SUB TOTAL OF FOOD & SERVICE

rental items   AT END - ALL RENTALS STACKED IN GARAGE READY FOR RENTAL COMPANY TO PICK UP

White Samsonite Chairs	48	
Buffet Tables	5	Buffet tables - 1 for hors d'oeuvre station / dessert
Banquet Table Cloths WHITE WITH EXTRA TO CHANGE HORS D' TABLE TO DESSERT	7	3 for Beverage Station - 2 in front to serve from - 1 in back for equipment, etc.
Umbrella Tables with White Umbrellas	8	
Table Cloths for Umbrella Tables WHITE	8	
Champagne Glasses per rack of 25 When glasses run out switch to plastic	3	When glasses run out switch to plastic
Water / All purpose glasses per rack of 25 When glasses run out switch to plastic	3	
Cloth Napkins CHOCOLATE - INCLUDES BREAD BASKETS	84	
Paper Goods		Bring all unopend paper goods back to restaurant

Off-site notes for 60th birthday brunch

THE BOTTOM LINE

THE CLIENT'S CONCERNS HAVE BEEN ADDRESSED AND THE CONTRACT HAS BEEN FINALIZED; now we need to look at the event from our side of the table and work out the kitchen production plan, including the ordering of raw materials, scheduling prep workers and wait staff, arranging for rentals and deliveries, and overseeing the setup.

Who will work the day of the event?

- Schedule

- Extra kitchen prep

- Delivery and setup

- Wait staff requirements

What special equipment, training, and food will be needed?

- Rentals/purchases

When do the ordering, prepping, and setup begin?

- Separate timeline for each component

Where will the buffet be? On-premises? Off-premises? Indoors? Outdoors?

- Site visit for visual inspection of equipment and physical layout

- Kitchen or cooking location vis-à-vis buffet tables and guest seating

How will the food be prepared, displayed, and maintained?

- Special directions, specialty dishes, replenishment, temperature holding

And why? Why must the plan be so thorough? It's all about hospitality, being warm and welcoming through food and the service offered around it. It comes with a tacit guarantee of seamless performance rather than the notion of a quick-fire challenge cobbled together at the last minute.

Knowing that every aspect of the food has been covered, that the kitchen is well oiled, that the setup is complete, that the overall vision is intact, allows us to attend to the guests rather than worry about what should have been done yesterday. Because, according to plan, it was done yesterday. Thus executing the buffet and supervising the event become one process, fluid and orderly, exact and efficient. Yet with so many supporting roles clamoring for attention, the focus must remain on the star; without the limelight, the food flounders in a sea of unrelated details while unifying thematic elements scatter.

It's all about this event as preparation for the next event. As the planning process becomes second nature, it's directed by a learning curve that allows streamlining and adaptation. As it evolves, sometimes through trial and error, sometimes through intuition and gut instinct, sometimes through a bit of luck, but always through meticulous attention to detail, this planning process builds upon past performance by learning from, improving upon, and eliminating mistakes. This is why planning the modern buffet is so important, after all. Not only does it provide for the current event, but it also sets in motion the opportunity for a better next event through delicious food and remarkable service. Reputation is everything.

Designing the buffet to be both intriguing and interactive can be a daunting task. The chef, as architect, builder, decorator, and event planner, must unite the client's vision with all the functions of the kitchen. The layout of the buffet and how it fills the space includes not only the location of the buffet line itself and its stations, but also tables and chairs, plates and flatware, and everything necessary to make the event run as smoothly as possible. How this layout ultimately impacts the guest's experience is the primary concern of this chapter.

2

DESIGNING
the **BUFFET**

PAIRINGS
palate + plate

Beef Fajitas
Pico de Gallo
Guacamole

walnut • south • cranford, nj . 908.276.4026

PAIRINGS
palate + plate

Herbed Beer Batter Shrimp
and Vegetables

UNFORGETTABLE

AN UNFORGETTABLE BUFFET IS OUR GOAL, GRANTED, BUT ALL TOO OFTEN IT IS DEEMED ALL TOO FORGETTABLE. The usual assumption holds that it won't wow, that it's been done before, that it's the same old stuff. For the buffet experience to be made unforgettable, it doesn't just need its batteries recharged—it needs a total makeover. It needs a reimagining of menus, a redesign of layouts, a revamping of equipment, and a reintroduction of service.

But before we can do this, we have to forget a few things. We have to forget that it's merely lots of choices of lots of food for lots of people. We have to forget those who complain that it's outmoded, with limp food and long lines. We have to forget the dazed and confused looks of the self-servers, the slopping, and the spilling. And we have to forget the notion that it's mass-produced, that it's never quite as good as it should be. Forget this never-never land and awaken to a new world built on flavor that's fresh and vibrant, layer upon intriguing layer, internationally influenced yet inviting and comforting. Welcome to the new world of modern buffet design.

OUTSIDE THE BOX

A variety of crudités is anything but ordinary served on a vertical display.

TO BE SURE, THE MODERN BUFFET MUST SHAKE OFF ITS COBWEBS AND BE REINVENTED. It must offer a taste of the exotic, of the new and exciting, in addition to the traditional and comforting. Of course, this does not supplant traditional methods and applications; rather, it is an integration of them with what has developed in the world around us. The embracing of ethnic foods, the technological improvements in equipment, and the manner in which these two are combined to serve the guests' needs is the new reality.

Once there was only the predictable long table, the horizontal buffet overflowing with chafers and silver platters from which guests served themselves. But it's a new and interactive world now for both guest and chef. Now vertical is in, pedestals and risers of varying heights and composition lend interest, and newly designed vessels can contain either hot or cold foods. Now satellite stations break up the linear path, with intoxicating flavors and aromas inviting the guests to partake. Now smaller tasting plates, precious in perception, pay homage to the fresh, to the local, and to the artisanal. Now the kitchen is brought out to the guests as dishes are made à la minute, focusing on the food on a more intimate level. Now all the comforts of home, wherever it may be, are allowed to come together and interact.

Thinking outside the box requires imagination and creativity. This makes the buffet experience stand out and tell a story, and, consequently, be remembered and talked about. The modern buffet should be energetic and allow guests to socialize and inter-mingle beyond what may occur during a served dinner. It should flow smoothly, with an interaction of guest and chef that reflects the client's vision. And, through our own brand of customization and service, it should provide an air of sophistication and exclusivity.

THE BIG PICTURE

EVEN BEFORE WE CAN DISCUSS THE NUMBER AND PLACEMENT OF THE BUFFET LINES AND STATIONS, WE NEED TO DETERMINE HOW MUCH SPACE IS AVAILABLE FOR THE BUFFET EITHER ON- OR OFF-PREMISES. This means we must know the various components that the event demands of the space in locating tables and chairs, stages and dance floors, head table or band. This is the big picture; nothing stands independently. Each component has an impact on the next and on the space itself. A domino effect occurs when making any placement deci-sion, and the client should be included in this process.

Obviously, the look and feel and flow of the space change according to how it is set up, and each arrangement has its own impact on guest traffic and ease of service. Thus, we often need to back into our use of the space by penciling in and prioritizing these other components and then maximizing the space left for the buffet.

Lay of the Land

Design of the buffet and room layout can only be done in conjunction with menu de-velopment and client input, as each one hinges upon the other. To design the layout of the buffet, start with a menu in mind and physically sketch the space, indicating length and width, height and shape. This may be evident when at our own location but must be carefully considered for off-site events. By starting with these basics, the physical layout can be plotted and pertinent details added. Use exact dimensions and include anything peculiar that affects the use of the space, such as:

- All doorways, aisles, and paths

- Windows, main entrances, and fire exits

- Distances to and from the kitchen

- Pillars and other impediments

- Locations of restrooms

- Electrical outlets, panels, and utility closets

- Stairwells, bleachers, stages, or anything hanging from the ceiling

Make notes about the atmosphere: indoor or outdoor, open to the elements or tented, a single large room or a combination of smaller ones. Is it bright and airy or dark and cozy? What will it require from our staff beyond basic setup? When surveying an outdoor space, include notes on the patio, paths, shrubs, and uneven areas that may cause tripping hazards or wobbly tables.

BLOCK IT OUT

Figuring out how to use a large space to its best advantage may seem overwhelming, but it's easily managed by dividing the whole into smaller equal sections. Divide the space into 10-foot square blocks and assign a specific function to each block.

We can assume that each 10-foot square block accommodates:

- One 60-inch round table with 10 chairs

- One 8-foot table (buffet, head table, or bar)

- A stand-up reception or dance area for 20 to 25

Because our goal is to have every guest through the line in about 15 minutes, keep in mind this general rule: A traditional 16-foot straight-line buffet comfortably accommodates 50 to 75 guests.

With these assumptions in mind, we can quickly determine what is doable: How much of the space can be or should be devoted to the buffet? Is there room for everyone to be seated? Is there only room for a stand-up reception? Or is the best alternative somewhere in between?

Let's plan the high school sports award dinner and determine how the menu and layout impact one another:

High School Sports Award Dinner Logistics	*Menu*		
200 people plus head table for 12	Mâche Salad with Basil Vinaigrette	Rigatoni al Forno	Vanilla Cake, Chocolate Mousse, Chocolate Whipped Cream
7:00 P.M. opening remarks	Bread Basket	Roasted Vegetable Tower Milanese, Macadamia-Pignoli Pesto, Sun-Dried Tomato Jam	Pizzelles
Dinner served immediately after	Chicken Milanese; Lemon Sauce; Artichoke, Caper, and Lemon Sauce	Roasted New Potatoes and Balsamic-Onion Jam	Coffee, Tea, Decaf
8:30 P.M. coffee and dessert served	Sweet Italian Sausage and Peppers	Garlicky Wilted Spinach	Iced Tea, Lemonade, Water
8:45 awards begin	Italian Meatballs in Herbed Tomato Sauce	Orange Spiked Carrots	
Have to be out by 11:00			

We have the menu and the timeline and are now ready to evaluate how the menu and layout impact one another. Start with a detailed sketch of the area on graph paper (see illustration below).

We make a detailed map of the space indicating length and width; height and shape; doorways, aisles, and paths; windows, main entrances, and fire exits; distances to and from the kitchen; pillars and other impediments; locations of restrooms; electrical outlets, panels, and utility closets; stairwells; bleachers; stages; and anything hanging from the ceiling.

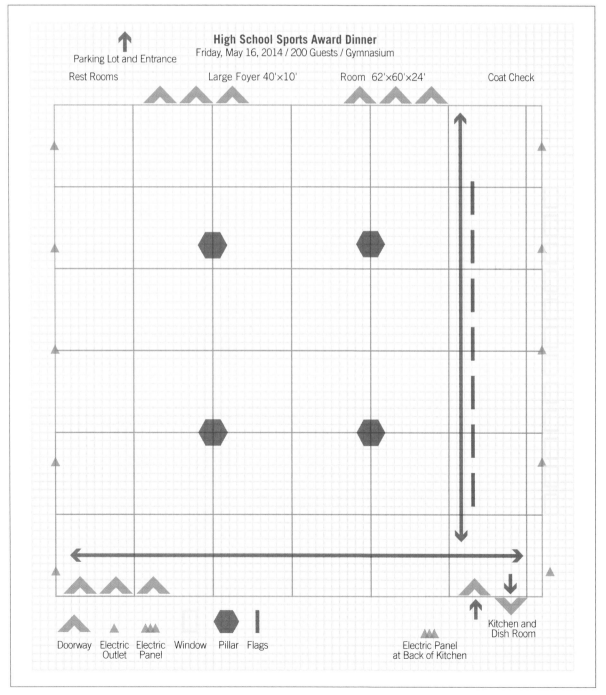

FILL IN THE BLANKS

With the sketch blocked out and a tentative menu selected, possible setups become clearer. Identify each physical element needed for the event and fill in corresponding blocks on the grid; for this event, we need to fill in areas for the buffet, beverages, head table, and seating. Start with the focal points and assess the options. Once the locations of the buffet and head table are determined, everything else will fall into place.

Since a 16-foot buffet line accommodates 50 to 75 guests, we can safely assume that we need three or four lines for 212 guests. And since one 8-foot table seats four when configured as a head table, we assume we need three tables. Placing the buffet lines in the middle of the room, blocking views of the head table and podium, is not an option. Placing them at opposite ends of the room works, but it also means crossing in front of the head table when serving and clearing. The buffet works against the back wall or under the windows, since both are close to the kitchen; however, the head table looks best under the windows and framed by the flags. Furthermore, the buffet placed near the back wall can be cleared unobtrusively as the awards are presented. Now we can fill in these blanks: three squares for the head table under the windows and eight squares for the four buffet lines near the back wall.

An elegant and economical use for this space is the 60-inch round table with ten chairs, so we assume we need at least twenty tables. Generally, a bar with two bartenders services 100 guests, so assume two bars. Now we can fill in these blanks: twenty squares for the tables and chairs that have a view of the head table, and one square for each beverage area placed at opposite sides of the room (see illustration on facing page).

SHARPEN YOUR PENCIL

Let's look at our plan and how it works so far. Does the space accommodate everything comfortably? Is there room enough for circulation? Are all entrances and emergency exits and doors clearly accessible? What can be streamlined, moved to a better location, or eliminated? What else needs to be added? For example, other needs to consider might include a dance floor, a table to display a cake or to hold gifts, coat racks, or a DJ or band area. Evaluate, prioritize, and adjust.

The awards ceremony is the most important aspect of this event, so first we pencil in the head table. We need to add a podium. To maintain symmetry, it is placed in the center and a 4-foot and an 8-foot table are placed on each side. Keep in mind that the podium must be accessible to everyone at the head table and that clear paths must be kept open for those coming forward to receive awards. To ensure that everyone has a clear view, risers are warranted. These standard 4-foot squares, 1 foot high, are used two deep to accommodate a table, chair, and aisle, so fourteen are needed. Pencil them in butted up against the back wall for safety, with a 6-foot-wide aisle in front of them (see illustration on page 34). Note that the head table must be skirted and that there is an electrical outlet for the microphone. Room is tight for one beverage area, so it is moved to the other side of the buffet. Not ideal, but it's a temporary option.

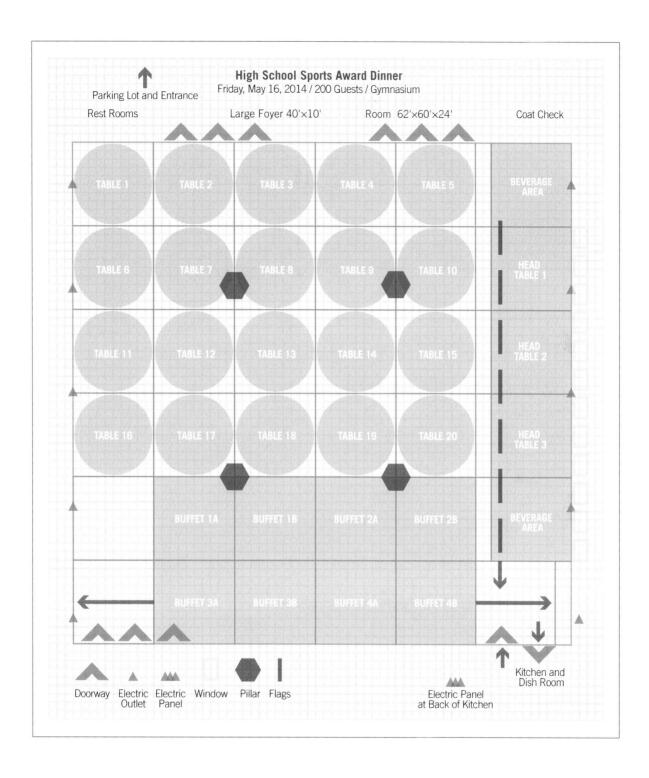

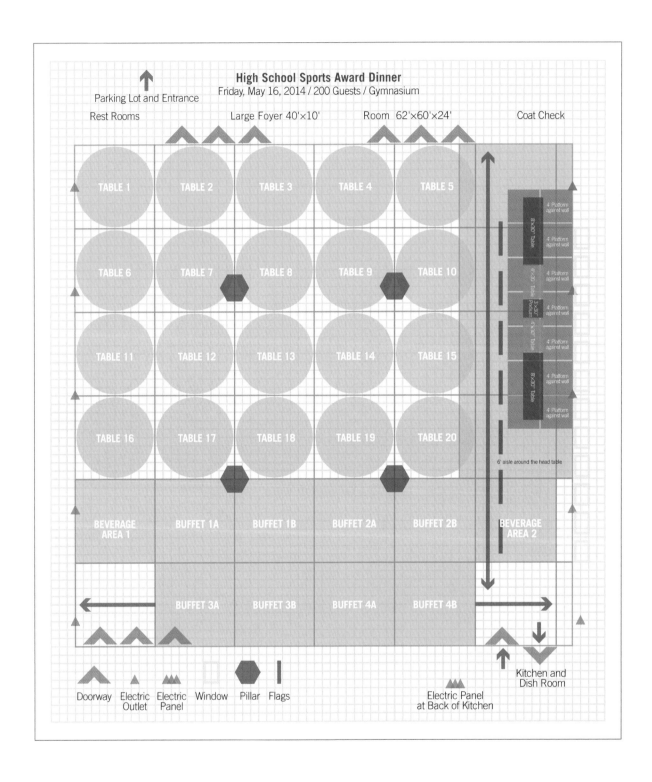

High School Sports Award Dinner
Friday, May 16, 2014 / 200 Guests / Gymnasium

Parking Lot and Entrance

Rest Rooms   Large Foyer 40'×10'   Room 62'×60'×24'   Coat Check

TABLE 1   TABLE 2   TABLE 3   TABLE 4   TABLE 5

TABLE 6   TABLE 7   TABLE 8   TABLE 9   TABLE 10

TABLE 11   TABLE 12   TABLE 13   TABLE 14   TABLE 15

TABLE 16   TABLE 17   TABLE 18   TABLE 19   TABLE 20

4' Platform against wall
8'×30" Table
4' Platform against wall
4'×30 Table
4' Platform against wall
3'×30" Podium
4' Platform against wall
4'×30" Table
4' Platform against wall
8'×30" Table
4' Platform against wall

6' aisle around the head table

BEVERAGE AREA 1   BUFFET 1A   BUFFET 1B   BUFFET 2A   BUFFET 2B   BEVERAGE AREA 2

BUFFET 3A   BUFFET 3B   BUFFET 4A   BUFFET 4B

Kitchen and Dish Room

Doorway   Electric Outlet   Electric Panel   Window   Pillar   Flags   Electric Panel at Back of Kitchen

THE LINE ON BUFFETS

The most common buffet setup is a straight line where food is served from one side or self-served from both sides. For large crowds, multiple lines presenting the same dishes can be placed together or on opposite sides of the room and allow the chef to close one as the initial push to be served dies down. A pair of buffet lines side by side saves space while moving guests along the line quickly. Aesthetically, the overall stretch of the line should not exceed 16 linear feet without a break. The addition of a carving or specialty station, which also adds energy to the line through the interaction between guest and chef, remedies this.

Although a straight-line buffet may be the most ordinary, it can be made extraordinary by using tables and risers of varying heights, tall centerpieces, and tiered food vessels. Height pulls the eye upward and captures the guests' attention from the second they enter the room. A vertically styled buffet, therefore, renders the entire view more contemporary and invites guests into the space to anticipate what's to come.

A two-tiered semicircular table adds a three-dimensional pop to this hors d'oeuvre station with a great use of space.

Serpentine tables are added to create an intriguing layout, but without height, this buffet not only makes it more difficult for guests to see and reach every dish, but it also has no wow factor.

Configuring the buffet into H, L, T, or V shapes breaks up the monotony of the straight line while helping to control the flow of traffic. To further soften the absolute straightness of this line, serpentine or quarter round tables are added to create intriguing layouts. Large circular, rectangular, or horseshoe-shaped configurations allow the open centers to be used as grand displays or as points from which attendants can serve. Ovals, semicircles, and serpentines are more fluid, more sophisticated, and often hold more items than straight-line buffets.

Satellite stations are another way to enhance a buffet and can be operated in conjunction with or independently of a line to showcase or demonstrate specialty items. Because they can be located in different areas of the room, stations encourage grazing and mingling and become the stars of the show by adding flashes of fire and heat. Traffic flow is more leisurely paced, however, as guests return for items they find most appealing and linger for demos.

Personality and functionality are added to the same buffet with the exact same equipment by simply setting some of the vessels on risers and stands.

The Picture Develops

The menu, style of service, head count, room size, and timeline all directly impact the final menu and configuration of the buffet. Each of these components needs to be examined independently, yet all must work in unison. Many of these details need to be brainstormed with the client before final decisions are made.

Since the sports award dinner starts at 7:00 P.M. with the awards following, this buffet must be especially efficient and quickly paced. We want to have 212 people through the line in twenty minutes in order for all to enjoy their meals at the same time. This is doable when the layout has four buffet lines, each prepared to serve fifty guests. The menu is a straightforward self-service buffet with no hors d'oeuvre or cocktail hour. We determine that two double-sided buffets back to back are the best option for this event given the space limitation. Pencil them in. Make note that a table riser can run down the middle of the buffet, adding height and drama and calling attention to its location in the space.

A plated and served dish adds a feeling of personalized service and eliminates crowding along the buffet.

To ease traffic flow, the beverage areas should always be located away from the buffet, obviously an issue with this plan so far. Iced tea and lemonade are the only options, so it's decided to nix the beverage areas altogether and place carafes on the tables.

A salad station is proposed to add the feel of more personalized service and allow more room on the buffet. Upon closer evaluation, however, this station takes up too much space and causes bottlenecks. We recommend setting the tables with napkins and flatware and individually plating the salads to be served with the bread and butter once guests are all seated (see photo at left). This not only quickens the pace of the event but also adds a first course, shortens the time required to go through the line, and frees up additional circulation space. To end the event with personalized service, cake, coffee, tea, and decaf will be served tableside.

Next, address the seating area. Pencil in the tables with chairs and 2½-foot circulation aisles around each. Shift these tables closer to the buffet to allow for a larger entrance area into the gym.

While penciling in these details, always optimize the use of space for the guests' convenience and then consider the proximity to the kitchen for ease of service. To accommodate the guests and keep everything flowing smoothly, double-check the size appropriateness of paths leading to and from the focal points and eliminate any choke points. Make sure the guests can intuitively understand how to proceed through the space without any crisscrossing, crowding, or herding effects detracting from their overall experience. Evaluate, prioritize, and adjust.

With our plan, illustrated on the facing page, setting up on the day of the event is efficient and straightforward. However, once everything is in place, before the event begins, we need to walk the room in the guests' shoes. See what they see, hear what they hear, and feel what they feel. Experience what they experience. Once again, evaluate, prioritize, and adjust. When it all works without a hitch, chance has little to do with it.

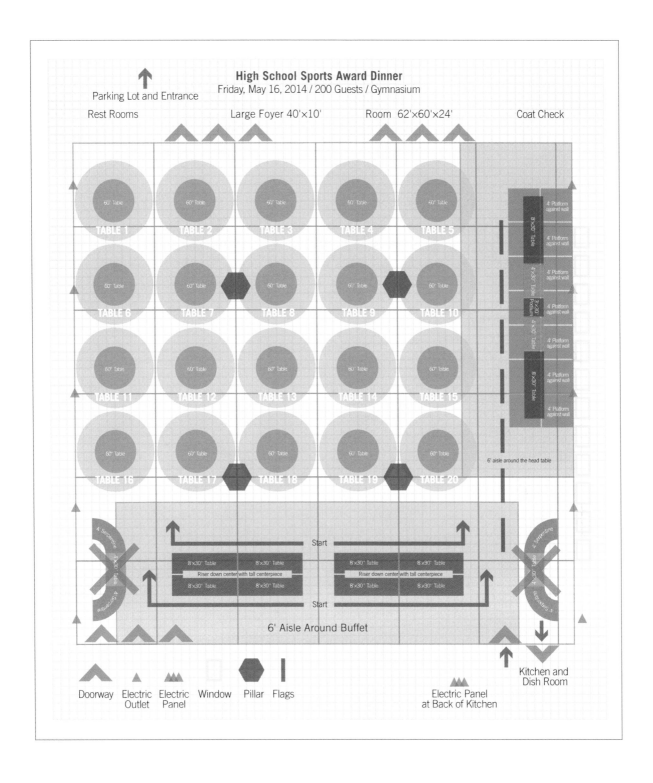

Providing a designated place for used plates and glasses makes cleaning easier and keeps the buffet tidier.

Waste Management

A tasty little appetizer is graciously served, and then what happens to the frilled pick and crumpled napkin? Heading to the buffet, what's to be done with the empty glass? With no alternative, they are plopped down amid the clean plates on our elegantly appointed buffet; our carefully arranged displays, and perhaps some appetites, are ruined just like that. Since there is no obvious place for the capture and removal of remains, the buffet becomes a mess.

Like soiled linens, spotted table settings, or haphazard service, this sets the tone for the event. Yet the fix is so easy. A simple solution to the debris dilemma is a tray on a skirted stand near the approach to the buffet. Seeded with a few empties and placed strategically, a tray signals to the guest, "Here's a place for the junk." A place for discards, including plates and glasses, must be obvious to the guests and part of our plan. After setup is complete, a walk-through inspection of the room makes sure this tray is in its place.

Textures, colors, and shapes in clear bowls call guests to a buffet that screams "fresh." The smaller platters of chicken, beef, and shrimp assure that every piece is juicy or crispy. The smaller vessels also make for easy replenishment, keeping all of the dishes at their peak of attractiveness.

Keep It Fresh

Do more with less. Though large mirrors, serving platters, and silver chafers make stunning statements initially, they become messy and unappetizing after only a few guests help themselves. While oversized platters offer a bountiful presentation to the first few, those further back get a different view. Heaping platters imply old-fashioned mass production, whereas the same food composed on smaller platters suggests contemporary craftsmanship. And it's about much more than the size of the vessel.

Our objective is not only to offer the last guest the same choice that the first guest enjoyed, but also for the last guests to feel as if they were first in line. The goal is to keep everything looking fresh and attractive by providing a clear method of replenishment. This is achieved with the more fashionable use of smaller vessels, replaced more often, more rapidly, and more readily, which also allows quick adaptation to guests' tastes. When a particular dish is in high demand, more platters can be at the ready, while any dish that is not moving can be swapped out and returned to the kitchen. Although larger quantities of the same style serving vessels are needed, the smaller quantities of foods sitting on display reduce food costs.

Safe food-handling practices can also be reinforced by the use of smaller-scale displays. Since smaller vessels are replaced rather than added to or topped off, the tendency to combine fresh items with picked-over ones is avoided. Using several smaller vessels to arrange and serve foods means smaller quantities are on display at any given time. This allows the greater portion to be held at the correct temperature in the oven or refrigerator.

Because all foods need to be served at the correct temperature, because they need to look their best and freshest at all times, and because the distance from the prep area to the serving area must be factored in as a timeline issue, the buffet's proximity to the kitchen almost always outranks other concerns. A short sprint beats a marathon for runners while navigating around guests and other hazards.

Proper procedures eliminate potentially unsafe behavior and ensure that only the freshest and most attractive food is served. Obviously time is of the essence when serving guests from a buffet line, and having a procedure for "when to" and "how to" replenish makes sense. Every operation must have standards for replacement. Some replace strictly at half-full time; others let it play out until closer to the end. This replacement procedure must work in sync with the servers, the runners,

Using smaller vessels keeps food looking fresh and attractive, because they can be easily and quickly replaced with new platters.

and the kitchen to keep the buffet fresh. The kitchen should be prepared to supply fresh platters promptly to avoid disrupting service and make replenishing unobtrusive and efficient.

The Icing on the Cake

It's all in the details. It's going that extra mile. It's adding that little something. It's all just common sense until we realize that it's not really common at all. In fact, it's pretty rare. It's what sets us apart. It doesn't cost much more, but it adds a lot more.

Guests today want to be in the know. They want to know what the dish is, naturally, but they want to know more. They want to know something of provenance, husbandry, and stewardship. They want to know about ingredients, sources, and preparation. They want to know about regional specialties and treasured family recipes. But mostly, they want to be privy to the kitchen's insider information.

With printed signage and an informative staff, the guest's need to know is addressed. Apt descriptions shine light on the composition of dishes. They alert guests to potential allergy issues with ingredients like dairy, wheat, eggs, shellfish, nuts, and nut oils. And they enrich the entire experience with educational and entertainment elements perceived as value added to the bottom line.

PAIRINGS
palate + plate

Fruit Salad
Scented with Ginger and Lime

walnut + south · cranford, nj · 908-276-4026

LEFT: **The aroma of sweet Italian sausage and peppers cooking on an induction burner fills the room with a wonderful aroma, turning a relatively inexpensive dish into a sought-after one.**

RIGHT: **Clear signage not only communicates the type of dish to guests but also alerts them to potential allergy issues.**

Guests today demand an exceptional experience; that they are the priority should be evident in the buffet design. With a direct impact on how food and service are perceived, the buffet should function clearly, without confusion or complication. It should be designed to encourage guests to proceed intuitively along the line without ever feeling awkward or uninformed. There should be no "what is it" menu choices and no "what to do with it" procedural issues.

Providing exceptional hospitality means thinking strategically:

- There should be ample space to approach the line, and the direction of flow should be obvious.

- Everything must fit the table securely, with no chance of falling or spilling or collapsing if bumped.

- At least one attendant should be assigned to each line to maintain it and to assist guests with any needs.

- Food should be arranged in a logical order. First, decide how the food should look if it were plated in the kitchen. Then back into the food arrangement on the buffet to achieve that look. If it is ratatouille on polenta, the polenta has to be first. And it usually makes sense to start the buffet with cold food so that hot food is enjoyed as hot as possible, not sitting on a plate getting cold as you wait to go through the rest of the line.

■ The size of the vessel and serving spoon should correlate to the size of the finished portion. Place pasta in a large bowl with a 4 fl-ounce serving spoon and grated cheese in a much smaller bowl with a teaspoon.

■ Correctly sized plates should be stacked neatly at the beginning of the line, signaling to the guests to "start here." Use smaller plates for tasting stations and larger plates for full meals.

■ A printed menu at the front of the line helps with decision-making, and labeling each dish speeds movement through the line. An attendant describing the dish adds personalized attention.

■ Napkins and flatware should be located at the end of the line so there is no juggling. Better yet, setting tables with flatware whenever possible is a more elegant approach that reduces space needed for the buffet and, more importantly, puts the guests' needs first.

■ The design should maintain correct serving temperatures. Keep hot with hot and cold with cold. A salad quickly goes limp next to a steaming chafing dish.

■ Group all similar items in the same area; carrots, cauliflower, and broccoli, for instance, should be displayed in concert so guests see all vegetable choices. They should also be placed in the order they need to go on the plate: Lettuce greens go first, then tomatoes, then dressing, then chicken.

■ Sauces and condiments should be placed directly with the foods they accompany so that guests understand how to use them. Raspberry Coulis (page 305) is placed alongside the Pecan-Studded Chicken (page 230), not the Herb-Crusted Lamb Duo with Burgundy Reduction (page 251).

- All food on the buffet should be sliced, cut, plated, or marked to indicate portion. If the dish is costly or complicated, it's often best to plate or skewer it for effective portion control. Shrimp and scallop kebobs cut down on the amount of seafood needed. Individual soup shooters speed the line along with their "grab-n-go" portions.

- If there is no table seating, the food should be bite-size or small enough so that no cutting is necessary. It's impossible to use a knife while standing with a plate.

Tiered vessels not only look more interesting, but they are also more easily reached and allow more to fit on the buffet. With lower tiers in front and higher in back, we make sure nothing is blocked or can get knocked over. Ideally, drippy foods should go in front to prevent any dripping into other foods.

Individually portioned salads are easy for guests to grab and enjoy.

This buffet is beautiful but is missing a few details vital to the guest's experience. The buffet is lacking proper signage, napkins and utensils should be at the end, the salads need utensils that guests can use with one hand, and dessert plates should be before the dessert. These simple alterations make a big difference.

- Vessels themselves should be placed far enough apart so that a guest can put a plate down if necessary.

- Every dish on the buffet needs its own utensil with a landing pad. A small plate, for example, indicates to the guest where to place the utensil without messing the tablecloth.

- Utensils should not only be the correct type for the dish but should also be appropriately sized to the portion they will serve. A 4-ounce serving of soup needs a 4-ounce ladle. A 2-inch square of lasagna needs a 2-inch spatula.

- All utensils should be designed for single-handed use. Use tongs for a salad, not a salad server set.

A well-organized buffet signals to the guest that care was taken in the food preparation. Higher bowls are in the back, attractive signage is next to each dish, ample room is between each dish, appropriately sized serving utensils have plates underneath them to catch drips, condiments are placed after the dishes that they belong with, and foods are in the logical order that they are meant to go on the plate.

■ If the serving vessel has a lid, clearly indicate where it goes or remove it before service begins.

There are no minor details. As we did with the room setup, we must walk this line, imagining we are the guests, with a plate in hand. Each food display must be checked and rechecked. Make sure each one is balanced and eye-catching. Make sure each one can be reached without catching a sleeve. Make sure it is all in the right order without the need for backtracking. These personal touches make the food taste better. They are the icing on the cake.

Shining a spotlight on the buffet allows us to see what makes it come alive. As with any theatrical presentation, the possibility of a gaffe, a forgotten line, or a missed cue is always present. There are no stops, edits, takes, or retakes. It has to be so well rehearsed that the show goes on without the audience ever being aware of a glitch.

BUFFET STATIONS: EQUIPMENT, SERVICE, *and* SETUP

ALL THE WORLD'S A STAGE

DIRECTIONS FROM THE STAGE MANAGER OR THE CHEF PULL TO-GETHER OUR DRAMATIC ACTION. With a supporting cast of equipment, utensils, and servers, our star is ready for its close-up. There is only one chance to get it right, to surge beyond the ordinary. But before zooming in to get this close-up, food safety must be addressed.

Safety First

The triumvirate of time, temperature, and food handling govern the methods for setting up the buffet; it does not matter how beautiful the buffet looks if the food is not safe to eat. The primary function of buffet equipment is to maintain food at the correct temperature for the entire time that it is on display: hot foods above 135°F/57°C and cold foods below 41°F/5°C. Foods that are set out without this temperature control should be plated in small portions, continuously monitored, and never left out for more than 2 hours at room temperature. If the ambient conditions are above 78°F/26°C, caution must be exercised.

Food prepared ahead of time for reheating must move through the danger zone as rapidly as possible and be brought to 165°F/74°C for a minimum of 15 seconds. Hot holding equipment, such as chafing dishes, cannot be used for cooking or reheating. A steam table will adequately hold already heated foods above 135°F/57°C, but it is not able to bring foods out of the danger zone quickly enough and therefore should never be used to bring food up to temperature. All hot food must be brought to the proper temperature over direct heat from a burner, flattop, grill, or oven, and instant-read thermometers must always be used to check food temperatures on a regular basis.

Hot foods must be held above 135°F/57°C at all times to ensure proper food safety.

SAFETY CONSIDERATIONS

- Do use proper food service equipment that can hold food at correct temperatures.

- Do keep hot foods at or above 135°F/57°C and check temperatures using an instant-read thermometer at least every hour.

- Do keep cold foods at or below 41°F/5°C and check temperatures using an instant-read thermometer at least every hour.

- Do keep a time limit of 2 hours for food to be on the buffet at normal ambient temperature without temperature control and have a policy for discarding food that exceeds this time limit.

- Do use gloves, tongs, spatulas, and appropriate serving utensils.

- Do keep the buffet clean and tidy throughout service.

- Do have extra plates for seconds; do not allow guests to reuse plates.

- Do not allow guests to touch, sneeze, or cough on food.

- Do not display foods outdoors directly in the sun.

- Do not allow utensils to migrate from one dish to another.

- Do not combine food fresh from the kitchen into food already on the buffet.

Sleek, modern vessels are available that keep cold foods at the proper temperature, such as this insulated bowl with a hidden ice pack.

The presentation of the modern buffet must be meticulously planned for the service and equipment style to complement the food. Cold salads are grouped together on matching elevated platters, while hot soups are in bouillabaisse pots set on chafing dish alternatives.

THE STATION

From the intimate to the huge, from the basic to the intricate, from the local to the exotic, the experience is made more memorable when guests are encouraged to become part of the action. Breaking the straight-line buffet into separate stations further infuses guest involvement with vitality and movement. By adding personality and flair, we showcase our creativity not only in the menu, but also in its presentation; not only in the use of the event space, but also in its overall ambience; not only in the personnel present, but also in the warm way the guest is welcomed to be a part of the action. It's not just the diversity of foods on display that makes the buffet modern; it's the addition of an entertainment aspect, which is the interaction that occurs between the guest and the chef when food is the catalyst.

An hors d'oeuvre station creates a welcoming focal point but is flexible enough to be part of the buffet or stand on its own.

A station is a food presentation area that can be part of the buffet line or that can stand on its own and operate independently. It reflects the same view to the guest, albeit on a micro scale, as the open kitchen. A station functions as the focal point of the event by selecting special food items and allowing them to shine in their own spotlight rather than letting them blend indistinctly into the line. A station should also add decorative and entertainment aspects, and, when separated from the main line, get people to mingle and interact during an event.

When planning out the buffet line and integrating a station, keep in mind how much room is required. Although a station may not need as much square footage as the main buffet line itself, it actually requires more planning to function effectively. In sketching the layout of the space, keep the following elements in mind: proximity to the kitchen for ease of service, aisle space for guest access, and overall decorum and appearance. Since service must continue unabated during replenishing and cleaning, setting up as near the kitchen as practical saves time and energy. Furthermore, understanding the manner in which guests circulate becomes critical, as materials, preparation and service equipment, servers, chefs, and lines of guests will crowd available space quickly.

Cooks should practice how long it will take to prepare a dish on a station so that they can anticipate traffic flow.

THE STATION

Guest traffic flow is directly impacted by how long it takes to serve a particular dish at a station compounded by how long it takes for each guest to pick up a plate and move along comfortably. The dish should never be new to the staff; rather, it should be a well-practiced dish that has been made several times before the event takes place. Practice the procedure of making the dish at the station and time it carefully. With staff members acting as guests, cook, plate, and serve the dish. Make sure there is time enough to perform every step, including having to answer guests' questions about the food and preparation methods. Establish a plan in case the line backs up so that the kitchen is ready to replenish without any chance of a hiccup. For example, if fish is being sautéed à la minute in front of the guests, the kitchen must be prepared to sauté fish and deliver it to the station.

The setup of a station requires the attendants to be aware of the surroundings at all times, because guests notice everything. Cleanliness and sanitation rules must be observed: Uniforms, caps, and gloves are required before attendants can actually man the station. Nowhere else is mise en place and efficiency as important. Only the necessary equipment should be present, but nothing should be forgotten. Every piece of preparation equipment must be spotless, with a way to keep it that way as it is used. Every guideline that applies to the buffet as a whole applies to the station in particular. It must be intuitive to the guest which direction to follow, food must be in the correct order with any dips and/or condiments positioned nearby with properly sized serving utensils, and there must be adequate room for guests to be served or to serve themselves. This brings us back to menu development, layout, and equipment, for which ease of service is a major component. Staff should perform a complete walk-through, a dress rehearsal, from both the guest side and the service side of the station. Even with these organizational demands, a station engages the crowd with a showcase of the chef's techniques and skills as individual plates are crafted.

The Satellite Station

In its most basic form, a satellite station is set up away from the main buffet. As a classic example, beverages are usually separated from the main line so that major traffic tie-ups are avoided. This better use of space allows a guest to return again and again while not having an impact on more labor-intensive or time- and temperature-sensitive items.

The satellite station can be staffed or self-served, depending on what is being offered. For example, a full bar with mixed drinks requires at least one bartender, while a wine bar with appropriate signage can generally be left unattended. An attendant at a dessert station can slice the cake and plate it for guests who may be reluctant to slice their own, whereas an unattended coffee station can be adequate for most events. One side of the juice bar can be left unattended, while the other side, offering Bellinis, mimosas, and other cocktails, should be attended. The raw bar can be set apart to be a self-service type, or it can be made more elaborate and alluring with an attendant actively shucking and plating oysters in front of the guests. The number of attendants

Satellite stations can be self-service or staffed with an attendant to assist guests. Here, an employee slices cake for guests as they pass the station.

needed and the type of stations possible are determined by the client's vision for the event and the budget available.

It may be more intriguing to have an entire event planned around satellite stations instead of one uninterrupted line. This is yet another common element of the modern buffet that enhances the diversity of dishes while spreading the crowd throughout the event space. This idea can be especially appealing because it helps alleviate the stress of all guests heading for a single buffet line at once. One approach for such a plan is to contemplate a separate "bar" for as many items as space permits. With a series of these separate bars or islands strategically placed throughout the space, guests are encouraged to mingle and interact while they stroll and taste different dishes. The individual stations might feature pasta, sushi, or tapas, or adhere more to a specific theme, such as a trip through Spain with stations featuring Miniature Chicken and Pepper Empanadas (page 115), Garlicky Smoked Paprika Shrimp (page 117), Tortilla Española (page 140) with Romesco (page 322), Spanish Tomato Bread (page 113), and Quince Gastrique (page 318).

It cannot be stressed enough, though, that each station must have a plan for replenishing, cleaning, and collecting used items. The setup plan must include a method for easy replenishing so that there is no interruption of service or appearance of disorganization. Since replenishing is often a two-person operation, with one to remove the used or empty vessel and one to replace it with a new or full one, appoint specific staff members in appropriate attire. A harried line cook with a soiled jacket and side towel, for instance, should not be expected to do this. Used items such as plates; flatware and glasses; and toothpicks, napkins, and leftovers must be cleared continuously during the event, and a specific person should be in charge of this task.

These side dishes take a starring role at a satellite station while encouraging guests to move about the room.

SAMPLE SATELLITE STATIONS

Self-Serve Satellite Hors d'Oeuvre Station

Gougères (page 139)

Lemony Hummus (page 134) with Cashew-Studded Naan (page 262)

Grilled Vegetable Platter (page 181) and Red Pepper Rouille (page 324)

Alsatian Pizza with Sun-Dried Tomato Pesto, Montrachet, and Fresh Mozzarella (page 109)

Cheddar-Kissed Potato Pancakes (page 143) with crème fraîche and chives

Side Dish Satellite Station

Broccoli with Cashew Butter (page 179)

Orange-Spiked Carrots (page 182)

Creamy Polenta Marbled with Taleggio (page 211)

Potatoes au Gratin (page 215)

Mini Cupcake and Fruit Salad Bar

Chocolate Lovers' Cake (page 274) with Chocolate Whipped Cream Icing (page 305)

Vanilla Cake (page 283) with Lemon Curd (page 306)

Banana Spice Cake (page 276) with Brown Sugar Glaze (page 303)

Fruit Scented with Ginger and Lime (page 166)

Raw Bar Action Station

Oysters

Mussels

Clams

Shrimp

Crab

Lemons and limes

Horseradish, Tabasco, vinegars

Cocktail sauce, mignonette sauce, salsas

Action Stations

At the action station there is some active preparation of the food in full view of the guest, whether it is slicing the roast, saucing the pasta, or dressing the salad. A classic example is a carving station where the premier roast, or *grosse pièce*, is sliced as each guest approaches. It can offer one or more of the main proteins, such as Crusted Beef Tenderloin (page 229), Turkey Roulade with Sausage, Carrot, and Spinach Stuffing (page 246), or Herb-Crusted Lamb Duo with Burgundy Reduction (page 251). Since slicing à la minute presents meat at its peak with no loss of color or juiciness, the carving station becomes the center of attraction; guests can see the quality offered and decide on the quantity they desire.

Typically a carving station has an integrated heat lamp and cutting board from which guests are served. An alternative to the heat lamp, if electricity is not available, is to keep the *grosse pièce* warm in a chafing dish and to slice it on a cutting board set into a sheet pan: moistened side towel down, sheet pan down, another moistened side towel set into the sheet pan, then the cutting board on top. A tablecloth can be draped around the setup to give it a finished look. This will keep the station neat and clean without giving the guest a view of anything messy. Regardless of the setup, the cutting

Carving station setup: carving tools on a tray with hot water and side towels (left), carving station with heat lamp and cutting board (center), plates for carved portions (front right), and bowls for garnishes and sauces (back right).

board has to be clean and sanitary and set atop a moist towel to prevent slippage when slicing. Additional mise en place for a carving station includes a hot water bucket to keep the knife blade clean, side towels or paper towels to clean the blade and general area, a steel, a slicing knife and fork, a platter or a roasting pan to hold the *grosse pièce*, serving bowls and pieces for the condiments, and plates for the guests. In addition, the station needs a sanitation bucket and trash container, both of which should be kept out of view of the guest.

The action station is usually constructed with most of the food already prepared and held at the appropriate temperature. The chef, cook, or attendant then finishes the dish in view of the guest. At a crêpe action station, for instance, the crêpes and filling are already made and held at temperature before being assembled. At a salad action station, dressing the delicate greens à la minute prevents them from wilting too quickly and turning an unappetizing color. At a pasta action station, the pasta and the sauce or toppings are already made, but then are finished in a sauté pan on a direct heat source. Precooked dried pasta presents the textural problem of how to keep it al dente. For the action station application, dried pasta can be undercooked by a few minutes and chilled, and then for each guest, reheated in sauce à la minute. Though these are considered action stations, the actual "cooking" required at the station is kept to a minimum, since it is mostly slicing, heating, and/or finishing.

COFFEE ACTION STATION

The aroma of brewing coffee is intoxicating. A Melitta or French press coffee brewing system transforms the usual coffee urn station into something special. Smaller, brew-by-the-cup vessels present the opportunity to give guests individual attention, especially with a trained attendant discussing a particular bean, where it is grown, how it is roasted, and the method for brewing the best cup. This interaction projects the cachet that smaller is better, fresher, and handcrafted, and gives undivided attention to the guest's needs. Accompaniments, from flavored syrups and creams to alcohols and sugars, add another dimension.

This Melitta coffee system brews one cup at a time, allowing an attendant to brew the exact cup a guest would prefer, while discussing the details of the bean and brewing method.

GRILL ACTION STATION

The addition of a grill action station, for example, can elevate a simple grilled chicken breast to the "freshly made just for me" level. Buttermilk Grilled Chicken (page 242) is more delicious at an outdoor event when cooked to order, and doing this in front of the guests adds to the show. Chicken is certainly more mouthwatering hot off the grill than from a platter or chafer, even if it might have been sitting for only a minute. Since it needs to be grilled anyway, there is no large expense for new equipment or more personnel. There should be, however, a refocused attention to the maintenance of the grill and the training of the cook. The addition of freshly made Grilled Vegetable Platter (page 181) and sauces such as Sun-Dried Tomato Jam (page 325), Macadamia-Pignoli Pesto (page 323), or Fig-Onion Jam (page 326) propels the station's effectiveness even further. Emphasis, however, should always remain on cleanliness, organization, and efficiency.

ACTION STATION EXAMPLES

CARVING ACTION STATION

Turkey Roulade with Sausage, Carrot, and Spinach Stuffing (page 246), Cranberry-Bourbon Relish (page 317), and Turkey Gravy (page 313)

Crusted Beef Tenderloin (page 229) with Horseradish Crème (page 321)

Herb-Crusted Lamb Duo with Burgundy Reduction (page 251)

CRÊPE ACTION STATION

Crêpes (page 289)

Chocolate-Zinfandel Ganache (page 300) and sliced strawberries

Cherries in Blueberry Sauce (page 305)

COFFEE MELITTA BREWING SYSTEM ACTION STATION AND DESSERT BAR

Café Grand Marnier

Kona French-roasted coffee beans

Grand Marnier, whipped cream, orange peel, sugar

Coffee, tea, decaf

Milk, cream, sugars

Montazzoli Chiffon Cake (page 277) "Happy 60th Birthday Marie" with Lemon Curd (page 306), Whipped Cream Icing (page 304), and toasted coconut (see page 114)

Chocolate Lovers' Cake "Happy Mother's Day" (page 274) with

Mocha Mousse filling (page 307) and Chocolate Whipped Cream Icing (page 305)

Fruit Scented with Lime and Mint Kebobs (page 166) with Bittersweet Chocolate Sauce (page 304)

SAUSAGE AND PEPPER ACTION STATION

Sauté pan on induction burner as part of buffet

Sweet Italian Sausage and Peppers (page 249)

PASTA ACTION STATION

Butternut Squash Malfatti with Crispy Pumpkin Seeds (page 201) and Balsamic Molasses (page 318)

Black Pepper–Speckled Fettuccine Marsala with Chicken (page 196)

GRILLED TO ORDER ACTION STATION

Five-Spice Beef Satay Kebobs with Red Onion, Peppers, Zucchini, and Mushrooms (page 133)

Rosemary-Sage Grilled Lamb Kebobs (page 237)

Shrimp and Scallop Skewers in Dill-Dijon Marinade (page 253)

CREATIVE ACTION STATIONS

The action station can be ramped up to include not only ingredients chosen by the guest but also the actual cooking of the dish in front of the guest. The omelet station is a classic example of a "design your own" or creative action station. At this creation station, a cook creates an omelet to the exact specifications of the guest, such as "add mushrooms, onions, and peppers, but no cheese." The cook has all necessary ingredients set up for ease of service and prepares the omelet on a heating element or induction burner per each guest's instruction.

At a crêpe creative action station, for example, the crêpe is made à la minute, with the guest indicating how much of which filling to use. At a seafood creative action station, a cook pan-sears the seafood of choice, while the finishing sauce is determined in conversation with the guest.

Because guests can connect with the chef while their food is being cooked à la minute, the creative action station dishes are as far from mass production as

At this creative action station, a cook makes crêpes à la minute, allowing the guests to pick the filling of their choice.

It is critical to be neat and organized when cooking in front of guests. Here the cook sets up everything needed to prepare the crêpes without overcrowding the station with unnecessary tools and equipment.

can be. This type of station provides a higher level of skill, showmanship, knowledge, and organization. The cook needs the ability to multitask: to serve foods while describing ingredients and preparation methods to the guests. Of course, this added interaction requires training, not only in technique and execution, but also in basic public speaking skills, including eye contact, appropriate tone and inflection, and correct vocabulary usage. The selection of staff for guest interaction positions at stations is more critical than anywhere else and should be based on their experience and demeanor, their grace and poise. It is the chef's skill and personality that enhances the flavor of the food and elevates the atmosphere through a confident description of technique and execution.

SMOOTHIE CREATIVE ACTION STATION

Another step in the modernization of the buffet and its satellite stations is to sensationalize things in a more definitive, bold way. An example is a smoothie yogurt action station, where the guests take complete control over selecting their ingredients. All guests start with a large cup or container that they fill with their choices from a fruit and yogurt buffet. Each guest chooses only the fruit and yogurt in the desired proportion. Then, having been filled with the desired ingredients, the cups are handed to the barista or bartender, who pours the fruit-yogurt mix into the blender, locks it tight, and lets it whirl. The results are smoothies as unique as the guests designing them. Keep in mind that the size of the glass or vessel that the guests fill establishes the portion and that, once blended, it must fit into the serving glass.

Yogurt should be given considerable thought, as freshness and quality count here as much as they do with the fruit. Always include the local and the farm fresh. Offer Greek yogurt or *dahi*, both of which have fuller flavor than plain American-style yogurt. To sweeten the smoothies, consider options such as local clover or wildflower honey, maple syrup, agave, or raw or brown sugar. To sensationalize it even further, more exotic selections like mangosteens, açai berries, and Ugli fruit may be included, and their bright natural colors make eye-catching displays. To entice health-conscious guests, consider having whey and protein powders available at the blend-in station.

This idea is infinitely adaptable. The smoothie action station can also be the sensationalized adult frozen drink station with little effort. A simple alteration allows guests to enjoy frozen cocktails they've helped to make. The sensational aspect is that there is no limit to the variations. The guests can choose the fruit to blend in while the bartender is responsible for the addition of any alcohol, which can be kept to a minimum.

ABOVE LEFT: **At this interactive smoothie station, guests enjoy the opportunity to make their own by choosing the types and amounts of fruit, yogurt, and sweetener.**

ABOVE RIGHT: **The attendant blends and then serves the finished smoothie to the guest.**

The addition of any alcoholic beverages adds a legal and liability dimension to the mix. While covered at large venues by the legal department, it is imperative for the small operator to stay on top of local ordinances controlling the use and service of alcohol and to be sure that TIPS-trained (Training for Intervention Procedures) personnel are on hand.

GNOCCHI CREATIVE ACTION STATION

Gnocchi is another item that can be sensationalized at the creative action station. The guests start the line with an appropriately sized single-portion sauté pan instead of a plate and fill it with their desired vegetables and sauces: asparagus and broccoli, mushrooms and onions, tomato ragù, or creamy vodka sauce. They spoon their selections into their small sauté pan and hand it to the chef. With gnocchi already browning on one burner, the chef heats the sauce in the guest's pan on another burner before combining and plating the dish. The guest can then select a Macadamia-Pignoli Pesto (page 323) or a drizzle of extra-virgin olive oil to finish.

Imagine the entertainment and educational value of the gnocchi itself being made at this station. Guests see the gnocchi being rolled into snake-like strands, cut into bite-size pieces, and thumbed off the back of a fork. This process also holds true for a sensationalized pasta station where malfatti or fettuccine, for example, can be rolled out in front of the guests as they select their own sauces. By watching and learning before tasting, the guest is captivated by the heightened level of artisanal craftsmanship. Of course, the gnocchi or pasta for the guest meals should be prepped ahead of time so that the staff does not have to rely solely on what is produced during the demonstration.

FRESH MOZZARELLA CREATIVE ACTION STATION

Making fresh mozzarella from curds takes less than 10 minutes from start to finish. Notice steam wafting off the water, curds being stretched and kneaded ever so gently. See the still-dripping whey on the glistening orbs. Who can resist such freshness?

The fresh mozzarella creative action station can be offered as part of a garden salad, a pasta salad, a hot pasta entrée, or a bruschetta, or as part of a cheese station. As a demo, making the fresh mozzarella has an enthralling entertainment value. The simplicity of setup makes this a hit for the house as well. A few bowls of hot water and a thermometer make the setup easy. The attendant gently kneading and stretching the curd in front of the guests becomes a shining star of the event—after, of course, the fresh mozzarella itself.

BELOW LEFT: **The attendant at the gnocchi creative action station is secure knowing that the cooking process was well organized and practiced and will work for the event. So confident, she will be able to engage in conversation and entertain the guests.**

BELOW RIGHT: **Making fresh mozzarella is a dynamic and cost-effective action station. Guests watch the process and select their garnish for the warm cheese.**

CREATIVE ACTION STATION EXAMPLES

Tortilla Española and Tortilla Torcal (page 140) Creative Action Station

All of the ingredients are available in separate bowls for the guest to design their own.

Eggs

Onions

Potatoes

Serrano ham

Peas

Piquillo peppers

Chorizo

Crêpe Creative Action Station

The crêpes are made in front of the guest, who picks the fillings.

Crêpes (page 289)

Day Boat Scallops Provençal (page 120)

Ratatouille (page 182)

Cream Cheese Soufflé Filling (page 288)

Strawberries in Blueberry Sauce (page 305)

Seafood Creative Action Station

The fish is sautéed à la minute in front of the guest, who selects the accompanying pan sauce.

Ahi tuna

Black bass

Day boat scallops

Jumbo white shrimp

Mediterranean Sauce (page 256)

Provençal Sauce (page 120)

Red Pepper Rouille (page 324)

Green Onion–Wasabi Sauce (page 125)

Churro Creative Action Station

The churros are fried à la minute in front of the guest, who picks the sauces and ice creams.

Churro Pâte á Choux (page 284)

Cinnamon Sugar (page 284)

Dulce de Leche (page 303)

Bittersweet Chocolate Sauce (page 304)

Candied Pecans (page 331)

Espresso ice cream

French vanilla bean ice cream

Yukon Gold Gnocchi (page 210) Creative Action Station

Yukon Gold Gnocchi/ Dough (page 210)

Sautéed asparagus

Roasted broccoli

Sautéed Mushrooms (page 178)

Roasted Tomato Ragù (page 209)

Herbed Tomato Sauce (page 312)

Creamy Vodka Sauce (page 312)

Macadamia-Pignoli Pesto (page 323)

Grated Pecorino Romano cheese

Extra-virgin olive oil

Capers

Olives

Fruity Yogurt Smoothie (page 273) Creative Action Station

Bananas

Blueberries

Mangos

Melons

Strawberries

Mangosteens

Açai berries

Ugli fruit

Whey and protein powders

Yogurt

Honey, maple syrup, agave, raw or brown sugar

Vanilla extract

Milk

Ice

Fresh Mozzarella (page 113) Creative Action Station

Mozzarella curd

Crostini (page 333)

Roma Salsa (page 316)

THE STAGE IS SET

FOR THE BUFFET, ALL THE TABLETOP IS THE STAGE. The spotlight shines on the food and the service, while chafers and risers, bowls and platters, linens and centerpieces are the supporting players. The tabletop serves as the staging area for the dramatic action, whose prime directive is to maintain the integrity of the food, keeping hot foods hot and cold foods cold while serving guests easily and elegantly.

THE STRAIGHT EIGHT

THE STRAIGHT BUFFET TABLE WITH A PLAIN CLOTH ACROSS THE TOP HAS BEEN THE OLD RELIABLE, GO-TO, QUICK-AND-READY DESIGN OF EVERY CATERER AND EVENT PLANNER. No matter what the occasion or where it is held, the 8-foot-long table is the industry-wide standard, or the stage. There are alternatives, of course, but the straight 8-footer fits the bill as the most versatile table for the buffet and complementary stations. Though it has been around for a long time, it need not be boring, old-fashioned, or tired. Rather, every setup using "old reliable" can be contemporary, evocative, and even trendy.

Traditional dining room tables and farmhouse tables provide an intimate setting for smaller-size banquets. For larger banquets, the space can be set up using standard wooden tables in various shapes to best fit the room and seat the crowd. Straight and round tables still dominate since they are the most versatile for serving and seating, but serpentines and smaller bar/cocktail tables break the room into specific functional areas. For the cocktail reception, bar tables at standing height make the entire space feel more open and inviting and encourage movement in the room.

Half-circle and serpentine tables create unlimited ways of accommodating different room sizes and numbers of guests. By allowing for buffet setups that are different from the usual straight line, these shaped tables are one small and easy way to add excitement to the buffet. (For more information, see page 36 in Chapter 2.)

Serpentine tables are generally used in 3-foot to 4-foot multiples to create a wavy shape or to encircle a serving area. Cocktail tables generally have a 28-inch base with a 30-inch round top and are available in heights of 30 inches and 42 inches.

Standard Table Sizes and Shapes

RECTANGULAR	ROUND
4 feet x 30 inches (seats 4 to 6)	48 inches (seats 4 to 6)
6 feet x 30 inches (seats 6 to 8)	60 inches (seats 8 to 10)
8 feet x 30 inches (seats 8 to 10)	72 inches (seats 10 to 12)

There are many Web sites that have contemporary table designs to fit every conceivable need, including lighter-weight plastic tables that fold for easy storage, which are ideal for off-site caterers. Also available are buffet tables with high-end surfaces, negating the need for tablecloths. While this reflects the current trend of exposed wood or granite, it appears less elegant for a full-service function. The trend, however, seems to be gaining traction as traditional skirting is increasingly replaced by fabrics partially draping the table.

There is an assortment of tables available today that have been designed to be lightweight, strong, and portable. You can also find Web sites that offer a wide selection of high-end furniture with built-in chafers and induction burners. These communal tables, or "furniture that works," are functional convertible buffet systems suitable for the most elegant reception.

Heated tables are an innovative approach to extending the outdoor season. A heater is built into the center post of the table, directing heat toward the legs of the guests. Whereas other patio-style heaters broadcast inefficiently, this innovation directs the heat where it is most effective.

Varying the heights of serving vessels and platters on top of the table leads the eye upward. Tiered vessels are available in all shapes, sizes, and heights; see the Resources on page 347 for Web sites that offer beautifully made items that add a touch of class and height to the buffet.

BELOW LEFT: **Some modern table options feature sleek skirting and high-end surfaces that do not require tablecloths.**

BELOW RIGHT: **Tiered shelving provides a beautiful and streamlined way to display glasses.**

Tabletop risers are another way to add interest. However, risers do not have to be complicated or costly add-ons since they can be made from many materials. Even basic boxes, milk crates, or glass racks covered in fabric can be used to lift food to new heights, as can inverted bowls or other items already in-house. Some Web sites offer self-contained risers with nonskid bottoms, while others offer a wide variety of buffet displays and riser sets.

Another creative approach is to raise the heights of the tables themselves by putting lifts under the legs. Leg lifters are available from many sources, but bricks, blocks, or even #10 cans have been used to raise one table a little higher than another. By having the center table a little higher, emphasis is lent to the items on the raised table. Conversely, raising two flanking tables adds emphasis to the lower center table. Each method breaks up the straight line and creates a visually interesting display. Whatever way these risers are used, the added dimension makes the entire setup, including the food, look more sophisticated. See the Resources on page 347 for tables with two or three tiers.

GOT IT COVERED

THE EVENT SPACE TAKES ON A DRAMATIC NEW FEEL WHEN SEEN THROUGH THE PRISM OF A BRIGHT AND COLORFUL PALETTE OF TABLECLOTHS AND SKIRTING. While white linen has been a mainstay, countless colors, patterns, and textures are available to enhance every décor. With the contemporary flair of cascading fabrics popularized by current designers, the buffet table itself has to make its own statement as being both "hot" and "cool." Prints, stripes, bold colors, and geometric shapes have been used to add colorful drama to the table, while the accompanying napery is shaped to add height and a contrasting burst of color.

Regardless of color and texture, all linens must be clean and crisp.

Pleated skirting clipped onto the table not only hides the underside and whatever is stored there but also gives a finished look. There are hundreds of luxurious and decorative linens, skirts, and chair covers available. Skirting made of spandex and Lycra fits over the tabletop and stretches below to cover the entire leg area in a contoured shape. This all-in-one concept presents a cleanly tailored system, a fresh look that pops with color. Stretch-to-fit table, chair, and other covers are completely customizable and can even be screen-printed with logos to match the event theme.

The most important consideration for linens, no matter their style, color, or intended use, is that they are clean and crisp.

EQUIPMENT FOR HOT HOLDING

THE CHAFING DISH, OR ITS STEAM TABLE EQUIVALENT, HAS BEEN THE WORKHORSE OF THE INDUSTRY, AND WITH MINOR CHANGES TO THE FINISH OF THE PRODUCT, THE BASIC PRINCIPLE REMAINS UNCHANGED. A heat source from below heats water to produce steam, which in turn heats the pans of food on top. Basic perhaps, simple without doubt, but it's the effective go-to choice of high-volume catering halls and hotels as well as smaller shops. From disposable foil pans and wire racks to gleaming and ornate silver plate, chafers abound.

Chafers are available in ovals, squares, rectangles, and tureens. The most common chafer is the size of a hotel pan, roughly 12 inches by 20 inches by 4 inches. Generally this full-size pan is used as the water pan, with a full pan of food measuring 12 inches by 20 inches by 2 inches or two half-size pans of food placed atop the deeper one. This portable steam table arrangement can thus be configured to offer the entire menu for a large crowd. However, the menu should be customized to include only foods that sit well in a steamy environment for as long as 2 hours.

Little has changed in this portable steam table concept, but improvements have been made to accentuate the food on the line. Available are the following:

- Mirror stainless-steel finish with fingerprint resistance

- Self-closing hinges on roll-top attached covers

- Condensation-catching ridges that prevent soggy foods

- Interiors that accept ceramic or plastic inserts

- Inserts colored black or white, not just stainless steel

- Insert shapes in ovals or in a yin-yang complement

- Attached holders for serving utensils

- Cool-to-the-touch handles

Chafing dishes will always be an important tool for the buffet simply because they are versatile, functional, and cost-effective. The more modern buffet, however, leans toward replacing the institutional, high-volume chafing dish with homier-feeling non-commercial oven-to-tableware such as roasting pans, Dutch ovens, and pewter platters. When hot from the oven, these replace the chafer with a "cooked just for me" feeling.

As a chafing dish alternative, consider the following:

- Stainless-steel flame guards, which are attractive metal rounds that conceal the canned heat below.

- Chafer alternatives; these racks look like authentic mini grills while concealing the canned heat source placed within.

Heavy weight pewter or stainless platters can be used on top of either of these. If the weight of the platter is not heavy enough and the food browns, use two of the same platter, setting one inside the other with a wet side towel between them. Then place on the heat source under the trays, remembering to maintain the water level for the side towel within. See the Resources on page 347 for stainless-steel flame guards and chafer alternatives.

Another alternative to the chafing dish is the wide selection of "cook-'n'-serve" systems, complete with rack, wire grill, and a canned heat or butane fuel source. The basic butane cassette burner remains a ready option for caterers. Instead of purchasing an entire system, however, one may opt to construct a framework of bricks or glass blocks around the heat source. This will support the pans of food, keeping them at temperature while presenting a unique look.

For casual, off-site deliveries and setup, an innovative way to replace the chafing dish is with the insulated display box. Delivering pans of foot hot from the oven in insulated display boxes to maintain temperature is a faster and easier alternative to setting up wire-rack chafers.

Another inventive addition to chafing dish design is the "knockdown" frame, which presents solid sides all around, effectively preventing gusts of wind from blowing out the flame under the food. These allow a cleaner, more contemporary look and add a touch of color.

Fuel Sources

Canned heat has been the core heat source of the chafer for years. These gel fuels are made from a variety of compounds, but all have an alcohol component that makes initial lighting easy. While the usual brands, both with and without wicks, still lead the way in sales, new eco-friendly developments include the "green" biodegradable and water-soluble fuels rather than denatured alcohol or ethanol-based ones. These clean-burning, plant-based biofuels are smoke- and odor-free, a definite boon to the buffet, and are made from renewable resources and recycled packaging. Some of these chafing dish fuels meet the rigorous standards of the Green Restaurant Association, which require a safer and cleaner environment. By earning the GRA endorsement, these brands go to the head of the line as green fuel suppliers for the modern buffet. Electromagnetic heating elements provide a clean heat source for the chafer and are also considered eco-friendly. These magnetic systems hold the electric heating element to the underside of the chafer, safely out of the water pan, but they require an electrical outlet.

On the Rocks

Hot rocks are a cool display idea that keep more delicate items like skewered shrimp warm. These are high-luster black porcelain rocks that provide even heating at buffet stations where food can be placed directly on the rocks. The rocks heat up quickly and evenly. Used hot from the oven to maintain temperature, they make spectacular presentations. Pizza stones, bricks, smooth large stones, ceramic tiles, slate, and the

Hot rocks display food and keep it warm.

like are used on the buffet as "hot plates" to extend "hot from the oven" tableware's actual hot time. When placed atop a canned heat source, all of these present unique alternatives to the usual chafing dish.

Portable hot holding cabinets are enclosed racks that allow trays of food to be kept warm with electric heating elements or canned heat. Some are insulated, many are not, but all are versatile performers during a large event. For banquets and buffets, these heat boxes are indispensable, as they hold food at temperature, keep plates warm, and can be wheeled close to the site of service. Insulated totes and boxes are another option for maintaining temperature while transporting foods to off-premises sites.

Induction Burner

Induction burners and their required pots and pans have become extremely popular as prices have become more reasonable. Induction cooking transfers heat through a specially designed cooktop made of a smooth ceramic material over an induction coil. The induction coil creates a magnetic current that causes a metal pan on the cooktop to heat up quickly, yet the cooktop itself remains cool. Heat is then transferred to the food in the pan through conduction.

THE OLD SALT: IT'S NEW

A new use of a very old substance, salt, has made its way to buffet presentation.

Large slabs of Hawaiian pink or black salt, Murray River salt, or French gray sea salt make stunning presentation platters with their naturalness of color and texture and their translucence when seen in light. Of course, the slabs themselves are pricey, but smaller ones can be used to highlight a specific item without breaking the budget.

Induction burners provide a safe and attractive way to cook at a buffet station.

Single induction burners are easily transported and set up for stations along the buffet line; they are ideal for off-site catering. More elaborate setups include quartz or granite countertops where the actual burner is integrated and not noticeable to the eye. These units heat and cook rapidly while looking attractive. Less expensive alternatives that just maintain temperature are also available.

Induction burners are offered in all sizes and shapes, from the simple to the extravagant. These not only make the modern buffet appear sleek, they also allow for continuous and easy change in the setup. By incorporating them into the buffet line, there is little chance that it will be perceived as usual, tired, or boring. There are also mobile buffet stations with varying configurations and color patterns of interchangeable plastic panels. Some offer colorful backlighting to grab attention and create buzz throughout the room.

BE COOL

THE VERSATILE CHAFING DISH CAN BE USED TO KEEP FOOD HOT OR COLD. IN ORDER TO KEEP COLD FOOD COLD, CHAFERS ARE FILLED WITH ICE, RATHER THAN HOT WATER WITH A HEAT SOURCE. One drawback is the condensation that forms on the outside and drips onto the table. Many caterers wrap the chafer with a tablecloth to absorb this excess water, but when renting linens this can get expensive and still look messy. Cold display equipment, such as freezer-safe tiered displays with reusable ice packs, eliminates the mess. There are also complete and portable ice tabletops that can be skirted and look elegant while maintaining cold food at temperature. These plastic-topped tables come with a molded well that holds ice and has a drain line underneath. They are lightweight, black or white, hold up to 100 pounds of ice, and are ideal for off-site events.

Insulated bowls, crocks, and trays can be placed in the freezer overnight, and the refrigerant gel within can then maintain temperature below 41°F/5°C for up to 4 hours. These multipurpose performers fit the buffet, salad, or beverage bar and are available in many shapes, colors, and sizes. Other options include fabricated ceramics and ice pack–type inserts. These hold temperature for longer than 4 hours and, since they don't melt or mess, they add pizzazz. Insulated containers hold ice cream for up to 4 hours with no messy melting or waste. They come in sizes to accommodate the standard 3-gal/11.4-L tub as a single, double, or even triple station with condiment containers to match; they are a classy dress-up addition to any décor.

Polished aluminum alloy and hammered copper presentation pieces are freezer-to-oven and oven-to-table safe and have stands to vary their heights and hold canned heat. They can be used as chafer replacements for a cleaner look. As oven-ready and freezer-ready presentation platters, their versatility is unmatched.

This serving platter is freezer-to-oven and oven-to-table safe, making it both versatile and ideal for replenishing. The stand is both decorative and utilitarian, providing a stylish way to cover a canned heat source.

LESS IS MORE

THE HUGE MIRRORED PLATTER WAS ONCE THE CENTER OF ATTEN-
TION, BUT THERE ARE NOW SMALLER VESSELS THAT ARE MORE EASILY
MAINTAINED. Larger overflowing platters can be replaced by smaller bowls that
allow less on the buffet; not less in selection or choice of dishes, but less in the actual
quantities needed to be on display at a given time. Since less of an item needs to be out
on display, adhering to the food safety laws of time, temperature, and handling is easier.
This style of presentation also keeps the guest's impression of the food as more appetizing, fresh, and not picked over.

The plated individual serving has a firm grip on the buffet, and with the popularity of
tapas and meze, this "small plates" approach has solidified its hold on center stage.
Individual plates and grab-and-go containers add dimension and movement. They make
the experience more interesting because guests can sample, graze, and try a little of this
and a little of that. These portioned items are self-contained and neat to eat. The attraction of being easy for the guest to identify, pick up, walk with, and consume is obvious.
Being plated and portion-controlled also allows the item to be completed ahead of time.

Shot glasses, cones, spoons, and other small products sized for hors d'oeuvre are
tailored to this new sensibility that less is more. Cones take things to a new level by
making the usual humdrum hors d'oeuvre unusual in its individual serving presenta-

These elegant cups are a
unique way to serve individually sized portions.

LESS IS MORE

ABOVE LEFT: **This "tasting spoon wall" holds bite-size portions in a dramatic and easily accessible way.**

ABOVE RIGHT: **This plate has a cutout for a wineglass, making it easy for a guest to maneuver around a cocktail party with an hors d'oeuvre buffet.**

tion. The "tasting spoon wall" makes a dramatic addition to any buffet, as do weighted-bottom shot glasses for individual servings.

New designs for individual servings also include push-up pops and test tubes with racks to hold them all. Passed plates with cutouts for dip cups and beverage glasses have lightened the load for guests at the buffet and are available in plastic, bamboo, and china. A concern is making the guest carry too many items at once. Other than separating the china, flatware, and glassware, not much attention had been given to this problem other than the compartmentalized plate with a notch for a cup. But now plates with cutouts for wine glasses, plastic plates that fit over bottles or cans, and plates with spoons and forks attached are available.

Serving pieces and utensils also add character to the buffet and must be sized appropriately for each food item. A 2-ounce ladle for dressing, a 6-ounce ladle for soup, tongs for salad or bread, and slotted spoons, serving spoons, and forks must be part of the plan. There must also be a landing pad for each to prevent migration from one dish to another and to keep the table clean.

Serve It Safe

The self-serve area at the breakfast buffet or the breadboard at the salad buffet presents a multitude of contamination issues when many hands pick through rolls or bagels or slice from a loaf on a cutting board. Exposure to many individuals allows for increased risks, and many guests refuse these offerings on principle, germophobes or not. As with dry cereals and juices, dispensers now used for bagels, muffins, and cupcakes limit access and exposure with an interactive acrylic display. Other interactive buffet display items come in acrylic, glass, wood, and stainless steel.

THE IMPORTANCE OF RENTALS

ALL CATERERS, ESPECIALLY OFF-SITE ONES, NEED TO ESTABLISH A RELATIONSHIP WITH A LOCAL RENTAL COMPANY. Since this rental company often has direct contact with the client and thus, in essence, represents the caterer, it is important to find one that delivers not only clean operational equipment but exceptional customer service as well. For the first few client visits, the caterer should accompany the rental representative as measurements for tents are taken and options for layouts of dance floors, bars, tables, and seating are discussed. The rental company should be expected to provide a written contract detailing layout and all rental items. Once a comfort level with the customer service of the rental representative is achieved, a working relationship between a caterer and rental company is established and a commission may be extended for all items rented.

Usually rental equipment, including tents, tables, chairs, dance floors, china, flatware, glasses, and linens, is delivered to the site a day or two before the event. Every item of the rental manifest must then be checked to make sure it meets standards of cleanliness, functionality, and count. This requires diligent attention, as not all rental companies are willing to go beyond dropping the delivery on-site according to their schedule.

Occasionally, however, something may break just before the event begins or, worse yet, after the event has started, and the rental company must be relied upon to respond immediately. Many don't. Developing a relationship with a company that provides this "freedom from worry" assurance is definitely worth the effort. One that does come through with perfect linens and working equipment, and that responds to urgent calls from the field, is priceless.

PRACTICE MAKES PERFECT

IN ORDER TO PERFORM AS PERFECTLY AS POSSIBLE ON-SITE AND ESPECIALLY OFF-SITE, IT PAYS TO CHECK AND RECHECK MISE EN PLACE: Test your ability to think fast, work under pressure, and demonstrate knowledge of flavors, food affinities, and presentation principles.

- Equipment: Try it; turn it on to ensure that it works correctly and gets hot or cold enough; check to see if it requires any special instructions.

- Ingredients: Check that every item needed for the recipe is present in the correct form.

- Kitchen procedure: Create a plan for backup and replenishing in case any problems emerge on the buffet line or at the station.

- Skill level: Ensure time for training and practicing is allotted for the staff.

Check, double-check, and triple-check everything. Practice and perfect all cooking techniques required for the station.

It is essential that staff members who will be cooking and interacting with guests at action stations are thoroughly trained.

THE MODERN BUFFET

THE PRESENTATION OF FOOD IN A CREATIVE AND SENSATIONAL WAY THAT THE GUESTS MAY NOT HAVE EXPERIENCED BEFORE IS THE POINT. Everything is far more special than the usual as guests enjoy a personalized cooking experience. Being creative is not about adding to the workload; rather, it's using the staff, resources, and skills already at hand to their fullest. It is truly a series of small tweaks or little improvements to countless details, a constant and consistent striving toward perfection. The point is to maximize the impact of everyone's abilities, to reinforce the end results of their collective efforts, and to realize their fullest potential. This is, of course, the goal—to surpass the guests' expectations. Becoming more efficient, more entertaining, and more enthusiastic is, in the end, a fortunate by-product of the synergy created by a team-oriented staff.

The pivotal step in ensuring that what we are building is not only a modern but also a memorable buffet is to pick and choose the pieces that work for the particular event and incorporate them into a seamless whole. Not every innovation will be used from the outset, nor will each new piece of equipment fit within every budget, nor will each current trend apply to every occasion. However, keeping up on these developments enables us to customize accordingly and ensure that whatever is adapted to fit the buffet performs for that application perfectly and completely. It's covering even the minutest of details. It's maintaining the standard of quality. It's, ultimately, doing a million little things right.

This seafood bar engages the guest with elegant simplicity. This cold food system keeps the seafood looking as delicious as it tastes.

Hospitality is built on warmth and sincerity. Being passionate about hospitality sets us apart, while merely providing an excellent meal does not. The buffet must offer a wide-ranging display of foods and embody exceptional service. All the diligence and determination that went into planning, all the mise en place and preparation in the kitchen, all this effort and energy now hinge on warmth and consideration, service with a smile, the "power of nice."

4

EXECUTING
the BUFFET

PAIRINGS
palate + plate

**Black and White Sesame
Crusted Tuna with Green
Onion Wasabi Sauce Green
Apple-Ginger Salsa**

walnut + south · cranford, nj · 908-276-8025

HOSPITALITY MATTERS

A BASIC TENET OF BUSINESS SCHOOL STATES THAT KEEPING CUR-
RENT CUSTOMERS IS MORE ECONOMICAL THAN TRYING TO CAPTURE
NEW ONES. Every customer, therefore, must be encouraged to return, to advocate
that our food, presentation, and service rise above all others. Offering the best food at
the best price is, obviously, the first way to attract customers, but more is needed to
keep them coming back. Hospitality and service working in unison succeed because all
focus centers on the guest's experience.

Mi Casa Es Su Casa

How a guest is greeted sets the tone for the event. The staff, therefore, presents the first
impression; they are not merely attendants and servers, neaten-uppers and refillers.
They are the front line, the traffic directors, the meal deliverers—and, ultimately, their
personalities provide whatever it takes to make the guest's experience memorable. The
key to locking up new customers is service—attentive and polite, informed and informative. A well-trained staff is the secret ingredient.

Buffet line attendants must not only embody the
proper style of service, they also must be well versed on
all menu selections and able to describe in detail the
food and preparation methods. All guests now want to
feel that they are being included in the cooking action,
that they have a role in the way their meal is made. Vivid
descriptions of ingredient origin and cooking techniques become part of the entertainment, and action
stations entice the guest to join in. Consider this as
value added to the entire process.

By engaging the guest, the professional attendant at
the line becomes as important to the overall success of
the event as the food itself. Buffet wait staff should be
trained to have the same versatility with the menu and
its execution as any "best restaurant" dining room attendant. It's the ambience. It's the aroma. It's the noise level.
It's the attitude. It's the service. It's how a guest is made
to feel. Focus must remain on the food, but it is the service provided that makes the guest feel at home.

**Actively sautéing at a station
engages and excites guests.**

Savvy employers understand the value of common sense, friendliness, and compassion, and hire passionate and dedicated people. They take this passion and dedication and shape it through a culture of training. Each server's role is clear, the style of service is understood, and interaction with a guest is practiced before any service actually begins. Providing necessary training and routinely reviewing all menu selections encourage the employee to take ownership of his or her role for the event.

Because we have a plan, we have viable alternatives at the ready and are prepared to make on-the-spot decisions. Much of what we need to do, however, comes under the guise of "winging it." Problems will always arise, naturally. Even the most minutely detailed plan may encounter a bump along the way, and the only remedy possible may have to be accomplished on the fly. But since everything has been so carefully planned and prepared, there is time to deal with the unexpected, and the impact, though felt by the staff, is minimized for the guest, who should have no inkling of an issue. That the staff can handle this in stride is the result of careful planning and detailed training.

All service personnel must work as a team aiming for the same goal: to surpass the expectations of the guests by welcoming them willingly and warmly. This includes every worker, from the valet parker, coat checker, and busperson right up to the maître d'hôtel and executive chef. When the service staff is skilled, well trained, and well groomed, and the kitchen surpasses itself in every detail, food is more than prepared and served. It is showcased.

General Guidelines for Basic Staffing

	DINNER BUFFET WITH SEATING ON-SITE	DINNER BUFFET WITH SEATING OFF-SITE	COCKTAIL BUFFET ON-SITE	COCKTAIL BUFFET OFF-SITE	STATIONS ONLY ON-SITE	STATIONS ONLY OFF-SITE
Set-up Team (Part of Servers)	1 per 50 guests	1 per 25 guests	1 per 150 guests	1 per 50 guests	1 per 50 guests	1 per 25 guests
Captain/Maître d'hôtel	1 per 150 guests	1 per 150 guests	1 per 250 guests	1 per 250 guests	1 per 250 guests	1 per 100 guests
Servers	1 per 25 guests	1 per 25 guests	1 per 50 guests	1 per 35 guests	1 per 75 guests	1 per 50 guests
Bartenders	1 per 50 guests	1 per 50 guests	1 per 35 guests	1 per 35 guests	1 per 50 guests	1 per 50 guests
Chefs/Culinary	1 per 50 guests and 1 per station	1 per 50 guests and 1 per station	1 per 100 guests	1 per 50 guests	1 per 150 guests and 1 per station	1 per 75 guests and 1 per station
Utility/ Dishwasher	1 per 50 guests	2 per 50 guests	1 per 100 guests	1 per 75 guests	1 per 50 guests	1 per 35 guests
Housekeeping	1 per 150 guests	1 per 100 guests	1 per 150 guests	1 per 150 guests	1 per 100 guests	1 per 100 guests

VARIETY IS THE SPICE OF LIFE

A SUCCESSFUL EVENT IS BUILT AROUND A PLENTIFUL SELECTION OF FOODS BOTH INTERESTING TO EAT AND EFFICIENT TO MAKE. To determine the correct amounts of food and develop a production plan, recheck the buffet planning worksheet (see Appendix A, page 336) for the number of guests, the time of day, the duration, and the client's vision.

A general rule for twenty to fifty guests is that they be offered a minimum of two entrée/protein dishes, two pasta/potato/rice dishes, two vegetable dishes, a green salad, and bread. For every twenty-five to fifty guests thereafter, it is advisable to add more selections (see Chapter 1, page 10). But how do we translate this into how much food to make? As a starting point, assume that each person will consume about 1 pound of food plus hors d'oeuvre, beverages, and desserts. To be confident that there is plenty, analyze each dish individually. Start with the proteins and calculate amounts based on raw weight. Analyze the pasta, rice, and grains that swell when cooked, using prepared weights and the potatoes and vegetables using edible weights. This translates into:

WEIGHTS FOR ENTRÉES/PROTEINS NEEDED PER PERSON FOR BUFFET

- Plan for 6 to 8 oz/170 to 227 g total trimmed raw protein with two entrées.

  For example, serve 3 oz/85 g poultry, and 4 to 5 oz/113 to 142 g beef, pork, or fish because they tend to shrink more with cooking.

- For three entrees, plan for 8 to 10 oz/227 to 284 g total trimmed raw protein per person.

  For example, per person, calculate 2 oz/57 g poultry, and 3 to 4 oz/85 to 113 g beef or pork, and 3 to 4 oz/85 to 113 g fish per person in total for the entrées.

PREPARED WEIGHTS FOR SIDE DISHES PER PERSON FOR BUFFET

- For pasta/potatoes/rice, prepare 6 oz/170 g total with two choices; prepare 8 oz/227 g total if there are three or more choices.

- For vegetables, prepare 6 oz/170 g total trimmed and peeled for two or more choices.

- Prepare 2 oz/57 g of undressed salad per person, or 4 oz/113 g salad per person if being individually plated.

- Allow 1 or 2 pieces of bread per person.

Experience will help tweak these amounts. Obviously, the profit margin is of concern, but always err on the side of plenty. And, because the profit margin is a major concern, keep track of actual production and actual consumption for future calculations and menu price adjustments.

To calculate a holiday buffet for 100 people, start with the proteins. Suppose the menu includes three proteins for a total of 8 to 10 oz/227 to 284 g raw protein per person. This breaks down to be 2 oz/56 g turkey, 3 oz/85 g beef, and 3 oz/85 g salmon per person. How much turkey do we need? Let's calculate for Turkey Roulade with Sausage, Carrot, and Spinach Stuffing (page 246):

Determining the portion size for each dish is crucial to setting prices and developing detailed plans for a buffet. The number of slices from each roulade was determined in advance and clearly communicated to the cook at the station.

- Once the amount needed per person is established (2 oz/56 g), multiply that by the number of people (100). Therefore, 2 oz/56 g trimmed raw turkey breast per person x 100 people = 200 oz/5,670 g.

- Divide that total (200 oz) by 16 to get the number of pounds: 200 oz ÷ 16 oz = 12 lb 8 oz (or 5,670 g ÷ 1,000 g = 5.67 kg) turkey needed.

- Divide that amount (12 lb 8 oz/5.67 kg) by the amount needed to make the recipe once (4 lb 8 oz/2.04 kg; see recipe on page 246). So, 12 lb 8 oz ÷ 4 lb 8 oz = 2.77 (or 5.67 kg ÷ 2.04 kg = 2.77), the number of times the recipe needs to be made.

- Always round up, so triple the recipe, which then requires 13 lb 8 oz/6.12 kg turkey. Base the amount of garnishes/stuffings/sauces on the amount of the main ingredient.

Suppose a menu includes two vegetables for a total of 6 oz/170 g snipped and peeled edible vegetable per person. This breaks down to be 3 oz/85 g Vegetable Medley with Garlic Chips (page 185) and 3 oz/85 g Charred Brussels Sprouts, Almonds, Grapes, and Pancetta (page 177). How much Vegetable Medley do we need? Let's calculate:

- Once the amount needed per person is established (3 oz/85 g), multiply that by the number of people (100). Therefore, 3 oz/85 g trimmed vegetables per person x 100 people = 300 oz/8,505 g.

- Divide that total (300 oz) by 16 to get the number of pounds: 300 oz ÷ 16 oz = 18.75 lb (or 8,505 g ÷ 1,000 g = 8.5 kg).

- Divide that amount (18.75 lb/8.5 kg) by the amount needed to make the recipe once (when we add up the asparagus, carrots, snap peas, red peppers, and zucchini, it equals 48 oz or 3 lb/1,361 g or 1.36 kg; see recipe on page 185). So, 18.75 lb ÷ 3 lb = 6.25 (or 8.5 kg ÷ 1.36 kg = 6.25), the number of times the recipe needs to be made.

VARIETY IS THE SPICE OF LIFE

- Always round up, so multiply the recipe by 7, which then requires 4.3 lb/1.95 kg asparagus, 5.25 lb/2.38 kg carrots, 4.3 lb/1.95 kg snap peas, 2.6 lb/1.18 kg red peppers, and 4.3 lb/1.95 kg zucchini. Base the amount of garnishes/sauces on the amount of the main ingredient.

Suppose a menu includes two starches for a total of 6 oz/170 g per person: Cinque Formaggio Manicotti (page 204) and Sweet Potato Mash with Pecan Crumble (page 217).

This, of course, breaks down to be 3 oz/85 g of each starch. But the manicotti is by the piece, so we need 100 pieces of that. The recipe makes 36 pieces and they can be made well in advance and frozen, so we plan on making at least three batches for the freezer in advance. We know from experience that the manicotti is filling and rich, as is the Sweet Potato Mash with Pecan Crumble, so we decrease the amount of sweet potato to 2 oz/57 g per person. Let's calculate for Sweet Potato Mash with Pecan Crumble:

- Once the amount needed per person is established (2 oz/57 g), multiply that by the number of people (100). Therefore, 2 oz/ g sweet potato per person x 100 people = 200 oz/5,670 g.

- Divide that total (200 oz) by 16 to get the number of pounds: 200 oz ÷ 16 oz = 12 lb 8 oz (or 5,670 g/1,000 g = 5.67 kg) sweet potato pulp needed. We see in step 1 of the recipe (page 217) that the assumption is made that 5 lb /2.27 kg raw sweet potato yields about 4 lb /1.81 kg pulp (the peeled weight).

- Divide that amount (12 lb 8 oz/5.67 kg) by the amount needed to make the recipe once (4 lb/1.81 kg; see recipe on page 217). So, 12 lb 8 oz ÷ 4 lb = 3.13 (or 5.67 kg ÷ 1.81 kg = 3.13), the number of times the recipe needs to be made. We round up and multiply the recipe by 4.

SANDWICHES AND SALADS

- For a sandwich and salad buffet, assume one whole sandwich, which is a 3- to 4-oz/ 85- to 113-g portion of bread or rolls and a 4 oz/113 g portion of cooked meat, poultry, fish, vegetable, charcuterie or cheese, plus condiments like cheese slices, lettuce, tomato, and mayo and 8 oz/227 g total of prepared side salads per person.

DESSERTS

- For desserts, prepare a 4- to 6-oz/113- to 170-g slice of cake, 4 oz/113 g ice cream, and/ or 3 to 4 cookies per person.

Hors d'Oeuvres

If a party starts with a cocktail hour and is followed by dinner, three to five individual hors d'oeuvre pieces per person are sufficient, unless the client has specified a more substantial menu, for example a wedding reception. Each hors d'oeuvre should be no more than one or two bites and should be neat and tidy to eat. The purpose of the pre-dinner hors d'oeuvre is to stimulate the appetite, not to satiate it. When too much food is consumed at the beginning, dinner enjoyment is diminished. Be prepared, though, to actually exhaust the supply of hors d'oeuvre and remove empty platters quickly. This is totally acceptable when dinner follows immediately thereafter.

An eclectic selection of hors d'oeuvre creates intrigue

Avoid hors d'oeuvre that compete with dinner by leading the client to those that complement the theme without repetition of major ingredients. For example, Gingered Confetti Shrimp (page 123) as an hors d'oeuvre and Crunchy Coconut Shrimp (page 119) as the first course are too much alike. Also select lighter hors d'oeuvre options; for example, Lumpy Cajun Crab Cake Sliders (page 129) might be too filling, while bite-size Lumpy Cajun Crab Cakes (page 129) are more appropriate. Think about the party in total and use the hors d'oeuvre to contribute to the variety and balance of the meal.

The Cocktail Party

Although clients may at first think that the cocktail party is a way to help control costs, caution them that this is not usually the case. In reality, it costs much more to make many smaller items than a single large one. For example, fifty Miniature Quiche Hors d'Oeuvre (page 186) are much more labor-intensive to make than one large Deep-Dish Vegetable Quiche (page 186). What a cocktail party does allow, however, is for more people to attend than if it were a sit-down dinner. In a home, for example, the maximum for a traditional buffet dinner with seating might be twelve people, whereas with an hors d'oeuvre party, seventy-five guests may be the maximum. Furthermore, the hors d'oeuvre party is an opportunity to interweave many styles of food into one theme: Think of tapas, meze, antipasti, and dim sum—and how small bites can enhance the theme.

For a typical business party that starts before dinner or a Saturday night house party that starts after dinner, eight to ten individual hors d'oeuvre pieces per person are needed. This type of party implies that the guests plan to eat dinner afterward or have eaten before arriving, and small bites paired with cocktails and mingling are expected. The menu is substantial enough, however, to satisfy. Since it is difficult to hold a glass, napkin, and plate and still be able to meet and greet friends, finger foods that do not require plates or flatware are the norm. The key to this style of party is that all hors d'oeuvre are neat and tidy bite-size pieces. As with all finger foods, keep plenty of beverage napkins and toothpicks on hand and make sure the staff clears continually as they serve.

The Hors d'Oeuvre Dinner

The hors d'oeuvre dinner is especially effective for the off-site buffet with space and equipment limitations. The hors d'oeuvre dinner begins in the same manner as the full-scale dinner, proceeding from lighter to heavier fare: First come strictly finger foods

The principles of modern buffet design require that we do more with less, that presentations favor a minimalist approach to appear more approachable and current, that smaller portions be offered with appropriately sized vessels, and that painstaking hand craftsmanship be obvious.

like Gooey Gougères (page 139) or Grilled Vegetable Platter (page 181), which may be passed. Then more substantial entrée-type hors d'oeuvres like miniature Cinque Formaggio Manicotti (page 204) or Black and White Sesame-Crusted Tuna with Green Onion–Wasabi Sauce (page 125) are set up on the buffet with small grab-and-go plates and flatware. And, just like a dinner buffet, the hors d'oeuvre buffet should end with a selection of cookies and bite-size pastries.

For the hors d'oeuvre dinner, plan at least fifteen different individual hors d'oeuvre pieces plus dessert per person. This is essentially the same amount of food as a traditional dinner buffet or seated dinner, but in a different format. In fact, for this type of party a favorite entrée item can be reworked so that it is smaller, neater, and easier to eat. Instead of Crusted Beef Tenderloin (page 229) and Burgundy Reduction (page 251), think Beef Tenderloin with Peppercorn Crust on a toasted Crostini with Horseradish Crème (page 226). The key to this style of dinner is that all portions are small, with a plentiful variety. Allow one of each hors d'oeuvre per person, except for popular items like shrimp, where two per person are needed. Running out of one type of hors d'oeuvre is compensated for by the many others that are changed out constantly. For dinner, plan seven or eight individual lighter hors d'oeuvre pieces per person to start, eight or nine individual pieces of the more substantial ones for the "entrée," and four or five individual finger desserts per person to end. Variety is the spice of life, so plan to make a wide variety of hors d'oeuvre to stimulate the palate.

CHEAT THE CLOCK

ALWAYS BEGIN PRODUCTION AS FAR OUT AS PRACTICAL; 1 HOUR OF PREP TIME THE DAY BEFORE IS WORTH AT LEAST 3 HOURS ON THE DAY OF THE EVENT. As chefs and caterers, we understand that the days before an event are valued differently than the day of the event. All of the recipes in this book indicate when to start making recipe components so as to maximize time management. Every time a recipe is made, notes should be kept on how long it took to prepare and how long it will keep at its peak of freshness. Keep detailed notes as to what technique or recipe worked well and what should be improved upon. Everything that can be made in advance should be made in advance; the day before the event is not over until all mise en place is completed. Nothing should need to be made on the fly during the event because prep time ran out or insufficient quantities were made. This implies a failure in time management and menu design. There should be a balanced selection of items that can be made in advance and frozen, items that can be made a few days ahead and refrigerated, and only a few that must be made from start to finish on the day of the event. Such an "ahead of time" production schedule allows the caterer to cheat the clock but never the quality of the food.

Production Schedule

This is a holiday hors d'oeuvre dinner party menu for 100 people, along with the number of each hors d'oeuvre needed. Because the menu is so substantial, it is determined that none of the more popular items need to be doubled, such as the shrimp, scallops, or tuna. Without an efficient production schedule in place, this menu would require quadrupling the normal number of staff members, and for a smaller organization it would be impossible to prepare.

HOLIDAY HORS D'OEUVRE DINNER PARTY MENU

Lighter Hors d'Oeuvre

50 Chèvre Grapes with Toasted Pistachios and 50 Roquefort Grapes with Toasted Walnuts (page 138)

100 Miniature Chicken and Pepper Empanadas (page 115), Romesco (page 322)

100 Lumpy Cajun Crab Cakes (page 129), Rémoulade (page 319)

100 Spanish Tomato Bread (page 113)

100 Mini Quiche Hors d'Oeuvre (page 186)

100 Red Potatoes with Gorgonzola Cream, Bacon, and Walnuts (page 114)

100 Tortilla Española (page 140), Fire-Roasted Red Pepper Coulis (page 327)

100 Mini Turkey and Spinach Meatballs (page 131), Balsamic-Onion Jam (page 214), Sun-Dried Tomato Jam (page 325)

Entrée Hors d'Oeuvre

100 Garlicky Smoked Paprika Shrimp (page 117), Avocado-Mango Guacamole (page 321)

100 Day Boat Scallops Provençal (page 120) on Shaved Fennel, Arugula, Avocado, and Orange Salad (page 166)

100 Wild Mushroom Soup Shooters with Madeira Crème Fraîche (page 150)

100 Rosemary-Sage Grilled Lamb Kebobs (page 237)

100 Peppercorn-Crusted Beef Tenderloin Crostini with Horseradish Crème (page 226)

100 Moroccan Chicken and Carrot Sauté (page 234)

100 Black and White Sesame-Crusted Tuna with Green Onion–Wasabi Sauce (page 125), Green Apple–Ginger Salsa (page 314), Sweet and Sour Sushi

Rice Cake (page 213)

Action Station

Yukon Gold Gnocchi Sensation Station for 100 appetizer portions

Blanched Asparagus (page 185)

Blanched Broccoli (page 179)

Sautéed Wild Mushrooms and Onions (page 178)

Yukon Gold Gnocchi (page 210)

Roasted Tomato Ragù (page 209)

Herbed Tomato Sauce (page 312)

Creamy Vodka Sauce (page 312)

Macadamia-Pignoli Pesto (page 323)

Fresh Mozzarella (page 113)

Grated Pecorino Romano cheese

Balsamic Molasses (page 318)

White truffle oil

Extra-virgin olive oil

Toasted macadamia nuts

Toasted pignoli nuts

Capers

Olives

Desserts

50 Double Cinnamon-Apple Phyllo Turnovers and 50 Vanilla-Scented Pear (page 302), Phyllo Turnovers (page 299)

100 Chocolate–Peanut Butter Bonbons (page 288)

100 Mini Tiramisù (page 278)

Every single menu item must be analyzed and included on the production schedule, leaving nothing to chance. During the event, only the absolutely necessary à la minute preparation should be needed.

THIS IS THE PRODUCTION SCHEDULE:

Production up to 3 months ahead of time, made in large batches for multiple parties and frozen:

Miniature Chicken and Pepper Empanadas

Mini Quiche Hors d'Oeuvre

Miniature Turkey and Spinach Meatballs

Sun-Dried Tomato Jam

Yukon Gold Gnocchi

Double Cinnamon-Apple Phyllo Turnovers and Vanilla-Scented Pear Phyllo Turnovers

Chocolate–Peanut Butter Bonbons

Chiffon Cake for Mini Chocolate Tiramisù

All nuts and seeds toasted

All herb purées made

Bread crumbs

All stocks

Production from 1 to 3 days ahead of time and refrigerated:

Romesco

Rémoulade

Roquefort Cream Cheese

Chèvre Cream Cheese

Gorgonzola Cream, Bacon, and Walnuts for the Red Potatoes

Turkey Gravy for Miniature Turkey and Spinach Meatballs

Fire-Roasted Red Pepper Coulis and roasted peppers for Lumpy Cajun Crab Cakes

Toast baguette for Day Boat Scallops Provençal on Shaved Fennel, Avocado, and Arugula and Peppercorn-Crusted Beef Tenderloin Crostini

Balsamic-Onion Jam

Wild Mushroom Soup and also make extra Sautéed Mushrooms and Onions and extra onions and garlic for Sautéed Asparagus for gnocchi station

Madeira Crème Fraîche

Chive Butter

Marinade for Rosemary-Sage Grilled Lamb Kebobs, without herbs

Beef Tenderloin Marinade

Horseradish Crème

Moroccan Rub for chicken

Green Onion–Wasabi Sauce for Tuna

Roasted Tomato Ragù

Herbed Tomato Sauce and Creamy Vodka Sauce

Macadamia-Pignoli Pesto

Fresh Mozzarella

Grate cheeses

Balsamic Molasses

Tiramisù Filling, Espresso Syrup, and any garnish for Mini Chocolate Tiramisù

Complete anything not in the freezer

Production from 1 to 2 days ahead of time and refrigerated:

Provençal Sauce for Day Boat Scallops Provençal

Marinate beef tenderloin for Crusted Beef Tenderloin Crostini

Green Apple–Ginger Salsa

Fabricate all meat and poultry and keep it on ice: lamb, beef tenderloin, poultry

Prep all vegetables, such as carrots for Moroccan Chicken and Carrot Sauté and broccoli and asparagus for gnocchi station

Complete anything not completed the day before

Production 1 day ahead of time and refrigerated (everything on this list must be done before the day is over):

Chèvre Grapes with Toasted Pistachios and Roquefort Grapes with Toasted Walnuts and have stored ready to plate

Form Lumpy Cajun Crab Cakes

Toast the bread and rub with garlic for Spanish Tomato Bread; slice the Manchego

Slice Tortilla Española and have stored on sheet pan ready to bake

Make garlic chip oil sauce; make marinade; skewer shrimp for Garlicky Smoked Paprika Shrimp

Prep everything but the avocado for Avocado-Mango Guacamole

Place frozen hors d'oeuvre on sheet pans, wrap with plastic, and refrigerate:

Miniature Chicken and Pepper Empanadas

Mini Quiche Hors d'Oeuvre

continued

CHEAT THE CLOCK

Production 1 day ahead of time, *continued*

Put the frozen Miniature Turkey and Spinach Meatballs in the cold Turkey Gravy so they are ready to bake

Double Cinnamon-Apple Phyllo Turnovers and Vanilla-Scented Pear Phyllo Turnovers

Chocolate–Peanut Butter Bonbons

Skewer lamb for Rosemary-Sage Grilled Lamb Kebobs

Grill beef tenderloin for Crusted Beef Tenderloin Crostini

Moroccan Chicken and Carrot Sauté

Clean scallops

Fabricate tuna

Sweet and Sour Sushi Rice Cakes

Blanch asparagus and broccoli for gnocchi station

Gather all ingredients for gnocchi station

Production that morning and refrigerated (everything on this list must be done before the party starts):

Fry Lumpy Cajun Crab Cakes

Bake the potatoes for the Red Potatoes with Gorgonzola Cream, Bacon, and Walnuts; when cooled, pipe on topping and store in container ready to plate

Chop chives, parsley, rosemary, thyme, sage,

cilantro, green onions, lime zest, and wash basil to finish all dishes and sauces

Finish Avocado-Mango Guacamole

Assemble salad for Day Boat Scallops Provençal on Shaved Fennel, Avocado, and Arugula Salad with avocado scored in skin

and put back together with seed in middle

Marinate Rosemary-Sage Grilled Lamb Kebobs

Cook chicken for Moroccan Chicken and Carrot Sauté and put together with carrots

Marinate Black and White Sesame-Crusted Tuna with Green Onion–Wasabi Sauce

Mise en place to demo gnocchi making

Make Chocolate Whipped Cream Icing and assemble Mini Chocolate Tiramisù

During event:

Chèvre Grapes with Toasted Pistachios and Roquefort Grapes with Toasted Walnuts **PLATE**

Miniature Chicken and Pepper Empanadas **FRY/ PLATE/SERVE**, Romesco **PLATE/SERVE**

Lumpy Cajun Crab Cakes **BAKE /PLATE/SERVE,** Rémoulade **PLATE/SERVE**

Spanish Tomato Bread **BAKE/RUB WITH TOMATO/ TOP WITH CHEESE/ BAKE/PLATE/SERVE**

Mini Quiche Hors d'Oeuvre **BAKE/PLATE/SERVE**

Red Potatoes with Gorgonzola Cream, Bacon, and Walnuts **PLATE/SERVE**

Tortilla Española **BAKE / PLATE/SERVE,** Fire-Roasted Red Pepper Coulis **PLATE/SERVE**

Miniature Turkey and Spinach Meatballs **BAKE/ PLATE/SERVE,** Balsamic-Onion Jam **HEAT/PLATE/ SERVE,** Sun-Dried Tomato Jam **HEAT/PLATE/SERVE**

Garlicky Smoked Paprika Shrimp **MARINATE/GRILL/ FINISH/ SAUCE/PLATE/ SERVE,** Avocado-Mango Guacamole **PLATE/SERVE**

Day Boat Scallops Provençal on Shaved Fennel, Arugula, and Avocado Salad **SEAR SCALLOPS/FINISH SAUCE/ TOSS SALAD/PLATE/SERVE**

Wild Mushroom Soup Shooters with Madeira Crème Fraîche **HEAT/ PLATE/SERVE**

Rosemary-Sage Grilled Lamb Kebobs **GRILL/ PLATE/SERVE**

Peppercorn-Crusted Beef Tenderloin Crostini with Horseradish Crème **ASSEMBLE/PLATE/SERVE**

Moroccan Chicken and Carrot Sauté **HEAT/PLATE/SERVE**

Black and White Sesame-Crusted Tuna with Green Onion–Wasabi Sauce, Green Apple–Ginger Salsa, Sweet and Sour Sushi Rice Cake **GRILL/SEAR/PLATE/SERVE**

Yukon Gold Gnocchi Sensation Station **SET UP STATION AND GNOCCHI-MAKING DEMO COOK/PLATE/SERVE**

Double Cinnamon-Apple Phyllo Turnovers and Vanilla-Scented Pear Phyllo Turnovers **BAKE/PLATE/SERVE**

Chocolate–Peanut Butter Bonbons **PLATE/SERVE**

Mini Chocolate Tiramisù **SERVE**

MAKE IT OR BREAK IT

THUS WE ENTER THE FINAL "PUBLIC" STAGE OF OUR EVENT, ENCOMPASSING ALL THE PREVIOUS PHASES: the reason for the event, the location and setup of the venue, the development of the menu and production list, the training and scheduling of staff, and the collection of all necessary equipment and accoutrements. The actual production of the meal, the display of the food, and the ability to serve it to the guests efficiently and elegantly are now in full swing.

Food arrangement is one of the bigger challenges facing the banquet chef. This is because large quantities of food must be prepared and then arranged into smaller portions that are both at the correct temperature and manageable for service. Added to this is the self-service factor, which can easily turn a carefully crafted arrangement into a mess.

From a food safety standpoint, it is critical to avoid contaminating the food as you work. Gloves, tongs, spatulas, and other tools keep you from touching the food with your bare hands and prevent cross-contamination. They also cut down on the number of smudges or fingerprints that might mar the food or the platter. Regardless of the overall design, cleanliness and order are crucial to successful food presentation and assure guests that the food has been properly and professionally handled.

Spaced Out

The spacing and sequencing of food items require diligent attention. All slices should be sized according to the appropriate portion and spaced for ease of service and pickup. Precise cutting skills and knife work is critical to showcase the colors, textures, and shapes of the food on display.

A large item, or *grosse pièce*, partially sliced onto a platter can look impressive by providing a focal point within the display. However, it requires forethought in portion sizing, slicing direction, and sequencing of slices. Slicing and sequencing foods that have tapered shapes, such as turkey breasts, or that have an internal garnish, such as a terrine, make it possible to create strong lines from foods that are not perfectly regular in shape and size.

Large items, like this Turkey Roulade with Sausage, Carrot, and Spinach Stuffing (page 246), **are sliced into uniform pieces and displayed on a platter or in a chafing dish.**

Begin slicing from the end of a roast that will provide the best slices; slice evenly from this end, keeping it all together in numerical, logical order so that their arrangement on the service platter follows the same pattern. Keep the outer side of each slice facing the same way and with the same side up. Follow each slice in the order and direction it is sliced onto the serving platter, and end with the last piece sliced closest to the *grosse pièce*. This ensures that the display pattern is uniform to the eye.

Food items that have irregular or tapered shapes should follow the natural shape of the food in sequence. Slices should be arranged in a uniform direction so the internal view and shape appear consistent. Reversal of slices weakens the presentation and makes it look sloppy.

Height is another important element of the buffet's visual presentation. Height can be accomplished in a variety of ways: with a *grosse pièce* unsliced; with a rack or bones on which to stack sliced meat; with a mold of rice, polenta, or quinoa; or with tall functional vessels filled with accompaniments. To give height to foods that are naturally flat, roll or fold them, arrange them in piles or pyramids, or use serving pieces such as pedestals, columns, or baskets.

Chicken breast is an example of an irregular and/or tapered food item. Here, the Chicken Fajitas (page 226) **are uniformly sliced and plated in the natural sequence of the original form.**

The shape and height of the food itself can be altered into three-dimensional forms like cubes, cylinders, spheres, and pyramids. Alternating or repeating shapes in a design is another way to add visual interest to food arrangements.

The design principles at the chef's disposal include symmetrical or asymmetrical compositions, the use of lines to create patterns or indicate motion, and contrasting or complementary arrangements. In creating a balanced presentation, consider the accessibility of each item to be placed on the platter; larger items should be placed in the rear and lower items in front. Of course, individual pieces such as crab cakes or canapés should maintain uniformity of size, shape, and spacing for the most attractive visual arrangement.

When the focal point is positioned in the center and the lines radiating from it are the same length, it gives the impression that both sides of the arrangement are in equilibrium or symmetrical. The platter's layout is asymmetrical when the position of the focal point on a platter is off-center and the lines extending away from it are different lengths, so that one side of the arrangement appears to have more weight than the other. Asymmetrical arrangements tend to look natural and more modern, while symmetrical arrangements look formal and classic.

Giving a dish height is an excellent way to create visual appeal.

Strong, clean lines with the food neatly and logically arranged introduce a sense of flow or motion into the arrangement. Lines can be straight, curved, or angled to create different moods on a platter.

A certain amount of regularity and repetition is comfortable and appealing, but too much of anything becomes monotonous. Introducing contrasts in color, flavor, texture, or shape, for example, adds energy and motion to an arrangement. However, when every element seems to stand on its own, the effect can be chaotic. Simplicity is usually the best approach.

ROUND AND OVAL PLATTER ARRANGEMENTS

**Some options for plating hors d'oeuvre
on circular and oval platters**

SQUARE AND RECTANGULAR PLATTER ARRANGEMENTS

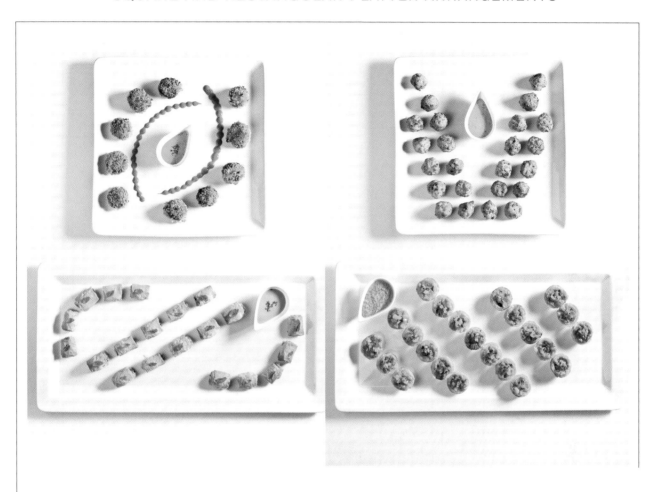

Some options for plating hors d'oeuvre on square and rectangular platters

Individual Spinach Ensaladas with a Poached Quail Egg (page 151) controls both portion size and guests' traffic flow.

GRAB AND GO

Individual servings lend a contemporary look to the buffet and create elegance and ease of service for the guest. Although this food is prepared and plated en masse, smaller plating styles and portions lend an artisanal and handcrafted look. With the ready-to-serve items artfully arranged in a contemporary grab-and-go order, the buffet line is constantly moving.

GARNISHING PLATTERS

Clean space on the plate helps emphasize the main ingredient. Think of the edge of the platter as a picture frame. As with any artistic project, white, empty, or negative space works to reinforce the featured element by adding a visually impressive backdrop to make the art pop off the plate. The border of the plate should be clear of any food, smudges, or fingerprints.

Too many extras, actually take away from the overall appearance of the dish. In the dark ages of the tired buffet, large platters heaped with food were often lined with lettuce leaves or surrounded by orange, lemon, or lime slices; some had large branches of rosemary stuck into them, and others were smothered in parsley. Stay away from these nonfunctional detractors. If garnish is added, keep it simple and use only ingredients that are part of the dish to add color, texture, taste, and interest to the plate.

When the only purpose for a garnish is to add a shape or a color, find a better option. Sprigs of parsley or watercress added to a platter simply for a bit of green color are nonfunctional garnishes. But if the watercress is actually a bed for a marinated salad or other item, and the flavor and texture of the watercress become a significant element in the dish, it is a functional garnish. The selection of a garnish for individual items may be governed by tradition, but it is often the development of an original garnish that creates the impression of a "new" item, something that is modern and fashionable, such as ice cream garnished with a Pizzelle (page 296).

Appropriate garnishes include a vegetable, a bread or starch item, a sauce or a dip, a chutney or a relish. An individual salad component can be used to highlight that salad. Each item may be used to garnish a dish either as a stand-alone hinting at the ingredient in the main dish, or as a separate part that complements the serving. In each case, the texture and color of the main dish, and its flavor profile, must be enhanced and complemented by the addition of the ingredient garnish.

The border of any platter should be completely clean and free of food, smudges, or fingerprints.

EXAMPLES OF APPROPRIATE GARNISHES

VEGETABLES ADD COLOR AND FLAVOR:

- Tuscan Braised Pork Shanks (page 238) garnished with Broccoli Rabe and Cannellini Bean Sauté (page 193)

- Pork Chop Milanese (page 233) garnished with Braised Red Cabbage and Apples (page 174)

- Moroccan Chicken garnished with Carrot Sauté (page 234)

- Cinque Formaggio Ravioli (page 205) garnished with Asparagus Ragoût (page 192)

- Curried Zucchini Soup garnished with Corn and Crab Relish (page 149)

NUTS AND SEEDS ADD TEXTURE AND RICHNESS:

- Butternut Squash Malfatti garnished with Crispy Pumpkin Seeds (page 201)

- Cinnamon Churros (page 284) garnished with Candied Pecans (page 331)

- Honey-Lacquered Ribs (page 222) garnished with Chili-Roasted Peanuts (page 332)

- Spinach Ensalada garnished with pine nuts and pomegranate seeds (page 151)

- Waldorf Caesar Salad (page 152) garnished with toasted walnuts

- Sweet Potato Mash garnished with Pecan Crumble (page 217)

STARCHES ADD TEXTURE AND RICHNESS:

- Black and White Sesame-Crusted Tuna (page 125) garnished with a Crispy Sweet and Sour Sushi Rice Cake (page 214)

- Beef Tenderloin with Peppercorn Crust (page 226) garnished with Cheddar-Kissed Potato Pancake (page 143)

- Broccoli Rabe Mineste (page 173) garnished with Crispy Polenta Cake (page 211)

BREAD OR BREAD ITEMS ADD TEXTURE AND VARIETY:

- Wild Mushroom Soup with Madeira Crème Fraîche (page 150) garnished with Sausage en Croute (page 133)

- Lemony Hummus (page 134) garnished with Cashew-Studded Naan (page 262)

- Tomato-Basil Soup (Caprese Zuppa) with Mozzarella (page 147) garnished with Cheese Sticks (page 264)

- Beef Tenderloin garnished with Herbed Crust (page 229)

- Mango-Stuffed French Toast garnished with Coconut Crunch (page 273)

SAUCES CAN BE USED AS A GARNISH:

- Coconut Shrimp (page 119) garnished with Honey Mustard (page 327)

- Tortilla Torcal (page 140) garnished with Fire-Roasted Red Pepper Coulis (page 327)

- Roasted Beets Stuffed with Herbed Chèvre (page 169) garnished with Pistachio Pesto (page 323)

- Lemon-Horseradish-Dill Crusted Salmon (page 255) garnished with Arugula-Cucumber-Spinach Tzatziki (page 319)

- Lumpy Cajun Crab Cakes (page 129) garnished with Rémoulade (page 319)

- Pecan-Studded Chicken (page 230) garnished with Raspberry Coulis (page 305)

- Cinque Formaggio Manicotti (page 204) garnished with Herbed Tomato Sauce (page 312) and Macadamia-Pignoli Pesto (page 323)

SALAD COMPONENTS CAN ADD VARIETY AND COLOR:

- Phyllo Spring Rolls with Chicken and Shiitake Mushrooms (page 137) garnished with Bibb lettuce

- Black and White Sesame-Crusted Tuna (page 125) garnished with Green Apple–Ginger Salsa (page 314)

- Individual Deep-Dish Quiche (page 186) garnished with Mâche Salad (page 158)

- Day Boat Scallops Provençal (page 120) garnished with Shaved Fennel, Arugula, Avocado, and Orange Salad (page 166)

COMPOTES, CHUTNEYS, AND RELISHES ADD FLAVOR, CONTRAST, AND COLOR:

- Garlicky Smoked Paprika Shrimp (page 117) garnished with Avocado-Mango Guacamole (page 321)

- Buttermilk Grilled Chicken (page 242) garnished with Cranberry-Bourbon Relish (page 317)

- French Toast Baked in Maple Butter (page 271) garnished with Vanilla-Scented Pears (page 302)

- Fresh Mozzarella (page 113) garnished with Roma Salsa (page 316)

- Barolo-Braised Short Ribs (page 221) garnished with Horseradish Gremolata (page 315)

- Duck Confit garnished with Blueberry-Port Sauce (page 245)

A Balancing Act

Balance is an important concept in food presentation. When we particularly like a dish, we consider it balanced. But what does this mean? It means that the ingredients are used in proportion—that the right amount of salt, pepper, or lemon has been used, for example. And it means that the correctly sized vessels have been chosen for the amount of food to be plated. Each item complements the others, yet nothing overpowers. They work in harmony to enhance the buffet as a whole.

Cooking methods should also be in balance. The buffet should not present all grilled or all sautéed or all fried food. A variety of cooking methods will automatically add a variety of textures to the presentation; for example, oven-roasted Lemon-Horseradish-Dill Crusted Salmon (page 255), pan-seared Charred Brussels Sprouts with Almonds, Grapes, and Pancetta (page 177), and uncooked creamy Arugula-Cucumber-Spinach Tzatziki (page 319). The cooking methods should complement the entire presentation while not becoming monotonous.

Likewise, the shapes of the plated items should lend cohesion. Rather than offering too many of the same shapes on one plate, vary the look by mixing it up so that everything is not all round or all square. Custards, purées, coulis, and gastriques can alleviate similarities on each platter because the various textures can be smooth or coarse, solid or soft, and add more color.

Texture is another important consideration in plating. Too much of the same texture when you look at it or bite into it is boring. Also, the food's surface texture will have a tendency to either reflect light or absorb it, making some foods appear glossy while others look matte.

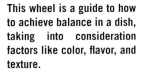

This wheel is a guide to how to achieve balance in a dish, taking into consideration factors like color, flavor, and texture.

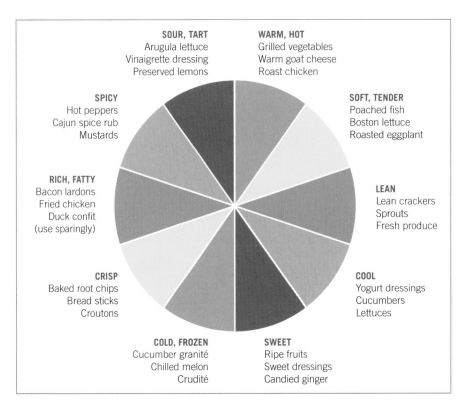

SOUR, TART
Arugula lettuce
Vinaigrette dressing
Preserved lemons

WARM, HOT
Grilled vegetables
Warm goat cheese
Roast chicken

SPICY
Hot peppers
Cajun spice rub
Mustards

SOFT, TENDER
Poached fish
Boston lettuce
Roasted eggplant

RICH, FATTY
Bacon lardons
Fried chicken
Duck confit
(use sparingly)

LEAN
Lean crackers
Sprouts
Fresh produce

CRISP
Baked root chips
Bread sticks
Croutons

COOL
Yogurt dressings
Cucumbers
Lettuces

COLD, FROZEN
Cucumber granité
Chilled melon
Crudité

SWEET
Ripe fruits
Sweet dressings
Candied ginger

Herbs and spices provide flavor, but they should neither overwhelm the dish nor be served in every single dish. Avoid, for instance, commonly overused herbs such as parsley or chives. Keep in mind complementary flavor profiles that work together: rich with lean, spicy with mild, salty with sweet, sweet with spicy.

Color is, of course, always important when dealing with food, especially when considering presentation. Color reinforces freshness, quality, and proper cooking technique. By incorporating warm, earthy tones with more vibrant colors from fruits and vegetables, a desired complementary effect is achieved. This natural affinity of brightly colored foods as "good for you" has moved into the forefront of the average consumer's mind.

A food's natural color is one important tool in platter presentation. The color of a food can be used as an element in design. We associate with colors in very specific ways. Greens give the impression of freshness and vitality. Browns, golds, and maroons are warming, comforting, and rich. Orange and red are intense, powerful colors.

On this buffet, the food on the three-tier display draws you in.

Colors that harmonize are those that touch each other on the color wheel; for example, green, blue, and violet are complementary colors, while blue and orange are contrasting. Clashing colors are rarely a problem. A more common concern is the overuse of one color on a single display.

This centerpiece is tall and elegant without taking up much of the valuable table space.

The Centerpiece

The eye is attracted to odd shapes that can be symmetrical or asymmetrical, tall or short, wide or thin. These shapes are intriguing because they add depth and dimension. The arrangement of tall in back, short in front is a natural progression that is barely noticeable—that is, until something is out of place or unbalanced.

Centerpieces create interest and excitement for the eye and pull attention toward them. The focal point adds excitement and interest to the presentation, much as a garnish adds them to a dish. They improve the entire experience by reinforcing the theme. As the eye scans the event space, it naturally alights on the centerpiece, the focal point of the buffet. This can be a floral arrangement, an ice sculpture, or an arrangement of fruits, vegetables, or breads.

The contemporary approach leans toward sleek and clean lines that rise upward, pulling the eye higher and higher. Tall and thin is in. Real flowers and greens are in, especially edible ones that are part décor, part meal ingredient. Ice sculptures add a wow factor that compares with nothing else. Fruits and vegetables add vibrant colors and scream "fresh and natural," and they should be on the menu. Freshly baked breads awaken more than just the eye.

Though the centerpiece may be tall, it should not be intrusive or obstructive of the view from any point in the space. It should interfere neither with the guest's access to the buffet nor with the attendant's ability to service the line. As complement to the theme, the centerpiece acts in a supporting role to enhance the look and feel of the space. By contributing a stunning point of interest that just cannot be missed, the centerpiece acts as an anchor, as the bull's-eye to which the eye is naturally drawn. And radiating outward from this visual line to enrich each guest, the buffet builds momentum.

CENTER PIECE IDEAS AND EQUIPMENT

- Ice Carvings
- Vegetable Carvings
- Flower Arrangements/ Plants
- Fruits and Vegetables
- Wine and Other Beverages

- Linens
- Cookware
- Hot Rocks
- Action Stations
- Candles
- Serving Vessels

- Display Columns
- Fountains
- Sculpture/Artwork
- Lighting
- Risers

ICE IS COOL

- When designing and setting up any ice sculpture for the buffet, remember that it will need to be set into a container to collect whatever water melts and runs off. This may be as simple as a hotel pan covered with a tablecloth, but a better alternative is to add large slabs of ice as the base set into the pan. This helps maintain a lower temperature for the ice sculpture and thus prolongs its life. Consider that ice bowls containing food need to be easily reached by the guests while not melting in front of them.

- One of the most dazzling displays uses large slabs of crystal-clear ice as the table on which the food is directly displayed. These ice-slab displays are more than magnificent and add excitement and entertainment far beyond the usual stylized ice sculpture, however costly. There are several Web sites that sell ice-carving saws, chisels, and other implements for those serious about their ice centerpieces.

THE FOOD

WHAT WAS ONCE CONSIDERED STREET FOOD AND RELEGATED TO NEAR OBSCURITY HAS BEEN TRANSFORMED INTO CUTTING-EDGE COMFORT FOOD AS GLOBAL FLAVORS ARE INCORPORATED INTO THE BUFFET. As trends toward healthier eating habits gain traction and become ingrained in consumers' minds, the buffet itself must be adaptable to provide what is wanted. Think about the culinary trends forming now as the newest additions to the buffet and highlight them as special areas or stations. Think smaller. Think greener. Think organic, local, and artisanal.

Careful planning of similar menu items with different clients enables us to handle multiple parties at once while maintaining a completely personalized feel for each client. All of the recipes in this book not only maximize time management by indicating when to start making components, they also maximize efficiency by having a single recipe do double duty on more than one buffet. Every menu must be planned with a timeline in mind; sort them by items that can be made well in advance, items that can be made a few days ahead, and items (only a few) that must be made from start to finish on the day of the event.

The versatility of all of these recipes is that they can be modified to fit many visions and many buffets. We make recommendations on how to modify each recipe: they can be portioned or positioned as individual servings; they can be sized appropriately to function as appetizers, first courses, or entrées; and they can be highlighted at action stations.

As global boundaries blur, menus that reflect a cross-cultural heritage and stations that highlight these varied dishes and cooking methods energize the entire buffet experience. International ingredients sourced from our quick-paced, well-traveled world are the tools we use to modernize the buffet. At the same time, however, foods fit for the modern buffet have to be appealing, aromatic, and appetizing while remaining servable and serviceable. Dinner is served.

Appetizers and hors d'ouevre are so much more than mere nibbles and bites. They are the first edible representation of our hospitality, setting the tone for every event. And in this ever-smaller world, representing our ancestral heritage or ethnic affiliation can open doors to new clients and expand our business in new directions. It helps to think of these little wonders as money in the bank, as so many can be made in quantity and frozen without affecting their quality on the plate. Many are sourced from more elaborate and costly entrées and recast as small bites, which can help stretch a client's budget while adding to our bottom line. Knowing that the freezer banks are full enables us to jump at opportunities that may have otherwise been elusive.

5

APPETIZERS *and* HORS D'OEUVRE

Alsatian Pizzas with Sun-Dried Tomato Pesto, Montrachet, and Fresh Mozzarella. Slate serving stone by CAL-MIL (see Resources, page 347).

ALSATIAN PIZZAS WITH SUN-DRIED TOMATO PESTO, MONTRACHET, AND FRESH MOZZARELLA

YIELD: 12 SERVINGS OR 96 PIECES

2 lb/907 g Fresh Mozzarella, sliced into 60 thin slices (1 batch; page 113)

12 oz/340 g Montrachet Cream Cheese (2 cups/480 mL or 1 batch; page 138)

Crispy Thin Pizza Crust, scaled into twelve 3-oz/85-g, 6-in/15-cm rounds and prebaked (½ batch; page 263)

32 fl oz/960 mL Sun-Dried Tomato Pesto (1 batch; page 324)

84 basil leaves

1. Place the mozzarella slices on a sheet pan lined with paper towels. Top with another layer of paper towels and repeat until all the mozzarella is between paper towel layers. Top with a sheet pan to weigh it down and refrigerate for 30 minutes to 8 hours to absorb excess moisture from the mozzarella.

2. Evenly spread 1 oz/28 g (2 tbsp) of the Montrachet cream cheese on each pizza crust, leaving a thin border. Evenly spread a 2⅔-oz/73-g (2½-tbsp/37.5-mL) layer of tomato pesto over the Montrachet cream cheese on each pizza. *The pizza can be assembled to this point 1 day in advance. Store wrapped in the refrigerator.*

3. Position a pizza stone in the bottom of the oven and heat to 475°F/246°C. If you don't have a pizza stone, place inverted sheet pans in the heated oven and warm them for 15 to 20 minutes. Place the pizzas on the pizza stone and bake until the edges are golden brown and the bottom is crispy, 8 to 12 minutes. Top each pizza with 5 slices fresh mozzarella and 7 basil leaves and bake until the cheese is melted, 2 to 3 minutes more.

If serving the pizzas as an hors d'oeuvre, cut each pizza into 8 pieces before baking. Cut the mozzarella slices into ½-in/1.25-cm strips, and chiffonade the basil. Place the individual pizza slices onto a sheet pan without touching each other and bake as directed.

FRENCH ONION CHECKERBOARD TART

YIELD: 12 SERVINGS
---

1 lb 10 oz/737 g Lager Pastry Dough, cold
from the refrigerator (1 batch; page 308)

Bench flour as needed

Butter, soft, as needed to prepare parchment

8 fl oz/240 mL Onion Marmalade,
cooled (1 batch; page 326)

8 oz/227 g Gruyère, cut into 1-in/3-cm squares
about ⅛ in/3 mm thick (about 48 squares)

1. Place the chilled dough on a lightly floured cold surface and dust the top of the dough and rolling pin with flour. Roll out the dough into an even rectangle about 12½ in by 17½ in by ⅛ in/30.5 cm by 44 cm by 3 mm. Place it in an ungreased half sheet pan and trim it and/or patch it in to completely cover the bottom and sides and overhang by ¼ in/6 mm. Roll the overhang over and flute the edges. Dock the dough by lightly pricking it with a fork or dough docker several times so it does not form blisters as it bakes. Place it in the freezer until firm, about 30 minutes. See accompanying box, "How to Roll Out Pastry Dough." *The crust can be rolled out and frozen in advance. Store wrapped in the freezer for 3 months.*

2. Position a rack in the bottom third of the oven and heat to 425°F/218°C. Butter one side of a piece of parchment paper large enough to cover the dough. Line the dough with the parchment paper, butter side touching the dough, and fill the parchment paper with enough rice or pie weights to completely fill the well. Bake until the crust is completely cooked and golden brown, about 25 minutes. Cool the crust with the rice on it at room temperature for 30 minutes. Remove the parchment paper and rice. (The rice can be used over and over again as pie weights.) *The crust can be baked in advance. Store wrapped in the refrigerator for 3 days or in the freezer for 3 months.*

3. Evenly top the crust with the onion marmalade. Top with rows of cheese squares placed 1 in/3 cm apart so that they form a checkerboard pattern. *The tart can be assembled 1 day in advance. Store wrapped in the refrigerator.*

4. Adjust the oven to 350°F/177°C. Bake the tart until piping hot and the cheese is melted, 10 to 12 minutes.

HOW TO ROLL OUT PASTRY DOUGH

To ROLL PASTRY DOUGH, lightly dust a cold work surface, the top of the dough, and rolling pin with bench flour. Press the dough from the center, roll it out in one direction, and then roll it out from the center again in another direction. Turn the dough, using a bench scraper to unstick it and dusting the board with bench flour as needed, and roll it from the center again. As the dough is rolled out, it should move on the work surface and not stick to it. Continue until it is the correct size.

For easier rolling: Take one disk out of the refrigerator and roll it out between 2 sheets of lightly floured parchment or waxed paper. Press the dough from the center, then roll it out in one direction and then from the center again in another direction. If the dough sticks to the paper and is difficult to roll out, remove the paper from one side, lightly flour the dough, replace the paper, flip over, lightly flour the other side, then continue rolling. As the dough is rolled out, it should move on the paper and not stick to it.

To ensure evenly rolled dough, use bamboo skewers, which are normally ⅛ in/3 mm thick, as gauges on either side of the dough. Place them alongside the dough, not wider than the rolling pin, and roll until the pin rests only on the skewers.

For very thin dough, use a pasta machine. Start by cutting the dough into about 6½-oz/184-g pieces. Keep the dough not being used in the refrigerator. It is difficult to use if it is not very cold. Place one dough piece on a lightly floured cold surface and dust the top and rolling pin with flour. Roll out into a rectangle about 4 in/10 cm wide and ¼ in/6 mm thick so it fits into the pasta machine roller. Re-dust both sides with flour. Run the dough through the pasta machine roller on the widest setting. Adjust the roller to the next thinner setting and run the dough through again. (This is setting 2 on a KitchenAid pasta roller.)

French Onion Checkerboard Tart. Cast-iron griddle with brackets by CAL-MIL; Satin Swirl buffet table by Southern Aluminum (see Resources, page 347).

Fresh Mozzarella is delicious served on Crostini (page 333) **and topped with Roma Salsa** (page 316). **Tavola plate by Fortessa Tableware** (see Resources, page 347).

FRESH MOZZARELLA

1 gal/3.84 L cold water

3½ oz/99 g kosher salt (¾ cup/180 mL)

16 fl oz/480 mL buttermilk

2 lb/907 g fresh mozzarella curds, cut into ¼-in/6-mm dice

1. In an 8-qt/7.68-L sauce pot, bring the water and salt to 170°F/77°C and stir to dissolve the salt. Remove the pot from the heat. Place the buttermilk into a 4-qt/3.84-L bowl and stir 2 cups/480 mL of the hot salted water into the buttermilk.

2. Place the cheese curds in a colander and place the colander in the pot of hot salted water so the cheese is completely submerged. Let the curd melt in the water undisturbed for 1 minute, then gently stir with a wooden spoon until it becomes a smooth yet stringy mass. Rewarm the water if needed to maintain a temperature of 155°F/68°C.

3. Wearing a double set of food-grade plastic gloves, carefully gather 4-oz/113-g handfuls of the cheese and form it into 8 smooth balls, being careful not to overwork them, as they will become tough. Let the balls cool in the water for 20 minutes.

4. Place the mozzarella balls in the buttermilk mixture and let them rest for 5 minutes. *The mozzarella can be stored in the buttermilk and covered in the refrigerator for 4 days.*

SPANISH TOMATO BREAD

12 baguette slices, cut ½ in/1 cm thick on the diagonal

2 garlic cloves, or as needed to rub over bread (¼ oz/7 g)

3 very ripe tomatoes, such as beefsteak, halved crosswise, plus as needed to rub over bread (about 10 oz/284 g)

1 fl oz/30 mL extra-virgin olive oil, Spanish preferred

Scant ¼ tsp/1 g salt

Scant ¼ tsp/0.5 g ground black pepper

12 slices Manchego or Drunken Goat cheese (about 6 oz/170 g)

1. Heat the grill to high. Clean and oil the grates. Reduce the heat to medium and grill the bread until it becomes golden and crispy, 1½ minutes on each side. When cool enough, rub the garlic roughly over one side of each grilled bread slice, as if grating the garlic on the bread. *The bread can be prepared 1 day in advance. Store wrapped in the refrigerator.*

2. Rub the cut sides of the tomatoes over the same side of each slice of bread, just like the garlic, squeezing the tomato so the juice and pulp soak into the bread. Discard the tomato skins. Top each slice with ½ tsp/1 mL olive oil, a pinch of salt and pepper, and a cheese slice. Grill or bake until the cheese melts and the bottom is crunchy, 1 to 2 minutes.

RED POTATOES WITH GORGONZOLA CREAM, BACON, AND WALNUTS

YIELD: 4 DOZEN PIECES

POTATOES

24 red potatoes, about 1 in/3 cm in diameter

2 fl oz/60 mL olive oil

½ tsp/1.5 g kosher salt

¼ tsp/0.5 g Cajun Spice (page 333)

GORGONZOLA CREAM, BACON, AND WALNUTS

8 oz/227 g block cream cheese, not whipped
or spreadable (1 cup/240 mL)

2 oz/57 g toasted shelled walnut pieces
(½ cup/120 mL; see Box)

2 oz/57 g crumbled Gorgonzola (½ cup/120 mL)

¾ oz/21 g cooked thick-sliced bacon that was cut into
¼-in/6-mm pieces before cooking (¼ cup/60 mL)

1 tbsp/3.5 g minced chives

¼ tsp/1.25 mL Tabasco sauce, plus as
needed to adjust seasoning

¼ tsp/0.5 g finely ground black pepper,
plus as needed to adjust seasoning

Kosher salt, as needed to adjust seasoning

GARNISH

1 tbsp/3 g minced chives

1. For the potatoes, position a rack in the bottom third
of the oven and heat to 375°F/191°C. Cut the potatoes in
half and place them on a sheet pan. Toss the potatoes
with the oil, salt, and Cajun spice. Turn cut side down.
Bake until the cut sides are golden and the potatoes are
tender when pierced with a fork, 20 to 25 minutes. Cool at
room temperature for 20 minutes. *The potatoes can be
baked 4 hours in advance. Store wrapped in the refrigerator.*

2. For the Gorgonzola cream, process the cream cheese
in a food processor fitted with a steel blade until smooth,
20 seconds. Add the walnuts, Gorgonzola, bacon, chives,
Tabasco, and black pepper and pulse the motor until
combined, ten 3-second on/off pulses, scraping down the
bowl a few times. The mixture should still be quite
chunky. Taste and adjust the seasoning, adding salt if necessary. *The Gorgonzola cream can be prepared 3 days in
advance. Store wrapped in the refrigerator.*

3. Fit a pastry bag with a No. 4 star piping tip and fill
with the Gorgonzola cream, bacon, and walnuts. Pipe
onto the flat side of each potato half. Garnish with the
chives.

WHY TOAST NUTS, SEEDS, AND COCONUT?

TOASTING INTENSIFIES FLAVOR because it brings
the essential oils to the surface of nuts and seeds
and caramelizes coconut.

To toast raw nuts, seeds, or coconut:

1. Position a rack in the middle of the oven and
   heat to 325°F/163°C. Distribute the nuts,
   seeds, or coconut on a sheet pan (about 4
   cups/960 mL per sheet pan.)

2. Toast in the oven, tossing several times, until
   fragrant and golden, 12 to 15 minutes. Cool
   completely. *The nuts, seeds, or coconut can be
   toasted in advance. Store in a plastic bag at
   room temperature for 3 days, in the refrigerator
   for 3 weeks, or in the freezer for 3 months.*

MINIATURE CHICKEN AND PEPPER EMPANADAS

YIELD: 6 DOZEN PIECES

1 lb 10 oz/737 g Lager Pastry Dough (1 batch; page 308)

Bench flour, as needed

2 eggs

2 fl oz/60 mL water

1 lb 4 oz/567 g Chicken Empanada Filling (about ⅕ batch; page 226)

32 fl oz/960 mL canola oil

1. Place the chilled dough on a lightly floured cold surface and dust the top of the dough and rolling pin with flour. Roll out the dough into an even ¹⁄₁₆-in/2-mm-thick circle and cut into 3-in/8-cm rounds, about ½ oz/ 14 g each, reserving the scraps. Combine all the scraps and repeat until 36 rounds are prepared. As the batches of dough are prepared, place them on a sheet pan and keep wrapped in the refrigerator. Refrigerate all the rounds for 30 minutes before filling. See page 110 for tips on rolling out dough.

2. Whisk the eggs and water in a 2-cup/480-mL bowl. Line 2 sheet pans with parchment paper. Place 1 tbsp/ 15 mL filling on each dough circle. With a pastry brush, lightly coat the edges with the egg wash, fold the dough in half over the filling, and seal and crimp the seams with fork tines. Place on the prepared sheet pans and refrigerate for at least 30 minutes. *The empanadas can be assembled in advance. Store wrapped in the refrigerator for 1 day or in the freezer for 3 months. Thaw in the refrigerator.*

3. Pour the oil into a 4-qt/3.84 L saucepan. The oil should never go more than one-quarter up the side of the pan but should be deep enough so that the empanadas can be submerged and not touch the bottom. Over medium heat, heat the oil to 350°F/177°C. It is hot enough when an empanada causes the oil to immediately sizzle but takes 45 seconds to start browning.

4. Carefully place 6 empanadas into the oil, one at a time. Deep-fry, turning several times until the empanadas are golden brown, 4 to 5 minutes. Place the cooked empanadas on a cooling rack lined with paper towels. Repeat with all the empanadas.

Empanadas can also be baked. Position racks in the top third and bottom third of the oven and heat to 425°F/218°C. Brush the outside of each empanada with egg wash and make several air vents with fork tines. Bake on parchment-lined sheet pans 2 in/5 cm apart until hot and crispy, 10 to 12 minutes.

The Red Pepper Rouille on page 324 makes a great dipping sauce.

CHICKEN PECORINO ON A STICK

YIELD: 4 DOZEN PIECES

PECORINO ROMANO CRUST

8 oz/227 g freshly toasted bread crumbs (4 cups/960 mL; see Box) or panko

6 oz/170 g grated Pecorino Romano (2 cups/480 mL)

4 tsp/8 g cumin

DIJON BUTTER

1 lb/454 g unsalted butter (2 cups/480 mL)

10 oz/284 g Dijon mustard (1¼ cups/300 mL)

½ tsp/1 g cayenne

¼ tsp/1 g kosher salt

CHICKEN

3 lb/1.36 kg trimmed boneless skinless chicken breast

1. For the Pecorino Romano crust, combine the bread crumbs, cheese, and cumin in a 2-qt/1.92-L shallow bowl. *The seasoned bread crumbs can be made in advance. Store them in a plastic bag in the refrigerator for 3 days or in the freezer for 3 months.*

2. For the Dijon butter, melt the butter in a 1½-qt/1.44-L saucepan over medium heat. Remove from the heat and whisk in the mustard, cayenne, and salt to make a smooth, thick emulsion. Cool in the pan for 5 minutes.

3. For the chicken, soak 48 bamboo skewers in warm water for 20 minutes. Pound the chicken between 2 sheets of waxed paper to an even ¼-in/6-mm thickness. Cut the chicken into forty-eight ½-in/1-cm-wide strips. Blot dry and thread onto the skewers, ¼ in/6 mm from the end. Dip the chicken into the Dijon butter, completely coating it and letting the excess drip back into the pan. Press the chicken into the bread crumbs, patting on as much as possible to both sides, letting the excess fall back into the bowl. Lay the chicken skewers on sheet pans 1 in/3 cm apart. Repeat with all the chicken. *The chicken can be breaded 1 day in advance. Store wrapped in the refrigerator.*

4. Position racks in the top third and bottom third of the oven and heat it to 425°F/218°C. Bake the chicken until it has a deep golden edge and bottom, the center is opaque and firm, and it reaches an internal temperature of 165°F/74°C, 15 to 20 minutes, rotating the sheet pans halfway through baking time from front to back and top to bottom. They will make a sizzling sound when close to being done.

This is also great as an entrée or on a sandwich: Pound the chicken into cutlets, but do not cut it into strips. Bake as directed, increasing the time to 25 to 30 minutes.

WHY MAKE YOUR OWN BREAD CRUMBS?

STORE-BOUGHT BREAD CRUMBS ARE STALE and powdery and, as a coating, can have a pasty finish. Besides, making bread crumbs yourself uses up bread that otherwise might end up in the garbage. If making them is not possible, substitute panko, a Japanese flaky bread crumb.

To make bread crumbs:

1. Position a rack in the middle of the oven and heat to 350°F/177°C. Rip day-old bread into 2-in/5-cm pieces. Process small batches of the bread in a food processor fitted with a steel blade until coarse bread crumbs form, 30 seconds. Distribute the bread crumbs on a sheet pan (about 8 oz/227 g bread crumbs per sheet pan).

2. Toast in the oven, tossing several times, until crunchy and light golden, 20 to 25 minutes. Cool completely. *The bread crumbs can be toasted in advance. Store in a plastic bag at room temperature for 3 days, in the refrigerator for 3 weeks, or in the freezer for 3 months.*

3 lb/1.36 kg firm day-old bread yields 2 lb/907 g or 16 cups bread crumbs

GARLICKY SMOKED PAPRIKA SHRIMP

YIELD: 1 DOZEN SKEWERS

MARINADE AND SHRIMP

1 fl oz/30 mL extra-virgin olive oil

1 fl oz/30 mL lime juice

½ oz/14 g garlic paste (4 tsp/20 mL or 4 cloves) made with ¼ tsp/0.75 g kosher salt

2 tsp/8 g packed dark brown sugar

1½ tsp/6 g Spanish smoked paprika

¾ tsp/2 g kosher salt, plus as needed to adjust seasoning

¼ tsp/0.5 g ground black pepper, plus as needed to adjust seasoning

⅛ tsp/0.25 g cayenne, plus as needed to adjust seasoning

24 shrimp (16/20 count), peeled and deveined, tails removed, patted dry with paper towels

Canola oil, to oil grill grates

GARLIC CHIPS

2 fl oz/60 mL olive oil

1 oz/28 g thinly sliced garlic (8 cloves)

1 oz/28 g cold unsalted butter, cut into ¼-in/6-mm pats (2 tbsp/30 mL)

½ oz/14 g chopped flat-leaf parsley (¼ cup/60 mL)

½ tsp/2 g lime zest

1. Soak twelve 6-in/15-cm wooden skewers in warm water for 30 minutes. For the marinade, whisk the extra-virgin olive oil, lime juice, garlic paste, sugar, paprika, salt, pepper, and cayenne in a 1-qt/960-mL bowl. Thread 2 shrimp onto each wooden skewer, positioning them ¼ in/6 mm from the end, and place on a sheet pan. Repeat with the remaining shrimp and skewers. *The marinade can be made 1 week in advance and the shrimp skewered 1 day in advance. Immediately store both wrapped separately in the refrigerator.*

2. Pour the marinade over the shrimp to evenly coat. Marinate the shrimp wrapped in the refrigerator for 30 minutes and up to 1 hour.

3. For the garlic chips, put the olive oil and sliced garlic into a cold 6-in/15-cm sauté pan. Cook the garlic over very low heat until golden, 10 to 15 minutes. Set aside. *The garlic can be cooked 1 day in advance. Immediately store wrapped in the refrigerator.*

4. To grill the shrimp and finish the sauce, heat the grill to high. Clean, then oil, the grates with canola oil. Place a sheet of aluminum foil on the center of the grill. Drain the shrimp and discard the marinade. Just before placing the shrimp on the grill, lower the heat to medium. Place the skewers on the grill so the shrimp is directly on the grates but the exposed skewers are over the foil to prevent them from burning. Leave the shrimp undisturbed for 1 to 2 minutes. Turn the shrimp over and grill until they are uniformly pink on the outside and are opaque in the center, 1 to 1½ minutes more.

5. Reheat the garlic chips and oil in a saucepan over low heat, 3 minutes. Remove the pan from the heat and swirl in the butter until the sauce is emulsified. Add the parsley and lime zest. Drizzle the sauce over the shrimp. Taste and adjust the seasoning.

Crunchy Coconut Shrimp with Honey Mustard (page 327) and Orange-Horseradish Salsa (page 314). Oblong bamboo tray by Willow Group, Ltd. (see Resources, page 347).

CRUNCHY COCONUT SHRIMP

YIELD: 4 DOZEN PIECES

EGG WASH

4 eggs

½ tsp/2 g kosher salt

½ tsp/1 g ground black pepper

FLOUR COATING

7½ oz/212 g unbleached all-purpose
flour (1½ cups/360 mL)

TEMPURA BATTER

2 eggs

3¾ oz/106 g unbleached all-purpose flour (¾ cup/180 mL)

1 tbsp/6 g cornstarch

½ tsp/2 g baking powder

1 tsp/3 g kosher salt

8 fl oz/240 mL cold water

COCONUT COATING

1 lb 8 oz/680 g unsweetened coconut
(6 cups/1.44 L, lightly packed)

SHRIMP

48 shrimp (16/20 count), peeled and deveined, tails removed, patted dry with paper towels (about 3 lb/1.36 kg)

32 fl oz/960 mL canola oil, plus as needed, to fry the shrimp

1. For the egg wash, whisk the eggs, salt, and pepper in a 2-qt/1.92-L shallow bowl until thoroughly combined. For the flour coating, put the flour into another 2-qt/1.92-L shallow bowl. For the tempura batter, whisk the eggs, flour, cornstarch, baking powder, salt, and water in a third 2-qt/1.92-L shallow bowl. For the coconut coating, put the coconut into a fourth 2-qt/1.92-L shallow bowl. Line up the bowls in the order they were filled for the standard breading procedure.

2. Toss all the shrimp with the egg in the first bowl and evenly coat. Lift one shrimp out of the egg and evenly coat with the flour in the second bowl, shaking off any excess. Drop into the third bowl, completely coat with the batter, and let the excess drip back into the bowl. Press the shrimp into the coconut in the last bowl, patting on to evenly coat. Lay the shrimp on a parchment-lined sheet pan. Repeat, evenly coating the remaining shrimp (any coconut that becomes wet from the batter is still fine to use). Refrigerate, wrapped, for at least 30 minutes before frying. *The shrimp can be coated 1 day in advance. Immediately store wrapped in the refrigerator.*

3. Pour the oil into a wide-mouth 4-qt/3.84-L saucepan. The oil should never go more than one-quarter up the side of the pan but should be deep enough so the shrimp can be submerged and not touch the bottom. Over medium heat, heat the oil to 350°F/177°C. It is hot enough when a shrimp causes the oil to immediately sizzle but takes 45 seconds to start browning. Carefully place 6 shrimp into the oil, one at a time. Deep-fry, turning several times until the coconut is golden brown and the shrimp is opaque in the center, about 4 minutes.

4. Place the cooked shrimp on a cooling rack lined with paper towels. Repeat with all the shrimp. Between batches, skim all loose pieces of coconut and batter from the oil with a fine-mesh strainer and discard. Adjust the heat so the oil does not smoke or burn. *The shrimp can be fried 4 hours in advance. After frying, cool completely at room temperature, 15 minutes. Immediately store wrapped in the refrigerator. Bake on a sheet pan in a single layer 2 in/5 cm apart at 425°F/218°C until hot and crispy, 3 to 4 minutes.*

Serve with Honey Mustard (page 327) and Orange-Horseradish Salsa (page 314).

COCONUT CHICKEN: Replace the shrimp with 2 lb/907 g trimmed, boneless skinless chicken breast. Pound the breasts between 2 sheets of waxed paper with a mallet to an even ½-in/1.25-cm thickness. Cut the chicken into forty-eight 1½-in/4-cm pieces.

DAY BOAT SCALLOPS PROVENÇAL

YIELD: 3 DOZEN PIECES

PROVENÇAL SAUCE

1 lb 8 oz/680 g plum tomatoes or canned peeled whole plum tomatoes in tomato juice, no salt added (5 ¾ cups/1.38 L or about 8 tomatoes)

12 fl oz/360 mL Chablis

1 fl oz/30 mL olive oil

3¾ oz/106 g minced shallots (¾ cup/180 mL)

½ tsp/1.5 g kosher salt, plus as needed to adjust seasoning

¼ tsp/0.5 g finely ground black pepper, plus as needed to adjust seasoning

⅜ oz/11 g finely minced garlic (1 tbsp/15 mL or 3 cloves)

1½ tsp/6 g minced thyme

SCALLOPS

36 dry-pack day boat scallops (U10 count), muscle tabs removed (about 3 lb 8 oz/1.6 kg)

¾ tsp/3 g sweet Spanish paprika

1½ tsp/5 g kosher salt

¾ tsp/1.5 g ground black pepper

1½ fl oz/45 mL olive oil

3 oz/85 g unsalted butter, cold, cut into ¼-in/6-cm pats (6 tbsp/90 mL)

¼ oz/7 g basil chiffonade (2 tbsp/30 mL) or 2 tsp Basil Purée (page 323)

¼ oz/7 g chopped flat-leaf parsley (2 tbsp/30 mL)

¼ oz/7 g minced chives (2 tbsp/30 mL)

1. For the Provençal sauce, if using fresh plum tomatoes, roast the tomatoes over an open gas flame or on a hot grill, turning every 10 seconds, until the skin starts to blister. Cool at room temperature for 10 minutes. Peel off and discard the skin. Chop the tomatoes into fine dice, keeping all seeds and juice with tomatoes. *The tomatoes can be roasted 3 days in advance. Store wrapped in the refrigerator.*

2. In a 12-in/30-cm sauté pan over medium-low heat, slowly reduce the Chablis to 3 fl oz/88 mL, about 45 minutes. *The wine can be reduced 2 weeks in advance. Store wrapped in the refrigerator.*

3. Heat a 12-in/30-cm sauté pan over medium heat for 1 minute. Add oil to the pan and heat to hot but not smoking, about 10 seconds. Add the shallots, salt, and pepper and cook, tossing frequently, until soft and translucent, about 5 minutes. Add the garlic and thyme and cook until fragrant, about 1 minute more. Reduce the heat to medium-low. Add the tomatoes and reduced wine and cook until the sauce is reduced by one-third, about 5 minutes. Set aside. *The sauce can be made 2 days in advance. Store wrapped in the refrigerator.*

4. For the scallops, blot the scallops dry and toss with the paprika, salt, and pepper. Heat a 12-in/30-cm nonstick sauté pan over medium heat for 1 minute. Add ½ fl oz/ 15 mL of the olive oil (1 tbsp) to the pan, adjust the heat to high, and heat until hot but not smoking, 20 seconds, so that a scallop sizzles when it hits the pan. Carefully place about one-third of the scallops into the pan so they fill the pan but are not touching, and give each a gentle press so all its surface area touches the pan. Cook the scallops undisturbed until the bottoms are browned, 1½ to 2 minutes. Adjust the heat, if necessary, so the pan is as hot as possible but does not scorch. Flip the scallops over, add ½ oz/14 g of the butter (1 tbsp/15 mL), and cook, basting the scallops with the butter, until evenly browned, firm to the touch, and opaque in the center, 1 to 1½ minutes more. Place the cooked scallops on a platter and tent with foil.

5. Remove the pan from the heat, add about half of the reserved sauce, scraping up any fond on the bottom of the pan, and pour back into the reserved sauce. Wipe out the pan with a paper towel. Repeat with the remaining scallops, adding oil and butter as needed, and when cooked, place on the platter with the other cooked scallops.

6. Put all the reserved sauce in the sauté pan and, over medium heat, cook the sauce until it starts to bubble, 5 minutes. Remove from the heat and stir in the remaining 1½ oz/43 g butter (3 tbsp/45 ml), 2 pieces at a time,

Day Boat Scallops Provençal. Glass cone with square glass sampler by Front of the House (see Resources, page 347).

until the butter is fully incorporated and the sauce has thickened. Add the basil, parsley, and chives. Place the scallops and any accumulated juices in the sauce. Taste and adjust the seasoning.

Dry-pack means the scallops have not been processed with sodium tripoly phosphate (STP). Phosphate-treated or wet-pack scallops are usually a little cheaper and look whiter and plumper, ironically looking more delicious raw than the dry-pack ones. But beware: When they hit a hot pan, all the excess water held in by the phosphate pours out, resulting in shriveled, tough, fishy scallops. Nothing worse. So, if your only choice is wet-pack scallops, change your plans and make another dish.

These scallops make a great first course served with an individual portion of Shaved Fennel, Arugula, Avocado, and Orange Salad (page 166). For crunch, add Crostini (page 333). Or, pair the scallops and sauce with Black Pepper–Speckled Fettuccine (page 199).

TIPS FOR A SUCCESSFUL SAUTÉ

- Let the food come to room temperature for a few minutes before cooking.

- Dry the food, then season it.

- Heat the pan first, and then add only enough fat to coat the bottom of the pan.

- The pan must be very hot so that the food sizzles when it hits the pan.

- Do not crowd the food in the pan. There should be at least ½ in/1.25 cm between each piece so the food does not steam.

- Put the best-looking side down first. The pan is at its hottest and will make that side look the most mouthwatering.

- Color is flavor, so let the food cook undisturbed. It will pull away from the pan when it is ready to be turned.

- Adjust the heat so the fond, or the browned bits on the bottom of the pan, does not scorch. Tent the food with foil and let it rest.

- Make a sauce with the fond.

GINGERED CONFETTI SHRIMP

YIELD: 4 DOZEN PIECES

SHRIMP

2 fl oz/60 mL extra-virgin olive oil, plus
as needed, to cook the shrimp

1½ oz/43 g minced peeled ginger (¼ cup/60 mL)

¾ oz/21 g minced garlic (2 tbsp/30 mL or 6 cloves)

48 shrimp (16/20 count), peeled and
deveined (about 2 lb 8 oz/1.13 kg)

½ tsp/1.5 g kosher salt

CONFETTI GARNISH

1 roasted red pepper, cut into brunoise (2 oz/57 g; see Box)

1 oz/28 g green onions, sliced ⅛ in/3 mm
thick on the bias (about 4 green onions)

¼ oz/7 g chopped flat-leaf parsley
or cilantro (2 tbsp/30 mL)

1 fl oz/30 mL lime juice (about 2 limes),
plus as needed to adjust seasoning

1 tsp/5 mL Tabasco sauce, plus as
needed to adjust seasoning

¼ tsp/0.5 g ground black pepper, plus
as needed to adjust seasoning

Kosher salt, as needed to adjust seasoning

1. For the shrimp, put 1 fl oz/30 mL of the olive oil, the ginger, and the garlic in a 12-in/30-cm nonstick sauté pan and cook over medium-low heat until slightly golden and fragrant, 3 minutes. Add the contents to a 4-qt/3.84-L bowl.

2. Blot the shrimp dry and toss with the salt. Add the remaining 1 fl oz/30 mL olive oil to the same pan and heat over medium-high to hot but not smoking, about 1 minute, so the shrimp sizzles when it hits the pan. Carefully place 10 to 12 shrimp into the pan so they fill the pan but are not touching. Cook the shrimp, undisturbed, until the bottoms are lightly browned, 45 seconds. Adjust the heat if necessary so that the pan is as hot as

possible but does not scorch. Flip the shrimp over and cook until evenly browned, about 45 seconds more, and then stir-fry until pink, curled, and opaque in the center, about 30 seconds more. Place the cooked shrimp into the bowl with the garlic and ginger and combine. Repeat with the remaining shrimp, adding oil as necessary. *The shrimp can be cooked up to 1 day in advance. Rapidly cool, then immediately store wrapped in the refrigerator.*

3. For the garnish, add the roasted pepper, green onions, parsley, lime juice, Tabasco, and pepper to the shrimp. Toss, taste, and adjust the seasoning, adding salt if necessary. *The shrimp can be prepared up to 4 hours in advance. Rapidly cool, then immediately store wrapped in the refrigerator. Bring to room temperature for 10 minutes before serving.*

HOW TO ROAST A PEPPER

PLACE THE PEPPER OVER AN OPEN GAS FLAME OR under the broiler, turning every 45 seconds until evenly charred. Immediately place the peppers in a 2-qt/1.92-L bowl and cover to steam at room temperature for at least 15 minutes. Remove the charred skin, seeds, and ribs. Cut as desired. *The peppers can be prepared 3 days in advance. Immediately store wrapped in the refrigerator.*

Black and White Sesame-Crusted Tuna with Green Onion–Wasabi Sauce and Green Apple–Ginger Salsa (page 314). **Double tasting spoon by Front of the House** (see Resources, page 347).

BLACK AND WHITE SESAME-CRUSTED TUNA WITH GREEN ONION–WASABI SAUCE

YIELD: 4 DOZEN PIECES

WASABI SAUCE

4 fl oz/120 mL water

4 fl oz/120 mL soy sauce

4 fl oz/120 mL mirin

½ oz/14 g honey (2 tsp/10 mL)

1¾ oz/3½ g wasabi powder (½ cup/120 mL)

¾ oz/21 g finely minced ginger (2 tbsp/30 mL)

3 fl oz/90 mL canola oil

1 fl oz/30 mL dark sesame oil

TUNA

2 lb 4 oz/1 kg trimmed tuna, cut into twelve 3-oz/85-g rectangular portions

1¼ oz/35 g Toasted black sesame seeds (¼ cup/60 mL; page 114)

1¼ oz/35 g toasted white sesame seeds (¼ cup/60 mL; page 114)

1 fl oz/30 mL canola oil, plus as needed to oil grill grates

½ oz/14 g green onions, sliced ⅛ in/3 mm thick on the bias (¼ cup/60 mL or about 2 green onions)

1. For the wasabi sauce, put the water, soy sauce, mirin, honey, wasabi powder, and ginger into a blender. Run the motor until smooth, first on the lowest setting for about 30 seconds and then on the highest setting for about 30 seconds. Slowly drizzle in both oils with the motor running on the lowest speed, about 1 minute. Continue to blend until thick and emulsified, about 30 seconds more. *The wasabi sauce can be prepared 3 weeks in advance. Store wrapped in a sealed bottle in the refrigerator. Shake to emulsify before using.*

2. Place the tuna pieces in a 2-gal/7.5-L zip-close plastic bag set into a 2-qt/1.92-L bowl for support. Pour 6 fl oz/180 mL of the wasabi sauce into the bag and evenly coat the fish. Squeeze the air out of the bag and seal. Refrigerate for 30 minutes.

3. Pour 4 fl oz/120 mL unused wasabi sauce into a flat-bottomed 1-qt/960-mL bowl. Pour the black and white sesame seeds into another flat-bottomed 1-qt/960-mL bowl. Heat the grill to high. Clean, then oil, the grates. After 30 seconds, re-oil the grates several times.

4. Remove the tuna pieces from the bag, drain and discard the marinade. Blot the tuna dry and brush with the canola oil. Place the tuna on the hot grill and cook undisturbed for 30 seconds to 1 minute. Turn the tuna over and grill each of the remaining sides until rare to medium-rare, about 2 minutes more total.

5. Roll the tuna in the bowl of wasabi sauce and then in the sesame seeds to evenly coat all sides. Slice each piece into about 6 bite-size pieces. Add the green onions to the remaining wasabi sauce. Serve alongside the tuna.

This is delicious served with a Sweet and Sour Sushi Rice Cake (page 213) and Green Apple–Ginger Salsa (page 314). For an entrée, use a 6 oz/170 g portion of tuna.

HERBED BEER BATTER SHRIMP AND LEMON

YIELD: 4 DOZEN PIECES

SHRIMP AND LEMON

48 shrimp (16/20 count), peeled and deveined, inner curve of shrimp scored several times, patted dry with paper towels (3 lb/1.36 kg)

24 slices lemon, ⅛ in/3 mm thick, pressed dry between paper towels (about 2 lemons)

½ fl oz/15 mL olive oil

¼ tsp/1 g kosher salt

¼ tsp/0.5 g ground black pepper

32 fl oz/960 mL canola oil, plus as needed, to fry shrimp

BEER BATTER

5 oz/142 g unbleached all-purpose flour (1 cup/ 240 mL), plus as needed to adjust viscosity of batter

2 tbsp/24 g cornstarch

2 tsp/6 g kosher salt

¾ tsp/1.5 g Cajun Spice (page 333)

6 fl oz/180 mL ice-cold beer, plus as needed to adjust viscosity of batter

3 fl oz/90 mL ice-cold vodka

1 tbsp/3.5 g marjoram, sage, chive, cilantro, or basil chiffonade

GARNISH

12 servings Crispy Capers and Parsley Pluches (page 332)

1. For the shrimp and lemon, place the shrimp and lemon slices into a 1-qt/960-mL bowl and toss with the olive oil, salt, and pepper to evenly coat.

2. For the beer batter, whisk the flour, cornstarch, salt, and Cajun spice in a 2-qt/1.92-L shallow bowl until combined. Whisk the beer and vodka into the flour until smooth, about 30 seconds. The batter should be the viscosity of cake batter. If not, adjust with flour or beer 1 tbsp/15 mL at a time. Mix in the marjoram. Set the bowl over an ice bath to keep very cold. *The dry ingredients can be mixed 3 weeks in advance. Store in plastic. The beer batter can be mixed 4 hours in advance. Immediately store wrapped over ice in the refrigerator.*

3. Pour the canola oil into a 4-qt/3.84-L saucepan. The oil should never go more than one-quarter up the side of the pan but should be deep enough so the shrimp can be submerged and not touch the bottom. Over medium heat, heat the oil to 350°F/177°C, about 10 minutes. When the oil is hot enough or when a little batter causes the oil to immediately sizzle but takes about 45 seconds for browning to begin, hold one shrimp by the tail and dunk it into the beer batter so it is evenly coated. Do not dunk the tail. Lift the shrimp out of the batter, letting any excess drip back into the bowl, and carefully place it into the oil. Repeat with about 5 more shrimp and deep-fry in small batches, turning several times until the coating is golden and the shrimp are opaque in the center, 2 to 2 ½ minutes.

4. Place the cooked shrimp on a cooling rack lined with paper towels. Repeat with all the shrimp and then with the lemon slices. Fry the lemon slices carefully, because if they are too wet the oil will splatter. Between batches, skim all loose pieces of batter from the oil with a fine-mesh strainer and discard. Adjust the heat as needed so that the oil does not smoke or burn. Garnish with capers and parsley pluches.

Leaving the tail on the shrimp certainly makes for a beautiful presentation when guests are seated. But, if it's a stand-up event, the tails can cause a cleanup issue. In this case, always opt to take them off so that the guests don't have to worry about what to do with them.

For an Asian theme, serve with Green Onion–Wasabi Sauce (page 125).

HERBED BEER BATTER CHICKEN: Replace the shrimp with 2 lb/907 g trimmed, boneless skinless chicken breast. Pound the breasts between 2 sheets of waxed paper to an even ½-in/1.25 cm thickness. Cut the chicken into forty-eight 1½-in/4-cm pieces.

HERBED BEER BATTER VEGETABLES: Replace the shrimp and lemon with 48 trimmed 1-in/3-cm vegetable pieces, such as asparagus, broccoli, cauliflower, carrots, green beans, mushrooms, onions, peppers, and/or squash.

Herbed Beer Batter Shrimp and Lemon and Herbed Beer Batter Vegetables with Red Pepper Rouille (page 324). Coppered linked bowls with inserts, copper linked risers, "Mod Ideal" platter, and round footed sampler by Front of the House (see Resources, page 347).

Lumpy Cajun Crab Cake Sliders. Kyoto nine-square taster by **Fortessa Tableware** (see Resources, page 347).

LUMPY CAJUN CRAB CAKES

YIELD: 3 DOZEN PIECES

CRAB CAKES

½ cup/120 mL mayonnaise (4 oz/113 g)

1 egg

2 tbsp/30 mL Dijon mustard (1 oz/28 g)

1 fl oz/30 mL lemon juice (about 1 lemon)

½ fl oz/15 mL Worcestershire sauce

½ tsp/2 mL Tabasco sauce

½ tsp/2 mL lemon zest (about ¼ lemon)

¼ tsp/0.5 g Cajun Spice (page 333)

¾ tsp/2 g kosher salt, plus as needed to adjust seasoning

¼ tsp/0.5 g ground black pepper, plus as needed to adjust seasoning

3¼ oz/85 g roasted red pepper, cut into brunoise (½ cup/60 mL; page 123)

1 oz/28 g green onions, sliced ⅛ in/3 mm thick (½ cup/120 mL or about 4 green onions)

½ oz/14 g minced flat-leaf parsley (¼ cup/60 mL)

1 lb/454 g jumbo lump crabmeat, picked through

2 oz/57 g freshly toasted bread crumbs (1 cup/240 mL; page 116) or panko

8 fl oz/240 mL canola oil, plus as needed, to fry crab cakes

GARNISH

4 eggs

2 oz/57 g freshly toasted bread crumbs, plus as needed, to coat crab cakes (1 cup/240 mL; page 116) or panko

1. For the crab cakes, whisk the mayonnaise, egg, mustard, lemon juice, Worcestershire sauce, Tabasco, lemon zest, Cajun spice, salt, and pepper in a 4-qt/3.84-L bowl until combined. Fold in the roasted pepper, green onions, and parsley and mix until combined. Then gently fold in the crabmeat and bread crumbs, being careful not to break up the crabmeat lumps. Taste and adjust the seasoning.

2. Gently form the crab mixture into 36 loosely packed cakes, about ¾ oz/21 g (1 tbsp/15 mL) each. Refrigerate the crab cakes for at least 30 minutes to let them set. *The crab cakes can be formed 1 day in advance. Immediately store wrapped in the refrigerator.*

3. For the garnish, whisk the eggs in a 2-qt/1.92-L shallow bowl. Place the bread crumbs into another 2-qt/1.92-L shallow bowl. Evenly coat each crab cake with the egg and then with the bread crumbs. *The crab cakes can be coated 4 hours in advance. Immediately store wrapped in the refrigerator.*

4. Fill a 12-in/30-cm sautoir with oil deep enough to go two-thirds up the side of the crab cakes. Over medium heat, heat the oil to hot but not smoking, 3 minutes. It is hot enough when a little crab mixture causes the oil to immediately sizzle but it takes 45 seconds for it to start browning. Carefully place enough crab cakes into the oil to fill the pan without touching each other. Adjust the heat so the oil sizzles but does not smoke or burn. Fry the crab cakes until the edges and bottom are golden brown and the crab cakes are set, 1 to 1½ minutes. Turn over and continue cooking until evenly browned and firm to the touch, 1 to 1½ minutes more. As batches are cooked, place the crab cakes on a wire rack lined with paper towels. Repeat the process until all the crab cakes are fried, adding more oil as needed. *The crab cakes can be fried 4 hours in advance. Rapidly cool, then immediately store wrapped in the refrigerator. Warm in a 400°F/204°C oven until the bread crumbs are crispy, 10 to 12 minutes.*

For serving, try Lumpy Cajun Crab Cake Sliders with Avacado-Mango Guacamole (page 321) and Rémoulade (page 319), or Lumpy Cajun Crab Cakes on Shaved Fennel, Arugula, Avocado, and Orange Salad (page 166). For dips, serve the crab cakes with Fire-Roasted Red Pepper Coulis (page 327) and Rémoulade (page 319).

ITALIAN MEATBALLS

YIELD: 8 DOZEN MINI MEATBALLS OR
2 DOZEN LARGE ENTRÉE MEATBALLS

6 eggs

1½ tsp/5 g kosher salt, plus as needed to adjust seasoning

½ tsp/1 g ground black pepper, plus
as needed to adjust seasoning

3 oz/85 g freshly toasted bread crumbs
(1½ cups/360 mL; page 116) or panko

½ oz/14 g garlic cloves (4 cloves)

4½ oz/128 g chopped yellow onion (1 cup/240 mL)

2½ oz/71 g chopped red pepper (½ cup/120 mL
or ½ pepper)

½ oz/14 g chopped flat-leaf parsley (¼ cup/60 mL)

3 oz/85 g grated Pecorino Romano (1 cup/240 mL)

2 lb 8 oz/1.13 kg ground beef chuck, 85% lean

32 fl oz/960 mL canola oil, plus as
needed, to fry the meatballs

1. Whisk the eggs, salt, and black pepper in a 4-qt/3.84-L bowl until combined. Mix in the bread crumbs.

2. Drop the garlic cloves one at a time into a food processor fitted with a steel blade with the motor running and process until finely chopped, 10 seconds. Turn off the motor and add the onion, red pepper, and parsley. Pulse the motor until the vegetables are uniformly minced but not puréed, fifteen 2-second on/off pulses. Transfer the vegetables to the bowl with the bread crumb mixture. Add the Pecorino Romano and mix until combined. Add the ground beef and mix until combined. Sample a little of the meat mixture by frying or microwaving a small flat patty until it is fully cooked. Taste and adjust seasoning.

3. Roll all the meat mixture into ½-oz/14-g (1-tbsp/15-mL) loosely packed balls for mini meatballs or 2-oz/57-g (¼-cup/60-mL) balls for entrée meatballs.

4. Fill a 12-in/30-cm sautoir with oil deep enough to go two-thirds up the side of the meatballs. Over medium heat, heat the oil to 350°F/177°C, about 10 minutes. It is hot enough when a meatball causes the oil to immediately sizzle but takes 1 minute to begin browning. Carefully place enough meatballs into the oil to fill the pan without touching. Adjust the heat so the oil does not smoke or burn. Pan fry the meatballs until the bottoms are brown, 3 minutes. Turn over and continue cooking until evenly browned and firm to the touch, and they reach an internal temperature of 165°F/74°C, about 3 minutes more. Place the cooked meatballs on a sheet pan. Repeat with all the meatballs. Between batches, skim all loose pieces of meat from the oil with a fine-mesh strainer and reserve for enriching the sauce, if appropriate. Adjust the heat so the oil does not smoke or burn.

The meatballs can be prepared in advance. Store meatballs wrapped in the refrigerator for 2 days or in the freezer for 3 months. Warm before serving.

Simmer the meatballs in Herbed Tomato Sauce (page 312) for 20 minutes on medium-low heat or bake in the oven at 350°F/177°C for 45 to 50 minutes. They can be placed in the sauce 1 day in advance, refrigerated, and then baked before serving.

MINI TURKEY AND SPINACH MEATBALLS

YIELD: 8 DOZEN PIECES

4 eggs

2 tsp/6 g kosher salt, plus as needed to adjust seasoning

¾ tsp/1.5 g ground black pepper, plus
as needed to adjust seasoning

4 oz/113 g freshly toasted bread crumbs
(2 cups/480 mL; page 116) or panko

¼ oz/7 g garlic cloves (2 cloves)

2¼ oz/64 g chopped yellow onion (½ cup/120 mL)

2½ oz/71 g chopped red pepper (½ cup/120 mL)

4 oz/113 g squeezed dry and coarsely chopped
spinach (1⅓ cups/320 mL packed)

2 oz/57 g grated Pecorino Romano (⅔ cup/160 mL)

2 lb/907 g ground turkey breast, 99% fat-free

32 fl oz/960 mL canola oil, plus as
needed, to fry the meatballs

1. Whisk the eggs, salt, and black pepper in a 4-qt/
3.84-L bowl until combined. Mix in the bread crumbs.

2. Drop the garlic into a food processor fitted with a
steel blade with the motor running and process until
finely chopped, about 10 seconds. Turn off the motor and
add the onion and red pepper. Pulse the motor until the
vegetables are uniformly minced but not puréed, about
fifteen 2-second on/off pulses. Transfer the vegetables to
the bowl with the bread crumb mixture. Add the spinach
and Pecorino Romano and mix until combined. Add the
ground turkey and mix until combined. Sample the meat
mixture by frying or microwaving a small flat patty until it
is fully cooked. Taste and adjust seasoning.

3. Roll all the meat into ½-oz/14-g (1-tbsp/15-mL)
loosely packed balls.

4. Fill a 12-in/30-cm sautoir with oil deep enough to go
two-thirds up the side of the meatballs. Over medium
heat, heat the oil to 350°F/177°C, about 10 minutes. It is
hot enough when a meatball causes the oil to immediately sizzle but takes about 1 minute to begin browning.
Carefully place enough meatballs into the oil to fill the
pan without touching. Adjust the heat so the oil does not
smoke or burn. Pan fry the meatballs until the bottoms
are brown, about 3 minutes. Turn over and continue
cooking until evenly browned and firm to the touch, and
they reach an internal temperature of 165°F/74°C, about
3 minutes more. Place the cooked meatballs on a sheet
pan. Repeat with all of the meatballs. Between batches,
skim all the loose pieces of meat from the oil with a fine-
mesh strainer and reserve for enriching the sauce, if
appropriate. *The meatballs can be prepared in advance.
Store wrapped in the refrigerator for 2 days or in the freezer
for 3 months.*

For multiple batches: Cool the meatballs on sheet pans
in the refrigerator for 2 hours to eliminate condensation
in the freezer. For inventory control, it is helpful to store
the same amount of meatballs in each plastic bag; for
example, 100 mini meatballs per bag.

Turkey Meatballs are great simmered in Herbed Tomato
Sauce (page 312) or in Turkey Gravy (page 313).

PAN FRYING AND DEEP-FRYING ON THE STOVETOP

- Heat the correct amount of fresh oil to a minimum of 325°F/163°C and a maximum of 375°F/191°C in a heavy pan. The pan has to be heavy enough to conduct and retain heat evenly, and the volume of the pan needs to safely hold the correct amount of oil.

- For pan frying, use a heavy sautoir with straight sides.

- For deep-frying, use a heavy wide-mouth saucepan or stockpot.

- The oil temperature is critical because smoking hot oil is not only dangerous and unhealthy but also burns the exterior crust without cooking the interior. Oil that's not hot enough makes greasy food.

- Always use fresh oil with a high smoke point so that it does not break down quickly during the cooking process. For example, canola or peanut oil can withstand high prolonged temperatures.

- For pan frying, fill the pan so the oil goes about two-thirds up the side of the food. The food should touch the bottom of the pan but appear as if it is floating. Touching the bottom encourages browning. Never fill the pan more than one-quarter full with oil, because it can bubble over when the food is added. Replace oil as needed to maintain the correct depth.

- For deep-frying, fill the pot so the food can be completely submerged or swim in the oil. Again, never fill the pot more than one-quarter full with oil, because it can bubble over when the food is added. Replace oil as needed to maintain the correct depth.

- Use a candy/frying thermometer to gauge the oil temperature. Or place a small piece of bread into the oil. At 350°F to 375°F/177°C to 191°C, the oil around the food should immediately bubble, but the food should take at least 45 seconds to begin browning.

- Keep the oil clean by skimming all loose pieces of food from the oil with a very fine-mesh spider and discarding them.

- Cook the same size food in several batches. Too much food added to the pan at once lowers the temperature. The food should not touch, because this prevents uniform browning. Use tongs to turn the food so that the crust is not pierced. For the best flavor and even cooking, turn pan-fried food once but deep-fried food several times.

- Blot excess oil from the food on a wire rack lined with paper towels set over a sheet pan. Airflow under the rack maintains crispiness by reducing the condensation that happens when food is placed directly on a sheet pan lined with paper towels.

FIVE-SPICE BEEF SATAY

YIELD: 4 DOZEN PIECES

FIVE-SPICE MARINADE

4 fl oz/120 mL mirin

4 fl oz/120 mL toasted sesame oil

4 fl oz/120 mL soy sauce

3 oz/85 g honey (¼ cup/60 mL)

1½ oz/43 g finely minced ginger (¼ cup/60 mL)

1 oz/28 g thinly sliced green onions
(½ cup/120 mL, about 4)

½ oz/14 g garlic paste (4¾ tsp/23.75 mL or 4 cloves) made with ¾ tsp/2 g kosher salt

1 tsp/2 g Chinese five-spice powder

1½ tsp/3 g ground black pepper, plus as needed to adjust seasoning

BEEF

3 lb/1.36 kg trimmed beef flank steaks

4½ fl oz/135 mL canola oil, plus as needed, to oil grill grates

GARNISH

½ oz/14 g chopped cilantro or parsley leaves (¼ cup/60 mL)

1¼ oz/35g toasted sesame seeds
(¼ cup/60 mL; page 114)

1. Soak 48 wooden skewers in warm water for 20 minutes. For the marinade, whisk the mirin, sesame oil, soy sauce, honey, ginger, green onions, garlic paste, five-spice powder, and pepper in a 2-gal/7.52-L zip-close plastic bag set in a 2-qt/1.92-L bowl for support. For the beef, cut the beef into forty-eight 1-in/3-cm-wide strips on the bias and against the grain. Blot dry and thread onto the skewers, ¼ in/6 mm from the end. *The marinade can be made 1 week in advance and the beef skewered 1 day in advance. Immediately store both wrapped separately in the refrigerator.*

2. Place the beef in the bag, coat with the marinade, and seal. Marinate, refrigerated, for 20 to 30 minutes.

3. Heat the grill to high. Clean, then oil, the grates. Place a folded sheet of aluminum foil on the center of the grill. Remove the beef from the bag, drain and discard the marinade, and blot the beef dry. Brush the oil on the beef. Place the skewers on the grill so the beef is directly on the grates and the exposed skewers are over the foil to prevent them from burning. Adjust the heat if necessary to control flare-ups or burning. Leave the beef undisturbed for 1 to 2 minutes, then turn over and continue to grill until the beef is pink in the middle, 1 to 2 minutes more. Garnish the beef with the cilantro and/or sesame seeds.

For an entrée, use the marinade on kebobs made with beef cubes, red onion, peppers, zucchini, and mushrooms.

SAUSAGE EN CROUTE

YIELD: 4 DOZEN PIECES

1½ fl oz/45 mL canola oil

2 lb/907 g sweet Italian sausage, casings removed

16 fl oz/480 mL Fig-Onion Jam, cold from refrigerator (½ batch; page 326)

Kosher salt, as needed to adjust seasoning

Ground black pepper, as needed to adjust seasoning

1 lb 10 oz/737 g Lager Pastry Dough, cold from refrigerator (1 batch; page 308)

Bench flour as needed

1 egg

2 fl oz/60 mL milk

1. Heat a 12-in/30-cm sauté pan over medium heat, about 1 minute. Add the oil to the pan, and heat to hot but not smoking, about 10 seconds. Add the sausage, breaking it into very small pieces. Adjust the heat to medium-low and cook, tossing occasionally until well browned, about 30 minutes. Put the sausage into a 1-qt/960-mL bowl, discarding the fat. Quickly cool. Add the fig-onion jam to the sausage and mix until evenly combined. Taste and adjust seasoning then refrigerate

until ready to assemble the pastries. *The sausage can be cooked in advance and stored alone or combined with the fig jam. Cool quickly and store wrapped in the refrigerator for 1 day or in the freezer for 3 months.*

2. Line 4 baking sheets with parchment paper. Place the chilled dough on a lightly floured cold surface and dust the top of the dough and a rolling pin with flour. Roll out an even ¹⁄₁₆-in/1.5-mm-thick rectangle and cut into 2½-in/6-cm squares, about ¼ oz/7 g each, reserving the scraps. Combine all the scraps and repeat until 48 squares are cut. Place the pans in the refrigerator until the dough is firm, at least 30 minutes. See page 110 for tips on rolling dough. *The crust can be rolled out and cut in advance. Store wrapped in the freezer for 3 months.*

3. Combine the egg and milk for an egg wash. Place 1 heaping tsp/5 mL of sausage mixture onto the center of each dough square. Brush two opposite edges of the dough with the egg wash and fold one over the other to encase the sausage, gently pressing them together. *The sausage en croute can be assembled in advance. Store wrapped in the refrigerator for 2 days or in the freezer for 3 months.*

4. Position racks in the top third and bottom third of the oven and heat to 350°F/177°C. Bake until the crust is set and golden, 15 to 20 minutes.

These pair well as a cunchy element alongside Wild Mushroom Soup with Madeira Crème Fraîche (page 150).

LEMONY HUMMUS

YIELD: 48 FL OZ/1.44 L

---

2 fl oz/60 mL extra-virgin olive oil to cook garlic and 2½ fl oz/75 mL to blend into hummus, plus as needed to adjust viscosity

¾ oz/21 g garlic cloves (6 cloves)

2 tsp/4 g ground cumin, plus as needed to adjust seasoning

½ tsp/1 g ground black pepper, plus as needed to adjust seasoning

⅛ tsp/0.25 g cayenne

4 fl oz/120 mL water

1¼ oz/35 g tahini paste (2 tbsp/30 mL)

2 fl oz/60 mL lemon juice

¼ oz/7 g lemon zest (1 tbsp/15 mL)

1½ tsp/5 g kosher salt, plus as needed to adjust seasoning

2 lb 5 oz/1.04 kg drained, cooked chickpeas (4¾ cups/1.14 L; see Box)

GARNISH

½ fl oz/15 mL extra-virgin olive oil

1 tsp/3 g Tabasco sauce

½ tsp/1 g coarsely grated lemon zest

1. Put 2 fl oz/60 mL olive oil and the garlic into a 6-in/15-cm sauté pan. Cover with a tight-fitting lid and cook over very low heat until soft and golden but not browned, about 10 minutes. Remove from the heat and add the cumin, pepper, and cayenne. Cool to room temperature.

2. Put the seasoned oil and garlic, the water, the tahini paste, lemon juice, lemon zest, salt, the remaining 2½ fl oz/75 mL oil, and the chickpeas into the bowl of a food processor fitted with a steel blade. Run the motor until the mixture is smooth, scraping down the bowl as necessary, about 2 minutes. Add more water and olive oil as needed to adjust viscosity and flavor. Taste and adjust seasoning. *The hummus can be prepared 1 day in advance. Store in the refrigerator with plastic wrap pressed onto the surface area, completely sealing it, to prevent drying and discoloring.*

3. To garnish, combine the olive oil and Tabasco, then drizzle over the hummus. Sprinkle with the lemon zest.

CANNELLINI BEAN AND BASIL PURÉE: Replace the chickpeas with the same amount of cannellini beans. Eliminate the tahini and cumin. Decrease the water to 2 fl oz/60 mL. Add ¾ oz/21 g basil chiffonade (6 tbsp/90 mL) or 2 tbsp/30 mL Basil Purée (page 323) and ¼ oz/7 g minced flat-leaf parsley (2 tbsp/30 mL) to the food processor.

HOW TO COOK CHICKPEAS

WHY COOK DRIED CHICKPEAS? Simple: They're hands-down better than canned.

YIELD: 2 LB 5 OZ/1.04 KG COOKED
CHICKPEAS (4¾ CUPS/1.14 L)

1 lb/454 g dried chickpeas (2¼ cups/540 mL)

1 peeled onion, halved

1 tsp/10 g salt

1 sachet d'épices (containing 8 cracked black peppercorns, 5 parsley stems, 2 bay leaves, 1 sprig thyme, and 1 garlic clove)

1. Remove any pebbles and discolored beans and rinse several times. In a 6-qt/5.76-L bowl, cover the chickpeas with 4 in/10 cm cold water, and discard any beans that float. Add 2 tsp/6 g salt and bring to a boil over high heat for 2 minutes, skimming off any foam. Remove from the heat and soak at room temperature for 1 hour. Drain and rinse, discarding the water.

2. Cover the chickpeas again with cold water by 4 in/10 cm in the same saucepan. Addthe onion, salt, and the sachet d'épices in a 6-qt/5.76-L saucepan. Bring the water to a boil, adjust the heat to medium-low, and simmer until tender, skimming off any foam, 2 to 2½ hours, adding water as necessary to maintain depth.

3. Cool in the cooking liquid at room temperature for 1 hour. *The chickpeas can be cooked 3 days in advance. Store in the cooking liquid wrapped in the refrigerator.*

GRILLED ASPARAGUS WITH MANCHEGO AND JAMÓN SERRANO

YIELD: 2 DOZEN PIECES

1 fl oz/30 mL extra-virgin olive oil, plus more as needed to oil grill grates

24 asparagus spears, trimmed to 5 in/13 cm long and peeled

½ tsp/1.5 g kosher salt

¼ tsp/1 g Cajun Spice (page 333)

12 very thin slices jamón serrano

24 slices Manchego, cut into bâtonnet

1. Heat a grill to high. Clean and oil the grates. Place the asparagus into a 2-qt/1.92-L bowl. Add the oil, salt, and Cajun spice and toss to evenly coat. Place the vegetables on the hot grill grates. Leave undisturbed for 1 to 1½ minutes. Adjust the heat if necessary to control flare-ups or burning. Turn the vegetables over and grill until tender, 1 to 1½ minutes more. Cool at room temperature for 10 minutes.

2. Slice the ham slices in half lengthwise. Place a piece of ham on the work surface. On top of it, place an asparagus spear so the bottom of the asparagus when wrapped with the ham will be visible by ¼ in/6 mm. Place a piece of cheese parallel to the asparagus. Tightly roll the ham around the cheese and asparagus, concealing all of the cheese but leaving the tip of the asparagus exposed. Repeat with the remaining ham, asparagus, and cheese. *The asparagus can be prepared 1 day in advance. Immediately store wrapped in the refrigerator.*

3. Place the ham-wrapped asparagus on the hot grill grates. Leave undisturbed for 30 to 45 seconds. Adjust the heat if necessary to control flare-ups or burning. Turn the vegetables over and grill until the cheese is soft and the meat is slightly charred, 30 to 45 seconds more.

Serve with Balsamic Molasses (page 324) or Red Pepper Rouille (page 318).

Phyllo Spring Rolls with Chicken and Shiitake Mushrooms. Aluminum leaf dish by Willow Group, Ltd. (see Resources, page 347).

PHYLLO SPRING ROLLS WITH CHICKEN AND SHIITAKE MUSHROOMS

YIELD: 6 DOZEN PIECES

---

2 fl oz/60 mL canola oil

1 lb/454 g finely minced trimmed boneless skinless chicken breast

¾ tsp/2.5 g kosher salt, plus as needed to adjust seasoning

½ tsp/1 g ground black pepper, plus as needed to adjust seasoning

½ oz/14 g finely minced ginger (1 tbsp/15 mL)

¼ oz/7 g finely minced garlic (2 tsp/10 mL or 2 cloves)

2 oz/57 g shiitake mushroom caps, cut into julienne (1 cup/240 mL)

5 oz/142 g chopped spinach (1⅔ cups/400 mL packed)

5 oz/142 g shredded zucchini (1 cup/240 mL or about 1 medium zucchini)

5 oz/142 g shredded carrot (1 cup/240 mL or about 3 medium carrots)

¾ oz/21 g thinly sliced green onions (¾ cup/180 mL or about 3 green onions)

½ oz/14 g finely minced jalapeño (2 tsp/10 mL)

1½ fl oz/45 mL soy sauce

1 fl oz/30 mL toasted sesame oil

1 lb/454 g phyllo dough

6 oz/170 g unsalted butter, melted (¾ cup/180 mL), plus as needed

1. Heat a 12-in/30-cm sauté pan over medium-high heat, 1 minute. Add 1 fl oz/30 mL canola oil to the pan, and heat to hot but not smoking, about 10 seconds. Add the chicken, ½ tsp/1.5 g salt, and ¼ tsp/0.5 g pepper and stir-fry until the chicken is cooked through but not browned, about 4 minutes. Place the chicken and any juices into a 2-qt/1.92-L bowl.

2. Add the remaining 1 fl oz/30 mL canola oil to the same sauté pan and coat the bottom. Add the ginger and garlic and stir-fry until soft and translucent, about 30 seconds. Add the mushrooms and the remaining ¼ tsp/1 g salt and ¼ tsp/0.5 g pepper. Cook, tossing occasionally, until all the liquid released from mushrooms evaporates and they are tender, 2 minutes. Add the spinach and cook, tossing frequently until wilted, about 2 minutes. Add the zucchini, carrots, green onions, and jalapeño. Cook until tender but still very crisp, 1 minute more. Place in the bowl with the chicken and add the soy sauce and sesame oil. Toss, taste, and adjust seasoning. Do not be alarmed if the flavor is assertive; it needs to be since it is a filling in the unseasoned phyllo. Rapidly cool, then immediately store wrapped in the refrigerator until ready to assemble. Just before the assembly of the spring rolls, drain and discard any liquid that may have accumulated in the bottom of the bowl and place the bowl over ice. *The filling can be made 1 day in advance. Store wrapped in the refrigerator.*

3. Open and unfold the phyllo and place it on the work surface. Immediately cover the phyllo completely with a dry kitchen towel topped with a damp kitchen towel. Line 2 sheet pans with parchment paper.

4. Place 2 phyllo sheets with long sides toward you on an adjacent work surface. Brush top layer with a thin, even coat of melted butter. Cut the phyllo from top to bottom into 5 even strips about 3¼ in/8 cm wide. Place ½ tsp/3 mL filling on the side of a strip closest to you. Fold one long edge over the filling to cover it by about ½ in/ 1 cm. Repeat with the other long side. Starting with the filling end, roll up the phyllo strip to completely enclose the filling and form a log. Brush the log with melted butter, seal the seam, and place on a prepared sheet pan. Repeat with all the filling and phyllo, placing the spring rolls on the pans 1 in/3 cm apart and in a single layer. Chill the spring rolls for at least 30 minutes before baking. *The spring rolls can be assembled in advance. Immediately store wrapped with 2 waxed paper sheets between layers in refrigerator for 1 day or in the freezer for 3 months. Spring rolls can be baked frozen.*

5. Position racks in the top and bottom third of the oven and heat to 350°F/177°C. Bake the spring rolls until golden and the center reaches an internal temperature of

165°F/74°C, 18 to 20 minutes, rotating the sheet pans halfway through the baking time from front to back and top to bottom.

For best results, thaw the phyllo in the refrigerator overnight. If time is of the essence, take the phyllo out of the box but leave it in sealed plastic and thaw it in a warm spot. Don't be tempted to rush this in the microwave; that does not work. Always keep phyllo completely covered with a dry kitchen towel topped with a damp kitchen towel when not in use.

To serve spring rolls Thai style, place a hot spring roll on a small piece of Bibb lettuce with 2 mint leaves and ¼ tsp/1.25 mL of Tahini Sauce (page 322).

PHYLLO SPRING ROLLS WITH DUCK CONFIT AND SHIITAKE MUSHROOMS: Replace the cooked chicken with ¾ lb/340 g shredded Duck Confit (page 245).

ROQUEFORT GRAPES WITH TOASTED WALNUTS

YIELD: 4 DOZEN PIECES

ROQUEFORT CREAM CHEESE

8 oz/227 g block cream cheese, not whipped or spreadable (1 cup/240 mL)

4 oz/113 g crumbled Roquefort cheese or other blue cheese (1 cup/240 mL)

1 fl oz/30 mL heavy cream

¼ tsp/1 g kosher salt, plus as needed to adjust seasoning

¼ tsp/0.5 g ground black pepper, plus as needed to adjust seasoning

GRAPES

10 oz/284 g toasted walnut pieces, finely chopped (2½ cups/600 mL; page 114)

48 seedless grapes (about 1 lb 8 oz/680 g)

1. For the Roquefort cream cheese, blend the cream cheese, Roquefort, heavy cream, salt, and pepper in a food processor fitted with a steel blade until smooth, scraping down the bowl a few times, 1 minute. Taste and adjust seasoning. Transfer to a 1-qt/960-L bowl and chill until firm, about 30 minutes. *The Roquefort mixture can be made 3 days in advance. Store wrapped in the refrigerator.*

2. For the grapes, place the nuts on a sheet pan. Scoop ¼ oz/7 g (about 1 tbsp/15 mL) cream cheese mixture and press a grape into it. With the palms of your hands, roll the cream cheese around the grape. Place onto the sheet pan and evenly coat with nuts. Repeat with all the cream cheese mixture, grapes, and nuts. *The Roquefort grapes can be made 1 day in advance. Store wrapped in the refrigerator.*

MONTRACHET CREAM CHEESE: Replace the Roquefort with an equal amount of Montrachet. Eliminate the heavy cream.

GOOEY GOUGÈRES

YIELD: 5 DOZEN PIECES

GOUGÈRES PÂTE À CHOUX

8 fl oz/240 mL milk

4 oz/113 g unsalted butter, cut into
½-in/1-cm pats (½ cup/120 mL)

½ tsp/1.5 g kosher salt

5¼ oz/149 g bread flour (1 cup/240 mL)

4 to 5 eggs, beaten, to total 8 oz/227 g (see Notes)

4 oz/113 g finely grated Gruyère (1 packed cup/240 mL)

1 tbsp/3.5 g minced chives

1 tsp/2 g dry mustard

¼ tsp/0.25 g minced thyme

¼ tsp/0.5 g Cajun Spice (page 333)

EGG WASH

1 egg

¼ cup/60 mL milk

Pinch kosher salt

CHEESE CENTER

1 lb/454 g Gruyère, cut into 60 cubes

1. For the pâte à choux, bring the milk, butter, and salt to a simmer over medium-high heat in a 1½-qt/1.44-L saucepan and cook until the butter is melted. Remove from the heat and add the flour all at once. Vigorously stir with a wooden spoon to form a smooth paste. Put back over medium heat and cook, stirring constantly, until a film develops on the bottom of the pan and the paste becomes shiny, about 2 minutes. You will hear a little sizzle on the bottom of the pan, but it should not burn.

2. Place the paste in the bowl of a stand mixer fitted with a paddle and beat on low speed for 1 minute to cool. Add the eggs, one at a time, and mix on low speed until fully incorporated and the paste comes back together, 20 seconds after each addition, scraping down the bowl as necessary. The pâte à choux should be smooth and shiny

and the consistency of toothpaste. Add the grated Gruyère, chives, mustard, thyme, and Cajun spice and mix on low speed until fully incorporated, 30 seconds. *The gougères choux can be made 1 day in advance. Immediately store wrapped in the refrigerator.*

3. Position a rack in the middle of the oven and heat to 375°F/191°C. Line 2 sheet pans with parchment paper. Fit a pastry bag with a No. 4 plain piping tip and fill with the pâte à choux. Pipe onto pans in even ⅜-oz/10-g mounds, about ¾ in/3 cm in diameter and 1½ in/4 cm apart.

4. For the egg wash, whisk all the ingredients together. Lightly brush each mound with egg wash, smoothing out any bumps. Too much egg wash on the baking pan can prevent the gougères from rising fully.

5. Place the pans in the oven, immediately raise the oven temperature to 400°F/204°C, and bake for 15 minutes. Without opening the oven door, lower the temperature to 350°F/177°C and bake for 20 minutes more. Turn the oven off and let the gougères finish baking for 10 minutes in the cooling oven. Do not open the oven door to check. The sudden change in temperature could cause the puffs to collapse. Remove from the oven and carefully cut a small slit in the side of each gougère to let steam escape. *The gougères can be baked in advance. Store wrapped in the refrigerator for 1 day or in the freezer for 1 month. They can be very fragile, so store in a firm plastic container.*

6. Adjust/heat the oven to 350°F/177°C. Poke a cube of cheese into the slit in the side of each gougère and return them to the sheet pans 1 in/3 cm apart. Warm in the oven until the cheese has melted and the exterior is crispy, 8 to 10 minutes.

Without a scale, measure exactly the same volume of water, flour, and eggs by using the same 1-cup/240-mL dry measure.

For a crispier exterior and a drier interior, change the eggs to 3 whole eggs plus enough egg whites (about 2) to total 8 oz/227 g.

As an alternative, stuff the Gougères with Fig-Onion Jam (page 326) and Gorgonzola, or Sweet Italian Sausage, Spinach, and Mozzarella Stuffing (page 248).

TORTILLA ESPAÑOLA

YIELD: 3 DOZEN PIECES

POTATO CONFIT

1 lb 8 oz/680 g peeled Yukon gold potatoes (5 to 6 medium potatoes), placed in water to prevent oxidization

9 oz/255 g Spanish onion, cut into julienne (2 cups/480 mL)

1 tsp/3 g kosher salt

24 fl oz/720 mL extra-virgin olive oil, Spanish preferred, plus as needed, to cover potatoes in saucepan

TORTILLA

12 eggs

1½ tsp/5 g kosher salt, plus as needed to adjust seasoning

½ tsp/1 g ground black pepper, plus as needed to adjust seasoning

1. For the potato confit, pat the potatoes dry with paper towels and slice them ¼ in/6 mm thick. Place them into a 1-gal/3.84-L bowl with the onion and salt and toss together.

2. Fill a 3-qt/2.88-L nonstick saucepan with the oil. Over medium heat, warm the oil for 5 minutes. Carefully place all the potatoes and onions into the oil. Add more oil if necessary to cover. Adjust the heat so the oil remains around 325°F/163°C and poach the potatoes until tender and fully cooked, 10 to 15 minutes. The potatoes should not become crispy or have any color. Check occasionally to make sure none are sticking to the bottom. Carefully pour the potatoes into a colander completely set over a 4-qt/3.84-L metal bowl, reserving the oil. Let the potatoes cool and drain for 15 minutes.

3. For the tortilla, whisk the eggs, salt, and pepper in a 4-qt/3.84-L bowl. Carefully pour the warm potatoes into the eggs and gently fold to evenly distribute. Taste and adjust seasoning. Let sit at room temperature for 15 minutes for the potatoes to absorb the egg. *The egg-potato mixture can be made 4 hours in advance. Store wrapped in the refrigerator.*

4. Put 3 tbsp/45 mL of the reserved oil into a 10-in/25-cm nonstick sauté pan, swirl to coat the pan, and, over medium heat, heat to hot but not smoking, about 30 seconds. When the eggs hit the pan, they should sizzle. Pour the mixture into the pan, lower the heat to medium-low, and cook gently, swirling the pan and lifting the edges with a heatproof spatula to allow any liquid to run to the bottom. In the end, the potatoes should be flat and compact.

5. Meanwhile, put 1 tbsp/15 mL reserved oil into a 12-in/30-cm nonstick sauté pan, swirl to coat the pan, and over medium heat, heat to hot but not smoking. If there is a puddle of olive oil in the pan, pour it back into the reserved oil.

6. When the tortilla center is a little more than halfway set, run the spatula around the edges and bottom to make sure they are not stuck. Cover the tortilla with the larger 12-in/30-cm nonstick pan, and quickly flip the tortilla over into it. Lower the heat to medium-low and cook until the interior is set, about 5 minutes. Place the tortilla on a platter, tent with aluminum foil, and let rest for 15 minutes before slicing. *The tortilla can be cooked 1 day in advance. Store wrapped in the refrigerator. It can be served at room temperature or rewarmed in the oven. Reserved oil can be used for any other recipe but must be stored in the refrigerator.*

Don't be turned off by the length of this recipe and the detailed technique. Here the simplest ingredients are transformed into an unforgettable dish. Garnishes can be Fire-Roasted Red Pepper Coulis (page 327), Sun-Dried Tomato Jam (page 325), or Fig-Onion Jam (page 326).

TORTILLA TORCAL (SERRANO HAM, CHORIZO, PEAS, AND PIQUILLO PEPPERS): Decrease the potatoes to 12 oz/340 g (2 cups/480 mL), decrease the salt added to the potatoes to ½ tsp/2 g, and decrease the oil to 12 fl oz/360 mL, plus as needed if necessary to barely cover the potatoes and onions. Decrease the salt added to the eggs to ½ tsp/2 g. After the potatoes sit in the eggs for 15 minutes, add 5½ oz/156 g diced serrano ham (1 cup/240 mL), 8 oz/227 g thawed frozen peas (1 cup/240 mL), 6 oz/170 g chopped dried Spanish chorizo sausage (1 cup/240 mL), and 6½ oz/185 g chopped piquillo peppers (1 cup/240 mL). Follow cooking directions.

Tortilla Torcal. Round footed sampler by Front of the House (see Resources, page 347).

JALAPEÑO CHEESE PUFFS

YIELD: 6 DOZEN PIECES

---

1 batch Lager Pastry Dough, cold from the refrigerator (1 lb 10 oz/737 g; page 308)

Bench flour as needed

3 eggs

1 tsp/2 g Cajun Spice (page 333)

1 tsp/2 g chili powder

¾ tsp/1.5 g ground cumin

¾ tsp/2.5 g kosher salt, plus as needed to adjust seasoning

¼ oz/7 g coarsely chopped garlic (2 tsp/10 mL or 2 cloves)

2 oz/57 g jalapeño, seeds and ribs removed, coarsely chopped (¼ cup/60 mL)

8 oz/227 g coarsely chopped plum tomatoes (1¾ cups/420 mL)

2 oz/57 g red pepper, seeds and ribs removed, coarsely chopped (½ cup/120 mL)

1 oz/28 g green onions, sliced ⅛ in/3 mm thick (½ cup/120 mL, about 4)

½ oz/14 g cilantro leaves, chopped (¼ cup/60 mL)

5 oz/142 g zucchini, cut into 1-in/3-cm lengths (about 1 medium zucchini)

4 oz/113 g sharp cheddar (1 cup/120 mL shredded)

4 oz/113 g provolone (1 cup/120 mL shredded)

1. Place the chilled dough on a lightly floured cold surface and dust the top of the dough and a rolling pin with flour. Roll out an even circle ¹⁄₁₆-in/1.5-mm thick and cut into 2½-in/6-cm rounds, about ¼ oz/7 g each, reserving the scraps. Combine all the scraps and repeat until 48 rounds are cut. See page 110 for tips on rolling dough. Press one into each well of ungreased nonstick mini muffin pans, filling well. Dock the dough by lightly pricking it with a fork or dough docker several times so it does not form blisters as it bakes. Place it in the freezer until firm, about 30 minutes. *The crust can be rolled out and frozen for 3 months. After it freezes enough to hold its shape, it can be removed from the pan and stored wrapped with 2 waxed paper sheets between the layers. Place crust back into mini muffin pan before filling.*

2. Whisk the eggs, Cajun spice, chili powder, cumin, and salt in a 4-qt/3.84-L bowl until combined. Drop the garlic into a food processor fitted with a steel blade with the motor running and process until finely chopped, about 10 seconds. Then drop in the jalapeño and process until finely chopped, about 10 seconds. Turn off the motor and add the tomatoes, red pepper, green onions, and cilantro. Pulse the motor until vegetables are uniformly minced but not puréed, about fifteen 2-second on/off pulses. Transfer the vegetables into the bowl with the egg mixture.

3. Shred the zucchini, cheddar, and provolone in a food processor fitted with a fine disk. Transfer them to the bowl with the egg mixture. Fold the ingredients together. Sample a little of the filling by microwaving a small amount until it is cooked. Taste and adjust seasoning. *The filling can be made 1 day in advance. Immediately store wrapped in the refrigerator.*

4. Position racks on the bottom third and top third of the oven and heat to 425°F/218°C. Spoon 2 tbsp/30 mL filling into each crust. Bake until the center is set and the crust is golden, about 25 minutes, rotating the pans from top to bottom and front to back halfway through the baking time. *The cheese puffs can be baked in advance. Cool completely. Stack the puffs no more than 2 layers high with 2 waxed paper sheets between the layers. Store wrapped in the refrigerator for 2 days or in the freezer for 3 months. Place ½ in/1.25 cm apart on sheet pans and reheat at 350°F/177°C until hot, about 10 minutes.*

CHEDDAR-KISSED POTATO PANCAKES

YIELD: 7 DOZEN PIECES

¼ oz/7 g garlic cloves (2 cloves)

4½ oz/128 g coarsely chopped Spanish onion
(1 cup/240 mL or ½ large onion)

8 oz/227 g block cream cheese, not whipped
or spreadable (1 cup/240 mL)

2 eggs

1¼ oz/35 g unbleached all-purpose flour (¼ cup/60 mL)

2¼ tsp/7 g kosher salt, plus as needed to adjust seasoning

1¾ tsp/4 g Cajun Spice (page 333), plus
as needed to adjust seasoning

8 oz/227 g shredded cheddar (2 cups/480 mL)

¼ oz/7 g minced chives (2 tbsp/30 mL)

2 lb 4 oz/1.02 kg peeled russet potatoes,
placed in water to prevent oxidization

16 fl oz/480 mL canola oil, plus as needed, to fry pancakes

1. Drop the garlic into a food processor fitted with a steel blade with the motor running and process until finely chopped, 15 seconds. Turn the motor off and add the onion. Pulse until the onion is uniformly minced but not puréed, about ten 2-second on/off pulses, scraping the bowl once. Transfer to a 3-qt/2.88-L bowl.

2. Blend the cream cheese, eggs, flour, salt, and Cajun spice in the food processor until smooth, scraping down the bowl a few times, about 1 minute. Combine in a bowl with the onion to make a batter. Fold in the cheddar and chives.

3. Shred the potatoes in a food processor fitted with a fine disk and place them into another 3-qt/2.88-L bowl. In small batches, squeeze the water out of the potato, reserving the potato water in the bowl it was in, and place the squeezed-dry potatoes into the batter. Periodically combine the potatoes with the batter to slow oxidation. When done squeezing the potatoes, pour the potato water out of the bowl, discarding it; but keep the potato starch settled in the bottom of the bowl. Add this to the batter and combine. Sample a little of the potato batter by frying or microwaving a small amount until it is cooked. Taste and adjust the seasoning. *The potato pancake batter can be prepared up to 12 hours in advance. Store wrapped in the refrigerator with plastic pressed onto the surface area, completely sealing it, to prevent oxidation. If the top does turn brown, scrape it off and discard.*

4. Fill a 12-in/30-cm nonstick sauté pan or griddle with oil so that it is ¼ in/6 mm deep. Warm the oil over medium heat to hot but not smoking, about 4 minutes. It is hot enough when a little batter causes the oil to immediately sizzle but takes about 45 seconds to begin browning.

5. Carefully place about eight ⅝-oz/17-g (1-tbsp/15-mL) mounds of batter into the oil to fill the pan, leaving enough space to gently flatten them into 2-in/5-cm rounds without touching. Adjust the heat so the oil does not smoke or burn.

6. Pan fry the potato pancakes until the edges and bottoms are golden brown and crispy and the tops look like they are starting to dry and set, about 2 minutes. Turn over and continue cooking until evenly browned, crispy, and completely set, about 2 minutes more. As batches are cooked, place the pancakes on a wire rack lined with paper towels. Repeat until all are fried, adding oil as needed. *The potato pancakes can be made in advance. Cool completely before wrapping, and place 2 pieces of waxed paper between each layer. Store the potato pancakes wrapped in the refrigerator for 2 days or in the freezer for 3 months. Place ½ in/1 cm apart on sheet pans and bake at 400°F/204°C until hot and crispy, about 10 minutes.*

SERVING IDEAS: Place a dollop of crème fraîche on one side of a hot potato pancake. Garnish with 3 pomegranate arils or a sliver of smoked salmon and a pluche of dill. Or as a creative brunch BLT, make larger potato pancakes and layer them with cooked bacon strips, arugula salad, and tomatoes. Honey Mustard (page 327) and Double-Cinnamon Apple Sauce (page 302) are failsafe accompaniments.

Soups, salads, and vegetables are no longer relegated to the sidelines of the buffet; rather, they are given a starring role as the new center of the plate. These recipes give a surprise to the taste buds by pairing savory with a sweet and a sour component and by providing a crunch, a crispiness, and a chewiness that lend fullness and satisfaction to even the heartiest of carnivores. By introducing ethnic ingredients, not only to create a balanced menu but also to create a balance of flavors, these recipes fully develop the eclectic menu for the modern buffet. So much more than just leafy field greens, the recipes incorporate beans and legumes, grains and cheeses, seeds and nuts, transforming mere salads into complete proteins. Easily vegetarian, vegan, or gluten-free, these options make "healthy" and "tasty" synonymous. As with all the recipes, suggestions are made for swapping out for seasonality, with instructions on how and what to prepare in advance.

6

SOUPS, SALADS, *and* VEGETABLES

AUSTRIAN POTATO AND WILD MUSHROOM SOUP

YIELD: 12 SERVINGS (6 FL OZ/180 ML EACH)

AUSTRIAN POTATO SOUP

4 fl oz/120 mL Austrian dry Riesling or dry white wine

2 oz/57 g unsalted butter, cut into ½-in/1.25-cm pats (¼ cup/60 mL)

3½ oz/99 g chopped leeks, white part only (1 cup/240 mL); green part reserved for sachet d'épices below

4½ oz/128 g chopped shallots (1 cup/240 mL)

1 tsp/3 g kosher salt, plus as needed to adjust seasoning

¼ oz/7 g minced garlic (2 tsp/10 mL or 2 cloves)

4½ tsp/22.5 mL chopped marjoram leaves or 1½ tsp/7.5 mL dried marjoram

1 tsp/2 g caraway seed

1 lb 8 oz/680 g peeled russet potatoes, cut into large dice and placed in water to prevent oxidization (5 or 6 medium potatoes)

48 fl oz/1.44 L chicken stock

1 sachet d'épices (containing 4 cracked black peppercorns, 3 parsley stems, 1 bay leaf, 1 sprig thyme, 1 cup/240 mL shiitake mushroom stems, and 2 green leek tops)

8 fl oz/240 mL light cream

½ fl oz/15 mL champagne vinegar

½ tsp/1 g ground black pepper, plus as needed to adjust seasoning

½ batch Sautéed Mushrooms and Onions (page 178)

CHIVE BUTTER

2¼ tsp/7 g kosher salt, plus as needed to adjust seasoning

½ oz/14 g chopped chives

¼ oz/7 g flat-leaf parsley (2 tbsp/30 mL)

2 oz/57 g unsalted butter (¼ cup/60 mL)

1. For the soup, heat the wine in a 10-in/25-cm sauté pan over medium-low heat, so there are wisps of steam and very tiny bubbles but it is not simmering. Reduce by half, about 6 minutes.

2. Melt the butter over medium-high heat in a stockpot and heat until hot. Add the leeks, shallots, and salt and cook, tossing occasionally, until soft and translucent, about 10 minutes. Move the vegetables to one side of the pan. Add the garlic, 4 tsp/20 mL of the marjoram, and the caraway seed to the empty space and cook until fragrant, about 1 minute. Stir all ingredients together and cook for 2 minutes more. Add the potatoes, stock, sachet d'épices, and reduced wine. Bring to a boil, reduce the heat to medium-low, and simmer until the potatoes are very tender and start to fall apart, about 30 minutes. Remove the sachet d'épices. Stir in the remaining ½ tsp/2.5 mL marjoram, the cream, vinegar, and pepper. Remove from the heat and cool at room temperature for 15 minutes.

3. Add half of the sautéed mushrooms and onion to the soup. Purée the cooled soup in a blender in small batches. Pour the purée into another stockpot. Repeat with all the soup. Add the remaining sautéed mushrooms and onions. Taste and adjust the seasoning. *The soup can be prepared 3 days in advance. Rapidly cool and immediately store covered in the refrigerator.*

4. For the chive butter, bring a 1½-qt/1.44-L sauce pot filled three-quarters with cold water to a boil. Add 2 tsp/6 g salt, the chives, and parsley and blanch. As soon as the water returns to a boil, remove the herbs, shock in an ice-water bath, drain, and pat dry with paper towels. Blend the herbs, the remaining ¼ tsp/1 g salt, and the butter in a food processor fitted with a metal blade until fully combined, about 30 seconds. Taste and adjust seasoning. Mound onto parchment paper and roll into a 3-in/8-cm log. *The chive butter can be made 1 week in advance. Store wrapped in the refrigerator.*

5. Bring the soup to a simmer over medium-low heat, stirring frequently. To serve, ladle the hot soup into bowls. Garnish each with a ¼-in/6-mm pat of chive butter.

CAUTION: Never fill the blender more than one-quarter full with hot liquid. The steam can cause the hot soup to spray you when the blender is turned on.

For a crunchy element, serve with a miniature Popover (page 260).

TOMATO-BASIL SOUP (CAPRESE ZUPPA) WITH MOZZARELLA

YIELD: 12 SERVINGS (8 FL OZ/240 ML EACH)

TOMATO SOUP

4 fl oz/120 mL olive oil

9 oz/255 g diced Spanish onion (about
1 large onion or 2 cups/480 mL)

¾ tsp/2 g kosher salt, plus as needed to adjust seasoning

5 oz/142 g chopped celery (1 cup/240 mL)

½ oz/14 g minced garlic (4 tsp/20 mL or 4 cloves)

3 oz/85 g tomato paste (2½ fl oz/75 mL)

2¼ tsp/9 mL dried oregano

¼ tsp/0.5 g crushed red pepper flakes

48 fl oz/1.44 L chicken stock

3 lb 8 oz/1.59 kg canned peeled whole plum
tomatoes in tomato juice, no salt added, broken
up into small pieces (13¼ cups/3.13 L)

1¾ oz/50 g granulated sugar (¼ cup/60 mL)

¾ oz/14 g basil chiffonade (6 tbsp/90 mL) or
2 tbsp/30 mL Basil Purée (page 323)

2 oz/57 g grated Pecorino Romano (¾ cup/180 mL),
plus as needed to adjust seasoning

2 tbsp/30 mL extra-virgin olive oil

GARNISH

12 oz/340 g fresh mozzarella, cut into
medium dice (3 cups/720 mL)

2 tbsp/30 mL Macadamia-Pignoli Pesto (page 323)

2 tbsp/30 mL extra-virgin olive oil

1. For the soup, heat a 6-qt/5.76-L stockpot over
medium heat, about 1 minute. Add the olive oil to the
pan, raise the heat to medium-high, and heat to hot but
not smoking, about 20 seconds. Add the onion. Lower the
heat to medium and cook until the onion is soft and
jammy, 20 minutes. Add the celery and cook until it is
soft, 10 minutes more. Move the vegetables to one side of
the pan. Add the garlic and cook until fragrant, about 1
minute. Add the tomato paste, oregano, and red pepper
flakes. Mix all the ingredients together and cook until the
tomato paste is a deep rust color and smells sweet, about
5 minutes. Add the chicken stock, tomatoes in tomato
juice, and sugar and stir all ingredients together. Simmer
for 1 hour. Stir frequently, especially at the beginning,
with a flat-sided wooden spoon. The tomato pulp can
stick to the bottom of the pan and burn, completely ruining the soup. Remove from the heat and cool at room
temperature for 15 minutes.

2. Add the basil. Carefully purée the cooled soup in a
blender in small batches. Run the motor until thoroughly
combined and smooth, first on the lowest setting for 30
seconds and then on the highest setting for 20 seconds.
Pour the puréed soup into another 6-qt/5.76-L stockpot.
Repeat with all the soup. Stir in the Pecorino Romano and
olive oil. Taste and adjust the seasoning. *The soup can be
prepared 3 days in advance. Rapidly cool and immediately
store covered in the refrigerator. Reheat in a saucepan over
medium heat, stirring constantly.*

3. To serve, place 1 oz/28 g mozzarella into each of 12
individual bowls. Ladle hot soup into each bowl. Garnish
each with ½ tsp/2.5 mL Macadamia-Pignoli Pesto and ½
tsp/2.5 mL extra-virgin olive oil.

CAUTION: Never fill the blender more than one-quarter
full with hot liquid. The steam can cause the hot soup to
spray you when the blender is turned on.

Curried Zucchini Soup with Corn and Crab Relish and Tomato-Basil Soup *(Caprese Zuppa)* **with Mozzarella** (page 147).

CURRIED ZUCCHINI SOUP WITH CORN AND CRAB RELISH

YIELD: 12 SERVINGS (8 FL OZ/240 ML EACH)

CURRIED ZUCCHINI SOUP

3 oz/85 g unsalted butter (6 tbsp/90 mL)

13½ oz/383 g diced Spanish onions (about 1½ large onions or 3 cups/720 mL)

2 tsp/6 g kosher salt, plus as needed to adjust seasoning

¼ oz/14 g minced garlic (2 tsp/10 mL or 2 cloves)

2¼ tsp/5 g curry powder

48 fl oz/1.44 L chicken stock

1 lb/454 g seeded zucchini, cut into large dice (about 1 qt/960 mL)

12 oz/340 g peeled russet potatoes, cut into large dice (about 2½ cups/600 mL)

6 fl oz/180 mL heavy cream

½ fl oz/15 mL lemon juice (about ½ lemon)

GARNISH

½ oz/14 g finely chopped flat-leaf parsley (¼ cup/60 mL)

2 oz/57 g unsalted butter, cut into ¼-in/6-mm pats, room temperature (¼ cup/60 mL)

½ batch Corn and Crab Relish (page 171)

1 fl oz/30 mL Basil Oil (page 323)

1. For the soup, heat a 6-qt/5.68-L stockpot over medium heat, about 1 minute. Add the butter to the pan, raise the heat to medium-high, and heat until the butter is foaming, about 20 seconds. Add the onions. Lower the heat to medium and cook until the onions are soft and jammy, about 20 minutes. Move the onions to one side of the pan. Add the garlic and cook until fragrant, about 1 minute. Add the curry powder and cook for 1 minute more. Add the chicken stock, zucchini, and potatoes, and stir all ingredients together. Simmer until the vegetables are tender, 30 to 35 minutes. Remove from the heat and stir in the cream and lemon juice. Cool at room temperature for 15 minutes.

2. Purée the cooled soup in a blender in small batches. Run the motor until thoroughly combined and smooth, first on the lowest setting for 10 seconds and then on the highest setting for 20 seconds. Pour the purée into another 6-qt/5.76-L stockpot. Repeat with all the soup. Taste and adjust seasoning. *The soup can be prepared 3 days in advance. Rapidly cool and immediately store covered in the refrigerator. Reheat in a saucepan over medium heat, stirring constantly.*

3. Bring the soup to a simmer over medium-low heat, stirring frequently. To finish, stir in the parsley and butter. Taste and adjust seasoning. To serve, ladle the hot soup into bowls. Garnish each with 2 tbsp/30 mL corn and crab relish and a drizzle of basil oil.

CAUTION: Never fill the blender more than one-quarter full with hot liquid. The steam can cause the hot soup to spray you when the blender is turned on.

WILD MUSHROOM SOUP WITH MADEIRA CRÈME FRAÎCHE

YIELD: 12 SERVINGS (8 FL OZ/240 ML EACH)

WILD MUSHROOM SOUP

6 fl oz/180 mL Chablis

2 fl oz/60 mL extra-virgin olive oil

4 oz/113 g unsalted butter, cut into ½-in/1.25-cm pats) (½ cup/120 mL)

4½ oz/128 g chopped shallots (1 cup/240 mL)

1 tsp/3 g kosher salt, plus as needed to adjust seasoning

¼ oz/7 g minced garlic (2 tsp/10 mL or 2 cloves)

1 lb 8 oz/680 g cremini mushrooms, sliced ¼ in/6 mm thick (9½ cups/2.28 L)

8 oz/227 g shiitake mushrooms, stems and caps separated, caps sliced ¼ in/6 mm thick (3¼ cups/780 mL), stems coarsely chopped and reserved for sachet d'épices below

2¾ oz/78 g porcini mushrooms sliced, ¼ in/6 mm thick (1 cup/240 mL) or ½ oz/14 g dried porcini mushrooms reconstituted in 8 fl oz/240 mL hot stock (see Notes)

48 fl oz/1.44 L chicken or vegetable stock, or as needed

1 sachet d'épices (containing 2 cracked black peppercorns, 2 parsley stems, 1 bay leaf, 1 sprig thyme, and shiitake mushroom stems from above)

½ tsp/1 g ground black pepper, plus as needed to adjust seasoning

MUSHROOM GARNISH

6 oz/170 g reserved sautéed mushrooms from soup preparation (¾ cup/180 mL)

2 oz/57 g enoki mushrooms, bottom trimmed and mushrooms separated (⅔ cup/160 mL)

¼ tsp/1 g kosher salt, plus as needed to adjust seasoning

½ tsp/1 g ground black pepper, plus as needed to adjust seasoning

MADEIRA CRÈME FRAICHE

8 oz/227 g crème fraîche (1 cup/240 mL)

1 fl oz/30 mL dry Madeira

¼ tsp/1 g kosher salt, plus as needed to adjust seasoning

⅛ tsp/0.25 g ground black pepper, plus as needed to adjust seasoning

GARNISH

2 fl oz/60 mL Chive Oil (page 323)

1. For the soup, heat the Chablis in a 10-in/25-cm sauté pan over medium-low heat, so there are wisps of steam and very tiny bubbles but it is not simmering. Reduce by half, 20 minutes.

2. Heat a 6-qt/5.76-L wide-mouth stockpot and a 12-in/30-cm sauté pan over medium-high heat, 1 minute. Divide the olive oil and 2 oz/57 g butter (¼ cup/60 mL) butter between the stockpot and pan, and heat to hot but not smoking, 10 seconds. Divide the shallots and salt between the pot and pan and cook, tossing occasionally, until soft and translucent, 6 minutes. Divide the garlic between the pot and pan and cook until fragrant, 1 minute. Divide all of the mushrooms between the pot and pan and cook, tossing occasionally, until all liquid released evaporates and the mushrooms are tender and golden, 20 minutes. Combine all of the mushrooms together in the stockpot. Remove 6 oz/170 g cooked mushrooms for garnish. Add the stock, sachet d'épices, and reduced Chablis to the stockpot, scraping up the fond from the bottom of the pot. Bring the stock to a boil, reduce the heat to medium-low, and simmer until reduced by one-quarter, about 30 minutes. Stir in the pepper. Remove from the heat and cool at room temperature for 15 minutes.

3. Purée 2-cup/480-mL batches of soup in a blender. Run the motor until thoroughly combined and smooth, first on the lowest setting for 30 seconds and then on the highest setting for 30 seconds. Pour the purée into another 6-qt/5.76-L stockpot. Repeat with all the soup. Stir in the remaining 2 oz/57 g butter (¼ cup/60 mL). Taste and adjust seasoning. *The soup and reserved mushrooms can be prepared 3 days in advance. Rapidly cool and immediately store covered in the refrigerator.*

4. For the mushroom garnish, warm the reserved mushrooms, enoki mushrooms, salt, and black pepper in an 8-in/20-cm sauté pan over medium heat. Combine and cook until hot, about 1 minute. Taste and adjust seasoning. Keep warm.

5. For the crème fraîche, combine the crème fraîche, Madeira, salt, and pepper in a squeeze bottle. Shake vigorously to combine. *The crème fraîche can be made 3 days in advance. Immediately store wrapped in the refrigerator.*

6. To serve the soup, ladle the hot soup into a tureen. Top with the mushroom garnish. Swirl in the chive oil and Madeira crème fraîche. The soup can also be ladled into 12 individual bowls. Garnish each portion with ⅔ oz/19 g mushrooms, ½ tsp/2.5 mL chive oil, and 1½ tsp/7.5 mL crème fraîche.

CAUTION: Never fill the blender more than one-quarter full with hot liquid. The steam can cause the hot soup to spray you when the blender is turned on.

For a crunchy element, serve with Sausage en Croute (page 133).

To reconstitute dried mushrooms, place the mushrooms in a 2-qt/1.92-L bowl and steep in hot stock for 20 minutes. Halfway through the soaking time, vigorously agitate the mushrooms so the sediment on them falls to the bottom of the bowl. Lift the mushrooms out of the stock and coarsely chop. Pour the mushroom stock through a fine-mesh strainer lined with a coffee filter into the pot with the remaining stock.

SPINACH ENSALADA

YIELD: 12 SERVINGS

PANCETTA AND MUSHROOMS

½ fl oz/15 mL olive oil

4 oz/113 g diced pancetta (1 cup/240 mL)

1 lb/454 g cremini mushrooms, sliced ¼ in/6 mm thick (about 5 cups/1.2 L)

½ tsp/1.5 g kosher salt

¼ tsp/0.5 g ground black pepper, plus as needed to adjust seasoning

SALAD

4 hard-boiled eggs

5½ oz/156 g pomegranate seeds or 4 oz/113 g dried cranberries or dried or pitted fresh cherries (1 cup/240 mL)

1 lb 8 oz/680 g baby spinach leaves, large stems removed (12 cups/2.84 L gently packed)

4 oz/113 g crumbled Gorgonzola (1 cup/240 mL)

1¼ oz/35 g toasted pine nuts (¼ cup/60 mL; page 114)

6 fl oz/180 mL Garlic Confit Vinaigrette (page 329), plus as needed to adjust seasoning

6 oz/170 g Croutons (page 333)

1. For the pancetta and mushrooms, warm a 12-in/30-cm sauté pan over medium heat, about 1 minute. Add the olive oil to the pan and heat to hot but not smoking, about 10 seconds. Add the pancetta, adjust the heat to medium-low, and cook, tossing occasionally until caramelized and crispy, 15 to 20 minutes. Transfer the pancetta to a 13-qt/12.30-L bowl, leaving about 2 tbsp/30 mL of the fat in the sauté pan and reserving the remainder for another use. *The pancetta can be browned in advance. Rapidly cool, then immediately store wrapped in the refrigerator for 2 days or in the freezer for 3 months.*

2. Add the mushrooms, salt, and pepper to the same sauté pan and cook over medium-high heat, scraping the fond from the bottom of the pan and tossing occasionally, until all liquid released evaporates and they are tender and golden, about 15 minutes. Place the mushrooms in the bowl with the pancetta. Cool at room temperature for 20 minutes. *The mushrooms can be cooked in advance. Store wrapped in the refrigerator for 2 days.*

3. For the salad, peel the eggs, chop them into small pieces, and place into the bowl with the pancetta. Layer the pomegranate seeds, spinach, Gorgonzola, and toasted pine nuts on top of the eggs. *The salad can be assembled 4 hours in advance. Do not toss, but rather leave the ingredients layered. Store wrapped in the refrigerator.*

4. To serve, toss the layered salad with the vinaigrette. Taste and adjust seasoning. Add more vinaigrette as needed. Then add the croutons and gently toss again.

For an elegant appetizer, eliminate the hard-boiled egg and top a small portion of the salad with a poached quail egg.

GORGONZOLA, BACON, AND TOASTED WALNUT CAESAR SALAD

YIELD: 12 SERVINGS

CREAMY PECORINO ROMANO DRESSING

8 fl oz/240 mL Garlic Confit Vinaigrette (page 329)

4 oz/113 g mayonnaise (½ cup/120 mL)

4 oz/113 g sour cream (½ cup/120 mL)

¼ tsp/0.5 g Cajun Spice (page 333), plus as needed to adjust seasoning

3 oz/85 g shredded Pecorino Romano (1 cup/240 mL), plus as needed to adjust seasoning

GORGONZOLA, BACON, AND TOASTED WALNUT SALAD

2 lb/907 g romaine lettuce hearts, cut into 1-in/2.5-cm pieces (16 cups)

1½ oz/43 g cooked thick-sliced bacon that was cut into ¼-in/6-mm pieces before cooking (½ cup/120 mL)

5 oz/142 g toasted walnuts, coarsely chopped (1¼ cups/300 mL; page 114)

6 oz/170 g crumbled Gorgonzola (½ cup/120 mL)

Kosher salt, as needed to adjust seasoning

Ground black pepper to adjust seasoning

6 oz/170 g Croutons (page 333)

1. For the dressing, whisk the vinaigrette, mayonnaise, sour cream, and Cajun spice in a 4-qt/3.84-L bowl. Fold in the Pecorino Romano. Taste and adjust the seasoning. *The dressing can be made 3 days in advance. Store wrapped in the refrigerator.*

2. For the salad, layer the romaine, bacon, walnuts, and Gorgonzola in a 13-qt/12.30-L bowl. *The salad can be assembled 4 hours in advance. Do not toss, but rather leave the ingredients layered. Store wrapped in the refrigerator.*

3. To serve, toss the layered salad with 12 fl oz/360 mL of the dressing. Taste and adjust seasoning. Add more dressing as needed. Then add the croutons and gently toss again.

WALDORF CAESAR SALAD

YIELD: 12 SERVINGS

12 oz/340 g diced Fuji or Honeycrisp apples (3 cups/720 mL or about 2 apples)

½ fl oz/15 mL lime juice

1 lb 2 oz/510 g romaine lettuce hearts, cut into 1-in/2.5-cm pieces (12 cups/2.88 L)

6 oz/170 g mâche (4 cups/960 mL)

5 oz/142 g toasted walnut pieces, coarsely chopped (1¼ cups/300 mL; page 114)

4 oz/113 g dried cranberries (1 cup/240 mL)

4 oz/113 g crumbled Gorgonzola (1 cup/240 mL)

8 fl oz/240 mL Lime-Honey Vinaigrette (page 330), plus as needed to adjust seasoning

Kosher salt, as needed to adjust seasoning

Ground black pepper to adjust seasoning

1. Toss the apples with the lime juice in a 13-qt/12.30-L bowl. Layer the romaine, mâche, walnuts, dried cranberries, and Gorgonzola on top of the apples. *The salad can be assembled 4 hours in advance. Do not toss, but rather leave the ingredients layered. Store wrapped in the refrigerator.*

2. Toss the layered salad with the vinaigrette. Taste and adjust seasoning. Add more vinaigrette as needed.

CARRIBEAN MANGO CAESAR SALAD: Replace the apples and lime juice with 5 oz/142 g diced mango (1 cup/240 mL or about ½ mango) and 6 oz/170 g diced pineapple (1 cup/240 mL or about ¼ medium pineapple). Replace the walnuts with 5 oz/142 g toasted sliced almonds (1¼ cups/300 mL) and the cranberries with 4 oz/113 g toasted sweetened coconut (1 cup/240 mL, lightly packed) (to toast nuts and coconut, see page 114). Prepare as directed.

Waldorf Caesar Salad (center), Caribbean Mango Caesar Salad (front), and Gorgonzola, Bacon, and Toasted Walnut Caesar Salad (back). Plaza deep square bowls by Fortessa Tableware (see Resources, page 347).

SALMON SALADE NIÇOISE

YIELD: 12 SERVINGS

POACHED SALMON

12 fl oz/360 mL Chablis or dry white wine

2 tbsp/30 mL canola oil

4½ oz/128 g coarsely chopped Spanish onion (about 1 cup/240 mL)

2 tsp/6 g kosher salt

2½ oz/71 g coarsely chopped carrots (about ½ cup/120 mL)

2½ oz/71 g coarsely chopped celery (about ½ cup/120 mL)

¼ oz/7 g garlic cloves (2 tsp or 2 cloves)

32 fl oz/960 mL cold water

1 tsp/1 g chopped tarragon

10 black peppercorns

3 bay leaves

2 parsley stems

4 lb 8 oz/2.04 kg center-cut salmon fillets, skin removed, cut into twelve 6-oz/170-g portions

NIÇOISE SALAD

6 oz/170 g mâche, cut into 1-in/2-cm pieces (3 cups/720 mL)

6 oz/170 g Bibb lettuce, cut into 1-in/2-cm pieces (3 cups/720 mL)

6 oz/170 g oak leaf lettuce, cut into 1-in/2-cm pieces (3 cups/720 mL)

4 oz/113 g watercress, cut into 1-in/2-cm pieces (2 cups/480 mL)

6 fl oz/180 mL Chablis Vinaigrette (page 329), plus as needed to adjust seasoning and garnish salmon

Kosher salt, as needed to adjust seasoning

Ground black pepper, as needed to adjust seasoning

1 batch Niçoise Potato and Haricots Verts Salad (page 164)

6 hard-boiled eggs, sliced in half

3 oz/85 g nonpareil capers, rinsed (½ cup/120 mL)

1. For the poached salmon, heat the wine in a 12-in/30-cm sauté pan over medium-low heat, so there are wisps of steam and very tiny bubbles but it is not simmering. Reduce to half the original volume, about 30 minutes. *The wine can be reduced 2 weeks in advance. Store wrapped in the refrigerator.*

2. Heat a heavy braising pan measuring 18 by 20 in/46 by 51 cm over medium heat, about 1 minute. Add the canola oil to the pan, raise the heat to medium-high, and heat to hot but not smoking, about 20 seconds. Add the onion is salt, lower the heat to medium, and cook until the onion is soft and jammy, about 20 minutes. Add the carrots and celery and cook until they are golden, about 10 minutes more. Move the vegetables to one side of the pan. Add the garlic and cook until fragrant, about 1 minute. Add the water, reduced wine, tarragon, peppercorns, bay leaves, and parsley stems and simmer for 30 minutes. Turn off the heat and let cool to 165°F/74°C.

3. Add the fish fillets in a single layer without crowding the pan. If necessary, cook in 2 batches. Be sure all of the fish is covered with liquid; if not, add enough water to do so. Return the heat to low, bringing the liquid to a very gentle simmer. Poach until the salmon is slightly firm, has lost its translucency, and reaches an internal temperature of 140°F/60°C, 10 to 15 minutes. Remove the pan from the heat and cool the salmon in the stock at room temperature for 30 minutes. *The salmon can be poached 1 day in advance. Rapidly chill the salmon, keeping it almost submerged in stock, and store wrapped in the refrigerator.*

4. For the salad, lightly toss all the lettuces with the vinaigrette. Taste and adjust seasoning with salt and pepper. Top with the Niçoise potato and haricots verts salad, poached salmon, and hard-boiled eggs. Garnish the salad with a drizzle of vinaigrette and the capers.

ASIAN CHICKEN SALAD

YIELD: 12 SERVINGS

POACHED CHICKEN

4 lb 8 oz/2.04 kg trimmed boneless skinless chicken breast, cut into ¼-in/6-cm-wide strips

48 fl oz/1.44 L chicken stock

2 fl oz/60 mL olive oil

1 tbsp/10 g kosher salt

ASIAN SALAD

1 tbsp/10 g kosher salt plus 1 tsp/3 g, and as needed to adjust seasoning

1 lb/454 g trimmed snow peas, strings removed (about 3⅓ cups/840 mL)

5 roasted red and/or yellow peppers, cut into ¼-in/6-mm-thick strips (page 123)

1 lb/454 g sliced water chestnuts, drained and rinsed

4½ oz/128 g red onion, cut into julienne (1 cup/240 mL or about 1 medium onion)

7½ oz/215 g toasted cashews (1½ cups/360 mL; page 114)

2½ oz/71 g toasted sesame seeds (½ cup/120 mL; page 114)

1½ oz/43 g green onions, sliced ⅛ in/3 mm thick on the bias (¾ cup or about 6 green onions)

8 oz/227 g peeled and cored Asian pear or peeled jícama, cut into julienne (2 cups/480 mL)

1 oz/28 g chopped cilantro (½ cup/120 mL)

½ tsp/1 g ground black pepper, plus as needed to adjust seasoning

16 fl oz/480 mL Tahini Sauce (page 322), without cilantro added, plus as needed to adjust seasoning

1. To poach the chicken, put the chicken, stock, olive oil, and salt into a 4-qt/3.84-L sauce pot, stir to combine, and over medium heat, bring the liquid to a simmer. Lower the heat so the liquid very gently simmers, stirring a few times so the chicken cooks evenly. Cook until the chicken center is opaque and firm and reaches an internal temperature of 165°F/74°C, 10 to 15 minutes. Remove the pot from the heat and cool the chicken in the stock at room temperature for 30 minutes. *The chicken can be cooked 1 day in advance. Rapidly chill the chicken, keeping it in the stock, and store wrapped in the refrigerator.*

2. For the salad, bring a 4-qt/3.84-L sauce pot filled two-thirds with cold water to a boil. Add 1 tbsp/10 g salt and the snow peas. Remove from the water after 30 seconds and shock them in an ice-water bath. Drain and place in a 2-qt/1.92-L bowl. *The snow peas can be blanched 1 day in advance. Immediately store wrapped in the refrigerator.*

3. Add the roasted peppers, water chestnuts, red onion, cashews, sesame seeds, and green onions to the bowl with the snow peas. *The salad can be assembled 1 day in advance. Do not toss and do not dress. Immediately store wrapped in the refrigerator.*

4. Drain the chicken, reserving the stock for another use, and put it in the bowl with the vegetables. Add the Asian pear, cilantro, 1 tsp/3 g salt, black pepper, and tahini sauce. Toss, taste, and adjust seasoning. Add more tahini sauce if needed. *The salad can be assembled 4 hours in advance. Immediately store wrapped in the refrigerator.*

Grilled Skirt Steak Salad with Asparagus, Potatoes, and Fire-Roasted Peppers.
Oval porcelain platter by Willow Group, Ltd. (see Resources, page 347).

GRILLED SKIRT STEAK SALAD WITH ASPARAGUS, POTATOES, AND FIRE-ROASTED PEPPERS

YIELD: 12 SERVINGS

MARINADE

2 fl oz/60 mL Burgundy or dry red wine

2 fl oz/60 mL soy sauce

2 fl oz/60 mL Worcestershire sauce

2 fl oz/60 mL lemon juice (about 2 lemons)

1½ oz/43 g honey (2 tbsp/30 mL)

SKIRT STEAK

4 lb 8 oz/2.04 kg trimmed beef skirt steaks

2 oz/57 g Dijon mustard (¼ cup/60 mL)

1 fl oz/30 mL canola oil, plus as needed to oil grill grates

VEGETABLE SALAD

3 lb/1.36 kg small waxy potatoes such as Klondike Rose, Yellow Finn, and/or purple Peruvian potatoes, 1 to 1½ in/3 to 4 cm in diameter

3 tbsp plus ½ tsp/32 g kosher salt, plus as needed to adjust seasoning

4 roasted red and yellow peppers, cut into bâtonnet (page 123)

12 fl oz/340 mL Basil Vinaigrette (page 329), plus as needed to dress salad

4½ oz/128 g red onion, sliced into ¼-in/6-mm-thick rings (1 cup/240 mL or about 1 medium onion)

1 tsp/3 g coarsely ground black pepper, plus as needed to adjust seasoning

1 lb 14 oz/850 g peeled and trimmed asparagus or haricots verts, cut into 2-in/5-cm pieces on the bias (about 6 cups/1.44 L)

1 lb 1 oz/482 g grape tomatoes or cherry tomatoes, sliced in half (1 qt/960 mL)

6 oz/170 g Pecorino Romano, 4 oz/113 g finely shredded (1⅓ cups/300 mL) and 2 oz/56 g sliced into curls for garnish (⅔ cup/180 mL)

1 oz/28 g green onions, sliced ⅛ in/3 mm thick on the bias (½ cup/120 mL, or about 4 green onions)

1½ oz/43 g chopped flat-leaf parsley (¾ cup/180 mL)

¼ oz/7 g basil chiffonade (2 tbsp/30 mL)

1. For the marinade, whisk the wine, soy sauce, Worcestershire sauce, lemon juice, and honey in a 2-gal/7.68-L zip-close plastic bag set in a 2-qt/1.92-L bowl for support. *The marinade can be made 1 week in advance. Store wrapped in the refrigerator.*

2. For the steaks, blot them dry. Rub the mustard all over the steaks. Place the steaks in the bag, coat with the marinade, and seal. Marinate, refrigerated, for at least 2 hours and up to 12 hours, turning occasionally.

3. Heat the grill to high. Clean, then oil, the grates. Remove the steaks from the bag, drain, and discard the marinade, and let the steaks come to room temperature for 20 minutes. Blot the beef dry and brush with the oil. Place the steaks on the hot grill grates, presentation side down. To mark the steaks with a crosshatch, press each steak gently against the grates. Grill undisturbed for 4 to 5 minutes. With the same side down, turn the steaks 90 degrees, press gently, and cook undisturbed for 4 to 5 minutes. Turn the steaks over and grill until medium-rare or to an internal temperature of 120° to 125°F/49° to 52°C, 4 to 5 minutes more. Place the steaks on a platter, tent with aluminum foil, and let rest for 10 minutes. *The steak can be grilled, but not sliced, 1 day in advance. Rapidly cool, then immediately store wrapped in the refrigerator.*

4. For the salad, place the potatoes and 1 tbsp/10 g salt in a 4-qt/3.84-L saucepan. Cover with cold water by 2 in/5 cm. Bring the water to a boil, then adjust the heat to simmer. Cook the potatoes until there is no resistance when pierced, 20 to 25 minutes. Drain the potatoes, split each in half while as hot as possible, and place in a bowl. Add the roasted peppers, vinaigrette, red onions, the remaining ½ tsp/2 g salt, and the pepper and toss together gently to combine. Marinate at room temperature for 1 hour. *The potatoes, peppers, and red onions can be marinated 1 day in advance. Immediately store wrapped in the refrigerator.*

5. Bring an 8-qt/7.68-L sauce pot filled three-quarters with cold water to a boil. Add 2 tbsp/20 g salt and half of the asparagus. As soon as the water returns to a boil,

remove the asparagus and shock in an ice-water bath. (If using haricots verts, increase the blanching time to 2 to 3 minutes, until tender). Drain and repeat with the remaining asparagus. *The asparagus can be cooked 1 day in advance. Immediately store wrapped in the refrigerator.*

6. Slice the beef against the grain and on a bias into ¼-in/6-mm-thick strips. Place the steak and any juices in the bowl with the marinated vegetables. Add the asparagus, tomatoes, shredded cheese, green onions, and parsley. Toss, taste, and adjust seasoning. Add more vinaigrette as needed. Garnish with the basil chiffonade and cheese curls. *The salad can be assembled 4 hours in advance. Immediately store wrapped in the refrigerator.*

MÂCHE SALAD WITH PEANUTS

YIELD: 12 SERVINGS

4 oz/113 g Pickled Red Onions (page 332)

8 oz/227 g Granny Smith apples, cut into medium dice (about 2 cups/480 mL)

8 oz/227 g red seedless grapes, halved (2⅓ cups/560 mL)

6 oz/170 g mâche, torn into 1-in/2-cm pieces (3 cups/720 mL)

6 oz/170 g Bibb lettuce, torn into 1-in/2-cm pieces (3 cups/720 mL)

6 oz/170 g oak leaf lettuce, torn into 1-in/2-cm pieces (3 cups/720 mL)

4 oz/113 g watercress, torn into 1-in/2-cm pieces (2 cups/480 mL)

8 fl oz/240 mL Georgia Peanut Dressing (page 331), plus as needed to adjust seasoning

Kosher salt, as needed to adjust seasoning

Ground black pepper, as needed to adjust seasoning

2 oz/57g Chili-Roasted Peanuts, toasted (⅔ cup/160 mL; page 332)

1. Layer the red onions, apples, grapes, mâche, Bibb lettuce, oak leaf lettuce, and watercress in a 13-qt/12.30-L bowl. *The salad can be assembled 4 hours in advance. Do not toss and do not dress. Immediately store wrapped in the refrigerator.*

2. To serve, pour the dressing over the salad. Toss, taste, and adjust seasoning with salt and pepper. Add more dressing if needed. Garnish with the chili-roasted peanuts.

COCONUT-ALMOND QUINOA SALAD

QUINOA

28 fl oz/840 mL coconut milk

12 fl oz/360 mL water

2 tsp/6 g kosher salt

1 lb/454 g quinoa, rinsed (2½ cups/600 mL)

SALAD

4 fl oz/120 mL canola oil

5 oz/142 g minced shallots (1 cup/240 mL)

1 tsp/3 g kosher salt, plus as needed to adjust seasoning

½ oz/14 g minced garlic (4 tsp/20 mL or 4 cloves)

4½ oz/128 g roasted red peppers, cut into small dice (¾ cup/180 mL or 2 peppers; page 123)

2 fl oz/60 mL lime juice (about 4 limes)

2½ oz/71 g toasted almonds (½ cup/120 mL; page 114)

1 oz/28 g chopped cilantro (½ cup/120 mL)

¼ oz/7 g minced chives (2 tbsp/30 mL)

¼ oz/7 g coarse lime zest (1 tbsp/15 mL, or about 3 limes)

1 tsp/5 mL Tabasco sauce

½ oz/14 g mint chiffonade (4 tbsp/60 mL) or 4 tsp/10 mL Mint Purée (page 323)

½ tsp/1 g ground black pepper

1. To cook the quinoa, heat the coconut milk, water, and salt in a 4-qt/3.84-L saucepan over medium heat to a simmer. Add the quinoa, cover with a lid, adjust the heat to low, and cook until all the liquid is absorbed, 15 to 18 minutes. Spread out on a sheet pan and cool at room temperature for 20 minutes. *The quinoa can be made 1 day in advance. Immediately store wrapped in the refrigerator.*

2. For the salad, heat a 12-in/30-cm sauté pan over medium heat, about 1 minute. Add 1 fl oz/30 mL canola oil and heat until hot but not smoking, about 10 seconds. Add the shallots and salt and cook, tossing frequently, until soft and translucent, about 10 minutes. Move the shallots to one side of the pan. Add the garlic to the empty space and cook until fragrant, about 1 minute. Combine and cook until the shallots are barely golden, about 5 minutes more. Put into a 4-qt/3.84-L bowl and cool at room temperature for 20 minutes. *The shallots and garlic can be cooked 1 day in advance. Immediately store wrapped in the refrigerator.*

3. Add the quinoa, the remaining 3 fl oz/90 mL canola oil, and the roasted peppers, lime juice, almonds, cilantro, chives, lime zest, Tabasco, mint, and black pepper. Taste and adjust the seasoning. *The salad can be made 4 hours in advance. Immediately store wrapped in the refrigerator.*

The salad can also be served warm.

BULGUR, CHICKPEA, AND LENTIL SALAD

YIELD: 12 SERVINGS

LENTILS

7 oz/198 g French green lentils (1 cup/240 mL)

½ tsp/1.5 g kosher salt

Sachet d'épices (containing ½ peeled onion, 8 cracked black peppercorns, 5 parsley stems, 2 bay leaves, 1 sprig thyme, and 1 garlic clove)

BULGUR AND SUN-DRIED TOMATOES

9 oz/255 g coarse-grain bulgur (1½ cups/360 mL)

½ tsp/1.5 g kosher salt

Sachet d'épices (same contents as above)

2¼ oz/64 g minced sun-dried tomatoes, dry packed (½ cup/120 mL packed)

PASTA

2 tsp/6 g kosher salt

7 oz/198 g acini di pepe pasta or Israeli couscous (1 cup/240 mL)

DRESSING AND GARNISH

1 lb 2½ oz/524 g drained cooked chickpeas (about 2⅓ cups/560 mL; page 135)

6 fl oz/180 mL Lemon and Fennel Seed Vinaigrette, plus as needed to adjust seasoning (page 330)

1½ oz/43 g chopped flat-leaf parsley (¾ cup/180 mL)

½ oz/14 g oregano (2 tbsp/30 mL)

Kosher salt, as needed to adjust seasoning

Coarsely ground black pepper, as needed to adjust seasoning

1. For the lentils, remove any pebbles and rinse the lentils several times. Put the lentils, 1 qt/960 mL cold water, salt, and sachet d'épices in a 3-qt/2.88-L saucepan. Bring the water to a boil, adjust the heat to medium-low, and simmer until tender but still intact, 25 to 35 minutes. The cooking liquid should almost be absorbed when the lentils are cooked. Cool at room temperature. *The lentils can be cooked 2 days in advance. Store wrapped in the refrigerator.*

2. For the bulgur, rinse the bulgur several times. Put the bulgur, 1 qt/960 mL cold water, the salt, and sachet d'épices in a 3-qt/2.88-L saucepan. Bring the water to a boil, adjust the heat to medium-low, cover, and simmer until tender, about 20 minutes. The cooking liquid should almost be absorbed when the bulgur is cooked. Add the sun-dried tomatoes and fluff through with a fork. Let rest covered for 20 minutes. Cool at room temperature. *The bulgur and sun-dried tomatoes can be cooked 2 days in advance. Store wrapped in the refrigerator.*

3. For the pasta, bring a 3-qt/2.88-L sauce pot filled three-quarters with cold water to a boil. Add the salt and the pasta. Cook until the pasta is al dente, about 12 minutes. Drain and cool at room temperature. *The pasta can be cooked 1 day in advance. Store wrapped in the refrigerator.*

4. To finish the salad, remove both the sachets and place the lentils, bulgur and sun-dried tomatoes, pasta, chickpeas, vinaigrette, parsley, and oregano in a 4-qt/3.84-L bowl. Toss, taste, and adjust seasoning. Add more vinaigrette as needed. *The salad can be tossed 4 hours in advance. Store wrapped in the refrigerator.*

WILD RICE, APPLE, AND DRIED CRANBERRY SALAD

YIELD: 12 SERVINGS

WILD RICE

64 fl oz/1.92 L chicken stock

9¾ oz/276 g wild rice (1½ cups/360 mL)

1 tsp/3 g kosher salt

CONVERTED RICE

24 fl oz/720 mL chicken stock

10½ oz/298 g converted white rice (1½ cups/360 mL)

1 tsp/3 g kosher salt

VEGETABLES

6 oz/170 g unsalted butter (¾ cup/180 mL)

2 fl oz/60 mL canola oil

13½ oz/383 g minced Spanish onions (3 cups/720 mL or 1½ large onions)

4 tsp/12 g kosher salt, plus as needed to adjust seasoning

½ tsp/1 g red pepper flakes

10 oz/284 g minced celery (2 cups/480 mL)

¾ oz/21 g garlic cloves (2 tbsp/30 mL or 6 cloves)

12 oz/340 g diced Granny Smith apples (3 cups/720 mL or about 2 apples)

2 fl oz/60 mL lime juice

2 fl oz/60 mL orange juice

4½ oz/128 g dried cranberries (¾ cup/180 mL lightly packed)

3 oz/85 g toasted walnut pieces (¾ cup/180 mL; page 114)

1½ oz/43 g green onions, sliced ⅛ in/3 mm thick on the bias (¾ cup/180 mL or about 6 green onions)

¾ oz/21 g minced flat-leaf parsley (6 tbsp/90 mL)

1 tsp/4 g orange zest

1 tsp/4 g lime zest

1 tsp/2 g ground black pepper, plus as needed to adjust seasoning

1. For the wild rice, in a 4-qt/3.84-L saucepan bring the stock to a boil over high heat. Add the wild rice and salt. If the stock has salt in it, reduce the salt accordingly. Stir, cover with a lid, adjust the heat to low, and simmer until tender, 1 to 1½ hours. If there is liquid left, remove the lid, drain excess, raise the heat to medium, and gently boil until almost dry. Fluff with a fork and cool on a sheet pan.

2. For the converted rice, in a 4-qt/3.84-L saucepan bring the stock to a boil over high heat. Add the converted rice and salt. If the stock has salt in it, reduce the salt accordingly. Stir, cover with a lid, adjust the heat to low, and simmer until tender, about 20 minutes. Fluff with a fork and cool on a sheet pan. *Both rices can be prepared 1 day in advance. Immediately store wrapped in the refrigerator in the same bowl.*

3. For the vegetables, melt the butter and canola oil over medium-high heat in a 12-in/30-cm sauté pan until hot but not smoking, about 10 seconds. Add the onions, salt, and red pepper flakes. Adjust the heat to medium-low and cook, tossing occasionally, until golden and jammy, about 20 minutes. Add the celery and cook until celery is tender, about 10 minutes. Move the vegetables to one side of the pan. Add the garlic to the empty space and cook until fragrant, about 1 minute. Combine and cook until the onions are golden, 10 minutes more. Cool at room temperature for 20 minutes. *The vegetables can be prepared 1 day in advance. Immediately store wrapped in the refrigerator.*

4. In a 4-qt/3.84-L bowl, toss the apples with the lime and orange juices. Add the cooked wild rice and converted rice. Add the cooked onions and celery, cranberries, walnuts, green onions, parsley, orange and lime zests, and black pepper. Toss, taste, and adjust seasoning. *The salad can be prepared 4 hours in advance. Immediately store wrapped in the refrigerator.*

The salad can also be served warm or as a stuffing.

Fig and Burrata Salad. Oval porcelain server by Willow Group, Ltd. (see Resources, page 347).

FIG AND BURRATA SALAD

6 fl oz/180 mL Quince Gastrique (page 318)

1 lb/454 g burrata, cut into 12 pieces

6 Black Mission figs, halved

2 fl oz/60 mL Rosemary-Scented Honey (page 317)

2 lb/907 g Bibb lettuce, torn into bite-size pieces (2 qt/1.92 L)

6 fl oz/180 mL Fig–Marcona Almond Vinaigrette (page 328), plus as needed to adjust seasoning

2½ oz/71 g coarsely chopped and toasted Marcona almonds (½ cup/120 mL; page 114)

1. On a large platter, spoon 12 individual ½ fl oz/15 mL puddles of the quince gastrique (1 tbsp/15 mL each). Place 1 piece of cheese on top of each puddle. Lean a fig half on each piece of cheese, then drizzle each fig with the rosemary-scented honey (1 tsp/5 mL each).

2. Dress the lettuce with the vinaigrette. Toss, taste, and adjust seasoning. Add more vinaigrette as needed. Plate alongside the figs. Garnish with the toasted almonds.

Use this salad as the base for individual cheese plates. For example, replace the burrata with Humboldt Fog cheese and replace the figs with Fig-Onion Jam (page 326).

MEDITERRANEAN WATERMELON SALAD

WATERMELON SALAD

4 lb 8 oz/2.04 kg seedless watermelon balls, drained in a colander in refrigerator for 1 to 8 hours, juice reserved for another use (12 cups/2.88 L)

10½ oz/298 g blueberries, picked over (1½ cups/360 mL)

4½ oz/128 g red onion, cut into fine julienne and soaked in ice water for 1 to 8 hours (1 cup/240 mL or about ½ onion)

5¼ oz/148 g feta, crumbled into large pieces (1 cup/240 mL)

VINAIGRETTE

2 fl oz/60 mL sherry vinegar

½ tsp/1.5 g kosher salt, plus as needed to adjust seasoning

¼ tsp/0.5 g ground black pepper, plus more to adjust seasoning

¼ tsp/1 g granulated sugar, plus more to adjust seasoning

4 fl oz/120 mL extra-virgin olive oil

¼ oz/7 g basil chiffonade (2 tbsp/30 mL) or 2 tsp/10 mL Basil Purée (page 323)

¼ oz/7 g mint chiffonade, tough ribs removed (2 tbsp/30 mL) or 2 tsp/10 mL Mint Purée (page 323)

1¼ oz/35 g toasted pistachios, coarsely chopped (¼ cup/60 mL; page 114)

1. For the watermelon salad, layer the watermelon, blueberries, onion, and feta in a 4-qt/3.84-L bowl *The salad can be assembled 6 hours in advance. Do not toss, but rather leave ingredients layered. Store wrapped in the refrigerator.*

2. For the vinaigrette, whisk the vinegar, salt, pepper, and sugar in a 1-qt/960-mL bowl. Slowly drizzle in the oil while whisking vigorously until emulsified. *The vinaigrette can be made 1 week in advance. Store wrapped in the refrigerator. Shake to emulsify.*

3. To serve, add the basil and mint to the vinaigrette, drizzle onto the salad, and gently toss. Taste and adjust seasoning. Garnish with the pistachios.

MEDITERRANEAN POTATO AND HARICOTS VERTS SALAD

YIELD: 12 SERVINGS

MARINATED POTATOES

2 lb/907 g small waxy potatoes such as Klondike Rose, Yellow Finn, and/or purple Peruvian potatoes, 1 to 1½ in/3 to 4 cm in diameter

1 tbsp plus ½ tsp/11.5 g kosher salt

4 fl oz/120 mL Balsamic Vinaigrette (page 329)

1½ oz/43 g nonpareil capers, rinsed (¼ cup/60 mL)

½ tsp/1 g coarsely ground black pepper

⅛ tsp/0.25 g red pepper flakes

HARICOTS VERTS SALAD

2 lb/907 g trimmed haricots verts or green beans (about 6 cups/1.44 L)

2 tbsp/20 g kosher salt to blanch vegetables, plus as needed to adjust seasoning

4 fl oz/120 mL Balsamic Vinaigrette, plus as needed to adjust seasoning (page 329)

8½ oz/240 g grape tomatoes or cherry tomatoes, sliced in half (2 cups/480 mL)

6 oz/170 g pitted oil-cured Gaeta olives (1 cup/240 mL)

1½ oz/43 g grated Pecorino Romano (½ cup/120 mL)

½ oz/14 g finely chopped flat-leaf parsley (¼ cup/60 mL)

¼ oz/7 g basil chiffonade (2 tbsp/30 mL) or 2 tsp/10 mL Basil Purée (page 323)

¼ oz/7 g minced chives (2 tbsp/30 mL)

Ground black pepper, as needed to adjust seasoning

GARNISH

Pecorino Romano curls

1. For the potatoes, place the potatoes and 1 tbsp/10 g salt in a 4-qt/3.84-L saucepan. Cover with cold water by 2 in/5 cm. Bring the water to a boil over high heat, then adjust the heat to a simmer. Cook the potatoes until there is no resistance when pierced, 20 to 25 minutes. Drain the potatoes, slice each into quarters while as hot as possible, and place into a 4-qt/3.84 L bowl. Immediately add the vinaigrette, capers, the remaining ½ tsp/1.5 g salt, black pepper, and red pepper flakes and gently toss until combined. Marinate at room temperature for 1 hour. *The potatoes can be marinated 1 day in advance. Store wrapped in the refrigerator.*

2. For the salad, bring an 8-qt/7.68-L sauce pot filled three-quarters with cold water to a boil. Add the haricots verts and 2 tbsp/20 g salt. Remove the haricots verts when tender, 2 to 3 minutes after the water returns to a boil. Shock in an ice-water bath, and drain. *The haricots verts can be blanched 1 day in advance. Store wrapped in the refrigerator.*

3. Add the haricots verts, vinaigrette, tomatoes, olives, Pecorino Romano, parsley, basil, and chives to the bowl with the potatoes. Toss, taste, and adjust seasoning. Add more vinaigrette as needed. Garnish with the cheese curls. *The salad can be tossed 4 hours in advance. Store wrapped in the refrigerator.*

NIÇOISE POTATO AND HARICOTS VERTS SALAD: Eliminate the Pecorino Romano. Replace the Balsamic Vinaigrette with the same amount of Chablis Vinaigrette (page 329). Replace the basil with the same amount of tarragon.

MARINATED ROASTED PEPPER AND HARICOTS VERTS SALAD

YIELD: 12 SERVINGS

---

3 oz/85 g golden raisins (½ cup/120 mL)

1½ fl oz/45 mL dry sherry

3 roasted red and/or yellow peppers (page 124)

4¼ oz/120 g heirloom tomatoes, cut into 1-in/2.5-cm chunks (1 cup/240 mL)

3 oz/85 g pitted oil-cured Gaeta olives, slivered (½ cup/120 mL)

1 oz/28 g shaved red onion (¼ cup/60 mL)

¼ oz/7 g finely minced jalapeño (1 tsp/ 10 mL or about ¼ jalapeño)

4 fl oz/120 mL Balsamic Vinaigrette, plus as needed to adjust seasoning (page 329)

2 tbsp/20 g kosher salt, plus as needed to adjust seasoning

1 lb/454 g trimmed haricots verts or green beans (about 5 ⅓ cups/1.28 L)

½ oz/14 g thinly sliced green onions (¼ cup/60 mL or about 2 green onions)

¼ oz/7 g finely chopped flat-leaf parsley (2 tbsp/30 mL)

½ oz/14 g chopped cilantro (¼ cup/60 mL)

Ground black pepper, as needed to adjust seasoning

1 oz/28 g toasted pine nuts (3 tbsp/45 mL; page 114)

1½ oz/64 g Parmigiano-Reggiano curls (about ¾ cup/180 mL loosely packed)

1. Plump the raisins in the sherry for 20 minutes. Drain, reserving the sherry for another use.

2. Toss the roasted peppers, raisins, tomatoes, olives, onion, jalapeño, and vinaigrette in a 4-qt/3.84-L bowl. Marinate covered at room temperature for 1 hour.

3. Bring an 8-qt/7.68-L sauce pot filled three-quarters with cold water to a boil. Add the salt and haricots verts. Remove the haricots verts when tender, 2 to 3 minutes after the water returns to a boil. Shock in an ice-water bath, and drain. *The haricots verts can be blanched 1 day in advance. Store wrapped in the refrigerator.*

4. Add the haricots verts, green onions, parsley, and cilantro to the bowl with the peppers. Toss, taste, and adjust seasoning. Add more vinaigrette as needed. Garnish with the pine nuts and cheese curls. *The salad can be tossed 4 hours in advance. Store wrapped in the refrigerator.*

FRUIT SCENTED WITH LIME AND MINT

YIELD: 12 SERVINGS

3 lb/1.36 kg ripe fruit, cut into bite-size pieces, balls, or wedges, such as blackberries, blueberries, grapefruit suprêmes, kiwi, mangos, melons, nectarines tossed with lime juice, orange suprêmes, pears tossed with lime juice, apples tossed with lime juice, pineapple, raspberries, seedless grapes, and/or strawberries

1½ oz/43 g honey (2 tbsp/30 mL)

1 fl oz/30 mL lime juice (about 2 limes)

1 tbsp/3 g mint chiffonade or 1 tsp/5 mL Mint Purée (page 323)

1 tsp/4 g lime zest

1. Place in a bowl the fruit that does not require lime juice to prevent oxidizing, starting with the firmest fruit and ending with the most delicate. *The fruit salad can be prepared to this point up to 1 day in advance. Store wrapped in the refrigerator.*

2. For fruits that were tossed with lime juice, drain the lime juice and place that fruit in the bowl with the rest. *The fruit salad can be prepared to this point up to 4 hours in advance. Store wrapped in the refrigerator.*

3. Whisk the honey and lime juice in a 4-qt/3.84-L bowl until combined. Add the mint chiffonade and lime zest. *The dressing can be prepared 4 hours in advance. Store wrapped in the refrigerator.*

4. Just before serving, strain the honey-lime dressing onto the fruit, discarding the solids. Gently combine the fruit until evenly distributed. Taste and adjust seasoning.

For a different presentation, make fruit kebobs by threading alternating fruit onto bamboo skewers.

FRUIT SCENTED WITH GINGER AND LIME: Add ¾ oz/21 g finely grated ginger (2 tbsp/30 mL) with the Mint Purée (page 323) and lime zest.

SHAVED FENNEL, ARUGULA, AVOCADO, AND ORANGE SALAD

YIELD: 12 SERVINGS

1 lb/454 g shaved fennel from small trimmed fennel bulbs (about 3 bulbs)

4 very ripe avocados, halved, pitted, peeled, sliced ⅛ in/3 mm thick

3 oz/85 g pitted and sliced oil-cured Gaeta olives (½ cup/120 mL)

6 fl oz/180 mL Chablis Vinaigrette, plus as needed to adjust seasoning (page 329)

1 lb/454 g arugula (about 8 cups/1.92 L)

½ oz/14 g chopped flat-leaf parsley (¼ cup/60 mL)

½ oz/14 g minced chives (¼ cup/60 mL)

Kosher salt, as needed to adjust seasoning

Ground black pepper, as needed to adjust seasoning

8 oz/227 g orange suprêmes (1 cup/240 mL or about 2 oranges)

2 oz/57 g toasted Marcona almonds (⅔ cup/160 mL; page 114)

1. In a 4-qt/3.84-L bowl, gently toss the fennel, half of the avocado, and olives with the vinaigrette. In a separate bowl, combine the arugula, parsley, and chives. *The salad can be prepared to this point up to 4 hours in advance. Store both bowls wrapped in the refrigerator.*

2. Gently toss the fennel mixture with the arugula salad. Taste and adjust seasoning. Add more vinaigrette if needed. Garnish with the remaining avocado, orange suprêmes, and toasted almonds.

Shaved Fennel, Arugula, Avocado, and Orange Salad. Ojo platter by Fortessa Tableware (see Resources, page 347).

Garden Salad with Roasted Beet Duo. Temptationz Tini-Martini glasses by Fortessa Tableware (see Resources, page 347).

GARDEN SALAD WITH ROASTED BEET DUO

YIELD: 12 SERVINGS

ROASTED BEETS

2 lb/907 g medium beets at least 2½ in/6.25 cm in diameter, greens removed and reserved for salad

HERBED CHÈVRE AND PISTACHIOS

12 oz/340 g crumbled chèvre (1½ cups/360 mL)

1 tbsp/4 g minced flat-leaf parsley

1½ tsp/2 g minced chives

1½ tsp/6 g lemon zest

¾ tsp/2 g kosher salt, plus as needed to adjust seasoning

¼ tsp/0.5 g ground black pepper, plus as needed to adjust seasoning

2 tbsp/30 mL Pistachio Pesto (page 323)

2½ oz/71 g toasted pistachios, very finely chopped into "dust" (½ cup; page 114)

CHILLED BEET SHOOTER

1 fl oz/30 mL olive oil

¼ oz/7 g garlic cloves (2 tsp/10 mL or 2 cloves)

1 tsp/1 g chopped thyme or scant ½ tsp/2.5 mL dried

1 lb/454 g roasted beets, using scraps from stuffed beets (about 2 cups/480 mL)

8 fl oz/240 mL chicken, duck, or vegetable stock, plus as needed to adjust viscosity

2 fl oz/60 mL orange juice

4 tsp/20 mL red wine vinegar

½ oz/14 g orange zest (2 tbsp/30 mL or about 1 orange)

1½ tsp/10 mL honey

½ tsp/1.5 g kosher salt

¼ tsp/0.5 g ground black pepper

Horseradish Crème (page 321)

GARDEN SALAD

4 oz/113 g Pickled Red Onions (page 332)

5¼ oz/149 g seeded English cucumber, thinly sliced (1 cup/240 mL or about ½ cucumber)

8½ oz/240 g grape tomatoes, halved (2 cups/480 mL)

6 oz/170 g beet greens, cut into 1-in/2.5-cm pieces, or arugula, stems removed (3 cups/720 mL)

6 oz/170 g mâche, torn into 1-in/2-cm pieces (3 cups/720 mL)

6 oz/170 g Bibb lettuce, torn into 1-in/2-cm pieces (3 cups/720 mL)

6 oz/170 g spinach, stems removed (3 cups/720 mL)

8 fl oz/240 mL Basil Vinaigrette, plus as needed to adjust seasoning (page 329)

Kosher salt, as needed to adjust seasoning

Ground black pepper, as needed to adjust seasoning

12 oz/340 g crumbled chèvre (1½ cups/360 mL)

5 oz/142 g toasted pistachios, coarsely chopped (1 cup/240 mL; page 114)

1. To roast the beets, position a rack in the bottom third of the oven and heat it to 400°F/204°C. Scrub the beets. Place 3 or 4 beets of the same size together in the center of an 18-in/46-cm square piece of aluminum foil. Pull the edges of the foil up so the beets are sealed in a foil pouch. Repeat with all the beets. Place the foil packs in a single layer on a baking tray and roast in the oven until the beets are tender and a fork easily pierces through the skin and into the center, 1 to 2 hours, depending on the size of the beets. Unwrap, and let the beets cool at room temperature for 30 minutes. Scrape the skin off all beets. Slice enough beets to make forty-eight ¼-in/6-mm-thick slices. Cut into 1½-in/4-cm rounds, reserving 1 lb/454 g scraps for soup. *The beets can be sliced 3 days in advance. Store wrapped in the refrigerator.*

2. For the herbed chèvre, combine the chèvre, parsley, chives, lemon zest, salt, and pepper with a fork to make a smooth paste. Taste and adjust the seasoning. Fill a pastry bag fitted with a #5 plain piping tip with the herbed chèvre. *The herbed chèvre can be prepared 3 days in advance. Store wrapped in the refrigerator.*

3. Spread ⅛ tsp/0.63 mL pistachio pesto on the top side of each beet round. Pipe ½ oz/14 g herbed chèvre

(1 tbsp/15 mL) onto 24 of the rounds, top with a beet slice, pesto against the chèvre, and gently flatten to make an even layer of filling. *The stuffed beets can be assembled up to 4 hours in advance. Store wrapped in the refrigerator.*

4. For the beet shooter, put the olive oil, garlic, and thyme in a 6-in/15-cm sauté pan and cook over medium-low heat until slightly golden and fragrant, 2 minutes. Pour the contents of the pan and the beets, stock, orange juice, vinegar, zest, honey, salt, and pepper into a blender. Run the motor until smooth, first on the lowest setting for 30 seconds and then on the highest setting for 1½ to 2 minutes. It should be thick and emulsified. If necessary, adjust the consistency with stock. Taste and adjust seasoning. Refrigerate for at least 2 hours. *The beet shooter can be prepared 3 days in advance. Store in the refrigerator.*

5. For the salad, layer the pickled red onions, cucumber, tomatoes, beet greens, mâche, Bibb lettuce, and spinach in a 13-qt/12.30-L bowl. *The salad can be assembled 4 hours in advance. Do not toss and do not dress. Immediately store wrapped in the refrigerator.*

6. To serve, pour the vinaigrette over the salad. Toss, taste, and adjust seasoning. Add more vinaigrette if needed. For each serving, place 1 heaping cup of salad on a plate. Top salad with chèvre and coarsely chopped pistachios. Place 2 stuffed beets alongside salad and top each of them with pistachio dust. Finally, place a 2 fl-oz/60-mL glass filled with the Chilled Beet Shooter topped with a dollop of Horseradish Crème alongside salad.

ROMANO BEAN SALAD WITH BOCCONCINI AND CHICKPEAS

YIELD: 12 SERVINGS (3 LB/1.36 KG)

6 oz/170 g cooked chickpeas (1 cup/240 g; page 135)

8½ oz/240 g assorted heirloom tomatoes, cut into 1-in/2.5-cm chunks, or grape tomatoes, halved (2 cups/480 mL)

6 oz/170 g bocconcini (about 1 cup/240 mL)

2¼ oz/63 g red onion, cut into julienne (½ cup/120 mL or about ½ medium onion)

4 fl oz/120 mL Basil Vinaigrette (½ cup; page 329), plus as needed to adjust salad

2 tbsp plus ¼ tsp/21 g kosher salt, plus as needed to adjust seasoning

1 lb 4 oz/567 g trimmed green, yellow, and/or purple Romano beans or Italian flat green beans or green beans, cut into 1-in/3-cm pieces (about 6 ⅔ cups/1.6 L)

½ oz/14 g basil chiffonade (¼ cup/60 mL) or 4 tsp/20 mL Basil Purée (page 323)

¼ oz/7 g minced chives (2 tbsp/30 mL)

¼ oz/7 g finely chopped flat-leaf parsley (2 tbsp/30 mL)

¼ tsp/0.5 g ground black pepper, plus as needed to adjust seasoning

1. Put the chickpeas, tomatoes, bocconcini, and onion into a 4-qt/3.84-L bowl. Add the vinaigrette, toss, and marinate at room temperature for 1 hour. *These vegetables can be marinated 3 hours in advance. Immediately store wrapped in the refrigerator.*

2. Bring an 8-qt/7.68-L sauce pot filled three-quarters with cold water to a boil. Add 2 tbsp/20 g salt and half of the beans. Remove the beans when tender, 2 to 3 minutes after the water returns to a boil. Shock in ice-water bath, and drain. Repeat with the remaining beans. *The beans can be blanched 1 day in advance. Immediately store wrapped in the refrigerator.*

3. Add the beans, basil, chives, parsley, the remaining ¼ tsp/1 g salt, and the pepper to the bowl with the chickpeas. Toss, taste, and adjust seasoning. Add more vinaigrette as needed. *The salad can be finished 4 hours in advance. Immediately store wrapped in the refrigerator.*

CREAMY CORN AND EDAMAME SUCCOTASH

YIELD: 12 SERVINGS

2 lb/907 g plum tomatoes (about 11 medium tomatoes)

2 fl oz/60 mL olive oil, plus as needed to oil grill grates

9 oz/255 g minced Spanish onion (2 cups/480 mL or about 1 large onion)

5 tsp/15 g kosher salt, plus as needed to adjust seasoning

¼ oz/7 g finely minced garlic (2 tsp/10 mL or 2 cloves)

½ tsp/1 g Cajun Spice (page 333)

½ tsp/1 g ground black pepper, plus as needed to adjust seasoning

½ tsp/1 g granulated sugar

12 ears corn, shucked and silk removed

6 oz/170 g shelled edamame (1 cup/240 mL)

6 fl oz/180 mL heavy cream

3 oz/85 g unsalted butter (¾ cup/90 mL)

½ oz/14 g basil chiffonade (¼ cup/60 mL) or 4 tsp/20 mL Basil Purée (page 323)

½ oz/14 g finely chopped flat-leaf parsley (¼ cup/60 mL)

1. Roast the tomatoes over an open gas flame or under a hot broiler, turning every 10 seconds until the skin starts to blister. Cool at room temperature for 10 minutes. Peel and discard the skin. Chop the tomatoes into large dice and place into a 2-qt/1.92-L bowl, including all juice and seeds. *The tomatoes can be prepared in advance. Store wrapped in the refrigerator for 3 days.*

2. Heat a 16-in/41-cm sauté pan over medium heat, about 1 minute. Add the oil to the pan, and heat until hot but not smoking, about 10 seconds. Add the onion and 2 tsp/6 g salt, adjust the heat to medium-low, and cook until translucent and tender, occasionally checking that the bottom is not burning, about 20 minutes. If the onions start to brown, add ½ fl oz/15 mL water. Move the onions to one side of the pan. Add the garlic to the empty space and cook for 1 minute. Combine and cook until the onions are golden, 5 minutes more. Add the tomatoes and cook until almost completely reduced, about 5 minutes more. Turn off the heat and add the Cajun spice, pepper, and sugar. *The onions and tomatoes can be prepared in advance. Store wrapped in the refrigerator for 3 days.*

3. Heat the grill to high. Clean, then oil, the grates. Place the corn on the hot grill grates and leave undisturbed until they start to char, 3 to 4 minutes. Adjust the heat if necessary to control flare-ups or burning. Turn the corn and cook until evenly charred, 3 to 4 minutes more. In the end there will be char marks on about one-quarter of the kernels. Cool the corn at room temperature for 10 minutes. Carefully cut the kernels off the cob. *The corn can be grilled in advance. Store wrapped in the refrigerator for 1 day. Do not combine with ingredients other than edamame.*

4. Bring a 2-qt/1.92-L sauce pot filled three-quarters with cold water to a boil. Add 1 tbsp/10 g salt and the edamame and blanch. Cook until tender, 5 to 6 minutes, then remove the edamame and shock in an ice-water bath. Drain. *The edamame can be blanched 1 day in advance. Store wrapped in the refrigerator.*

5. Heat a 16-in/41-cm sauté pan over medium heat, about 1 minute. Add the onions and tomatoes, corn, edamame, and cream to the sauté pan. Toss together and simmer until reduced by about half, about 5 minutes. Turn off the heat and swirl in the butter, basil, and parsley. Taste and adjust seasoning.

Add pasta or rice for a vegetarian summer entrée.

CORN AND CRAB RELISH: Eliminate the edamame and cream. Increase the butter to 4 oz/113 g and cook the succotash in the butter for 5 minutes. When adding the basil, also add 2 tbsp/30 mL lemon juice. Gently fold in 1 lb/454 g jumbo lump crab. Taste and adjust seasoning. This can also be served chilled.

Broccoli Rabe Mineste, Creamy Polenta Marbled with Taleggio (page 211), and Sun-Dried Tomato Jam (page 325). Cielo oval B&B plates by Fortessa Tableware (see Resources, page 347).

BROCCOLI RABE MINESTE

YIELD: 12 SERVINGS

3 lb 8 oz/1.59 kg trimmed broccoli rabe, chopped into 1-in/3-cm pieces (18½ cups/4.44 L packed)

2 tbsp plus 1¾ tsp/25 g kosher salt, plus as needed to adjust seasoning

4 fl oz/120 mL extra-virgin olive oil

1 lb/454 g sweet Italian sausage, casings removed

6¾ oz/191 g finely chopped onion (1½ cups/360 mL)

⅛ tsp/0.25 g red pepper flakes

1 oz/28 g minced garlic (8 tsp/mL or 8 cloves)

2 lb/907 g peeled sweet potatoes, cut into ½-in/1.25-cm cubes (8 or 9 potatoes)

32 fl oz/960 mL chicken or vegetable stock

1 lb 8 oz/680 g cooked cannellini beans (1 qt/960 mL)

1 oz/28 g unsalted butter (2 tbsp/30 mL)

2 oz/57 g shredded Pecorino Romano (⅔ cup/160 mL)

¼ tsp/0.5 g ground black pepper, plus as needed to adjust seasoning

1. Bring an 8-qt/7.68-L saucepan filled three-quarters with cold water to a boil. Add half of the broccoli rabe and 2 tbsp/20 g salt and blanch until tender, about 5 minutes. Shock in an ice-water bath. Drain. Repeat with the remaining broccoli rabe. *The broccoli rabe can be blanched 1 day in advance. Immediately store wrapped in the refrigerator.*

2. Heat a 12-in/30-cm sauté pan over medium heat, about 1 minute. Add 1½ fl oz/45 mL olive oil to the pan and heat to hot but not smoking, about 10 seconds. Add the sausage, breaking it into small pieces, adjust the heat to medium-low, and cook, tossing occasionally, until well browned, about 30 minutes. Remove the sausage, leaving 3 tbsp/45 mL fat in the pan and discarding the rest. Put the sausage into a 1-qt/960-mL bowl. *The sausage can be cooked in advance. Cool quickly and store wrapped in the refrigerator for 3 days or in the freezer for 3 months.*

3. Add the onions, ¾ tsp/2 g salt, and the red pepper flakes to the sausage sauté pan and scrape the fond from the bottom of the pan. Cook over medium-low heat, tossing occasionally, until soft and translucent, about 20 minutes. Move the onions to one side of the pan. Add ½ fl oz/15 mL oil and the garlic to the empty space and cook until fragrant, about 1 minute. Place the sweet potatoes on top of the onions, add the stock and the remaining 1 tsp/3 g salt (reduce the salt to ½ tsp/2 mL if the stock is salty), toss together, cover, and cook until the potatoes are tender, 15 to 20 minutes. Uncover and add the beans, combine, and cook until the liquid is almost all reduced. *The onions, potatoes, and beans can be cooked 1 day in advance. Cool quickly and store wrapped in the refrigerator. Reheat in a sauté pan over medium heat before proceeding.*

4. Add the sausage and simmer with the onions to marry the flavors, 5 to 6 minutes. Add the blanched broccoli rabe and toss until heated through. Add the butter and toss until melted, about 30 seconds more. Remove from the heat and add 1 oz/28 g cheese (⅓ cup/80 mL) and the black pepper. Toss, taste, and adjust seasoning. Garnish with 2 fl oz/60 mL olive oil and 1 oz/28 g cheese (⅓ cup/80 mL).

As an individual hors d'oeuvre, serve Broccoli Rabe Mineste on Crispy Polenta Cakes (page 211).

BRAISED RED CABBAGE AND APPLES

YIELD: 12 SERVINGS

½ fl oz/15 mL canola oil

8 oz/227 g thick-sliced bacon, cut into
½-in/1.25-cm pieces (1 cup/240 mL)

9 oz/255 g Spanish onion, cut into julienne
(2 cups/480 mL or 1 large onion)

1 tsp/3 g kosher salt, plus as needed to adjust seasoning

½ tsp/1 g ground black pepper, plus
as needed to adjust seasoning

2 lb/907 g red cabbage chiffonade (½ large head)

12 oz/340 g peeled and cored Granny Smith apples,
cut into ½-in/1.25-cm cubes and tossed with 1
tbsp/15 mL lemon juice to prevent apples from
oxidizing (3 cups/720 mL or 3 to 4 apples)

8 fl oz/240 mL chicken stock or water

1½ fl oz/45 mL dry red wine

1½ fl oz/45 mL red wine vinegar

1¼ oz/35 g granulated sugar (3 tbsp/45 mL)

1 tsp/2 g caraway seed

12 juniper berries

2 oz/57 g unsalted butter, cut into ½-in/
1.25-cm pats (¼ cup/60 mL)

1. Heat a heavy braising pan measuring 18 by 20 in/
45 by 50 cm over medium heat, about 1 minute. Add the
oil to the pan, and heat to hot but not smoking, 10 seconds. Add the bacon, adjust the heat to medium-low, and
cook, tossing occasionally, until caramelized and crispy,
15 to 20 minutes. Transfer the bacon to a 2-cup/480-mL
bowl, leaving about 2 tbsp/30 mL of the fat in the pan and
reserving the rest for another use. *The bacon can be
browned in advance. Rapidly cool, then immediately store
the bacon and fat, each wrapped separately, in the refrigerator for 3 days or in the freezer for 3 months.*

2. Add the onions, salt, and pepper to the same pan and
scrape the fond from the bottom of the pan. Cook over
medium-low heat, tossing occasionally, until translucent,
occasionally checking that the bottom is not burning,
about 20 minutes. If the onions start to burn, add 2 fl
oz/60 mL water to the pan and cook until the liquid
evaporates.

3. Position a rack in the bottom third of the oven and
heat it to 350°F/177°C. Add the cabbage, apples, stock,
wine, vinegar, sugar, caraway seed, and juniper berries.
Bring to a gentle simmer over medium heat. Cover the
braising pan with parchment paper and seal with aluminum foil and braise in the oven until the cabbage is tender, 1 to 1½ hours. If too much liquid remains, reduce it
on the stovetop, uncovered, over medium heat until syrupy. *The cabbage can be made 3 days in advance. Rapidly
cool, then immediately store wrapped in the refrigerator.*

4. Fold in the butter. Taste and adjust seasoning.
Garnish with the reserved bacon.

Braised Red Cabbage and Apples with Pork Chop Milanese (page 233). Oval porcelain platter by Willow Group, Ltd. (see Resources, page 347).

Charred Brussels Sprouts with Almonds, Grapes, and Pancetta

CHARRED BRUSSELS SPROUTS WITH ALMONDS, GRAPES, AND PANCETTA

YIELD: 12 SERVINGS

PANCETTA

½ fl oz/15 mL olive oil

2 oz/57 g pancetta, diced (½ cup/120 mL)

SHALLOTS

10 oz/284 g shallots, sliced ⅛ in/3 mm thick (2 cups/480 mL)

½ tsp/2 g kosher salt

½ fl oz/15 mL olive oil

¾ oz/21 g minced garlic (2 tbsp/30 mL or 6 cloves)

BRUSSELS SPROUTS

2 lb 8 oz/1.13 kg trimmed Brussels sprouts, sliced ½ in/1.25 cm thick

6 fl oz/180 mL olive oil

1½ tsp/5 g kosher salt

½ tsp/1 g ground black pepper, plus as needed to adjust seasoning

GARNISH

3 oz/85 g toasted sliced almonds (¾ cup/180 mL; page 114)

7½ oz/212 g red seedless grapes, halved (1½ cups/360 mL)

Kosher salt, as needed to adjust seasoning

Ground black pepper, as needed to adjust seasoning

1. For the pancetta, heat an 8-in/20-cm sauté pan over medium heat, about 1 minute. Add the olive oil to the pan, and heat to hot but not smoking, about 10 seconds. Add the pancetta, adjust the heat to medium-low, and cook, tossing occasionally, until caramelized and crispy, 8 to 10 minutes. Transfer the pancetta to a 1-cup/240-mL bowl, leaving about 2 tbsp/30 mL of the fat in the sauté pan and reserving the rest for another use. *The pancetta can be browned in advance. Rapidly cool, then immediately store wrapped in the refrigerator for 2 days or in the freezer for 3 months.*

2. For the shallots, to the same sauté pan over medium-low heat add the shallots and salt. (If there is not pancetta fat available, replace it with the same amount of olive oil.) Scrape the fond from the bottom and cook until soft and translucent, about 20 minutes. If the shallots start to burn, add 1 fl oz/30 mL water and cook until the water has evaporated. Move the shallots to one side and add the olive oil and garlic and cook until fragrant, 1 minute. Then combine the garlic with the shallots and cook for 5 minutes more. Put the contents into a 2-cup/480-mL bowl. *The shallots can be cooked in advance. Rapidly cool, then immediately store wrapped in the refrigerator for 3 days.*

3. Rinse and drain the Brussels sprouts, leaving them damp. Warm a nonstick 12-in/30-cm sauté pan over medium-high heat until you feel heat, 1 minute. Add 2 fl oz/60 mL oil to coat the bottom of the pan and heat to hot but not smoking, so a sprout sizzles and steams when it hits the pan. Carefully place about one-third of the sprouts into the pan to fill it in a single layer, sprinkle them with ½ tsp/2 g salt, and turn so the cut sides are down. Cook the sprouts undisturbed until golden brown, about 3 minutes. Adjust the heat, if necessary, so the pan is as hot as possible but does not scorch. Flip the sprouts over and cook until golden brown, about 2 minutes, and then stir-fry until tender but still bright green, about 1 minute more. Place the cooked Brussels sprouts onto a sheet pan and spread out to cool. Repeat with the remaining oil, Brussels sprouts, and salt. *The Brussels sprouts can be cooked in advance. Rapidly cool, then immediately store wrapped in the refrigerator for 1 day.*

4. Return all the Brussels sprouts to the same nonstick sauté pan. Add the cooked shallots, pepper, and pancetta. Sauté until everything is hot, about 4 minutes. Toss in the almonds and grapes at the last second. (If added too early, the acid in the grapes can change the color of the Brussels sprouts.) Taste and adjust seasoning.

Add cooked pasta for a fall or winter dish.

SAUTÉED MUSHROOMS AND ONIONS

YIELD: 12 SERVINGS

2 fl oz/60 mL canola oil

2 oz/57 g unsalted butter, cut into
¼-in/6-mm pats (¼ cup/60 mL)

9 oz/255 g Spanish onion, minced (2 cups/480 mL
or about 1 large onion)

2 tsp/6 g kosher salt, plus as needed to adjust seasoning

¼ tsp/0.5 g red pepper flakes

½ oz/14 g minced garlic (4 tsp/20 mL or 4 cloves)

2 lb/907 g cremini mushrooms, caps and stems,
sliced ¼ in/6 mm thick (about 10 cups/2.4 L)

1 lb/454 g shiitake mushrooms, stems and caps
separated, caps sliced ¼ in/6 mm thick (1 cup/240 mL)
and stems reserved to enrich stock, or wild mushroom
mix, sliced ¼ in/6 mm thick (about 5 cups/1.2 L)

1 tsp/1 g thyme

2 fl oz/60 mL dry sherry or dry white wine

1 tsp/2 g ground black pepper, plus as
needed to adjust seasoning

½ oz/14 g chives (¼ cup/60 mL)

1. In a 16-in/41-cm nonstick sauté pan, add the oil and butter and warm over medium heat until the butter melts and is foamy, about 2 minutes. Add the onions, salt, and red pepper flakes. Lower the heat to low and cook, tossing occasionally, until the onions are translucent and starting to brown, about 15 minutes. Move the onions to one side of the pan.

2. Add the garlic to the empty space and cook until fragrant, 1 minute. Combine and cook until the onions are golden, 10 minutes more.

3. Put all the mushrooms and the thyme in the pan with the onions. Cook, tossing occasionally, until all liquid released from mushrooms evaporates and the mushrooms are tender and golden, 20 minutes. Add the wine and reduce to almost dry. Add the black pepper. Toss, taste, and adjust seasoning. *The mushrooms can be cooked 3 days in advance. Rapidly cool and immediately store wrapped in the refrigerator.*

4. Add the chives. Toss, taste, and adjust seasoning.

BROCCOLI WITH CASHEW BUTTER

YIELD: 12 SERVINGS

CASHEW BUTTER

6 oz/170 g unsalted butter (¾ cup/180 mL)

3¾ oz/106 g toasted unsalted cashews, finely chopped (¾ cup/180 mL; page 114)

BROCCOLI

2 tbsp plus 1 tsp/23 g kosher salt, plus as needed to adjust seasoning

3 lb/1.36 kg trimmed broccoli florets, cut into 1-in/2-cm pieces (12 cups/2.88 L)

½ tsp/1 g ground black pepper, plus as needed to adjust seasoning

1. For the cashew butter, melt the butter over medium-low heat in a 1½-qt/1.44-L saucepan. Gently simmer until the moisture in the butter has evaporated and the milk solids on the bottom of the pan turn brown, about 15 minutes. Pour the butter through a very fine-mesh strainer into another 1½-qt/1.44-L saucepan, discarding the browned milk solids. Add the cashews to the butter and cook over medium-low heat, stirring constantly, until the butter is caramel in color and the nuts are golden, about 5 minutes. *The cashew butter can be made 1 week in advance. Cool quickly and store wrapped in the refrigerator.*

2. For the broccoli, bring an 8-qt/7.68-L sauce pot filled three-quarters with cold water to a boil. Add 2 tbsp/20 g salt and half the broccoli. As soon as the water returns to a boil, remove the broccoli and shock it in an ice-water bath. Drain. Repeat with the remaining broccoli. *The broccoli can be blanched 1 day in advance. Store wrapped in the refrigerator.*

3. Transfer half of the cashew butter to a 12-in/30-cm sauté pan over medium heat and warm. Add half of the broccoli and toss occasionally until hot, 3 minutes. Transfer the mixture to a 4-qt/ 3.84-L bowl. Repeat with the remaining cashew butter and broccoli. Sprinkle the remaining 1 tsp/3 g salt and the pepper over the broccoli. Toss, taste, and adjust seasoning.

GREEN BEANS WITH CASHEW BUTTER: Replace the broccoli with trimmed green beans. Blanch the green beans until tender, 4 to 5 minutes.

CAULIFLOWER WITH CASHEW BUTTER: Replace the broccoli with trimmed cauliflower florets.

THAI SPAGHETTI SQUASH SLAW

SPAGHETTI SQUASH SLAW

2 lb/907 g spaghetti squash (about 1 medium squash)

2 tbsp/30 mL canola oil

12 oz/340 g savoy cabbage chiffonade, soaked in ice water for 15 minutes

12¾ oz/361 g plum tomatoes, diced (3 cups/720 mL or about 3 medium tomatoes)

6 oz/170 g carrots, shredded (about 1 cup/240 mL)

4½ oz/128 g shaved red onion (1 cup/240 mL or about 1 medium onion)

THAI DRESSING

2 fl oz/60 mL lime juice (about 4 limes)

1 fl oz/30 mL fish sauce

2 tbsp/25 g granulated sugar

1 tsp/5 mL Thai chili paste

1 tsp/3 g kosher salt, plus as needed to adjust seasoning

1 oz/28 g chopped cilantro (½ cup/120 mL)

1 oz/28 g Thai basil chiffonade (½ cup/120 mL)

¾ oz/14 g mint chiffonade (6 tbsp/90 mL) or 2 tbsp Mint Purée (page 323)

GARNISH

5 oz/142 g toasted peanuts (page 114)

2 oz/57g g green onions, sliced ⅛ in/3 mm thick on the bias (1 cup/ 240 mL or about 8 green onions)

2 tbsp/17 g toasted sesame seeds (page 114)

1. For the spaghetti squash slaw, position a rack in the bottom third of the oven and heat it to 375°F/191°C. Cut the squash in half lengthwise and remove the seeds and rough pulp. Coat the flesh with the canola oil and place cut side down on a sheet pan. Bake in the oven until tender, 35 to 45 minutes. Cool at room temperature for 30 minutes. With a fork, scrape long strands of squash pulp into a 3-qt/2.88-L mixing bowl. *The squash can be cooked 3 days in advance. Store wrapped in the refrigerator.*

2. Layer the remaining slaw ingredients to the bowl with the squash. *The salad can be assembled 1 day in advance. Do not toss, but rather leave ingredients layered. Store wrapped in the refrigerator.*

3. For the Thai dressing, combine all the ingredients except for the herbs. *The vinaigrette can be made to this point 1 week in advance. Store wrapped in the refrigerator. Shake to emulsify.*

4. Toss the dressing with the cilantro, basil, and mint. Add to the slaw and gently toss, keeping as many as possible of the spaghetti squash strands intact. Taste and adjust seasoning. Garnish with the peanuts, green onions, and sesame seeds. *The salad can be finished 4 hours in advance. Immediately store wrapped in the refrigerator.*

GRILLED VEGETABLE PLATTER

YIELD: 12 SERVINGS

2 fl oz/60 mL extra-virgin olive oil, plus as needed to oil grill grates

2 tsp/6 g kosher salt

1 tsp/2 g Cajun Spice (page 333)

3 lb/1.36 kg mixed vegetables, such as asparagus, trimmed and peeled; baby carrots, peeled; broccoli florets; cauliflower florets; corn, husked, silk removed, cut into thirds; trimmed green beans; zucchini and/or yellow squash, trimmed and quartered lengthwise, seeds removed; red, yellow, or orange peppers, cored and quartered; red or Vidalia onions, peeled and quartered or cut into 1-in/2.5-cm-thick rounds; mushrooms, trimmed; potatoes, sliced ½ in/1.25 cm thick

GARNISH

1 fl oz/30 mL extra-virgin olive oil

1 oz/28 g chopped fresh herbs, such as flat-leaf parsley, cilantro, chervil, chives, tarragon, basil, and/or mint (½ cup/120 mL)

1. Heat a grill to high. Clean and oil the grates. Whisk the oil, salt, and Cajun spice together in a 4-qt/3.84-L bowl. Add the vegetables and toss to evenly coat.

2. Place the vegetables on the hot grill grates, presentation side down. To mark with a crosshatch, press each vegetable gently so its surface area is against the grates. Leave undisturbed for 2 to 3 minutes. Adjust the heat if necessary to control flare-ups or burning. With the same side down, turn each vegetable 90 degrees, press gently, and cook undisturbed for 2 to 3 minutes. Turn the vegetables over and grill until tender, 2 to 6 minutes more, depending on vegetable type. *The vegetables can be grilled in advance. Rapidly chill and immediately store the vegetables wrapped in the refrigerator for 1 day. To reheat, place the vegetables on sheet pans in a single layer barely touching and warm at 400°F/204°C until hot, 5 minutes.*

3. Garnish with the olive oil and herbs.

Lemony Hummus (page 134), Rémoulade (page 319), Fig–Marcona Almond Vinaigrette (page 328), and Honey Mustard (page 327) work well as dips for a crudité platter.

Balsamic Molasses (page 318), Lemon and Fennel Seed Vinaigrette (page 330), and Macadamia-Pignoli Pesto (page 323) are just a few examples of additional sauces or garnishes for a vegetable platter.

ROASTED VEGETABLES: Position a rack in the bottom third of the oven and heat it to 450°F/232°C. Season the vegetables with oil, salt, and Cajun spices as in step 1. Place the vegetables on a sheet pan in single layer, keeping each particular vegetable type together, as they take different times to become tender. Roast in the oven until tender and slightly browned, 10 to 20 minutes, turning the vegetables about halfway though the cooking time.

ORANGE-SPIKED CARROTS

YIELD: 12 SERVINGS

2 oz/57 g unsalted butter (¼ cup/60 mL)

3 lb/1.36 kg oblique-cut carrots or peeled baby carrots with ½ in/1.25 cm green stem left on

3½ oz/99 g dark brown sugar (½ cup/120 mL)

2 fl oz/60 mL orange juice

4 tsp/12 g kosher salt, plus as needed to adjust seasoning

Pinch cayenne

½ tsp/1 g ground black pepper, plus as needed to adjust seasoning

¼ oz/7 g finely chopped flat-leaf parsley (2 tbsp/30 mL)

1 tsp/3 g mint chiffonade or ⅓ tsp/1 g Mint Purée (page 323)

½ tsp/2 g orange zest

1. Melt the butter in a wide-mouth 6-qt/5.76-L sauce pot over medium-high heat. Add the carrots, brown sugar, orange juice, salt, and cayenne and toss to coat. Cover with a lid and cook, tossing occasionally, until barely tender, 10 minutes. Remove the lid, increase the temperature to high, and cook, tossing occasionally, until all liquid is evaporated and the carrots are caramelized, 10 to 15 minutes more. Add the pepper. Toss, taste, and adjust seasoning. *The carrots can be cooked 3 days in advance. Quickly cool, then store wrapped in the refrigerator. Reheat in a sauté pan until hot, 10 to 12 minutes.*

2. Garnish with the parsley, mint, and orange zest.

RATATOUILLE

YIELD: 12 SERVINGS

1 lb 4 oz/567 g peeled globe or Italian eggplant, cut into medium dice (6 cups/1.44 L or about 2 medium eggplants)

2 tbsp plus 2 tsp/26 g kosher salt, plus as needed to adjust seasoning

1 lb 8 oz/680 g plum tomatoes or canned peeled whole plum tomatoes in tomato juice, no salt added (5¾ cups/1.38 L or about 8 tomatoes)

5½ fl oz/165 mL extra-virgin olive oil

1 lb/454 g Spanish onions, cut into 1/2-in/1.25-cm dice (3½ cups/840 mL or about 1½ large onions)

1 oz/28 g minced garlic (8 tsp/mL or 8 cloves)

¼ tsp/1 g Cajun Spice (page 333)

⅛ tsp/0.25 g red pepper flakes

1 lb/454 g cremini mushrooms, halved or quartered (about 5 cups/1.2 L)

2 fl oz/60 mL tomato paste

4 fl oz/120 mL Pinot Noir or dry red wine

4 roasted red, yellow, and/or orange peppers, cut into ½-in/1.25-cm dice (page 123)

⅛ oz/3 g chopped oregano (1 tbsp/15 mL) or 1/2 tsp/0.5 g dried oregano

12 oz/340 g medium-diced seeded zucchini (1½ cups/360 mL or about 2 small zucchini)

12 oz/340 g medium-diced seeded yellow squash (1½ cups/360 mL or about 2 small squash)

1 fl oz/30 mL lemon juice

1 oz/28 g minced chives (½ cup/120 mL)

½ oz/14 g basil chiffonade (¼ cup/60 mL) or 4 tsp/20 mL Basil Purée (page 323)

½ oz/14 g chopped flat-leaf parsley (¼ cup/60 mL)

¼ oz/7 g lemon zest (1 tbsp/15 mL or about 1 lemon), plus as needed to adjust seasoning

¼ tsp/0.5 g ground black pepper, plus as needed to adjust seasoning

1½ oz/43 g grated Pecorino Romano (½ cup/120 mL)

3 oz/85 g pitted oil-cured Gaeta olives (½ cup/120 mL)

3 oz/85 g nonpareil capers, rinsed (½ cup/120 mL)

1 fl oz/30 mL extra-virgin olive oil

1. Toss the eggplant with 2 tbsp/20 g salt and place into a 3-qt/2.88-L colander set over a 4-qt/3.84-L bowl. Place a heavy plate over the eggplant and then a heavy can on top of the plate so the liquid is pressed out. Drain for 1 hour. Discard the liquid. Rinse the salt off with water and squeeze dry with paper towels.

2. Roast the tomatoes over an open gas flame or under a broiler, turning every 10 seconds, until the skin starts to blister. Cool at room temperature for 10 minutes. Peel and discard the skin. Chop the tomatoes into medium dice, reserving all juice and seeds. *The tomatoes can be prepared in advance. Store wrapped in the refrigerator for 3 days.*

3. Warm a 12-in/30-cm sauté pan over medium-high heat, 1 minute. Add 1 fl oz/30 mL oil to the pan and heat to hot but not smoking, about 10 seconds. Add the onions and 1 tsp/3 g salt. Lower the heat to medium and cook, tossing occasionally, until translucent and starting to caramelize, about 15 minutes. Move the onions to one side of the pan. Add ½ fl oz/15 mL oil, the garlic, Cajun spice, and red pepper flakes to the empty space and cook until fragrant, about 1 minute. Add the mushrooms, combine, and cook, tossing occasionally until all liquid released evaporates and they are tender and golden, about 15 minutes more. Add the tomato paste and wine and cook until the liquid is evaporated, about 10 minutes. Put contents into a 4-qt/3.84-L bowl.

4. Warm a nonstick 12-in/30-cm sauté pan over medium heat, 1 minute. Add 1 fl oz/30 mL oil to the pan and heat to hot but not smoking. Add the eggplant and cook undisturbed until the bottom is browned, 2 minutes. Adjust the heat, if necessary, so the pan is as hot as possible but does not scorch. Toss and cook until evenly browned and tender, about 6 minutes more. Add the roasted peppers, tomatoes and juice, and ½ tsp/2 g salt and cook until liquid released from the tomatoes is

reduced by half, 15 minutes. Add the oregano and cook for another 5 minutes. Add the contents of the pan to the bowl with the other vegetables. Toss, taste, and adjust seasoning. *The ratatouille can be prepared to this point 3 days in advance. Quickly cool, then store wrapped in the refrigerator. Reheat in a sauté pan, 10 to 12 minutes.*

5. Warm a nonstick 12-in/30-cm sauté pan over medium heat, 1 minute. Add 1 fl oz/30 mL oil to the pan, increase the temperature to high, and heat to hot but not smoking, about 10 seconds. Add the zucchini and ¼ tsp/ 1 g salt and cook undisturbed until the bottom is browned, about 1½ minutes. Adjust the heat, if necessary, so the pan is as hot as possible but does not scorch. Toss and cook until evenly browned and tender, about 3 minutes more. Place the cooked zucchini into a 1-qt/960-L bowl, leaving as much oil as possible in the pan. Repeat with the yellow squash and remaining ¼ tsp/1 g salt. *The zucchini and yellow squash can be cooked 1 day in advance. Do not combine with the other vegetables, as the tomato acidity will change the bright color of the squash. Quickly cool, then store wrapped in the refrigerator.*

6. Return all the cooked vegetables except the zucchini and yellow squash to a 16-in/41-cm sauté pan. Over medium heat, warm the vegetables, stirring occasionally. Add the zucchini, yellow squash, 1 fl oz/30 mL olive oil, the lemon juice, chives, basil, parsley, zest, and black pepper to the pan with the vegetables and stir until hot, 3 minutes. Add the garnish(es). Toss, taste, and adjust seasoning.

Vegetable Medley with Garlic Chips

VEGETABLE MEDLEY WITH GARLIC CHIPS

YIELD: 12 SERVINGS

3 fl oz/90 mL extra-virgin olive oil

½ oz/14 g garlic cloves, cut lengthwise into
1/16-in/1.5-mm-thick slices (4 cloves)

1 tbsp plus 1 tsp/13 g kosher salt, plus
as needed to adjust seasoning

10 oz/284 g peeled and trimmed asparagus,
cut on the bias into 2-in/5-cm pieces

12 oz/340 g peeled and trimmed carrots, cut
into bâtonnet (about 3 cups/720 mL)

10 oz/284 g sugar snap peas, strings removed,
or trimmed green beans, cut into 2-in/5-cm
pieces on the bias (about 3⅓ cups/800 mL)

6 oz/170 g seeded red peppers, cut into bâtonnet (1 pepper)

10 oz/284 g trimmed zucchini, cut into bâtonnet
(2 scant cups/480 mL or 2½ medium zucchini)

⅛ tsp/0.25 g red pepper flakes

2 oz/57 g unsalted butter, cut into
¼-in/6-mm pats (¼ cup/60 mL)

¼ tsp/0.5 g ground black pepper, plus
as needed to adjust seasoning

1. Place the oil and garlic into a cold 6-in/15-cm sauté pan. Heat the pan over low heat. Cook the garlic, tossing occasionally, until deep golden, about 15 minutes. With a slotted spoon, remove the garlic and drain on paper towels. Reserve the oil. *The garlic can be cooked 3 days in advance. Rapidly cool, then immediately store wrapped in the refrigerator. The garlic-infused oil can be stored in the refrigerator for 2 weeks.*

2. Bring a 6-qt/5.76-L sauce pot filled two-thirds with cold water to a boil. Add 1 tbsp/10 g salt and the asparagus. As soon as the water returns to a boil, remove the asparagus and shock in an ice-water bath. Drain the asparagus and place into a 6-qt/5.76-L bowl. Place the carrots into the same boiling water. Remove them when tender, 2 to 3 minutes after the water returns to a boil. Shock them in an ice-water bath, drain, and add them to the asparagus. Repeat with the sugar snap peas, but remove as soon as the water returns to a boil. If using green beans, repeat as with the carrots. *The vegetables can be blanched 1 day in advance. Store wrapped in the refrigerator.*

3. Heat a 16-in/41-cm nonstick sauté pan over medium-high heat, about 1 minute. Add 1 fl oz/30 mL reserved oil to the pan and heat to hot but not smoking, about 10 seconds. Add the red peppers and ½ tsp/2 g salt and cook, tossing occasionally, until the peppers are caramelized, 8 minutes. Rapidly cool, then transfer the peppers to the bowl with the blanched vegetables, leaving as much oil as possible in the pan. To the same pan over medium-high heat, add the zucchini, the remaining ½ tsp/2 g salt, and the red pepper flakes, and cook, tossing occasionally, until the zucchini is tender and caramelized, about 6 minutes. Add more reserved oil if needed. Rapidly cool, then transfer the zucchini to the bowl with the other vegetables. *The peppers and zucchini can be sautéed 1 day in advance. Immediately store wrapped in the refrigerator.*

4. Add all the vegetables to the sauté pan and heat over medium-high heat, 5 to 8 minutes. Add the butter and black pepper and toss until the butter is melted. Taste and adjust seasoning. Garnish with ½ oz/ 14 g reserved oil and the garlic chips.

DEEP-DISH VEGETABLE QUICHE

YIELD: 12 SERVINGS

CRUST

1 batch Lager Pastry Dough (page 308), cold from refrigerator

Bench flour as needed

CUSTARD

2 oz/57 g unsalted butter, plus as needed to cook vegetables (¼ cup/60 mL)

9 oz/255 g finely chopped Spanish onion (2 cups/480 mL or about 1 large onion)

2 tsp/6 g kosher salt, plus as needed to adjust seasoning

32 fl oz/960 mL heavy cream

8 eggs

1 tsp/2 g ground black pepper, plus as needed to adjust seasoning

4 cups/960 mL chopped and cooked vegetables (such as blanched broccoli, cauliflower, carrots, spinach, asparagus, and/or sautéed zucchini, peppers, or mushrooms)

12 oz/340 g cheese (such as cheddar, Monterey Jack, provolone, mozzarella, Fontina, or Gruyère) , cut into ¼-in/6-mm dice

1. For the crust, place the chilled dough on a lightly floured cold surface and dust the top of the dough and a rolling pin with flour. Roll out into a round about 18 in/46 cm in diameter and ⅛ in/3 mm thick. Place it in an ungreased 10-in/25-cm springform pan and trim it and/or patch it in to completely cover the bottom and sides of the pan and have an overhang of ½ in/1.25 cm. Roll the overhang over and flute the edges. Dock the dough by lightly pricking it with a fork or dough docker several times spaced evenly apart so it does not form blisters as it bakes. Place it in the freezer until firm, at least 30 minutes. See page 110 for tips on rolling dough. *The crust can be rolled out and frozen in the springform pan in advance. Immediately store wrapped in the freezer for 3 months.*

2. For the custard, melt the butter over medium-high heat in a 10-in/25-cm sauté pan and heat until hot but not smoking, about 10 seconds. Add the onions and ½ tsp/1.5 g salt. Adjust the heat to medium-low and cook, tossing occasionally, until golden and jammy, about 20 minutes. Cool at room temperature for 20 minutes.

3. Whisk the cream, eggs, pepper, and remaining 1½ tsp/4.5 g salt in a 4-qt/3.84-L bowl. Stir in the cooked onions, cooked vegetables, and cheese. Sample the custard by cooking a small amount. Taste and adjust seasoning. *The custard can be made 1 day in advance. Immediately store wrapped in the refrigerator.*

4. Position a rack in the bottom of the oven and heat to 425°F/218°C. Pour the custard into the frozen crust. Cover the top with parchment paper and seal with aluminum foil. Bake until the center is set, about 3 hours. Remove the foil and bake until the top is browned, about 15 minutes more. *The quiche can be baked in advance. Cool completely. Store in the refrigerator for 2 days or in the freezer for 3 months. Thaw in the refrigerator, and bake at 350°F/177°C until hot and re-crisped, about 30 minutes.*

QUICHE WITH MEAT, POULTRY, OR FISH: Replace 4 oz/113 g of the cheese with 4 oz/113 g cooked meat, poultry, or fish, such as bacon, sausage, chicken, shrimp, scallops, or smoked salmon.

INDIVIDUAL DEEP-DISH QUICHE: Yield: 1½ dozen pieces. Press the dough into the wells of 6-cup/1.44 L nonstick giant muffin pans. Follow directions, except do not cover with foil, and bake until the center is puffy and set and the crust is golden, 20 to 25 minutes. For a smaller portion, use regular-size cupcake pans.

MINI QUICHE HORS D'OEUVRE: Yield: 8 dozen mini quiche. Roll out the dough into an even 1⁄16-in/1.5-mm-thick circle and cut into 2½-in/6-cm rounds, about ¼ oz/7 g each. Press dough into the wells of ungreased nonstick mini muffin pans. Follow directions, except finely chop the vegetables and shred the cheese. Bake uncovered until the center is set and the crust is golden, 20 to 25 minutes.

Individual Deep-Dish Vegetable Quiche. Wavy porcelain
tray by American Metalcraft, Inc. (see Resources, page 347).

Individual Eggplant Parmigiana Towers. Nonstick 6-cup giant muffin pan by **Chicago Metallic Bakeware** (see Resources, page 347).

EGGPLANT PARMIGIANA

YIELD: 12 SERVINGS
---

6 eggs

7½ oz/212 g unbleached all-purpose
flour (1½ cups/360 mL)

10 oz/284 g freshly toasted bread crumbs
(5 cups/1.2 L; page 116) or panko

1 lb 8 oz/680 g peeled, trimmed, sliced globe eggplant, cut
into ¼-in/6-mm-thick rounds (about 2 medium eggplant)

24 fl oz/720 mL canola oil, plus as
needed, to fry the eggplant

48 fl oz/1.44 L Herbed Tomato Sauce
(can be cold) (page 312)

1 oz/28 g shredded Pecorino Romano (⅓ cup/80 mL)

1 lb/454 g low-moisture mozzarella, sliced ⅛ in/3 mm thick

1. Whisk the eggs in a 2-qt/1.92-L shallow bowl.
Combine the flour and bread crumbs in a 4-qt/3.84-L
shallow bowl. Line up the bowls in the order they were
filled for the standard breading procedure.

2. Dunk each eggplant slice into the eggs and evenly
coat, letting the excess drip back into bowl, then press
each side into the bread crumbs, patting on to evenly
coat. Shingle the eggplant on a parchment-lined sheet
pan. Repeat with all of the eggplant slices.

3. Fill a 12-in/30-cm sautoir one-quarter full with oil.
Over medium heat, heat the oil to 350°F/177°C, 10 minutes. It is hot enough when an eggplant slice causes the
oil to immediately sizzle but takes 45 seconds to begin
browning. Carefully place enough eggplant into the oil to
fill the pan without touching. Pan fry the eggplant until
the bottom is golden brown, about 2 minutes, then turn
over and continue frying until evenly browned, about 1½
minutes more. Place the cooked eggplant on a cooling
rack lined with paper towels. Repeat with all of the eggplant. Between batches, skim all loose pieces of bread
crumbs from the oil with a fine-mesh strainer and discard. Adjust the heat so the oil does not smoke or burn.
*The eggplant can be fried in advance. Cool completely
before wrapping. Place 2 sheets of waxed paper between
shingled layers of eggplant. Store the eggplant wrapped in
the refrigerator for 3 days or in the freezer for 3 months.*

4. Evenly distribute 16 fl oz/480 mL tomato sauce in the
bottom of a half hotel pan or equivalent-size baking pan.
Place one-third of the fried eggplant in a layer so it completely covers the bottom of the pan. Evenly top the eggplant with half of the Pecorino Romano, half of the mozzarella, and 8 fl oz/240 mL tomato sauce. Repeat the lay-
ering with another third of the fried eggplant, the remaining Pecorino Romano, the remaining mozzarella, and 8 fl
oz/240 mL tomato sauce. Top with the remaining eggplant and 16 fl oz/480 mL tomato sauce. Cover the eggplant with parchment paper and seal with aluminum foil.
*The eggplant parmigiana can be assembled 1 day in
advance. Store wrapped in the refrigerator.*

5. Position a rack in the middle of the oven and heat to
350°F/177°C. Bake until the center is hot and reaches an
internal temperature of 165°F/74°C, about 45 minutes.
Uncover and bake until the edges and top start to brown
and the sauce is bubbly, about 15 minutes more. Let the
eggplant set at room temperature tented with foil for
15 minutes.

INDIVIDUAL EGGPLANT PARMIGIANA TOWERS:
Yield: 1 dozen towers. Layer the Herbed Tomato Sauce,
fried eggplant, Pecorino Romano, and mozzarella in
twelve nonstick giant muffin pans. Cut the baking time
in half.

Roasted Vegetable Tower Milanese, Balsamic Molasses (page 318), Sun-Dried Tomato Jam (page 325), and frizzled basil chiffonade. Stainless-steel rectangular hammered platter by American Metalcraft (see Resources, page 347).

ROASTED VEGETABLE TOWER MILANESE

YIELD: 12 SERVINGS

SEASONED FLOUR

3¾ oz/106 g unbleached all-purpose flour (¾ cup/180 mL)

1½ tsp/4.5 g kosher salt

¼ tsp/0.5 g ground black pepper

¼ tsp/0.5 g Cajun Spice (page 333)

EGG WASH

4 eggs

¼ tsp/1 g kosher salt

¼ tsp/0.5 g ground black pepper

MILANESE CRUST

7 oz/198 g freshly toasted bread crumbs
(3½ cups/840 mL; page 116) or panko

5¼ oz/148 g finely shredded Pecorino
Romano (1¾ cups/420 mL)

VEGETABLES AND GARNISH

24 slices globe eggplant, in ¼-in/6-mm-thick
rounds (about 2 medium eggplant)

72 slices zucchini, in ¼-in/6-mm-thick
rounds (about 4 medium zucchini)

6 fl oz/180 mL Basil Vinaigrette (page
329), plus as needed for sauce

24 slices tomato, in ¼-in/6-mm-thick
rounds (about 5 large tomatoes)

1 tsp/3 g kosher salt

1 tsp/2 g ground black pepper

½ cup/120 mL basil chiffonade (1 oz/28 g)

24 slices fresh mozzarella, in ¼-in/6-mm-
thick rounds (about 2 lb/907 g)

1. For the seasoned flour, combine the flour, salt, pepper, and Cajun Spice in a 2-qt/1.92-L shallow bowl. For the egg wash, whisk the eggs, salt, and pepper in another 2-qt/1.92-L shallow bowl. For the Milanese crust, combine the bread crumbs and Pecorino Romano in a third 2-qt/1.92-L shallow bowl. Line up the bowls in the order they were filled for standard breading procedure.

2. Place racks in the upper and lower third of the oven and heat to 425°F/218°C. Line 3 sheet pans with parchment. For the vegetables, toss half of the eggplant with the flour in the first bowl and evenly coat. Lift 1 slice out of the flour, shake off the excess, and dip into the egg, letting the excess drip back into the bowl. Press into the bread crumbs in the last bowl, patting on to evenly coat both sides. Lay the breaded slices on a sheet pan. Repeat with the remaining eggplant and all of the zucchini, placing them on sheet pans in a single layer barely touching. Drizzle all the slices with the vinaigrette. Bake for 20 minutes. *The eggplant and zucchini can be baked up to 1 day in advance. Quickly cool, then immediately store wrapped in the refrigerator.*

3. Remove the eggplant (the zucchini can remain in the oven) and top each with a tomato slice. Sprinkle the tomatoes with the salt and pepper. Return the eggplant to the oven and continue baking until tender and the bread crumbs are golden, 10 minutes more. Remove from the oven and evenly divide basil on top of the eggplant, then top each with a slice of mozzarella. Return to the oven and bake until the cheese is melted, about 2 minutes more. Top each eggplant-tomato-mozzarella layer with 3 zucchini slices, then with another eggplant-tomato-mozzarella layer. If the stack is not hot enough, return to the oven for 2 to 3 minutes.

Other garnishes that pair well with the vegetable stack include Basil Vinaigrette (page 329), Balsamic Molasses (page 318) Macadamia-Pignoli Pesto (page 323), and Fire-Roasted Red Pepper Coulis (page 327).

ASPARAGUS RAGOÛT

YIELD: 12 SERVINGS

2½ fl oz/75 mL extra-virgin olive oil

1 lb 2 oz/510 g finely chopped Spanish onions
(4 cups/960 mL or about 2 large onions)

2 tbsp plus 2 tsp/26 g kosher salt, plus
as needed to adjust seasoning

1 oz/28 g chopped garlic (8 tsp/40 mL or 8 cloves)

1 lb 3 oz/539 g cremini mushrooms, halved
or quartered (about 6 cups/1.44 L)

2 oz/57 g unsalted butter (¼ cup/60 mL)

¼ tsp/1 g Cajun Spice (page 333)

⅛ tsp/0.25 g red pepper flakes

4 fl oz/120 mL dry white wine

3 lb 8 oz/1.59 kg canned, peeled whole plum tomatoes
in tomato juice, no salt added (13¼ cups/3.18 L)

1 lb 14 oz/851 g peeled and trimmed asparagus, cut
into ½-in/1.25-cm pieces on the bias (1 qt/960 mL)

4 roasted red and yellow peppers, cut
into ½-in/1.25-cm dice (page 123)

9 oz/255 g chopped spinach, tough stems
removed (3 cups/720 mL firmly packed)

¾ oz/21 g nonpareil capers, rinsed (2 tbsp/30 mL)

2 oz/57 g basil chiffonade (1 cup/240 mL) or
3 fl oz/90 mL Basil Purée (page 323)

½ tsp/1 g ground black pepper

GARNISH

6 oz/170 g finely shredded Pecorino
Romano (2 cups/480 mL)

2 fl oz/60 mL extra-virgin olive oil

1. Warm a 16-in/41-cm sauté pan over medium-high heat, about 1 minute. Add 2 fl oz/60 mL oil to the pan and heat to hot but not smoking, about 10 seconds. Add the onions and 2 tsp/6 g salt. Adjust the heat to medium-low and cook, stirring occasionally, until soft and translucent, about 20 minutes. If the onions start to brown, add 1 fl oz/30 mL water. Move the onions to one side of the pan. Add the remaining ½ fl oz/15 mL oil and the garlic to the

empty space and cook until fragrant, about 1 minute. Combine and cook until the onions are golden, about 10 minutes more. Add the mushrooms, butter, Cajun spice, and red pepper flakes, combine, and cook, tossing occasionally, until all liquid released evaporates and the mushrooms are tender and golden, about 15 minutes more. Add the wine and cook until evaporated, about 20 minutes. Pour into a 6-qt/5.76-L stockpot.

2. Pass the tomatoes through a food mill fitted with a coarse disk into a 2-qt/1.88-L bowl and discard the tough pulp. Rinse the cans out with 2 fl oz/60 mL water and add to the tomatoes. Add the tomatoes to the stockpot with the mushrooms and simmer until the sauce is reduced by one-quarter and thickened, about 20 minutes. Stir frequently, especially at the beginning, with a flat-sided wooden spoon. The tomato pulp can stick to the bottom of the pan and burn, completely ruining the sauce. Stir in the roasted peppers and simmer for 10 minutes. Taste and adjust seasoning. *The sauce can be cooked 3 days in advance. Store wrapped in the refrigerator. Bring back to a simmer before continuing with the recipe.*

3. Bring an 8-qt/7.68-L sauce pot filled three-quarters with cold water to a boil. Add 2 tbsp/20 g salt and half of the asparagus. As soon as the water returns to a boil, remove the asparagus and shock in an ice-water bath. Repeat the blanching process with the remaining asparagus. *The asparagus can be cooked 1 day in advance. Store wrapped in the refrigerator.*

4. Just before serving, stir in the spinach, capers, and blanched asparagus and simmer until the spinach is wilted, about 1 minute. Remove from the heat and stir in the basil and black pepper. Taste and adjust seasoning. Garnish with the cheese and olive oil.

GARLICKY WILTED SPINACH

YIELD: 12 SERVINGS

GARLIC CHIPS

3 fl oz/90 mL extra-virgin olive oil

1½ oz/43 g garlic cloves, cut lengthwise into
⅛-in/3-mm-thick slices (12 cloves)

SPINACH

1 tbsp/10 g plus ¾ tsp/2 g kosher salt,
plus as needed to adjust seasoning

3 lb/1.36 kg baby spinach

6¾ oz/191 g finely chopped Spanish onion (1½ cups/
360 mL or about ¾ large onion)

⅛ tsp/0.25 g red pepper flakes

½ oz/14 g minced garlic (4 tsp/mL or 4 cloves)

1 oz/28 g unsalted butter, cut into
¼-in/6-mm pats (2 tbsp/30 mL)

1 oz/28 g shredded Pecorino Romano

¼ tsp/0.5 g ground black pepper, plus
as needed to adjust seasoning

1. For the garlic chips, in a cold 6-in/15-cm sauté pan, combine the oil and sliced garlic. Over low heat, cook the garlic, tossing occasionally, until deep golden but not browned, about 15 minutes. With a slotted spoon, remove the garlic and drain on paper towels. Reserve the oil. *The garlic chips can be made 3 days in advance. Store wrapped in the refrigerator. The garlic-infused oil can be stored in the refrigerator for 2 weeks.*

2. For the spinach, bring a 6-qt/5.76-L sauce pot filled two-thirds with cold water to a boil. Add 1 tbsp/10 g salt and one-third of the spinach and blanch. As soon as the water returns to a boil, remove the spinach and shock it in an ice-water bath. Squeeze the spinach to remove all water. Repeat the blanching process with the remaining spinach. Set aside. *The spinach can be blanched in advance. Store wrapped in the refrigerator.*

3. Heat a 12-in/30-cm sauté pan over medium-high heat until it is hot, about 1 minute. Add 1½ fl oz/45 mL reserved garlic oil to the pan, and heat to hot but not smoking, about 10 seconds. Add the onions, ¾ tsp/2 g salt, and red pepper flakes. Adjust the heat to medium-low and cook, tossing occasionally, until soft and translucent, about 20 minutes. Move the onions to one side of the pan. Add ½ fl oz/15 mL reserved garlic oil and the minced garlic to the empty space and cook until fragrant, about 1 minute. Combine and cook until the onions are golden, about 12 minutes more. *The onions can be sautéed 1 day in advance. Store wrapped in the refrigerator. Reheat in a sauté pan over medium heat before proceeding.*

4. Add the blanched spinach, tossing it with the onions until it is hot, about 2 minutes. Add the butter and toss together until it is melted, about 30 seconds more. Remove the spinach from the heat and toss in the cheese and black pepper. Taste and adjust seasoning. Put on a serving platter and garnish with 1 fl oz/30 mL reserved garlic oil and the garlic chips.

SPINACH AND CHICKPEA SAUTÉ: Add 8¼ oz/234 g cooked chickpeas to the onions and garlic.

BROCCOLI RABE AND CANNELLINI BEAN SAUTÉ: Replace the spinach with trimmed broccoli rabe chopped into 1-in/3-cm pieces. Blanch the broccoli rabe until tender, 4 to 5 minutes. Do not squeeze dry, but drain well. Add 8¼ oz/234 g cooked cannellini beans to the onions and garlic.

SPINACH, KALE, AND CHICKPEA SAUTÉ: Replace 1 lb 8 oz/680 g of the spinach with 1 lb 8 oz/680 g chopped kale. Blanch the kale in boiling salted water until tender, 4 to 5 minutes. Add 8¼ oz/234 g cooked chickpeas to the onions and garlic.

The time-tested staples of the steam-powered buffet certainly still satisfy irresistibly: the Three-Cheese Baked Macaroni, the Yukon Gold Gnocchi with Roasted Tomato Ragù and Broccoli, and the Sweet Potato Mash with Pecan Crumble, while kid friendly, are adult rated. The recipes for our scratch-made fettuccine lend a giant "wow" factor to an à la minute action station, and the handmade ravioli, in particular, dazzles on the buffet on a long metal platter set over a canned heat source. These relatively inexpensive starches provide a blank canvas for the added color of vegetables and proteins. They provide the opportunity to shine with savory sauces and pestos.

PASTA, POLENTA, RICE, *and* POTATOES

BLACK PEPPER–SPECKLED FETTUCCINE MARSALA WITH CHICKEN

YIELD: 12 SERVINGS

CHICKEN

3 lb/1.36 kg trimmed boneless skinless chicken breasts, butterflied, trimmings and bones reserved for fortifying stock

48 fl oz/1.44 L chicken stock

12 fl oz/360 mL dry Marsala or dry sherry

5 oz/142 g unbleached all-purpose flour (1 cup/240 mL)

1 tbsp/10 g kosher salt, plus as needed to adjust seasoning

1½ tsp/3 g ground dried porcini mushroom powder (see Note)

½ tsp/1 g ground black pepper, plus as needed to adjust seasoning

4 fl oz/120 mL olive oil, plus as needed, to brown the chicken

2 oz/57 g unsalted butter, cut into ½-in/1.25-cm pats, plus as needed to brown the chicken (¼ cup/60 mL)

½ batch Sautéed Mushrooms and Onions (page 178)

12 fl oz/360 mL heavy cream

PASTA

2 tbsp/20 g salt, plus as needed to adjust seasoning

1 batch Black Pepper–Speckled Fettuccine (page 199) or dried fettuccine

3 oz/85 g grated Pecorino Romano (1 cup/240 mL), plus as needed to garnish pasta

¼ oz/7 g minced flat-leaf parsley (2 tbsp/30 mL)

1. For the chicken, pound the chicken between 2 sheets of waxed paper to an even ¼ in/6 mm thickness. Cut into 2-in/5-cm pieces.

2. Heat the chicken stock in a 2-qt/1.92-L saucepan over medium heat. Add any trimmings and bones from the chicken preparation and simmer while continuing with the recipe. Skim and degrease while simmering. Taste and adjust the seasoning of the stock. Add the Marsala to the chicken stock. Turn off the heat.

3. Combine the flour, salt, porcini mushroom powder, and pepper in a 2-qt/1.92-L shallow bowl. Heat a 12-in/30-cm sauté pan over high heat, about 1 minute. Add the olive oil and butter to the pan and heat to hot but not smoking, about 30 seconds, so the chicken sizzles when it hits the pan. Evenly coat the chicken with seasoned flour, shake off any excess, and carefully place it into the pan. Repeat with enough chicken so the pieces are not touching but fill the pan. Cook undisturbed until the bottom is golden brown, about 2 minutes. Turn the chicken over and cook until golden brown, about 2 minutes more. Shingle the browned chicken into a large hotel pan. Repeat with the remaining chicken, adding more butter or oil as needed.

4. Carefully strain the stock into the hotel pan with the chicken, discarding any solids. Cover the chicken with parchment paper, seal with aluminum foil, and bake in a 350°F/177°C oven for 45 minutes, or until the liquid bubbles and chicken is fork-tender. *The chicken can be baked 1 day in advance. Rapidly cool, then store with the chicken in the sauce wrapped in the refrigerator.*

5. Carefully pour the liquid from the chicken into a 6-qt/5.76-L wide-mouth saucepan, then place the saucepan over medium heat. Add the mushrooms and onions and simmer to marry the flavors, about 5 minutes. Add the cream and simmer over medium heat until thickened, about 10 minutes. Taste and adjust seasoning. Add the chicken to warm.

6. For the pasta, bring an 8-qt/7.68-L sauce pot filled three-quarters with cold water to a boil. Add the salt and the pasta. Stir, making sure the pasta does not stick, bring the water back to a boil, and cook for about 30 seconds if using fresh pasta or 1 minute less than the recommended time on the package if using dried pasta. Lift the pasta out of the water with a spider and add the pasta to the pot with the chicken. Cook together for 30 seconds while gently tossing the pasta. Turn off the heat. Add the cheese and parsley. Taste and adjust seasoning.

To make dried porcini mushroom powder, grind dried porcini mushrooms in a spice grinder until they are reduced to fine dust. Sift the dust through a fine-mesh strainer.

Black Pepper–Speckled Fettuccine Marsala with Chicken.
Cielo bone china plates and Schott Zwiesel glassware by
Fortessa Tableware (see Resources, page 347).

PASTA DOUGH

YIELD: 1 LB 8 OZ/680 G

7½ oz/212 g Italian "00" farina or unbleached all-purpose flour (1½ cups/360 mL)

6 oz/170 g durum semolina (1 cup/240 mL)

2½ oz/71 g white whole wheat flour (½ cup/120 mL)

8 oz/227 g eggs, beaten (4 or 5 eggs)

Bench flour as needed

1. Put all of the flours together in a food processor fitted with a steel blade. With the motor running, pour in the eggs, and then pulse the motor until the dough looks like moist dough crumbs that hold together when pinched, about six 5-second on/off pulses. The goal is not a cohesive dough ball, so if that is what results, add all-purpose flour a tablespoon at a time, processing for 10 seconds between additions, until it breaks into moist dough crumbs. If the dough is too dry to pinch and hold together, add beaten egg a tablespoon at a time, running the food processor for 10 seconds between additions, until moist dough crumbs are formed. If in doubt, it is better to err on the moister side.

2. Place the dough on a work surface and knead it into a smooth, cohesive ball, about 30 seconds. Do not dust with flour. The dough will be very stiff at this point but will soften as it rests. Wrap the dough in plastic wrap and let it rest for 20 minutes. Divide the dough in half and roll each half into a disk so it fits into a pasta roller on the widest setting, about ¼ in/6 mm thick. Wrap in plastic, and let rest again at room temperature for 1 hour.

3. Run one of the disks through the rollers of a pasta machine on the widest setting. Fold the dough in half, pat together, and pass the dough through the pasta machine on the widest setting again. Do not dust with flour while doing this. Repeat this "kneading" process 5 more times; the dough will lighten in color and become very smooth and elastic.

4. With the machine still on the widest setting, pass the dough through the rollers again, stop the dough halfway through, and overlap the ends of the dough and press them together. Continue passing the dough though the roller so the overlapped ends seal and form a continuous dough belt. Place a sheet pan under the rollers to catch the dough and any excess flour that may fall. Dust both sides of the dough belt with bench flour.

5. Continue running the dough belt through the rollers, progressively decreasing the setting, but passing the dough through 2 or 3 times at each setting, until the desired thinness is achieved. Lightly flour the dough whenever it is the least bit sticky. Support the dough where it is fed into the roller so gravity does not stretch it and it remains the same width as the rollers. When finished, the entire dough belt should be the full width of the rollers and an even thickness without any tears or holes. Cut the dough along the rollers and release from the machine.

6. Cut the dough into uniform sheets as needed for the recipe or about 17 in/42.5 cm in length. Lightly flour the dough sheets and place them on a sheet pan in stacks no more than 6 layers high, covered with plastic wrap and then a damp towel. Repeat with the remaining dough. The dough is now ready to be cut and/or filled. *Rolled pasta sheets can be stored wrapped in the refrigerator for 4 hours or in the freezer for 3 months. Layer dough sheets on a sheet pan with plastic wrap or waxed paper between each layer in stacks no more than 6 layers high.*

Cut pasta can be stored wrapped in the refrigerator for 6 hours or in the freezer for 3 months. After the pasta is cut, dust with flour, shake excess flour off, and put up to 1 lb/454 g pasta on each sheet pan. Once it freezes, it can be transferred to zip-close plastic bags or layered in plastic containers, with 2 waxed paper sheets between layers, no more than 2 layers high. Do not thaw before cooking.

Filled pasta can be stored wrapped in the refrigerator for 4 hours or wrapped in the freezer for 3 months. Put filled pasta in a single layer, not touching, on a sheet pan dusted with cornmeal. Once it freezes, it can be wrapped with 2 waxed paper sheets between layers, no more than 3 layers high. Do not thaw before cooking.

Place pasta straight from the refrigerator or freezer into salted boiling water. Boil until tender, 30 seconds to 2 minutes, then lift the pasta out of the water with a spider and add the pasta to the pot with the hot sauce it will be served with. Cook together for 30 seconds while gently tossing the pasta.

Don't be turned off by the length of this recipe and the detailed technique and descriptions. Flour and eggs are turned into silky pasta that will set you miles apart from the competition. Once you get the feel in your fingers for the dough and process, a pound of pasta can be rolled in less than10 minutes.

As an alternative, mix the pasta in a stand mixer with a dough hook. With the motor running, pour in the eggs and knead on low speed for 5 minutes. When done, the dough should be moist but not stick to the bowl.

BLACK PEPPER–SPECKLED PASTA: While kneading the dough, add ½ tsp/1 g butcher-grind coarse pepper.

THREE-CHEESE BAKED MACARONI

YIELD: 12 SERVINGS

CHEESE SAUCE

8 oz/227 g unsalted butter, cut into ½-in/1.25-cm pats, plus as needed for preparing pan (1 cup/240 mL)

3¾ oz/106 g unbleached all-purpose flour (¾ cup/180 mL)

64 fl oz/1.92 L milk, left at room temperature for 20 minutes

1½ tsp/5 g kosher salt, plus as needed to adjust seasoning

1½ tsp/3 g dry mustard

½ tsp/1 g ground black pepper, plus as needed to adjust seasoning

¼ tsp/0.5 g cayenne

¼ tsp/0.5 g ground nutmeg

1 lb/454 g cheddar, cut into ½-in/1.25-cm cubes

8 oz/227 g Monterey Jack, cut into ½-in/1.25-cm cubes

8 oz/227 g provolone, cut into ½-in/1.25-cm cubes

PASTA

1 lb 8 oz/680 g dried semolina pasta (elbows, ziti, penne, bow tie, or other short shape)

2 tbsp/20 g kosher salt

4½ oz/128 g coarsely ground firm white bread (about 3 slices)

1½ oz/43 g grated Pecorino Romano (½ cup/120 mL)

1. For the cheese sauce, melt the butter in a 6-qt/5.76-L sauce pot over medium-low heat. Add the flour and cook, whisking constantly, until it is a thin golden roux, about 4 minutes. Slowly add the milk while whisking. Once incorporated, raise the temperature to medium-high and bring the sauce to a simmer. Stir frequently with a flat-sided wooden spoon, as the sauce on the bottom of the pan can stick and burn easily. If it burns, discard and start over. Once the sauce has thickened, adjust the heat to medium-low and cook gently until any raw flour taste cooks out, about 10 minutes.

2. Whisk in the salt, mustard, pepper, cayenne, and nutmeg. Remove the sauce from the heat and stir in all the cheese cubes at once so they gently melt. The cheese does not need to completely melt.

3. To cook the pasta, bring an 8-qt/7.68-L sauce pot filled three-quarters with cold water to a boil. Add the pasta and salt. Stir, making sure the pasta does not stick, and cook 1 minute less than the recommended time on the package. Drain the pasta, discard the water, and pour into the pot with the cheese sauce. Fold together, taste, and adjust seasoning.

4. Grease the bottom and sides of a half hotel pan or an equivalent size baking pan with butter. Pour into the prepared baking dish. Combine the bread crumbs and Pecorino Romano in a 1-qt/960-mL bowl. Sprinkle over the top of the pasta. *The macaroni can be prepared 2 days in advance. Add an additional 8 fl oz/240 mL milk to the roux. Rapidly cool, then immediately store wrapped in the refrigerator.*

5. Position a rack in the middle of the oven and heat to 350°F/177°C. Bake until the bread crumbs are golden and crispy and the pasta reaches an internal temperature of 165°F/74°C, 45 to 55 minutes.

Butternut Squash Malfatti with Crispy Pumpkin Seeds. Plaza
rectangular plate by **Fortessa Tableware** (see Resources, page 347).

BUTTERNUT SQUASH MALFATTI WITH CRISPY PUMPKIN SEEDS

YIELD: 12 SERVINGS

5 lb/2.27 kg butternut squash

3½ fl oz/105 mL extra-virgin olive oil

2 tbsp plus 2½ tsp/28 g kosher salt, plus as needed to adjust seasoning

1 lb 4¼ oz/574 g diced Spanish onions (4½ cups/ 1.06 L or about 2¼ large onions)

1 oz/28 g minced garlic (8 tsp/40 mL or 8 cloves)

¼ tsp/0.5 g red pepper flakes

2 bay leaves

2 fl oz/60 mL balsamic vinegar

6 oz/170 g grated Gruyère or Manchego (1½ packed cups/360 mL)

4 oz/113 g mascarpone (½ cup/120 mL)

3 oz/85 g grated Pecorino Romano (1 cup/240 mL)

½ oz/14 g chopped flat-leaf parsley (¼ cup/60 mL)

¼ oz/7 g sage chiffonade (2 tbsp/30 mL)

½ tsp/1 g ground black pepper, plus as needed to adjust seasoning

1 batch Pasta Dough (page 198), cut into malfatti, or 2-in/5-cm dough strips cut into rough trapezoids or squares, or dry semolina wide noodles

GARNISH

2 fl oz/60 mL pumpkin seed oil

2 oz/57 g toasted pepitas (½ cup/120 mL; page 114)

1 oz/28 g Pecorino Romano curls (⅓ cup/80 mL, loosely packed)

1. Position a rack in the bottom third of the oven and heat it to 375°F/191°C. Cut the squash in half lengthwise and remove the seeds and rough pulp. Coat the flesh with 1 fl oz/30 mL olive oil and 1½ tsp/5 g salt and place cut side down on a sheet pan. Bake in the oven until tender, 45 to 60 minutes. Cool at room temperature for 20 minutes.

Scoop the flesh out of the squash, discarding the skin. *The butternut squash can be prepared 1 day in advance. Cool quickly, then store wrapped in the refrigerator.*

2. Warm a 12-in/30-cm sauté pan over medium-high heat, about 1 minute. Add 2 fl oz/60 mL olive oil and warm to hot but not smoking, about 10 seconds. Add the onions and 1 tsp/3 g salt. Lower the heat to medium-low, cover, and cook, tossing occasionally, until soft and jammy, about 30 minutes. If there is not enough liquid released from the vegetables to cook for this length of time without burning, add 1 fl oz/30 mL water and cook until the liquid evaporates. Move the onions to one side of the pan. Add ½ fl oz/15 mL olive oil and the garlic, red pepper flakes, and bay leaves to the empty space and cook until fragrant, about 1 minute, then combine with the onions. Add the vinegar, toss together, and cook until the vinegar evaporates, about 10 minutes more. Remove the bay leaves. Add the squash and combine. *The seasoned butternut squash can be prepared in advance. Cool quickly, then store wrapped in the refrigerator for 2 days or in the freezer for 3 months. Thaw in the refrigerator.*

3. Fold the Gruyère, mascarpone, Pecorino Romano, parsley, sage, and black pepper into the squash. Taste and adjust seasoning. Reserve half of the seasoned squash in a 1-qt/960-mL bowl.

4. Bring an 8-qt/7.68-L sauce pot filled three-quarters with cold water to a boil. Add the remaining 2 tbsp/20 g salt. Add half of the pasta and gently stir, making sure the pasta does not stick. Cook the pasta until al dente, about 30 seconds if using fresh pasta or 1 minute less than the recommended time on the package if using dried pasta. Lift the pasta out of the water with a skimmer and put into the sauté pan with the squash. Raise the heat to medium, being careful the bottom does not scorch. Add 1½ cups/360 mL pasta water, fold together, and simmer for 30 seconds. Pour into a large shallow serving bowl. Repeat with the remaining pasta, squash mixture, and 1½ cups/360 mL pasta water. Fold the batches together. Taste and adjust seasoning. Garnish with the pumpkin seed oil, pepitas, and Pecorino Romano curls.

CINQUE FORMAGGIO RAVIOLI CON L'UOVO

YIELD: 12 SERVINGS

CHEESE FILLING

1 lb/454 kg ricotta, drained in a colander in refrigerator for 2 hours to 1 day, whey discarded (2 cups/480 mL)

2½ oz/71 g shredded low-moisture mozzarella (½ cup/120 mL)

1¼ oz/35 g shredded Asiago pressato (young Asiago) (⅓ cup/80 mL)

¾ oz/21 g grated Parmigiano-Reggiano (¼ cup/60 mL)

½ oz/14 g grated Pecorino Romano (3 tbsp/45 mL)

3 egg whites

2 tsp/2 g minced basil or ⅔ tsp/3 mL Basil Purée (page 323)

2 tsp/2 g minced flat-leaf parsley

¼ tsp/1 g kosher salt, plus as needed to adjust seasoning

¼ tsp/0.5 g ground black pepper, plus as needed to adjust seasoning

RAVIOLI

Cornmeal as needed

Twenty-four 5½-in/14-cm squares Pasta Dough, rolled thin enough to see fingers through, and covered with plastic wrap and then a damp towel (page 198)

24 thin 4-in/10-cm square slices low-moisture mozzarella

12 pasteurized egg yolks, unbroken

1 tbsp/10 g kosher salt

1. Combine all the ingredients for the cheese filling in a 1-qt/960-mL bowl. Sample a little of the cheese mixture by microwaving a small flat patty until it is fully cooked. Taste and adjust seasoning. Refrigerate until ready to use. Set the filling over ice while assembling the ravioli. *The cheese filling can be made 1 day in advance. Store wrapped in the refrigerator.*

2. Line 2 sheet pans with parchment paper and sprinkle with cornmeal. Lay 1 pasta dough square on a lightly floured work surface. Place a slice of mozzarella in the center of the square. Gently place a 2½-in/6-cm ring, cutting side up, in the center of the mozzarella slice and fill with 1¾ oz/50 g cheese filling (¼ cup/60 mL). With the back of a spoon, make a well in the center and push the filling about 1 in/3 cm up the sides of the ring. Place a yolk in the well. Remove the ring and gently pat the filling around the yolk. Top the yolk with 1 mozzarella slice. Lightly brush all the dough surrounding the cheese with water. Place the second square over the filling, centering it over the yolk. Press the dough together around the filling, pushing out any air pockets and preventing as many wrinkles in the dough as possible. With a pastry cutter, trim the dough into a 5-in/13-cm square. Place on the prepared sheet pan. Repeat with all the dough squares and filling. *The ravioli can be assembled 4 hours in advance. Immediately store wrapped in the refrigerator.*

3. Bring a wide-mouth 6-qt/5.76-L sauce pot filled 4 in/10 cm deep with cold water to a gentle boil. Add the salt and 2 ravioli. Make sure the ravioli do not stick together and stay yolk side up. Cook until the yolks are soft boiled, 3 to 3½ minutes. Lift out of the water with a skimmer and repeat with the remaining ravioli.

Cinque Formaggio Ravioli con l'Uovo. Acqua Vortex bowl by **Fortessa Tableware** (see Resources, page 347).

CINQUE FORMAGGIO MANICOTTI

YIELD: 3 DOZEN MANICOTTI

---

3 lb/1.36 kg ricotta

7½ oz/213 g shredded low-moisture mozzarella

3 ¾ oz/106 g shredded Asiago

2¼ oz/64 g grated Parmigiano-Reggiano

1½ oz/43 g grated Pecorino Romano

3 egg yolks

¼ oz/7 g minced basil (2 tbsp/30 mL) or 2 tsp/10 mL Basil Purée (page 323)

¼ oz/7 g minced flat-leaf parsley (2 tbsp/30 mL)

1 tbsp plus ¼ tsp/11 g kosher salt, plus as needed to adjust seasoning

¼ tsp/0.5 g ground black pepper, plus as needed to adjust seasoning

36 Crêpes (page 289) or twelve 11-in/28-cm sheets of Pasta Dough (page 198)

72 fl oz/2.16 L Herbed Tomato Sauce, plus as needed to garnish the manicotti (page 312)

1. In a 6-qt/5.76-L bowl, combine the ricotta, mozzarella, Asiago, Parmigiano-Reggiano, Pecorino Romano, egg yolks, basil, parsley, salt, and pepper. Sample a little of the mixture by microwaving a small flat patty until it is fully cooked. Taste and adjust seasoning.

2. If using crêpes, place 2 oz/57 g pasta stuffing on the lower third of a crêpe. Fold the bottom of the crêpe over the filling and roll it up to form a cylinder. Place the manicotti onto a baking tray seam side down. Repeat with all the filling and crêpes. *The manicotti can be assembled in advance. They can be stacked 2 layers high with 2 pieces of waxed paper between layers. Store wrapped in the refrigerator for 2 days or in the freezer for 3 months.*

3. If using pasta dough, cut each sheet into thirds. Bring a 4-qt/3.84-L sauce pot filled three-quarters with cold water to a boil. Add 1 tbsp salt/10 g and the pasta, a few sheets at a time. Stir, making sure the pasta does not stick, As soon as the water returns to a boil, remove the pasta and shock it in an ice-water bath. Drain, leaving a little water on the pasta sheets so they do not stick. Repeat with all the pasta sheets. Fill the pasta as described in step 2.

4. Position a rack in the middle of the oven and heat it to 350°F/175°C. Place 1½ cups/360 mL tomato sauce in the bottom of each of 3 baking pans measuring 9 by 13 in/23 by 33 cm. Place 12 manicotti in a single layer in each pan on the sauce. Top each tray of manicotti with 1½ cups/360 mL tomato sauce. *The manicotti can be placed in the baking pans with the tomato sauce 1 day in advance. Store wrapped in the refrigerator.*

5. Bake until the manicotti edges are starting to brown, the center is very hot and reaches an internal temperature of 165°F/75°C, and the sauce is bubbly, 30 to 45 minutes.

Pasta, polenta, rice and potatoes not only balance an entrée menu but also make *petite* side dishes for the hors d'oeuvre dinner. For instance, to make miniature manicotti, simply cut the crêpes or pasta dough in half, reduce the filling to half and stuff as described. For baked dishes, such as the Three-Cheese Baked Macaroni, Rigatoni al Forno, Creamy Polenta Marbled with Taleggio, and Potatoes au Gratin, replace the large baking vessel with multiple 2½ oz to 8 oz individually sized vessels. The smaller sized portions and vessels save baking time during party time too.

CINQUE FORMAGGIO RAVIOLI

YIELD: 3 DOZEN RAVIOLI

CHEESE FILLING

1 lb/454 kg ricotta, drained in a colander in refrigerator for 2 hours to 1 day, whey discarded (2 cups/480 mL)

2½ oz/71 g shredded low-moisture mozzarella (½ cup/120 mL)

1¼ oz/35 g shredded Asiago pressato (young Asiago) (⅓ cup/80 mL)

¾ oz/21 g grated Parmigiano-Reggiano (¼ cup/60 mL)

½ oz/14 g grated Pecorino Romano (3 tbsp/45 mL)

2 eggs

2 tsp/2 g minced basil or ⅔ tsp Basil Purée (page 323)

2 tsp/2 g minced flat-leaf parsley

¼ tsp/1 g kosher salt, plus as needed to adjust seasoning

¼ tsp/0.5 g ground black pepper, plus as needed to adjust seasoning

RAVIOLI

6 strips Pasta Dough (page 198), 5½ in by 17 in/14 x 43 cm, rolled thin enough to see fingers through, and covered with plastic wrap and then a damp towel

Cornmeal, as needed

Bench flour, as needed

1 tbsp/10 g kosher salt

1. Combine all the ingredients for the cheese filling in a 1-qt/960-mL bowl. Sample a little of the cheese mixture by microwaving a small flat patty until it is fully cooked. Taste and adjust seasoning. Refrigerate until ready to use. Set the filling over ice while assembling the ravioli. *The cheese filling can be made 1 day in advance. Store wrapped in the refrigerator.*

2. Line 2 sheet pans with parchment paper and sprinkle with cornmeal. Lay 1 pasta strip on a lightly floured work surface. Using a pastry bag, place six ¾-oz/21-g filling mounds (1 tbsp/15 mL) evenly spaced across the center of the bottom half of each dough sheet. With a pastry brush, paint a very light coating of water around the entire rim of the dough and between each mound where the dough will be cut.

3. Fold the dough over the filling, lining up the top edge with the bottom. Starting with the middle vertical line and working out to each side, one at a time, press the dough together around the filling mounds, pushing out any air pockets. With a ravioli cutter, cut the dough around the entire rim and then between the filling, making 6 ravioli. Place the completed ravioli on the prepared baking sheets. Repeat the process for the remaining dough sheets. *The assembled ravioli can be stored in the refrigerator for up to 4 hours (after that the moisture from the filling will cause the dough to tear) or in the freezer for up to 3 months.*

4. Bring a wide-mouth 6-qt/5.76-L sauce pot filled 4 in/10 cm deep with cold water to a gentle boil. Add the salt and 6 ravioli. Make sure the ravioli do not stick together. Cook until the ravioli pasta is fully cooked, 3 to 3½ minutes. Lift out of the water with a skimmer and repeat with the remaining ravioli.

Square ravioli waste much less dough then those made with a round cutter. To help shape uniformly sized square ravioli, make a template with a sheet of parchment paper and a dark permanent marker. Place the long side of the paper lengthwise and vertically draw 7 straight lines 2¾ in/7 cm apart from top to bottom, so there are even 6 sections marked on the parchment. Draw one line horizontally from one short side to the other so the paper is divided in half. Turn the parchment over so the marker side faces the work surface and does not bleed onto the dough. A clear flexible cutting mat placed between the dough and the template aids in cutting the dough and helps preserve the template. Lay the dough sheet over the template so the dough is centered over the horizontal line from top to bottom and the left edge of the dough is lined up with the first vertical line marked on the left side of the template. Those lines indicate where the dough will be folded and then cut to make 6 ravioli. The filling should be piped between the center line and the bottom of the dough.

RIGATONI AL FORNO

YIELD: 12 SERVINGS

PASTA

1 lb 8 oz/680 g dried semolina mezzi rigatoni

2 tbsp/20 g kosher salt

48 fl oz/1.44 L Herbed Tomato Sauce, cold (page 312)

6 oz/170 g low-moisture mozzarella, cut into medium dice

6 oz/170 g Asiago pressato (young Asiago), cut into medium dice

RICOTTA TOPPING

1 lb/454 g ricotta (2 cups/480 mL)

1½ oz/43 g grated Pecorino Romano (½ cup/120 mL)

½ oz/14 g freshly toasted bread crumbs (¼ cup/60 mL; page 116) or panko

1 egg, beaten

⅛ tsp/0.5 g kosher salt

⅛ tsp/0.25 g ground black pepper

GARNISH

16 fl oz/480 mL Herbed Tomato Sauce, cold (page 312)

2 oz/57 g low-moisture mozzarella, sliced into ¼-in/6-mm-thick slices

1. For the pasta, bring an 8-qt/7.68-L sauce pot filled three-quarters with cold water to a boil. Add the pasta and salt. Stir, making sure the pasta does not stick, and cook 2 minutes less than the recommended time on the package. Drain the pasta, discard the water, and pour into a half hotel pan or an equivalent size baking pan. Pour the cold tomato sauce over the pasta. Add the cubed mozzarella and Asiago. Combine so all ingredients are evenly distributed.

2. For the ricotta cheese topping, combine the ricotta, Pecorino Romano, bread crumbs, egg, salt, and pepper in a 1-qt/960-mL bowl. Place 6 even mounds of the ricotta cheese topping on top of the pasta. Push the ricotta into the pasta so the ricotta is in distinctive clumps and looks marbled in the pasta. The ricotta should not be fully incorporated.

3. For the garnish, top the pasta with the tomato sauce and mozzarella slices. Cover the top with parchment paper and seal with aluminum foil. *The rigatoni can be prepared 2 days in advance. Immediately store wrapped in the refrigerator.*

4. Position a rack in the middle of the oven and heat to 350°F/177°C. Bake until hot in the center and the cheese is melted, 40 to 60 minutes. Remove the foil and bake until the top is browned, about 10 minutes more.

Rigatoni al Forno. Mini cocottes by Le Creuset
(see Resources, page 347).

Yukon Gold Gnocchi with Roasted Tomato–Broccoli Ragù. Cielo bone china bowl by Fortessa Tableware (see Resources, page 347).

YUKON GOLD GNOCCHI WITH ROASTED TOMATO RAGÙ AND BROCCOLI

YIELD: 12 SERVINGS

ROASTED TOMATO RAGÙ

1 lb 4 oz/567 g grape tomatoes or cherry tomatoes, sliced in half lengthwise (4¾ cups/1.14 L)

3¾ oz/106 g minced shallots (¾ cup/180 mL)

½ oz/14 g minced garlic (4 tsp/20 mL or 3 cloves)

3 fl oz/90 mL extra-virgin olive oil

1 fl oz/30 mL balsamic vinegar

2 tsp/10 g kosher salt

½ tsp/1 g ground black pepper

¼ tsp/1 g granulated sugar

⅛ tsp/0.25 g red pepper flakes

BROCCOLI

2 tbsp/20 g kosher salt

12 oz/340 g broccoli florets, cut into ½-in/1.25-cm pieces (5 cups/1.2 L)

GNOCCHI

2 fl oz/60 mL olive oil, plus as needed to brown gnocchi

2 oz/57 g unsalted butter, plus as needed to brown gnocchi (¼ cup/60 mL)

1 batch Yukon Gold Gnocchi (1 batch) (page 210)

8 fl oz/240 mL gnocchi water or chicken or vegetable stock

½ batch Sautéed Mushrooms and Onions (page 178)

6 fl oz/180 mL Basil Purée (page 323)

½ tsp/1.5 g kosher salt

½ tsp/1 g ground black pepper

6 oz/170 g fresh mozzarella, cut into medium dice

1½ oz/43 g shredded Pecorino Romano (½ cup/120 mL)

2½ oz/71 g toasted macadamia nuts (½ cup/120 mL; page 114)

2½ oz/71 g toasted pine nuts (½ cup/120 mL; page 114)

1. For the tomato ragù, position a rack in the bottom third of the oven and preheat to 350°F/177°C. Combine the tomatoes, shallots, garlic, olive oil, vinegar, salt, pepper, sugar, and red pepper flakes in a 2-qt/1.92-L bowl. Pour the seasoned tomatoes onto a sheet pan and evenly distribute. Bake the tomatoes for 20 minutes, then lower the heat to 300°F/149°C and continue to bake until they shrivel and caramelize, about 2 hours more. Turn the oven off and leave the tomatoes in the cooling oven for 1 hour. *The roasted tomatoes can be prepared 1 week in advance. Immediately store wrapped in the refrigerator.*

2. For the broccoli, bring an 8-qt/7.68-L sauce pot filled three-quarters with cold water to a boil. Add the salt and broccoli. As soon as the water returns to a boil, remove the broccoli and shock it in an ice-water bath. Drain. *The broccoli can be blanched 1 day in advance. Immediately store wrapped in the refrigerator.*

3. For the gnocchi, put ½ fl oz/15 mL olive oil and ½ oz/14 g butter into a 12-in/30-cm nonstick sauté pan. Warm over medium-high heat to hot but not smoking, about 3 minutes, so a gnoccho sizzles when it hits the pan. Carefully place small batches of gnocchi into the pan so the pieces are not touching but fill the pan. Cook the gnocchi, undisturbed, until the bottoms are browned, about 2 minutes. Adjust the heat so the gnocchi do not scorch. Flip the gnocchi over and cook until evenly browned, about 2 minutes more. Place the gnocchi into a 4-qt/3.84-L bowl and tent with aluminum foil to keep warm. Repeat with the remaining gnocchi, adding oil and butter as needed.

4. Add the gnocchi water to the same sauté pan. Turn the heat to high and simmer for 1 minute. Add the sautéed mushrooms and onions, basil pesto, salt, and pepper and stir until incorporated and warm, about 1 minute. Fold in the roasted tomatoes and blanched broccoli and warm, about 30 seconds. Pour over the gnocchi. Toss, taste, and adjust seasonings. Garnish with the mozzarella, Pecorino Romano, macadamia nuts, and pine nuts.

YUKON GOLD GNOCCHI

YIELD: 12 SERVINGS

(2 LB 12 OZ/1.25 KG DOUGH)

3 lb/1.36 kg Yukon gold potatoes, scrubbed, pierced with fork several times (about 8 large potatoes)

2 tbsp plus 1½ tsp/25 g kosher salt

7½ oz/212 g unbleached all-purpose flour (1½ cups/360 mL), plus about 1 cup/240 mL to roll out dough

2 oz/57 g very finely grated Pecorino Romano (⅔ cup/160 mL)

½ tsp/1 g ground black pepper

⅛ tsp/0.5 g ground nutmeg

1 egg

1 egg yolk

2½ fl oz/75 mL extra-virgin olive oil, plus as needed

1. Position a rack in the bottom third of the oven and preheat to 400°F/204°C. Place the potatoes on a sheet pan and bake until there is no resistance when the potatoes are pierced, 45 minutes to 1 hour. While as hot as possible, carefully slice each potato in half at the equator so it will fit into a potato ricer. Place flesh side down into the ricer and push through onto a baking sheet. Discard the skins. Repeat to get 2 lb/907 g riced potato (4½ lightly packed cups/1.08 L). Fluff the pulp out into an even layer on the baking sheet with a bench scraper. Cool at room temperature for 15 to 20 minutes.

2. Bring an 8-qt/7.68-L sauce pot filled two-thirds with cold water to a gentle boil. Add 2 tbsp/20 g salt.

3. Combine the flour, Pecorino Romano, the remaining 1½ tsp/5 g salt, pepper, and nutmeg in a 2-qt/1.92-L bowl. Evenly sprinkle over the potatoes. Gently combine with the bench scraper; scoop up the potatoes and toss with the dry ingredients, 30 seconds.

4. Whisk the whole egg and egg yolk together in a 1-cup/240-mL bowl and evenly drizzle over the potatoes. Combine the ingredients with the bench scraper; scoop up and toss together for 1 minute. Gather the crumbs and push/gently knead them into a cohesive dough, taking no more than 2 minutes. If the dough seems too sticky, add up to 1¼ oz/35 g flour to dough (¼ cup/60 mL). Scale the dough into ten 4⅓-oz/124-g pieces. Roll each into a rope 1 in/2 cm in diameter and 18 in/45 cm long. The dough may split, but just pinch it back together. Dust the ropes liberally with flour. Line up a few ropes, and with the bench scraper cut them into ½-in/1.25-cm pieces. In one hand, hold a fork by its handle, back side up. With the other hand, line up a dough piece with the closed end of the fork tines, cut side up. Press the top of the dough with the thumb and, pulling down, roll dough down the tines of the fork. This will make a tine indentation on the bottom side and a smooth curved shape on the topside. With the index finger and thumb, roll the gnocco off the fork and onto lightly floured parchment paper. Repeat with all dough.

5. Working in 5 batches, add the gnocchi to the gently boiling water, several at a time. The gnocchi should be cooked within a few minutes of being made. Gently stir, making sure they do not stick. Once the gnocchi float to the surface, cook for 1 minute more. Lift out of the water with a skimmer and put onto a sheet pan to cool. Gently fold each batch with ½ fl oz/15 mL olive oil to prevent sticking. Repeat with all the gnocchi. *The gnocchi can be prepared in advance. Store wrapped in the refrigerator for 1 day or in the freezer for 3 months. Thaw and warm before serving.*

When making dough, a light touch and the minimum flour makes for lighter gnocchi. The finished dough should feel moist but not sticky; if it is too sticky, sprinkle in the least flour necessary. The ingredients need not look fully incorporated; specks of egg yolk might still be visible.

Once dough is scaled into 10 pieces, wash, dry, and lightly flour hands. It is easier to roll the dough into ropes without any residue on hands.

TO ROLL INTO ROPES: Spread fingers across center of dough and, with light pressure, roll dough back and forth, moving fingers from center to end. Repeat, gently rolling from center to end several times until rope is an even thickness of about 1 in/3 cm and 18 in/45 cm in length. After the ropes are rolled out, flour them well. From this point on, flour is not being incorporated into dough and won't make the gnocchi heavy. Use what's necessary to prevent sticking.

CREAMY POLENTA MARBLED WITH TALEGGIO

YIELD: 12 SERVINGS

64 fl oz/1.92 L whole milk

32 fl oz/960 mL water

2 tsp/6 g kosher salt, plus as needed to adjust seasoning

½ tsp/1 g ground black pepper, plus as needed to adjust seasoning

11¼ oz/319 g stone-ground white cornmeal (2 cups/480 mL)

4 oz/113 g grated Pecorino Romano (1⅓ cups/320 mL)

10 oz/284 g Taleggio, cold from the refrigerator, cut into bâtonnet (2½ cups/600 mL)

1. Bring the milk, water, salt, and pepper to a boil in an 8-qt/7.68-L stockpot over medium-high heat. While whisking the liquid, slowly sprinkle in the cornmeal. Continue to whisk until the mixture comes to a simmer. Adjust the heat to maintain a simmer. Switch to a wooden spoon and stir the polenta for 2 minutes more, being careful of lava-like bubbles. Adjust the heat to low, cover, and cook, stirring frequently, until thick, shiny, and smooth to the taste, 5 to 20 minutes depending on the cornmeal's grind. Stir often, as the bottom can burn easily. Remove from the heat and stir in the Pecorino Romano until evenly incorporated. Taste and adjust seasoning.

2. Heat the broiler to high. Fold in 8 oz/227 g Taleggio strips so they are evenly dispersed but not incorporated into the polenta. The polenta should appear to be marbled with cheese. Place in a half hotel pan or an equivalent size baking pan and garnish the top with the remaining 2 oz/57 g Taleggio. Place under the broiler until the top is lightly browned, 1 to 2 minutes. *The polenta can be prepared 1 day in advance. Rapidly cool, then immediately store wrapped in the refrigerator. Bake at 350°F/177°C covered with parchment paper and sealed with aluminum foil until the cheese in the center is melted and reaches an internal temperature of 165°F/74°C, about 30 minutes. Then brown under the broiler.*

The polenta can also be marbled with other cheeses, including chèvre, Fontina, or Gorgonzola.

CRISPY POLENTA CAKES: Reduce the milk to 16 fl oz/480 mL and the water to 16 fl oz/480 mL. Eliminate the Taleggio. Coat the bottom and sides of a half hotel pan with 1 fl oz/30 mL olive oil. Carefully pour the hot polenta into the pan, spread into a smooth, even layer, and chill until firm, at least 1 hour and up to 2 days. With a 1-in/3-cm biscuit cutter, cut the polenta into 24 pieces. If putting a topping on the cakes, use a teaspoon to carve out a shallow well into one side of each cake.

Heat a nonstick 12-in/30-cm sauté pan filled with 2 fl oz/60 mL olive oil over medium-high heat. Heat to hot but not smoking, so a polenta cake sizzles when it hits the pan but takes a minute to begin browning. Carefully place about half of the cakes into the pan to fill it in a single layer without touching. Fry undisturbed until golden brown, about 2 minutes. Adjust the heat, if necessary, so they do not scorch. Flip the cakes over and fry until golden brown, about 2 minutes. Place the cooked polenta cakes on a sheet pan. Repeat with the remaining cakes. *Polenta cakes can be fried 4 hours in advance. Rapidly cool completely, then immediately store wrapped in the refrigerator. Place the cakes on a sheet pan in a single layer without touching and bake at 425°F/218°C until hot and crispy, 10 to 12 minutes.*

Saffron Risotto with Pistachios and Pan-Roasted Mediterranean Red Snapper (page 256). Cast-iron griddle with brackets by CAL-MIL (see Resources, page 347).

SAFFRON RISOTTO WITH PISTACHIOS

YIELD: 12 SERVINGS

72 fl oz/2.16 L chicken stock, plus as needed to adjust texture

½ tsp/0.25 g saffron threads

1½ tsp/5 g kosher salt, plus as needed to adjust seasoning

½ tsp/1 g ground black pepper, plus as needed to adjust seasoning

4 fl oz/120 mL extra-virgin olive oil

7½ oz/213 g minced shallots (1½ cups/360 mL)

½ oz/14 g minced garlic (4 tsp/20 mL or 4 cloves)

1 lb 8 oz/680 g Arborio rice (3 cups/720 mL)

4 fl oz/120 mL Pinot Grigio or dry white wine

3 oz/85 g unsalted butter (¾ cup/180 mL)

6 oz/170 g grated Pecorino Romano (2 cups/480 mL)

2½ oz/71 g toasted pistachios, coarsely chopped (½ cup/120 mL; page 114)

1. Heat the stock in a 4-qt/3.84-L sauce pan over medium-low heat to a simmer. Toast the saffron threads in a 6-in/15-cm sauté pan over low heat until fragrant, about 20 seconds. Be careful not to burn them. Add the saffron to the stock. If using unsalted stock, add 1 tsp/3 g salt and the pepper. Taste and adjust seasoning.

2. Heat a wide-mouth 4-qt/3.84-L saucepan over medium-high heat, about 1 minute. Add 2 fl oz/60 mL olive oil and heat until hot but not smoking, about 10 seconds. Add the shallots and the remaining ½ tsp/2 g salt and cook, tossing frequently, until soft and translucent, about 10 minutes. Move the shallots to one side of the pan. Add the garlic to the empty space and cook until fragrant, about 1 minute. Combine and cook until the shallots are barely golden, about 5 minutes more.

3. Add the rice, stir to coat with oil, and cook until glistening and translucent but not browned, about 3 minutes. Adjust the heat so the risotto does not burn but is as hot as possible, so there is a sizzle when liquids hit the pan. Add the wine and cook, stirring constantly with a flat-sided wooden spoon, until the risotto has absorbed all of the wine. Add 2 cups/480 mL chicken stock to the rice and stir every few minutes until almost all of the liquid has been absorbed and a trail can be seen on the bottom of the pan, about 6 minutes. Add 2 cups/480 mL more stock and again stir every few minutes until almost all of the liquid has been absorbed, about 6 minutes. *The risotto can be cooked to this point, or about halfway through, 2 days in advance. Spread the risotto out on a sheet pan, rapidly cool, then immediately refrigerate.*

4. Add 1 cup/240 mL stock at a time, stirring constantly from here on, until the rice is cooked but still has texture or is al dente, 7 to 8 minutes more. Not all of the stock may be used. Remove the risotto from the heat and stir in the remaining 2 fl oz/60 mL olive oil and the butter, cheese, and pistachios. Taste and adjust seasonings and add more stock if a looser texture is desired.

For a Spanish twist, replace the Arborio with Bomba rice, the Pecorino Romano with Manchego, and the pistachios with Marcona almonds.

SWEET AND SOUR SUSHI RICE CAKES

YIELD: 12 SERVINGS

2 lb/907 g short-grain Japanese sushi rice (4 cups/960 mL)

34 fl oz/1 L cold water, plus water to wash/soak rice

8 fl oz/240 mL Japanese unseasoned rice vinegar

2¼ oz/64 g granulated sugar (⅓ cup/80 mL)

4½ tsp/14 g kosher salt

1. Put the rice into a 2-qt/1.92-L colander set in a 3-qt/2.88-L bowl and fill so the rice is covered with water. Agitate the rice so the water becomes cloudy, then drain the water. Repeat washing the rice 5 or 6 times until the water is noticeably clear. Cover the rice with cold water

and let soak for 1 hour. Drain and discard the soaking water.

2. Place the rice and the 34 fl oz/1 L cold water into a 4-qt/3.84-L saucepan. Cover with a lid and bring to a boil over high heat. Adjust the heat to low and simmer for 20 minutes. Remove the saucepan from the heat, remove the lid, cover the pot with a towel, replace the lid, and let the rice rest for 10 minutes.

3. Put the vinegar, sugar, and salt into a 1½-qt/1.44-L saucepan over low heat, and stir until the sugar and salt dissolve. Do not bring to a boil. Cool to room temperature.

4. Pour the rice out onto a half sheet pan and gently fluff it out and fan until the steam dissipates. Sprinkle the vinegar mixture over the rice and, while fanning, fold over with a plastic spatula to combine, being careful not to break the rice, and cool completely, about 10 minutes. Gently press the rice onto the half sheet pan, evenly filling it into a cohesive rectangle, about 1 in/3 cm thick. Cut into 2½-in/6-cm rounds or into the desired size and shape. *The rice cakes can be prepared 1 day in advance. Immediately store wrapped in the refrigerator. Warm in a vegetable steamer for 1 minute.*

CRISPY SWEET AND SOUR SUSHI RICE CAKES:
Heat 2 fl oz/60 mL oil in a 12-in/30-cm nonstick sauté pan over medium heat until hot but not smoking, about 1 minute, so a rice cake sizzles when it hits the pan. Carefully place enough rice cakes into the oil to fill the pan without touching each other. Adjust the heat so the oil sizzles but does not smoke or burn. Fry the rice cakes until the edges and bottoms are golden and crispy, 1 to 2 minutes. Turn over and continue cooking until evenly browned and hot in the middle, about 2 minutes more.

NEW POTATOES WITH BALSAMIC-ONION JAM AND THYME

YIELD: 12 SERVINGS

BALSAMIC-ONION JAM

2½ fl oz/75 mL extra-virgin olive oil

11¼ oz/319 g chopped Spanish onions

2 tsp/6 g kosher salt, plus as needed to adjust seasoning

½ oz/14 g minced garlic (4 tsp/20 mL or 4 cloves)

1 fl oz/30 mL water

1 tsp/1 g chopped thyme or ½ tsp/1 g dried

½ tsp/2.5 g Cajun Spice, plus as needed to adjust seasoning

2 fl oz/60 mL balsamic vinegar

2 oz/57 g unsalted butter, cut into ½-in/1.25-cm-thick pats (¼ cup/60 mL)

½ tsp/1 g ground black pepper, plus as needed to adjust seasoning

NEW POTATOES

3 lb /1.36 kg Klondike Rose potatoes, about 1 in/3 cm in diameter

1 tbsp/10 g kosher salt

1. For the balsamic-onion jam, heat a 10-in/25-cm sauté pan over medium heat until it begins to get hot, about 1 minute. Add 2 fl oz/60 mL oil to the pan and heat until hot but not smoking, about 10 seconds. Add the onions and salt, adjust the heat to low, cover, and cook the onions until their liquid is released and evaporates, occasionally checking that the bottom is not burning, about 10 minutes. Move the onions to one side of pan. Add the remaining ½ fl oz/15 mL oil and the garlic to the empty space and cook for 1 minute. Stir in the water, scrape up any bits on the bottom of the pan, cover, and cook until the water is completely evaporated and the onion looks jammy and caramelized, 30 to 40 minutes more. Adjust the heat to medium, add the thyme and Cajun spice, and cook until fragrant, about 1 minute. Add the vinegar and cook until it is completely reduced and the oil separates from the purple jam, about 5 minutes. Remove from the

heat. Swirl in the butter and pepper. *The onion jam can be prepared 3 days in advance. Store wrapped in the refrigerator.*

2. For the new potatoes, place the potatoes and salt in a 4-qt/3.84-L saucepan. Cover the potatoes with cold water by 2 in/5 cm. Over high heat, bring the water to a boil, then adjust the heat to a simmer. Cook the potatoes until there is no resistance when pierced, 20 to 25 minutes. Drain the potatoes, split each in half while as hot as possible, and place in the sauté pan with the onion jam. Toss, taste, and adjust seasoning. *The potatoes can be tossed with the onion jam up to 2 days in advance. Store wrapped in the refrigerator. Reheat the potatoes in a sauté pan or covered in a baking pan in the oven at 400°F/204°C until hot, 30 to 40 minutes.*

SMASHED BALSAMIC RED POTATOES: Increase the butter to 4 oz/113 g (½ cup/120 mL). Place the whole potatoes into the Balsamic-Onion Jam and press down on them with a large fork, smashing them into small lumps.

POTATOES AU GRATIN

YIELD: 12 SERVINGS

8 oz/227 g unsalted butter, cut into ½-in/1.25-cm pats, plus as needed for preparing pan and parchment paper (1 cup/240 mL)

9 oz/255 g chopped Spanish onion (2 cups/480 mL or about 1 large onion)

3½ tsp/11 g kosher salt

¼ oz/7 g minced garlic (2 tsp/10 mL or 2 cloves)

1½ tsp/7 g mL Cajun Spice (page 333)

¼ tsp/0.5 g ground black pepper

28 fl oz/840 mL milk

4 lb 8 oz/2 kg peeled russet potatoes, placed in water to prevent oxidization (about 15 medium potatoes)

1 lb/454 g shredded extra-sharp cheddar cheese (3¼ cups/780 mL)

2¼ oz/64 g shredded Pecorino Romano (¾ cup/180 mL)

1. Grease a half hotel pan or a baking pan measuring 9 by 13 in/23 by 33 cm with butter. Grease parchment paper to cover the top of the casserole.

2. Heat a 16-in/41-cm nonstick sauté pan over medium heat, about 1 minute. Add the butter and heat until the butter melts and foams. Add the onions and salt, adjust the heat to medium-low, cover, and cook until translucent and tender, occasionally checking that the bottom is not burning, about 20 minutes. If the onions start to burn, add 2 fl oz/60 mL water to the pan and cook until all of the water is evaporated. Move the onions to one side of the pan. Add the garlic, Cajun spice, and pepper to the empty space and cook for 2 minutes. Adjust the heat to medium, stir in the milk, scraping up any bits on the bottom, and warm the milk until very hot, about 5 minutes.

3. Pat one-third of the potatoes dry and slice into ⅛-in/3-mm-thick rounds. Place them into the milk and simmer, covered, until parcooked, 12 to 15 minutes, occasionally stirring gently to check that the bottom is not burning. With a slotted spoon, lift the potatoes out of the milk and layer into the baking dish. Sprinkle with 5⅓ oz/150 g cheddar (about one-third of the cheese or 1 heaping cup/240 mL). Repeat until there are 3 layers of potatoes and 3 layers of cheddar. Pour the remaining liquid onto the potatoes. Press the potatoes with a wooden spoon to evenly distribute and make compact. Top with the Pecorino Romano. Cover the potatoes with the prepared parchment, buttered side pressed onto the potatoes, and seal with aluminum foil. *The potatoes can be assembled 1 day in advance. Quickly cool, then immediately store wrapped in the refrigerator.*

4. Position a rack in the middle of the oven and heat to 325°F/163°C. Place the baking dish on a sheet pan, because it will bubble over while baking, and bake until there is no resistance when the potatoes are pierced, 1 to 1½ hours. Uncover and bake until the top is browned, 15 minutes more. Let the potatoes set at room temperature tented with foil for 15 minutes before serving.

Sweet Potato Mash with Pecan Crumble.
Oval porcelain platter by Willow Group, Ltd.
(see Resources, page 347).

SWEET POTATO MASH WITH PECAN CRUMBLE

YIELD: 12 SERVINGS

SWEET POTATO MASH

5 lb/2.27 kg sweet potatoes, scrubbed, pierced with fork several times (about 12 large potatoes)

8 oz/227 g unsalted butter (1 cup/240 mL)

6 fl oz/180 mL heavy cream

1 oz/28 g peeled ginger, sliced into ¼-in/6-mm-thick pieces

1 vanilla bean

2 eggs, whisked

3½ oz/99 g dark brown sugar (½ cup/ 120 mL firmly packed)

1 tsp/3 g kosher salt

½ tsp/1 g ground black pepper

⅛ tsp/0.25 g ground nutmeg

PECAN CRUMBLE

5¼ oz/149 g brown sugar (¾ cup/180 mL firmly packed)

4 oz/113 g pecans, finely chopped (1 cup/240 mL)

2½ oz/71 g unbleached all-purpose flour (½ cup/120 mL)

2 oz/57 g unsalted butter, room temperature (¼ cup/60 mL)

½ tsp/1.5 g kosher salt

1. For the sweet potato mash, position a rack in the bottom third of the oven and preheat to 400°F/204°C. Place the potatoes on a sheet pan and bake until there is no resistance when the potatoes are pierced, 45 minutes to 1 hour. Carefully slice each potato in half at the equator so it will fit into a potato ricer. Place flesh side down into the ricer and push through into a 4-qt/3.84-L bowl. Discard the skins. Repeat with all the potatoes. There needs to be 4 lb/1.81 kg sweet potato pulp.

2. Put the butter, cream, and ginger into a 2-qt/1.92-L saucepan. Scrape the seeds from the vanilla bean and place the seeds and pod into the cream. Over medium heat, bring to a simmer. Turn off the heat and let steep for 10 minutes. Remove the vanilla pod and ginger pieces. In a 2-qt/1.92-L bowl, whisk the eggs, sugar, salt, pepper, and nutmeg together. Then whisk in the steeped cream. Pour the mixture over the riced potatoes. Combine, taste, and adjust seasoning.

3. For the pecan crumble, in a 2-qt/1.92-L bowl combine the brown sugar, pecans, flour, butter, and salt. *The pecan crumble can be stored wrapped in the refrigerator for 3 days or in the freezer for 3 months.*

4. Grease a half hotel pan or a baking pan measuring 9 by 13 in/23 by 33 cm with butter. Evenly distribute the potatoes in the pan and sprinkle on the pecan topping. *The sweet potato mash can be prepared 2 days in advance. Store wrapped in the refrigerator.*

5. Position a rack in the middle of the oven and heat it to 350°F/177°C. Bake the sweet potato mash until the center is hot and set, 45 to 60 minutes.

These recipes have been selected for their wide appeal—the crowd-pleasers—as well as for their production methods—the kitchen aiders. Many of the heartier meats are featured because they are braise-worthy; that is, they are often less expensive cuts, are better when made well in advance, and hold at temperature in a sauce or gravy. In fact, these chafer-friendly braises actually become tastier as they sit in a steamy environment. Braises prepared in advance with no temperature (as in rare, medium, well) required for service allow us to offer other more à la minute items, such as Crusted Beef Tenderloin and Pan-Roasted Mediteranean Red Snapper. Chicken remains the most versatile and expected entrée that everyone enjoys, while salmon is our go-to fish because its firm texture holds without breaking apart.

MEAT, POULTRY, and SEAFOOD

Barolo-Braised Short Ribs and Horseradish Gremolata (page 315)

BAROLO-BRAISED SHORT RIBS

YIELD: 12 SERVINGS

BRAISING LIQUID

64 fl oz/1.92 L Barolo or dry, un-oaky red wine such as burgundy

2 fl oz/60 mL canola oil

2 lb 9 oz/1.2 kg coarsely chopped onions (about 9 cups/2.16 L)

2 tbsp/20 g kosher salt, plus as needed to adjust seasoning

1 lb/454 g coarsely chopped carrots (about 3 cups/720 mL)

1 lb/454 g coarsely chopped celery (about 3 cups/720 mL)

1⅛ oz/32 g minced garlic (3 tbsp/45 mL or 9 cloves)

1½ fl oz/45 mL tomato paste

1 tsp/2 g dried porcini mushroom powder (see Note)

6 thyme sprigs

6 rosemary sprigs

6 oregano sprigs

4 bay leaves

8 black cracked peppercorns

32 fl oz/960 mL canned peeled whole plum tomatoes in tomato juice, no salt added, broken up into small pieces

88 fl oz/2.6 L brown veal stock or low-sodium beef broth

Ground black pepper, as needed to adjust seasoning

SHORT RIBS

5 oz/142 g unbleached all-purpose flour (1 cup/240 mL)

3 tbsp/30 g kosher salt

1 tsp/2 g ground black pepper

12 beef short ribs, lollipop-style preferred (about 1 lb/454 g each)

8 fl oz/240 mL canola oil, plus as needed, to brown the meat

1. For the braising liquid, slowly reduce the wine in a 12-in/30-cm sauté pan over medium-low heat, so there are wisps of steam and very tiny bubbles but it is not simmering, to half the original volume, about 1½ hours. *The wine can be reduced 2 weeks in advance. Store wrapped in the refrigerator.*

2. Heat a wide-mouth 6-qt/5.76-L saucepan over medium heat, about 1 minute. Add 1½ fl oz/22.5 mL canola oil to the pan, raise the heat to medium-high, and heat to hot but not smoking, about 20 seconds. Add the onions and salt. If using low-sodium broth, reduce the salt to 1 tsp/3 g. Lower the heat to medium and cook until the onions are soft and jammy, about 20 minutes. Add the carrot and celery and cook until they are deep golden, about 20 minutes more. Move the vegetables to one side of pan. Add the remaining ½ fl oz/15 mL canola oil and the garlic to the empty space and cook until fragrant, about 1 minute. Add the tomato paste, dried mushroom powder, thyme, rosemary, oregano, bay leaves, and peppercorns to the empty space with the garlic and cook until fragrant, about 2 minutes. Mix all the ingredients together and cook until the tomato paste is a deep rust color and smells sweet, about 5 minutes. Add the tomatoes in tomato juice and stir all the ingredients together. Simmer for 5 minutes more. Add the stock and reduced wine and scrape the bottom to incorporate any brown bits. Bring to a simmer and taste and adjust seasoning. *The braising liquid can be made 1 day in advance. Rapidly cool, then immediately store wrapped in the refrigerator. Reheat to a simmer before using.*

3. For the short ribs, combine the flour, salt, and pepper in a flat-bottomed 2-qt/1.92-L bowl. Blot the meat dry and evenly coat it in the flour mixture, shaking off any excess. Heat a 16-in/41-cm nonstick sauté pan over medium heat, about 1 minute. Add 2 fl oz/60 mL canola oil to the pan, raise the heat to medium-high, and heat to hot but not smoking, about 20 seconds, so the meat sizzles when it hits the pan. Carefully place enough beef ribs in a single layer so they fill the pan without touching and cook undisturbed until the bottom is deep brown, about 3 minutes. Adjust the heat, if necessary, so the pan does not scorch. Turn the beef and cook until deep brown on all sides, 8 to 10 minutes more. Place the browned beef into a braising pan measuring 18 by 24 in/45 by 60 cm in a single layer. Repeat with the remaining meat, adding more oil as needed. Remove the sauté pan from the heat,

drain the fat, and if the bottom of the pan has not burned, add about 2 cups/480 mL veal stock, scraping up any fond on the bottom of the pan, and pour back into the other stock.

4. Position a rack in the bottom third of the oven and heat it to 225°F/107°C. Pour the stock and all the vegetables into the braising pan with the beef. Cover the meat with parchment paper touching it and completely seal the pan with aluminum foil. Place it in the oven, braise for 1 hour, and then reduce the heat to as low as the oven will go or 200°F/93°C and continue to braise until fork-tender, 5 to 6 hours more.

5. Remove from the oven and allow the short ribs to rest in the sauce for 1 hour at room temperature. Then chill rapidly, wrap, and refrigerate until the meat has firmed, at least 2 hours. *The short ribs can be braised 3 days in advance. Actually, the dish is better the next day.*

6. Heat the oven to 300°F/149°C. Remove any grease that has hardened on the top of the sauce. Strain the sauce into a 6-qt/5.76-L saucepan, discarding any solids, and warm over medium-high heat until it starts to simmer.

7. If there is butcher's twine on the short ribs, remove and discard it and place the ribs back into the braising pan. Pour all but 4 cups/960 mL of the hot sauce over the short ribs, cover them with parchment paper, and seal the pan with aluminum foil. Warm the short ribs in the oven until hot, 45 to 55 minutes, turning them several times so they stay moist and form a glaze.

8. Continue to simmer the sauce remaining in the saucepan over medium heat until it has a good flavor and consistency as a finishing sauce. It should be nappé, or thick enough to coat the back of a spoon. Taste and adjust the seasoning, adjusting the viscosity or amount with the sauce the ribs were reheated in. Garnish the short ribs with the finishing Barolo sauce.

———

To make dried porcini mushroom powder, grind dried porcini mushrooms in a spice grinder until they are reduced to fine dust. Sift the dust through a fine-mesh strainer.

Horseradish Gremolata (page 315) is a terrific garnish for the short ribs.

HONEY-LACQUERED RIBS

YIELD: 12 SERVINGS

RIBS

24 fl oz/720 mL soy sauce

24 fl oz/720 mL dark beer

4 fl oz/120 mL canola oil

1 lb 5 oz/595 g dark brown sugar (3 firmly packed cups/720 mL)

1 lb 9 oz/765 g coarsely chopped Spanish onions (6 cups/1.44 L or about 3 large onions)

2½ oz/71 g garlic cloves (20 cloves)

4 racks St. Louis–style spare ribs, trimmed (12 lb/5.44 kg total)

HONEY LACQUER

2 fl oz/60 mL canola oil

¾ oz/21 g minced garlic (2 tbsp/30 mL or 6 cloves)

12 oz/340 g honey (1 cup/240 mL)

8 fl oz/240 mL soy sauce

1 tbsp/15 mL Tabasco sauce

1½ tsp/4 g coarsely ground black pepper

GARNISHES

1 oz/28 g green onions, sliced 3 mm/⅛ in thick on the bias (½ cup/120 mL or about 4 green onions)

1 oz/28 g chopped flat-leaf parsley (½ cup/120 mL)

2 tbsp/19 g toasted sesame seeds (page 114)

1. Combine the soy sauce, beer, canola oil, and brown sugar in a deep hotel pan. Stir in the onions and garlic. For the ribs, submerge them in the marinade and store them wrapped in the refrigerator for 1 day, turning occasionally.

2. Heat the oven to 300°F/149°C. Place a piece of parchment on top of the ribs in the marinade and then cover the hotel pan tightly with aluminum foil. Braise in the oven until the meat pulls away from the bone and is fork-tender, 4 to 5 hours. Uncover pan and cool at room temperature, about 1 hour. Drain and discard the marinade and cut into individual ribs. Arrange the ribs in a single layer on 3 baking sheets. *The ribs can be baked 3 days in advance. Immediately store wrapped in the refrigerator.*

Honey-Lacquered Ribs, Creamy Corn and Edamame Succotash (page 171), **and Mediterranean Watermelon Salad** (page 163). **Oval porcelain platter and round nickel servers with round white porcelain bowls by Willow Group, Ltd.** (see Resources, page 347).

3. For the honey lacquer, put the canola oil and garlic into a cold 1½-qt/1.44-L saucepan. Cook the garlic over low heat until golden, about 12 minutes. Add the honey, soy sauce, Tabasco, and pepper. Whisk until combined.

The honey lacquer can be prepared 1 day in advance. Store wrapped in the refrigerator.

4. Raise the oven temperature to 400°F/204°C. Glaze the ribs with the honey lacquer. Return to the oven and bake until the glaze is bubbly and caramelized, 12 to 15 minutes. Top with the garnish(es).

Beef Fajitas. Mod Ideal platter by Front of the House
(see Resources, page 347).

BEEF FAJITAS

YIELD: 12 SERVINGS

LIME MARINADE

4 fl oz/120 mL lime juice

4 fl oz/120 mL soy sauce

4 fl oz/120 mL Worcestershire sauce

2¼ oz/64 g brown sugar (⅓ cup/80 mL packed)

1⅛ oz/32 g garlic paste (3 tbsp/45 mL or 9 cloves)
made with ½ tsp/1.5 g kosher salt

BEEF

4 lb 8 oz/2.04 kg trimmed beef flank steaks

1 fl oz/30 mL canola oil, plus as needed to oil grill grates

1 tsp/3 g kosher salt, plus as needed to adjust seasoning

1 tsp/2 g coarsely ground black pepper,
plus as needed to adjust seasoning

VEGETABLE GARNISH

3 fl oz/90 mL canola oil

3 Spanish onions, cut into ¼-in/6-mm-thick bâtonnet

2 tsp/6 g kosher salt, plus as needed to adjust seasoning

½ oz/14 g minced garlic (4 tsp/20 mL or 4 cloves)

2 tsp/2 g dried oregano

6 green, red, yellow, and/or orange
peppers, seeded, cut into bâtonnet

½ tsp/1 g coarsely ground black pepper,
plus as needed to adjust seasoning

½ oz/14 g cilantro pluches

CONDIMENTS

24 flour tortillas, 8 in/20 cm in diameter

32 fl oz/960 mL Guacamole (page 321)

32 fl oz/960 mL Pico de Gallo (page 315)

12 oz/340 g shredded cheddar cheese (3 cups/720 mL)

12 oz/340 g sour cream (1½ cups/360 mL)

12 lime wedges

1. For the marinade, whisk the lime juice, soy sauce, Worcestershire sauce, brown sugar, and garlic paste in a 2-gal/7.68-L zip-close plastic bag set into a 2-qt/1.92-L bowl for support. *The marinade can be made 3 days in advance. Store wrapped in the refrigerator.* Place the beef in the bag, coat with the marinade, and seal. Marinate, refrigerated, for 2 hours, turning occasionally.

2. Heat the grill to high. Clean, then oil, the grates. Remove the beef from the bag, drain, and discard the marinade, and let the beef come to room temperature for 20 minutes. Blot the beef dry and season with the salt and pepper. Brush with the canola oil. Place the steaks on the hot grill grates, presentation side down. To mark the steaks with a crosshatch, press each steak gently so its surface area is against the grates. Leave the meat undisturbed for 4 to 5 minutes. Adjust the heat. Then with the same side down, turn the steaks 90 degrees, press gently, and cook undisturbed for 4 to 5 minutes. Turn the steaks over and grill until medium-rare or they reach an internal temperature of 120°F/49°C, 4 to 5 minutes more. Place the steaks on a platter, tent with aluminum foil, and let rest for 10 minutes. *The steak can be grilled, but not sliced, 4 hours in advance. Store wrapped in the refrigerator.*

3. For the vegetables, warm a 12-in/30-cm sauté pan over medium heat, about 1 minute. Add the canola oil to the pan, and heat to hot but not smoking, about 30 seconds. Add the onions and 1 tsp/3 g salt. Lower the heat to medium-low and cook, tossing occasionally, until translucent and starting to brown, about about 15 minutes. Move the onions to one side of the pan. Add the garlic and oregano to the empty space and cook until fragrant, 1 minute. Combine and cook until the onions are golden, 15 to 20 minutes more. Put the contents in a 4-qt/3.84-L bowl, leaving the excess oil in the bottom of the pan.

4. Put all the peppers and the remaining 1 tsp/3 g of salt into the same pan. Over medium-high heat, cook, tossing occasionally, until the peppers are tender and caramelized, about 15 minutes. Put the cooked onions back into the pan with the peppers and cook together for 5 minutes, lowering the heat if necessary. Add the black pepper. Toss, taste, and adjust seasoning. *The peppers and onions can be cooked 1 day in advance. Store wrapped in the refrigerator. Warm in a sauté pan before proceeding.*

5. To serve, slice the beef against the grain and on the bias into ¼-in/6-mm-thick strips. Place the hot vegetables on a large serving platter and top with the beef and any juices. If the beef is chilled, fold together with the vegetables. Taste and adjust seasoning. Garnish with the cilantro and serve with the condiments.

CHICKEN FAJITAS: Replace the steak with trimmed boneless skinless chicken breast. Grill until the center is opaque and firm and reaches an internal temperature of 165°F/74°C.

CHICKEN EMPANADA FILLING: Finely mince the chicken breast. Marinate refrigerated for 30 minutes, then drain and discard the marinade. Reduce the salt and pepper for the chicken by half and toss it with the chicken. Heat a 12-in/30-cm sauté pan over medium-high heat. Add 1 fl oz/30 mL canola oil to the pan and heat to hot but not smoking, about 10 seconds. Add one-quarter of the chicken and stir-fry until the chicken is cooked and slightly browned, about 4 minutes. Place the chicken and any juices into a 4-qt/3.84-L bowl. Repeat with the remaining chicken, adding more oil as needed. Mince the onions and peppers. Cook as directed, reducing the cooking time as needed.

BEEF TENDERLOIN WITH PEPPERCORN CRUST

YIELD: 12 SERVINGS

2 fl oz/60 mL Burgundy or dry red wine

2 fl oz/60 mL soy sauce

2 fl oz/60 mL Worcestershire sauce

2 fl oz/60 mL lemon juice (about 2 lemons)

1½ oz/43 g honey (2 tbsp/30 mL)

2 oz/57 g Dijon mustard (¼ cup/60 mL)

4 lb 8 oz/2.04 kg completely trimmed beef tenderloins, tied to hold their shape with butcher's twine

1 fl oz/30 mL canola oil, plus as needed to oil grill grates

1 tsp/3 g kosher salt

1 tbsp/6 g coarsely crushed black peppercorns

1. Whisk the wine, soy sauce, Worcestershire sauce, lemon juice, and honey in a 2-gal/7.68-L zip-close plastic bag set in a 2-qt/1.92-L bowl for support. *The marinade can be made 3 days in advance. Store wrapped in the refrigerator.* Rub the mustard all over the tenderloins. Place the tenderloins in the bag, coat with the marinade, and seal. Marinate, refrigerated, for at least 4 hours and up to 1 day, turning occasionally.

2. Heat the grill to high. Clean, then oil, the grates. Let the tenderloins come to room temperature for 30 minutes. Blot the beef dry, sprinkle on the salt, and brush with the canola oil. Place on the hot grill grates. Lower the grill cover or use an aluminum foil pan to cover the meat. Leave the meat undisturbed for 3 minutes. Adjust the heat to control flare-ups, keeping it as hot as possible. Give the meat a quarter turn and grill, covered, 2 to 3 minutes more. Then give a quarter turn 2 more times and grill until evenly charred, 2 to 3 minutes more for each turn. The beef should be very rare. Place the meat on a sheet pan. *The beef can be grilled 4 hours in advance. Cool rapidly and immediately store wrapped in the refrigerator.*

3. Position a rack in the bottom third of the oven and heat it to 450°F/232°C. Remove and discard the butcher's twine. Evenly pat on the crushed peppercorns. Roast in the oven until the beef is rare to medium-rare or reaches an internal temperature of 115° to 120°F/46° to 49°C, 10 to 15 minutes. Loosely tent with aluminum foil, and let the meat rest for 20 minutes before slicing against the grain.

For an hors d'oeuvre dinner party, prepare a Beef Tenderloin Crostini with Horseradish Crème: Thinly slice the beef. Spread 1½ tsp/7.5 mL Horseradish Crème (page 321) over a piece of Crostini (page 333). Top with a slice of the tenderloin and a dollop of Horseradish Crème and minced chives. Or, for another garnish, use Gorgonzola, Bacon, and Toasted Walnut Crème (page 320).

**Beef Tenderloin Crostini with Horseradish Crème. Oval por-
celain platter by Willow Group, Ltd.** (see Resources, page 347).

Crusted Beef Tenderloin with Green Beans with Cashew Butter (page 179)

CRUSTED BEEF TENDERLOIN

YIELD: 12 SERVINGS

CRUST

4 oz/113 g unsalted butter (½ cup/120 mL), plus as needed to adjust crust

¼ oz/7 g minced garlic (2 tsp/10 mL or 2 cloves)

1 oz/28 g freshly toasted bread crumbs, coarsely ground (1½ cups/360 mL; page 116) or panko

¼ oz/7 g chopped flat-leaf parsley (2 tbsp/30 mL)

⅛ oz/3 g chopped thyme leaves (1 tbsp/15 mL)

⅛ oz/3 g basil chiffonnade (1 tbsp/15 mL) or 1 tsp/5 mL Basil Purée (page 323)

1½ tsp/1 g chopped marjoram leaves

1 tsp/3 g kosher salt, plus as needed to adjust seasoning

½ tsp/1 g coarsely ground black pepper, plus as needed to adjust seasoning

¼ tsp/0.5 g red pepper flakes, plus as needed to adjust seasoning

MUSTARD COATING

4 oz/113 g Dijon mustard (½ cup/120 mL)

2 oz/57 g unsalted butter, room temperature (¼ cup/60 mL)

BEEF TENDERLOIN

4 lb 8 oz/2.04 kg completely trimmed beef tenderloins, tied to hold their shape with butcher's twine

1 fl oz/30 mL canola oil, plus as needed, for grill grates

4 tsp/12 g kosher salt

1½ tsp/3 g crushed black peppercorns, plus as needed to adjust seasoning

1. For the crust, melt the butter in a 10-in/25-cm sauté pan over low heat. Add the garlic and cook until the butter and garlic start to turn golden, about 10 minutes. Remove from the heat. Add the bread crumbs, parsley, thyme, basil, marjoram, salt, black pepper, and red pepper flakes. Toss, taste, and adjust seasoning. The bread crumbs should be moist and hold their shape when pinched together. If not, add more melted butter a tablespoon at a time until it does. *The herb crust can be made in advance. Store in a plastic bag in the refrigerator for 1 day or in the freezer for 3 months.*

2. For the mustard coating, stir the mustard and butter together until evenly combined. *The mustard coating can be made 1 week in advance. Store covered in the refrigerator.*

3. Heat the grill to high. Clean, then oil, the grates. Let the tenderloin come to room temperature for 30 minutes. Blot the beef dry, evenly season with the salt and pepper, and brush with the oil. Place on the hot grill grates. Lower the grill cover or use an aluminum foil pan to cover the meat. Leave the meat undisturbed for 3 minutes. Adjust the heat to control flare-ups, keeping it as hot as possible. Give the meat a quarter turn and grill, covered, 2 to 3 minutes, then give a quarter turn 2 more times and grill until evenly charred, 2 to 3 minutes more for each turn. The beef should be very rare. Place the meat on a sheet pan. *The beef can be grilled 4 hours in advance. Cool rapidly and immediately store wrapped in the refrigerator.*

4. Position a rack in the bottom third of the oven and heat it to 450°F/232°C. Remove and discard the butcher's twine. Evenly paint a thick mustard coating on top of the tenderloin. Pat the bread crumbs on top of the mustard, forming about a ¼-in/6-mm-thick crust. Roast in the oven until the bread crumbs are golden but the beef is rare to medium-rare or reaches an internal temperature of 115°/46° to 120°F/49°C, 10 to 15 minutes. If the crust is not crispy or golden enough, brown under the broiler on high heat for about 1 minute. Loosely tent with aluminum foil, and let the meat rest for 20 minutes before slicing against the grain.

PECAN-STUDDED CHICKEN

YIELD: 12 SERVINGS

SEASONED FLOUR

10 oz/284 g unbleached all-purpose flour (2 cups/480 mL)

4 tsp/12 g kosher salt

½ tsp/1 g ground black pepper

EGG WASH

6 eggs

1 tsp/3 g kosher salt

2 fl oz/60 mL milk

PECAN FLOUR

1 lb 6½ oz/638g unbleached all-purpose flour (4½ cups/1.06 L)

12 oz/340 g raw pecans, finely chopped (3 cups/720 mL)

4 tbsp/40 g kosher salt

2 tbsp/30 g Cajun Spice (page 333)

CHICKEN

4 lb 8 oz/2 kg trimmed boneless skinless chicken breasts

24 fl oz/720 mL canola oil, plus as needed, to pan fry the chicken

Kosher salt, as needed to adjust seasoning

1. For the seasoned flour, combine all the ingredients in a 2-qt/1.92-L shallow bowl. For the egg wash, whisk all the ingredients in a second 2-qt/1.92-L shallow bowl until thoroughly combined. For the pecan flour, combine all the ingredients in a third 2-qt/1.92-L shallow bowl. *The flours can be made in advance. Store in a plastic bag in the refrigerator for 2 days or in the freezer for 3 months.* Line up the bowls in order they were filled for standard breading procedure.

2. For the chicken, pound the breasts between 2 sheets of waxed paper to an even ¼-in/6-mm thickness. Cut the chicken into 1½-in/4-cm-wide strips lengthwise. Evenly toss half of the chicken with the seasoned flour in the first bowl. Lift 1 chicken strip out of the flour, shake off any excess, and dip into the egg wash, letting excess drip back into the bowl. Press into the pecan flour, patting on to evenly coat. Lay the coated chicken on a parchment-lined sheet pan. Repeat with the remaining chicken, using parchment paper to separate the layers.

3. Fill a 16-in/41-cm nonstick sautoir with oil so it is about 1 in/3 cm deep. The oil should be deep enough so the chicken strips float. Warm the oil over medium heat to 350°F/177°C, about 6 minutes. It is hot enough when a small piece of chicken causes the oil to immediately sizzle but takes about 1 minute to begin browning. The pecan coating is delicate and will burn if the chicken rests on the bottom of the pan or if the oil is too hot. Carefully place enough chicken strips into the oil to fill the pan without touching. Adjust the heat so the oil sizzles but does not smoke or burn. Fry the chicken, turning several times, until it is golden brown, the center is opaque and firm, and it reaches an internal temperature of 165°F/74°C, about 4 minutes. Place the cooked chicken on a cooling rack lined with paper towels. Finish with a sprinkle of salt. Repeat with all the chicken. Between batches, skim all loose pieces of batter from oil with a fine-mesh strainer and discard. Replace the oil as needed to maintain depth. The oil may have to be changed once between batches.

Serve with Raspberry Coulis (page 305) or Honey Mustard (page 327).

Pecan-Studded Chicken with Raspberry Coulis (page 305). **Mission chafer alternatives, cast-iron griddle with brackets by CAL-MIL** (see Resources, page 347).

Chicken Milanese, Artichoke, Caper, and Lemon Sauce (page 313), and Lemon Sauce (page 313). Ornate wrought-iron chafers by American Metalcraft, Inc. (see Resources, page 347).

CHICKEN MILANESE

YIELD: 12 SERVINGS

SEASONED FLOUR

10 oz/284 g unbleached all-purpose flour (2 cups/480 mL)

5 tsp/15 g kosher salt

1 tsp/2 g ground black pepper

EGG WASH

6 eggs

2 fl oz/60 mL milk

BREAD CRUMB COATING

12 oz/340 g freshly toasted bread crumbs
(6 cups/1.44 L; page 116) or panko

9 oz/255 g finely shredded Pecorino
Romano (3 cups/720 mL)

1½ tsp/5 g kosher salt, plus as needed to adjust seasoning

¼ tsp/0.5 g ground black pepper

CHICKEN

4 lb 8 oz/2.04 kg trimmed boneless skinless chicken breasts

16 fl oz/480 mL extra-virgin olive oil, Italian
preferred, plus as needed to fry the chicken

1 tsp/3 g kosher salt, plus as needed to adjust seasoning

¼ tsp/0.5 g ground black pepper

12 lemon wedges

1. For the seasoned flour, combine all the ingredients in a 2-qt/1.92-L shallow bowl. For the egg wash, whisk the ingredients in a second 2-qt/1.92-L shallow bowl until thoroughly combined. For the bread crumb coating, combine all the ingredients in a third 2-qt/1.92-L shallow bowl. Line up the bowls in the order they were filled for standard breading procedure. *The seasoned flour and bread crumb coating can be made in advance. Store in plastic bags in the refrigerator for 2 days or in the freezer for 3 months.*

2. Pound the chicken breasts between 2 sheets of waxed paper to an even ¼-in/6-mm thickness. Blot the chicken dry. Toss the breasts with 1 fl oz/30 mL olive oil and the salt and pepper to evenly coat. Coat 1 breast at a time with the flour in the first bowl. Lift out of the flour, shake off the excess, and dip into the egg, letting the excess drip back into the bowl. Press into the bread crumbs in the last bowl, patting to evenly coat both sides. Lay the coated chicken on a parchment-lined sheet pan. Repeat with the remaining chicken, using parchment paper to separate the layers. *The chicken can be breaded 4 hours in advance. Immediately store wrapped in the refrigerator.*

3. Fill a 12-in/30-cm sauté pan with about 8 fl oz/240 mL oil, to about ¼ in/6 mm deep. The oil should be deep enough to go two-thirds up the side of the chicken breasts. Heat the oil over medium heat to 350°F/177°C, 5 to 6 minutes. It is hot enough when a small piece of chicken causes the oil to immediately sizzle but takes 1 minute to begin browning. Carefully place enough chicken into the oil to fill the pan without touching. Adjust the heat so the oil sizzles but does not smoke or burn. Pan fry the chicken until the bottom is golden brown, 2½ to 3 minutes, then turn over and continue cooking until the chicken is evenly browned, the center is opaque and firm, and it reaches an internal temperature of 165°F/74°C, 2 to 2½ minutes more.

4. Place the cooked chicken on a cooling rack lined with paper towels. Finish with a sprinkle of salt. Repeat with all the chicken. Between batches, skim all loose pieces of batter from oil with a fine-mesh strainer and discard. Replace the oil as needed to maintain depth. The oil may have to be changed once between batches. Garnish with the lemon wedges. *The chicken can be fried 4 hours in advance. Rapidly cool completely, then store wrapped in the refrigerator. Bake at 425°F/218°C on a sheet pan in a single layer without touching until hot and crispy, 12 to 15 minutes.*

Chicken Milanese also makes great chicken fingers for an hors d'oeuvre. Possible dips are Sun-Dried Tomato Jam (page 325) or Cranberry-Bourbon Relish (page 317). It can also be prepared with veal cutlets, pork chops, or pork cutlets. Pan fry these meats to an internal temperature of 145°F/63°C.

MOROCCAN CHICKEN AND CARROT SAUTÉ

YIELD: 12 SERVINGS

CARROTS AND ONIONS

2 fl oz/60 mL olive oil

1 lb 2 oz/510 g Spanish onions, cut into julienne (4 cups/960 mL or about 2 large onions)

2 tsp/6 g salt

2 lb/907 g carrots, cut into julienne (8 cups/1.92 L)

2 tbsp/30 mL cold water

MOROCCAN RUB

4 fl oz/120 mL soy sauce

1½ oz/43 g finely minced ginger (¼ cup/60 mL)

¾ oz/21 g minced garlic (2 tbsp/30 mL or 6 cloves)

1 tsp/3 g kosher salt, plus as needed to adjust seasoning

4 tsp/9 g ground cumin

4 tsp/9 g ground turmeric

2 tsp/4 g ground coriander

1 tsp/2 g cayenne

CHICKEN

4 lb 8 oz/2.04 kg trimmed boneless skinless chicken breasts

Olive oil, as needed to cook chicken

¾ tsp/1.5 g ground black pepper, plus as needed to adjust seasoning

2 oz/57 g chopped cilantro or flat-leaf parsley (1 cup/240 mL)

2 oz/57 g green onions, sliced ⅛ in/3 mm thick on the bias (1 cup/ 240 mL or about 8 green onions)

GARNISHES

2 oz/57 g toasted sliced almonds (⅔ cup/160 mL; page 114)

2½ oz/71 g toasted sesame seeds (½ cup/120 mL; page 114)

1. For the carrots and onions, warm a 12-inch/30-cm sauté pan over medium-high heat, about 1 minute.

Add the olive oil and warm to hot but not smoking, about 10 seconds. Add the onions and 1 tsp/3 g salt. Lower the heat to medium-low and cook, tossing occasionally, until the onions are starting to brown, about 15 minutes. Add the carrots, the cold water, and 1 tsp/3 g salt. Raise the heat to medium-high, cover, and cook until the carrots are almost tender, about 10 minutes. Remove the lid and cook until the moisture evaporates and vegetables caramelize, about 10 minutes more. Transfer the contents to a 4-qt/3.84-L bowl. *The onions and carrots can be cooked 1 day in advance. Store wrapped in the refrigerator.*

2. For the Moroccan rub, whisk all the ingredients together in a 2-qt/1.92-L bowl. *The rub can be prepared 3 days in advance. Immediately store wrapped in the refrigerator.* Pound the chicken between 2 sheets of waxed paper to an even ¼-in/6-mm thickness. Cut the chicken into ¼-in/6-mm-wide strips.

3. Blot the chicken dry and coat it with the Moroccan rub. Add 2 fl oz/60 mL oil to a 16-in/30-cm nonstick sauté pan and warm over medium heat, about 2 minutes, so the chicken sizzles when it hits the pan. Carefully place small batches of chicken into the pan so the pieces are not touching but fill the pan. Cook the chicken, undisturbed, until the bottom is browned, about 1½ minutes. Adjust the heat, if necessary, so the pan is as hot as possible but does not scorch. Flip the chicken over and cook until it is evenly browned, about 1½ minutes more, and then stir-fry until the center is opaque and firm and reaches an internal temperature of 165°F/74°C, about 1 minute more. Place the cooked chicken into the bowl with the vegetables, leaving as much oil as possible in the pan. Repeat with the remaining chicken, adding oil as necessary. The pan may have to be rinsed and wiped between batches if it starts to blacken or scorch. *The chicken can be cooked 4 hours in advance and stored with the carrots. Quickly cool, then store wrapped in the refrigerator.*

4. Return the chicken and vegetables to the sauté pan and warm. Add the black pepper, cilantro, and green onions and toss, taste, and adjust seasoning. Garnish with the almonds and sesame seeds.

This can be served wrapped in a Naan (page 262) or with rice.

Moroccan Chicken and Carrot Sauté. 3.5-in tagine by Front of the House (see Resources, page 347).

Rosemary-Sage Grilled Chicken Kebobs. Mission chafer alternatives by CAL-MIL (see Resources, page 347).

ROSEMARY-SAGE GRILLED CHICKEN

YIELD: 12 SERVINGS

MARINADE

4½ fl oz/135 mL red wine vinegar

1½ oz/43 g Dijon mustard (3 tbsp/45 mL)

½ oz/14 g chopped garlic (4 tsp/20 mL or 4 cloves)

1¼ oz/43 g chopped shallot (¼ cup/60 mL)

2 tbsp/20 g kosher salt

¾ tsp/1.5 g ground black pepper

½ tsp/1 g granulated sugar

12 fl oz/360 g olive oil

1½ oz/43 g chopped flat-leaf parsley (¾ cup/180 mL)

¼ oz/7 g sage (2 tbsp/30 mL)

¼ oz/7 g rosemary (2 tbsp/30 mL)

¼ oz/7 g thyme (2 tbsp/30 mL)

CHICKEN

4 lb 8 oz/2.04 kg trimmed boneless skinless chicken breasts (twelve 6-oz/170-g breasts)

Canola oil as needed to oil grill grates

1. For the marinade, put the vinegar, mustard, garlic, shallot, salt, pepper, and sugar into a blender. Run the motor until smooth, first on the lowest setting for 30 seconds and then on the highest setting for 30 seconds. Slowly drizzle in the olive oil with the motor running on the lowest speed, taking about 1 minute. Continue to blend until thick and emulsified, about 30 seconds more. *The marinade can be made 1 week in advance. Store wrapped in the refrigerator and shake to emulsify. Add the herbs just before using.*

2. Just before using, whisk the parsley, sage, rosemary, and thyme into the marinade. Reserve 3 fl oz/90 mL of the marinade and pour the rest into a 2-gal/7.68-L zip-close plastic bag set into a 2-qt/1.92-L bowl for support. Pound the chicken between 2 sheets of waxed paper to an even ½-in/1.25-cm thickness. Place the chicken in the bag, coat with the marinade, and seal. Refrigerate for 2 to 6 hours.

3. Heat the grill to high. Clean, then oil, the grates. Remove the chicken from the bag, drain, and discard the marinade, and let the chicken drain on a rack for 20 minutes. Place the chicken on the hot grill grates presentation side down. To mark the chicken with a crosshatch, press each cutlet gently so its entire surface area is against the grates. Leave undisturbed for 2 to 3 minutes. Adjust the heat, if necessary, to control flare-ups or burning. Then, with the same side down, turn the chicken 90 degrees, press gently, and cook undisturbed for 2 to 3 minutes more. Turn the chicken over and grill until the center is opaque and firm and reaches an internal temperature of 165°F/74°C, about 3 minutes more. Place the chicken on a platter, tent with aluminum foil, and let rest for 10 minutes. Serve drizzled with the reserved marinade that did not come into contact with the chicken.

For a party without tables to sit at, serve kebobs: Cut the chicken into 1-in/3-cm cubes and prepare 1-in/3-cm cubes of red and yellow peppers and halved cremini mushrooms. To cook with bamboo skewers on a grill, see page 117.

The marinade also works well with lamb. Grill until the lamb is pink in the center and reaches an internal temperature of 140°F/60°C.

TUSCAN BRAISED PORK SHANKS

YIELD: 12 SERVINGS

BRAISING LIQUID

64 fl oz/1.92 L Chablis or other dry, un-oaky white wine

2 fl oz/60 mL canola oil

2 lb 9 oz/1.16 kg coarsely chopped onions (about 9 cups/2.16 L)

1 tbsp/10 g kosher salt, plus as needed to adjust seasoning

1 lb/454 g coarsely chopped carrots (about 3 cups/720 mL)

1 lb/454 g coarsely chopped celery (about 3 cups/720 mL)

1⅛ oz/32 g minced garlic (3 tbsp/45 mL or 9 cloves)

1½ fl oz/45 mL tomato paste

1 tsp/2 g dried porcini mushroom powder (see Note)

6 thyme sprigs

6 rosemary sprigs

6 oregano

4 bay leaves

8 black peppercorns

64 fl oz/1.92 L canned peeled whole plum tomatoes in tomato juice, no salt added, broken up into small pieces

88 fl oz/2.64 L chicken stock or low-sodium chicken broth

Ground black pepper, as needed to adjust seasoning

PORK SHANKS

5 oz/142 g unbleached all-purpose flour (1 cup/240 mL)

8 tsp/24 g kosher salt

1 tsp/2 g ground black pepper

12 pork shanks (about 1 lb/454 g each), knob removed

8 fl oz/240 mL canola oil

1 batch Roasted Tomato Ragù (page 209)

1 lb 8 oz oz/680 g cooked cannellini beans (4 cups/960 mL)

3 lb 8 oz/1.59 kg trimmed broccoli rabe, chopped into 1-in/3-cm pieces, blanched until tender (page 173)

Kosher salt, as needed to adjust seasoning

Ground black pepper, as needed to adjust seasoning

1. For the braising liquid, slowly reduce the wine in a 12-in/30-cm sauté pan over medium-low heat, so there are wisps of steam and very tiny bubbles but it is not simmering, to half the original volume, about 1½ hours. *The wine can be reduced 2 weeks in advance. Store wrapped in the refrigerator.*

2. Heat a wide-mouth 6-qt/5.76-L saucepan over medium heat, about 1 minute. Add 1½ fl oz/45 mL canola oil to the pan, raise the heat to medium-high, and heat to hot but not smoking, about 20 seconds. Add the onions. If using low-sodium broth, lessen the salt to 1 tsp/3 g. Lower the heat to medium and cook until the onions are soft and jammy, about 20 minutes. Add the carrot and celery and cook until they are deep golden, about 20 minutes more. Move the vegetables to one side of the pan. Add ½ fl oz/15 mL canola oil and the garlic to the empty space and cook until fragrant, about 1 minute. Add the tomato paste, dried mushroom powder, thyme, rosemary, oregano, bay leaves, and peppercorns to the empty space with the garlic and cook until fragrant, about 2 minutes. Mix all the ingredients together and cook until the tomato paste is a deep rust color and smells sweet, about 5 minutes. Add the tomatoes in tomato juice and stir all the ingredients together. Simmer for 5 minutes more. Add the stock and reduced wine and scrape the bottom to incorporate any brown bits. Bring to a simmer and taste and adjust seasoning. *The braising liquid can be made 3 days in advance. Rapidly cool, then immediately store wrapped in the refrigerator. Reheat to a simmer before using.*

3. For the pork shanks, combine the flour, salt, and pepper in a flat-bottomed 2-qt/1.92-L bowl. Blot the meat dry and evenly coat in the flour, shaking off any excess. Heat a 16-in/41-cm nonstick sauté pan over medium heat, about 1 minute. Add 2 fl oz/60 mL canola oil to the pan, raise the heat to medium-high, and heat to hot but not smoking, about 20 seconds, so the meat sizzles when it hits the pan. Carefully place enough pork shanks in a single layer so they fill pan without touching and cook undisturbed until the bottom is deep brown, about 3 minutes. Adjust the heat, if necessary, so the pan does not scorch. Turn the pork and cook until deep brown on all sides, 6 to 8 minutes more. Place the browned pork into a braising pan measuring 18 by 24 in/45 by 61 cm in a single layer. Repeat with the remaining meat, adding more oil as needed. Remove the

Tuscan Braised Pork Shanks. Oval porcelain platter by Willow Group, Ltd. (see Resources, page 347).

sauté pan from the heat, drain the fat, and if the bottom of the pan has not burned, add about 2 cups stock, scraping up any fond on the bottom of the pan, and pour back with the other stock.

4. Position a rack in the bottom third of the oven and heat it to 225°F/107°C. Pour the stock and all the vegetables into the braising pan with the pork. Cover the meat with parchment paper touching it, and completely seal the pan with aluminum foil. Place it in the oven and braise for 1 hour, then reduce the heat to as low as the oven will go or 200°F/93°C and continue to braise until fork-tender, 5 to 6 hours more.

5. Remove from the oven and allow the pork shanks to rest in the sauce for 1 hour at room temperature. Then chill rapidly, wrap, and refrigerate them until the meat has firmed, at least 2 hours. *The pork shanks can be braised 3 days in advance. Actually, the dish is better the next day.*

6. Heat the oven to 300°F/149°C. Remove any grease that has hardened on the top of the sauce. Strain the sauce into a 6-qt/5.76-L saucepan, discarding any solids, and warm over medium-high heat until it starts to simmer.

7. Pour all but 9 cups/2.16 L of the hot sauce over the pork shanks set in the braising pan, cover with parchment paper, and seal with aluminum foil. Warm in the oven until hot, 45 to 55 minutes, turning them several times so they stay moist and form a glaze.

8. Add the tomato ragù to the sauce remaining in the saucepan and simmer over medium heat until it has a good flavor and consistency as a finishing sauce. It should be nappé, or thick enough to coat the back of a spoon. Add the beans and simmer for 5 to 10 minutes. Just before serving, add the broccoli rabe and heat through. Taste and adjust seasoning, adjusting the viscosity or amount with the sauce the shanks were reheated in. Remove the pork shanks from the roasting pan and top with the broccoli rabe and cannellini bean sauce.

———

To make dried porcini mushroom powder, grind dried porcini mushrooms in a spice grinder until they are reduced to fine dust. Sift the dust through a fine-mesh strainer.

ROCK CORNISH GAME HENS STUFFED WITH WILD RICE, APPLES, AND DRIED CRANBERRIES

YIELD: 12 SERVINGS

12 Rock Cornish game hens, 1 lb 4 oz/567 g each

1 tbsp/10 g kosher salt, plus as needed to adjust seasoning

1½ tsp/3 g ground black pepper, plus as needed to adjust seasoning

1 batch Wild Rice with Apples and Dried Cranberries (page 161)

6 fl oz/180 mL clarified butter (¾ cup/180 mL)

½ batch Lemon Sauce, without parsley added (page 313)

1 oz/28 g minced flat-leaf parsley (½ cup/120 mL)

1. Trim any excess fat and skin from the hens. Remove the wing tips and reserve. Season the cavity of each hen with the salt and pepper and loosely stuff with the wild rice mixture. Truss each hen with butcher's twine. Place any extra stuffing in a separate baking pan, cover with parchment paper, seal with aluminum foil, and reserve in the refrigerator. Rub the skin of the hens with the butter and place on a rack in a roasting pan measuring 18 by 24 in/46 by 61 cm. Place the reserved wing tips in the bottom of the pan.

2. Roast in a 400°F/204°C oven, basting every 15 minutes with butter, until golden brown and the center of the stuffing reaches an internal temperature of 165°F/74°C, 45 to 55 minutes. Bake the reserved wild rice mixture to an internal temperature of 165°F/74°C, 20 to 25 minutes. Remove the hens from the roasting pan, loosely tent with foil, and let rest for 10 minutes.

3. Deglaze the roasting pan with the lemon sauce, scraping up all bits from the bottom. Strain the sauce through a fine-mesh strainer into a saucepan, discarding all solids, and return to a simmer until it is reduced to the correct viscosity. Degrease, taste, and adjust seasoning. Add the parsley. Serve with the hens and extra stuffing.

Rock Cornish Game Hens Stuffed with Wild Rice, Apples, and Dried Cranberries. Roasting pan by Le Creuset (see Resources, page 347).

BUTTERMILK GRILLED CHICKEN

YIELD: 12 SERVINGS

BUTTERMILK MARINADE

16 fl oz/480 mL low-fat buttermilk

4 tsp/12 g kosher salt

2 tsp/4 g Cajun Spice (page 333)

CHICKEN

4 lb 8 oz/2.04 kg trimmed boneless skinless chicken breasts (twelve 6-oz/170-g breasts)

2 fl oz/60 mL canola oil, plus as needed to oil grill grates

1. Whisk the buttermilk, salt, and Cajun spice in a 2-gal/7.68-L zip-close plastic bag set into a 2-qt/1.92-L bowl for support. Pound the chicken between 2 sheets of waxed paper to an even ¾-in/2-cm thickness. Place the chicken in the bag, coat with the marinade, and seal. Refrigerate for 6 hours to 3 days.

2. Heat a grill to high. Clean, then oil the grates. Remove the chicken from the bag, drain, and discard the marinade, and let the chicken drain on a rack and come to room temperature for 20 minutes. Brush both sides of the breasts with the canola oil. Place the chicken on the hot grill grates presentation side down. To mark the chicken with a cross-hatch, press each cutlet gently so its surface area is against the grates. Adjust the heat to medium to control flare-ups or burning. Lower the grill lid or cover the chicken with an aluminum foil pan and leave the meat undisturbed for 2 minutes. Then, with the same side down, turn the chicken 90 degrees, press gently, and cook covered and undisturbed for 2 to 3 minutes more. Turn the chicken over and grill covered again until the center is opaque and firm and reaches an internal temperature of 165°F/74°C, about 3 minutes more. Place the chicken on a platter, tent with aluminum foil, and let rest for 5 minutes before serving.

This simple chicken preparation lends itself to an assortment of sauces. Offer a seasonal trio from which each guest can choose, such as Roma Salsa (page 316), Guacamole (page 321), and Macadamia-Pignoli Pesto (page 323); Fire-Roasted Red Pepper Coulis (page 327), Sun-Dried Tomato Jam (page 325), and Fig-Onion Jam (page 326); or Cranberry-Bourbon Relish (page 317), Onion Marmalade (page 326), and Honey Mustard (page 327).

SOUTHERN FRIED CHICKEN STICKS: Double the buttermilk marinade. Pound the chicken in step 1 and then cut the breasts lengthwise into 1½-in/3-cm-wide strips. Marinate in buttermilk. For seasoned flour coating, combine 1 lb 6½ oz/637 g unbleached all-purpose flour (4½ cups/1.08 L), 2 tbsp/30 g Cajun Spice (page 333), and 1 tbsp/10 g kosher salt in a 2-qt/1.92-L shallow bowl. Lift 1 chicken strip out of the buttermilk, letting the excess drip back into the bowl and press into the seasoned flour, patting on to evenly coat. Dip back into buttermilk and then again into seasoned flour. Lay the coated chicken on a parchment-lined sheet pan. Repeat with the remaining chicken, using parchment paper to separate the layers. Pan fry as described in step 5 of Sesame Chicken on the following page.

SESAME CHICKEN

MARINADE

4 fl oz/120 mL sesame oil

2 fl oz/60 mL soy sauce

2 fl oz/60 mL mirin

2 fl oz/60 mL tahini paste

2¾ oz/78 g dark brown sugar (6 tbsp/90 mL firmly packed)

SESAME COATING

12 oz/340 g freshly toasted bread crumbs (6 cups/1.44 L; page 116) or panko

10 oz/284 g sesame seeds (2 cups/480 mL)

1½ tbsp/10 g ground ginger

1½ tbsp/10 g garlic powder

1½ tsp/4.5 g kosher salt

CHICKEN

4 lb 8 oz/2 kg trimmed boneless skinless chicken breasts

12 fl oz/360 mL canola oil, plus as needed, to fry the chicken

1. For the marinade, whisk all the ingredients in a 2-gal/7.5-L zip-close plastic bag set into a 2-qt/1.92-L bowl for support. *The marinade can be made in advance. Store wrapped in the refrigerator for 3 days.*

2. For the sesame coating, combine all the ingredients in a 4-qt/3.84-L bowl shallow bowl. *The coating can be made in advance. Store wrapped at room temperature for 2 days or in the freezer for 3 months.*

3. For the chicken, pound the chicken breasts between 2 sheets of waxed paper to an even thickness of ¼ in/ 6 mm. Place the chicken in the bag and coat with the marinade. Squeeze the air out of the bag and seal. Refrigerate for 2 hours, turning occasionally.

4. Take a piece of chicken out of the plastic bag, letting excess marinade drip back into the bag, and discard the marinade. Press it in the bread crumb mixture, patting on as much as possible. Lay the coated chicken on a sheet pan. Repeat with the remaining chicken, using parchment paper to separate the layers.

5. Fill a 16-in/41-cm nonstick sauté pan with oil about ¼ in/6 mm deep. The oil should be deep enough to go two-thirds up the sides of the chicken breasts. Over medium heat, heat the oil to 350°F/177°C, 5 to 6 minutes. It is hot enough when a small piece of chicken causes the oil to immediately sizzle but takes 1 minute to begin browning. Carefully place enough chicken into the oil to fill the pan without touching. Adjust the heat so the oil sizzles but does not smoke or burn. Pan fry the chicken until the bottom is golden brown, 2½ to 3 minutes, then turn over and continue cooking until evenly browned, the center is opaque and firm, and it reaches an internal temperature of 165°F/74°C, 2 to 2½ minutes more. Place the cooked chicken on a cooling rack lined with paper towels. Repeat with all the chicken. Between batches, skim all loose pieces of coating from the oil with a fine-mesh strainer and discard. Adjust the heat so the oil does not smoke or burn. Replace the oil as needed to maintain depth. The oil may have to be changed once between batches. *The chicken can be fried 4 hours in advance. Rapidly cool, then store wrapped in the refrigerator. Bake at 425°F/218°C on a sheet pan in a single layer without touching until hot and crispy, 10 to 12 minutes.*

To serve as an hors d'oeuvre, thread ½-in/1.25-cm-wide strips onto bamboo skewers that have been soaked in warm water for 20 minutes before pan frying.

Duck Confit with Blueberry-Port Sauce and Coconut-Almond Quinoa (page 159)

DUCK CONFIT WITH BLUEBERRY-PORT SAUCE

YIELD: 12 SERVINGS

CONFIT

24 Moulard duck leg quarters (leg and thigh)

16 fl oz/480 mL duck fat and canola
oil, as needed, to cover legs

CONFIT CURE MIX

2 oz/57 g garlic cloves (16 cloves)

1 lb 2 oz/510 g Spanish onions, coarsely
chopped (4 cups/960 mL or 2 onions)

1 bunch flat-leaf parsley, leaves and stems,
coarsely chopped (4 oz/113 g)

2¼ oz/64 g fine sea salt or table salt (not kosher salt)

1¼ oz/35 g black peppercorns (¼ cup/60 mL)

⅔ oz/17 g light brown sugar (2 tbsp/30 mL)

¼ oz/7 g thyme (2 tbsp/30 mL)

4 bay leaves

BLUEBERRY-PORT SAUCE

Duck thigh bones reserved from confit

1½ fl oz/45 mL canola oil

5 oz/142 g minced shallots (1 cup/240 mL)

½ tsp/1.5 g kosher salt, plus as needed to adjust seasoning

2½ oz/71 g chopped carrots (½ cup/120 mL)

2½ oz/71 g chopped celery (½ cup/120 mL)

¼ oz/7 g minced garlic (2 tsp/ mL or 2 cloves)

32 fl oz/960 mL cold water

2 flat-leaf parsley stems

2 sprigs thyme

5 cracked black peppercorns

1 bay leaf

3½ oz/99 g granulated sugar

3½ fl oz/105 mL port, plus as needed to adjust seasoning

2 fl oz/60 mL red wine vinegar

6 cups/1.44 L blueberries, picked over

½ tsp/2 g kosher salt, plus as needed to adjust seasoning

¼ tsp/0.5 g ground black pepper, plus
as needed to adjust seasoning

⅛ tsp/0.25 cayenne, plus as needed to adjust seasoning

2 oz/57 g unsalted butter, cut into
¼-in/6-mm pats (¼ cup/60 mL)

GARNISH

2 cups/480 mL blueberries, picked over

1. For the duck legs, remove the thigh bones from the duck legs, being careful not to cut through the skin. Reserve the thigh bones for the stock for the blueberry-port sauce below. Trim any excess fat and skin from the duck with kitchen shears. Place all fat and skin into a 2-qt/1.92-L pot and, over low heat, render the fat for 1 to 1½ hours. Strain, discarding all solids. *The duck fat can be rendered in advance. Store wrapped and in the refrigerator for 3 weeks or in the freezer for 3 months.*

2. For the confit cure mix, drop the garlic cloves one at a time into a food processor fitted with a steel blade with the motor running and process until finely chopped, about 10 seconds. Turn off the motor and add the onion, parsley, salt, peppercorns, brown sugar, thyme, and bay leaves. Run the motor until all the vegetables are puréed. *The cure mix can be made 1 day in advance. Store wrapped and in the refrigerator.*

3. Evenly divide the cure and the duck legs between two 2-gal/7.68-zip-close plastic bags, each set into a 2-qt/1.92-L bowl for support. Coat the duck well, rubbing the cure onto each leg. Press out the air and seal the bags. Cure the duck legs, refrigerated, for 1 to 2 days.

4. Position a rack in the bottom third of the oven and heat to 300°F/149°C. Remove the duck legs from the bags, discarding all cure mix. Rinse all the cure off of the legs and pat dry the legs dry with paper towels. Place the legs in a single layer in one shallow hotel pan. They can be touching. Heat the fat to a simmer and carefully pour enough over the legs to cover, adding canola oil if necessary. Bake in the oven until the meat falls off the bone, 3½ to 4 hours. Cool the duck legs in the fat at room temperature for 1 hour. Then rapidly chill and refrigerate the duck legs covered in fat. *The duck can be cooked 3 weeks in advance. Store wrapped and covered completely in duck fat in the refrigerator.*

5. For the blueberry-port sauce, rinse the duck thigh bones under cold water and pat dry with paper towels. Heat a 2-qt/1.92-L saucepan over medium heat until it begins to get hot, about 1 minute. Add the canola oil to the pan and heat until hot but not smoking, about 10 seconds. Add the thigh bones and sear until browned, 8 to 10 minutes. Add the shallots and salt, adjust the heat to low, and cook until the shallots are soft, about 10 minutes. Add the carrots and celery and cook until the vegetables are starting to caramelize, about 10 minutes. Move the vegetables to one side of the pan, add the garlic to the empty space, and cook for 1 minute more. Add the water, parsley, thyme, peppercorns, and bay leaf. Bring to a boil and then lower the heat to a simmer for 3 hours, skimming the surface as necessary. Strain the stock through a fine-mesh strainer, discarding all solids.

6. Pour 2 cups/480 mL of the stock into a 2-qt/1.92-L saucepan, reserving the remainder for another use, and bring to a simmer over medium-low heat. Stir in the sugar, port, and vinegar and reduce to one-quarter of its original volume, 30 to 40 minutes. It should be thick and syrupy. Add the blueberries and cook until tender, 5 to 10 minutes. Add the salt, pepper, and cayenne. Remove the pan from the heat and cool at room temperature for 20 minutes, then carefully process until smooth with an immersion blender or in a blender. Strain through a fine-mesh strainer. *The sauce can be made in advance. Store wrapped in the refrigerator for 3 days or in the freezer for 3 months.*

7. Just before serving the duck, position a rack in the top third of the oven and heat to 400°F/204°C. Line 2 sheet pans with parchment paper. Remove excess fat from the duck, being careful not to tear the skin. Place the duck on the sheet pans, at least 2 in/5 cm apart, skin side up. Roast until hot in the center and the skin is crispy, 15 to 20 minutes. Reheat the sauce over medium-low heat. Remove from the heat, swirl in the butter, and add the blueberry garnish. Taste and adjust seasoning.

The duck confit pairs well with many dishes, including Waldorf Caesar Salad (page 152), Bulgur, Chickpea, and Lentil Salad (page 160), Saffron Risotto with Pistachios (page 213), and Fig-Onion Jam (page 326).

TURKEY ROULADE WITH SAUSAGE, CARROT, AND SPINACH STUFFING

YIELD: 12 SERVINGS

CARROT STUFFING

1 egg

½ batch Orange-Spiked Carrots (page 182)

1 oz/ 28 g freshly toasted bread crumbs (½ cup/ 120 mL; page 116) or panko

SPINACH STUFFING

1 egg

½ batch Garlicky Wilted Spinach, without the garlic chip garnish (page 193)

1 oz/ g freshly toasted bread crumbs (½ cup/ 120 mL; page 116) or panko

SEASONED BUTTER

12 oz/340 g unsalted butter, room temperature (1½ cups/360 mL)

4 tsp/13 g kosher salt

1½ tsp/3 g ground black pepper

TURKEY

2 whole turkey breasts, boned, skin on, about 5 lb/2.27 kg each

½ batch Sweet Italian Sausage, Spinach, and Mozzarella Stuffing, without the spinach added (page 248)

Kosher salt, as needed to adjust seasoning

Ground black pepper to season turkey, plus as needed to adjust gravy

1 batch Turkey Gravy (page 313)

1 oz/28 g minced flat-leaf parsley (½ cup/120 mL)

1. For the carrot stuffing, whisk the egg in a 1-qt/960-mL bowl. Add the carrots and bread crumbs and combine with a fork, smashing the carrots so they form a thick but lumpy paste. Taste and adjust seasoning. *The carrot stuffing can be made in advance. Rapidly cool, then immediately store wrapped in the refrigerator for 1 day or in the freezer for 3 months.*

2. For the spinach stuffing, in another 1-qt/960-mL bowl whisk the egg. Add the spinach and bread crumbs and combine. Taste and adjust seasoning. *The spinach stuffing can be made in advance. Rapidly cool, then immediately store wrapped in the refrigerator for 1 day or in the freezer for 3 months.*

3. For the seasoned butter, combine the butter, salt, and pepper in a third 1-qt/960-mL bowl with a fork until it forms a smooth paste. *The butter can be made 1 week in advance. Store wrapped in the refrigerator.*

4. Remove the skin from the turkey breasts without tearing it. Reserve. Butterfly the turkey breasts. Pound each breast between 2 sheets of plastic wrap to an even ½-in/1.25-cm thickness. *The turkey can be prepped but not stuffed 1 day in advance. Store in plastic in the refrigerator.*

5. Position a rack in the bottom third of the oven and heat it to 450°F/232°C. Remove the top layer of plastic wrap on one of the breasts. Evenly coat the turkey with 2 oz/57 g of the seasoned butter. In the center of the breast on the buttered side, place enough of the sausage and mozzarella stuffing to form a long, compact line about 1 in/3 cm wide. On one side of the sausage stuffing, make a compact line of carrots, and on the other side of the sausage stuffing, make a compact line of spinach. With the help of the plastic wrap, lift one side of the turkey over the stuffing, then lift the other side over to seal in the stuffing as tightly as possible without smashing the pattern of the stuffing. Evenly coat the inside of one of the turkey skins with 2 oz/57 g seasoned butter. Carefully lift the stuffed breast off the plastic and onto the skin, so the seam side of the flesh and skin is lined up. Tie with butcher's twine to hold its shape and place seam side down on a rack in a roasting pan measuring 18 by 24 in/45 by 60 cm. Repeat with the other breast. Sprinkle both turkey roulades with salt and pepper.

6. Place the turkey in the oven, immediately reduce the temperature to 350°F/177°C, and roast, basting every 15 minutes with the extra butter and then the pan drippings, until the turkey is golden brown and the stuffing reaches an internal temperature of 165°F/74°C, 60 to 75 minutes. If the drippings in the bottom of the pan start to scorch, add enough water to the bottom of the pan to prevent this. Remove the turkey breasts from the roasting pan, loosely tent with foil, and let the breasts rest for 10 minutes.

7. Place any extra stuffing in a separate baking pan in the same pattern as the turkey breast, cover with parchment paper, seal with aluminum foil, and reserve in the refrigerator. Bake it in an oven at 350°F/177°C to an internal temperature of 165°F/74°C, 25 to 30 minutes.

8. Deglaze the roasting pan with the turkey gravy, scraping up all the bits from the bottom. Strain the sauce through a fine-mesh strainer into a 2-qt/1.92-L saucepan, discarding all solids, and return to a simmer until it is reduced to the correct viscosity and flavor. Degrease, taste, and adjust seasoning. Add the parsley. Remove and discard the butcher's twine from the breasts, slice, and serve with the gravy.

SWEET ITALIAN SAUSAGE, SPINACH, AND MOZZARELLA STUFFING

YIELD: 4 LB/1.81 KG

1 fl oz/30 mL olive oil

2 lb/907 g sweet Italian sausage, casings removed

4 oz/113 g unsalted butter (½ cup/120 mL)

9 oz/255 g finely chopped Spanish onion (2 cups/480 mL)

½ oz/14 g minced garlic (4 tsp/20 mL or 4 cloves)

4 oz/113 g finely chopped whole cremini mushrooms or cremini mushroom stems (1 cup/240 mL)

3 oz/85 g coarsely chopped spinach, tough stems removed (2 cups/480 mL firmly packed) (optional)

7½ oz/212 g shredded low-moisture mozzarella (1½ cups/360 mL) or shredded Fontina

3 oz/85 g freshly toasted bread crumbs (1½ cups/360 mL; page 116) or panko

1½ oz/43 g shredded Pecorino Romano (½ cup/120 mL)

2 eggs, beaten

½ oz/14 g finely chopped flat-leaf parsley (¼ cup/60 mL)

¾ oz/21 g basil chiffonade (6 tbsp/90 mL) or 2 tbsp/30 mL Basil Purée (page 323)

½ tsp/1 g ground black pepper, plus as needed to adjust seasoning

Kosher salt, as needed to adjust seasoning

1. Heat a 12-in/30-cm sauté pan over medium heat for 1 minute. Add the oil to the pan and heat to hot but not smoking, about 10 seconds. Add the sausage, breaking it into small pieces, adjust the heat to medium-low, and cook, tossing occasionally, until well browned and caramelized, about 30 minutes. Remove the sausage, discarding the fat, and transfer to a 4-qt/3.84-L bowl. *The sausage can be browned in advance. Rapidly cool, then immediately store wrapped in the refrigerator for 2 days or in the freezer for 3 months.*

2. Melt the butter in the same sauté pan. Add the onions and scrape the fond from the bottom of the pan. Adjust the heat to medium-low and cook until the onions are soft and translucent, about 15 minutes. If the onions start to burn, add 1 fl oz/30 mL water to the pan and cook until the liquid evaporates. Move the onions to one side of the pan. Add the garlic to the empty space and cook until fragrant, about 1 minute. Add the mushrooms and combine. Cook until all of the liquid released from the mushrooms has evaporated and they have started to caramelize, 10 minutes. Place the contents of the pan into the bowl with the sausage.

3. Add the spinach to the same sauté pan and, over medium-high, cook until wilted, about 2 minutes. Place into the bowl with the sausage. Also add the mozzarella, bread crumbs, Pecorino Romano, eggs, parsley, basil, and pepper and combine. Sample the stuffing by microwaving a small amount until it is fully cooked. Taste and adjust seasoning. Salt is not added until this point and may not be needed because many of the ingredients are salty. *The stuffing can be made in advance. Rapidly cool, then immediately store wrapped in the refrigerator for 1 day or in the freezer for 3 months.*

This is a versatile stuffing that can be used to stuff such foods as mushrooms, zucchini, turkey, chicken, and pork. For a party with a Spanish theme, substitute chorizo for the sweet Italian sausage and Garrotxa for the mozzarella.

SWEET ITALIAN SAUSAGE AND PEPPERS

YIELD: 12 SERVINGS

VEGETABLE GARNISH

2 fl oz/60 mL canola oil

1 Spanish onion, cut into bâtonnet

1 tsp/3 g kosher salt, plus as needed to adjust seasoning

¼ oz/7 g minced garlic (2 tsp/10 mL or 2 cloves)

6 green, red, and/or yellow peppers, seeded, cut into bâtonnet

½ tsp/1 g coarsely ground black pepper, plus as needed to adjust seasoning

SAUSAGE

2 fl oz/60 mL canola oil, plus as needed, to brown the sausage

4 lb 8 oz/2.04 kg sweet Italian sausage rope, cut into 1½-in/4-cm pieces on the bias

1. For the vegetable garnish, heat a 16-in/41-cm sauté pan over medium heat, about 2 minutes. Add the oil to the pan, raise the heat to medium-high, and heat until hot but not smoking, about 20 seconds. Add the onions and salt. Reduce the heat to medium and cook, tossing occasionally, until translucent and starting to brown, about 10 minutes. Move the onions to one side of the pan. Add the garlic to the empty space and cook until fragrant, about 1 minute. Combine and cook until the onions are golden, 10 minutes more. Put all the peppers into the pan with the onions. Over medium heat, cook, tossing occasionally, until the peppers are tender and caramelized, about 20 minutes. Add the black pepper. Toss, taste, and adjust seasoning. *The peppers and onions can be cooked 1 day in advance. Store wrapped in the refrigerator.*

2. For the sausage, add the oil to a 16-in/41-cm nonstick sauté pan and warm over medium heat, about 2 minutes. Add the sausage, lower the heat to medium-low, and cook, turning occasionally, until the sausage is evenly and well browned, 25 to 30 minutes, and the center reaches an internal temperature of 165°F/74°C. Drain and discard the oil. *The sausage can be cooked 1 day in advance. Store wrapped in the refrigerator.*

3. Add the sausage to the sauté pan with the peppers and, over medium heat, toss until hot, about 5 minutes. Drain and discard excess oil. Taste and adjust seasoning.

Herb-Crusted Lamb Duo with Burgundy Reduction and Spinach, Kale, and Chickpea Sauté (page 193). **Ojo platter by Fortessa Tableware** (see Resources, page 347).

HERB-CRUSTED LAMB DUO WITH BURGUNDY REDUCTION

YIELD: 12 SERVINGS

BURGUNDY REDUCTION

36 fl oz/1 L Burgundy

Meaty trimmings from Lamb Sirloin below

1 tsp/3 g kosher salt, plus as needed to adjust seasoning

½ fl oz/15 mL canola oil

9 oz/255 g minced shallots (2 cups/480 mL)

5 oz/142 g minced carrot (1 cup/240 mL)

5 oz/142 g minced celery (1 cup/240 mL)

1 tbsp/15 mL tomato paste

¼ oz/7 g garlic cloves (2 tsp/10 ml or 2 cloves)

3 thyme sprigs

2 bay leaves

10 black peppercorns

2 oz/57 g unsalted butter, cut into ½-in/1.25-cm pats, chilled (¼ cup/60 mL)

1¼ oz/35 g unbleached all-purpose flour (¼ cup/60 mL)

36 fl oz/1 L brown veal stock

Ground black pepper, as needed to adjust seasoning

HERB CRUST

6 oz/170 g unsalted butter (¾ cup/180 mL), plus as needed to adjust crust

¾ oz/21 g minced garlic (2 tbsp/30 mL or 6 cloves)

1 tsp/3 g chopped rosemary leaves

1 tsp/3 g chopped sage leaves

1 tsp/3 g chopped thyme leaves

6 oz/170 g freshly toasted bread crumbs, coarsely ground (3 cups/720 mL; page 116) or panko

¼ oz/7 g chopped flat-leaf parsley (2 tbsp/30 mL)

1½ tsp/5 g kosher salt, plus as needed to adjust seasoning

¾ tsp/2 g ground black pepper, plus as needed to adjust seasoning

MUSTARD COATING

8 oz/227 g Dijon mustard (1 cup/240 mL)

2 oz/57 g unsalted butter, room temperature (¼ cup/60 mL)

LAMB RIBLETS

24 individually cut Denver lamb riblets, also called lamb breast riblets

1 fl oz/30 mL canola oil

2 tsp/6 g kosher salt

½ tsp/1 g coarsely ground black pepper

LAMB SIRLOIN

12 lamb hip steaks, also called sirloin steaks, trimmed, reserving any meaty trimmings for Burgundy Reduction above

1 fl oz/30 mL olive oil

1 tbsp/10 g kosher salt

1 tsp/2 g ground black pepper

1. For the Burgundy reduction, slowly reduce the Burgundy in a 12-in/30-cm sauté pan over medium-low heat, so there are wisps of steam and very tiny bubbles, but it is not simmering, to half the original volume, 45 to 50 minutes. *The wine can be reduced 2 weeks in advance. Store wrapped in the refrigerator.*

2. Blot the lamb trimmings dry and season with ½ tsp/1.5 g salt. Heat a 2-qt/1.92-L saucepan over medium heat, about 1 minute. Add the canola oil to the pan, raise the heat to high, and heat to hot but not smoking, about 20 seconds, so the trimmings sizzle when they hit the pan. Carefully place the lamb trimmings in a single layer and cook, turning several times, until well browned, about 20 minutes. Adjust the heat, if necessary, so the pan is as hot as possible but does not scorch. Remove the trimmings from the pan and set aside. Lower the heat to medium and add the shallots and the remaining ½ tsp/ 1.5 g salt. Scrape the fond on the bottom of the pan and cook until the shallots are soft and translucent, about 5 minutes. Add the carrot and celery and cook until the vegetables are caramelized, about 10 minutes more. Move the vegetables to one side of the pan. Add the tomato paste, garlic, thyme, bay leaves, and peppercorns to the

empty space and cook until fragrant, about 2 minutes. Mix together and cook until the tomato paste is rust colored, 5 to 6 minutes more. Put the vegetables aside with the trimmings.

3. Add the butter to the same saucepan. When it melts, stir in the flour and cook until it is smooth and looks like wet sand, about 1 minute. Add the stock, ground pepper, meaty trimmings and vegetables, and reduced wine. Stir all the ingredients together, scraping up anything on the bottom of the pan. Over medium heat, bring to a low simmer and cook until it is reduced by half the original volume and is nappé, or thick enough to coat the back of a spoon, about 1 hour. Degrease and strain the sauce through a fine-mesh strainer into a 2-qt/1.92-L saucepan, discarding the solids. There should be about 24 fl oz/720 mL sauce. Bring the sauce back to a simmer. Taste and adjust seasoning. *The sauce can be made 3 days in advance. Rapidly cool, then store wrapped in the refrigerator.*

4. For the herb crust, melt the butter in a 10-in/25-cm sauté pan over low heat. Add the garlic and cook until the butter and garlic start to turn golden, about 10 minutes. Add the rosemary, sage, and thyme and cook until fragrant, about 30 seconds. Remove from the heat. Add the bread crumbs, parsley, salt, and pepper. Toss, taste, and adjust the seasoning. The bread crumbs should be moist and hold their shape when pinched together. If not, add more melted butter a tablespoon at a time until it does. *The herb crust can be made in advance. Store in a plastic bag in the refrigerator for 3 days or in the freezer for 3 months.*

5. For the mustard coating, stir the mustard and butter together until evenly combined. *The mustard coating can be made 1 week in advance. Store covered in the refrigerator.*

6. For the lamb riblets, heat the oven to 325°F/163°C. Place the riblets into a deep half hotel pan. Add the canola oil, salt, and pepper and toss to evenly coat. Pour ½ cup/120 mL water into the bottom of the pan. Place a piece of parchment on top of the riblets, and then seal the hotel pan with aluminum foil. Bake until the meat is fork-tender, 1½ to 2 hours. Uncover and cool at room temperature, about 20 minutes. Drain and discard the fat.

Remove any excess gristle or silverskin from the riblets and place on a sheet pan. *The riblets can be baked 2 days in advance. Quickly cool, then immediately store wrapped in the refrigerator.*

7. For the lamb sirloin, heat the grill to high. Clean, then oil, the grates. Position the racks in the bottom third of the oven and heat it to 450°F/232°C. Place the riblets on a sheet pan and roast in oven until browned, about 10 minutes. Meanwhile, blot the lamb sirloin dry, evenly season with salt and pepper, and brush with the olive oil. Place on the hot grill grates presentation side down. Lower the grill cover or use an aluminum foil pan to cover the meat. Leave the meat undisturbed for 3 minutes. Adjust the heat to control flare-ups, keeping it as hot as possible. Turn the sirloin over and grill covered until evenly browned, 3 to 4 minutes more. Place the sirloin on a sheet pan. Remove the riblets from the oven and evenly paint a thick mustard coating on top of the sirloin and on the meaty side of the riblets. Pat the herb crust on top of the mustard, forming about a ¼-in/6-mm-thick crust.

8. Roast in the oven until the bread crumbs are golden but the lamb is medium-rare or reaches an internal temperature of 120° to 125°F/49° to 52°C, 8 to 10 minutes. If crust is not crispy or golden enough, brown under the broiler on high heat for 30 seconds to 1 minute. Loosely tent with foil, and let the meat rest for 10 minutes before slicing. Serve with the Burgundy reduction.

SHRIMP AND SCALLOP SKEWERS IN DILL-DIJON MARINADE

YIELD: 12 SERVINGS

MARINADE

3 fl oz/90 mL lemon juice

1 oz/28 g Dijon mustard (2 tbsp/30 mL)

½ oz/14 g chopped garlic (4 tsp/20 mL or 4 cloves)

2 tsp/6 g kosher salt, plus as needed to adjust seasoning

¾ tsp/2 g coarsely ground black pepper, plus as needed to adjust seasoning

¼ tsp/0.5 g red pepper flakes

8 fl oz/240 mL olive oil

1 oz/28 g coarsely chopped dill (½ cup/120 mL)

SEAFOOD

24 dry-pack day boat scallops (U10 count), muscle tabs removed (about 2 lb 8 oz/1.13 kg)

36 shrimp (16/20 count), peeled and deveined, patted dry with paper towels (about 2 lb/907 g)

1 fl oz/30 mL canola oil, plus as needed to oil grill grates

1. For the marinade, put the lemon juice, mustard, garlic, salt, black pepper, and red pepper flakes into a blender. Run the motor until smooth, first on the lowest setting for 30 seconds and then on the highest setting for 30 seconds. Slowly drizzle in the olive oil with the motor running on the lowest speed. Continue to blend until thick and emulsified, about 30 seconds more. *The marinade can be made 1 week in advance. Store wrapped in the refrigerator and shake to emulsify. Add the herbs just before using.*

2. Soak 12 wooden skewers in warm water for 20 minutes. Thread alternating scallops and shrimp onto the skewers (2 scallops and 3 shrimp per skewer). *The seafood can be skewered 1 day in advance. Store wrapped in the refrigerator.*

3. Whisk the dill into the marinade. Reserve 2 fl oz/60 mL marinade in a separate container to garnish the cooked kebobs. Pour the remaining marinade into a 2-gal/7.68-L zip-close plastic bag set into a 2-qt/1.92-L bowl for support. Place the skewers into the bag, coat with the marinade, and seal. Refrigerate 10 to 20 minutes.

4. Heat the grill to high. Clean, then oil, the grates. Remove the skewers from the bag, drain, and discard the marinade. Brush the canola oil on the seafood. Place a folded sheet of aluminum foil on the center of the grill. Place the kebobs on the grill so the seafood is directly on the grate and the exposed skewers are over the foil. Gently press on each kebob so its entire surface area touches the grates. Adjust the heat, if necessary, to control flare-ups or burning. Leave undisturbed for 1½ to 2 minutes, turn over, and continue to grill until the seafood is evenly browned, firm to the touch, and opaque in the center, 1 to 1½ minutes more. Garnish with the reserved marinade that did not come into contact with the seafood.

LEMON-HORSERADISH-DILL CRUSTED SALMON

YIELD: 12 SERVINGS

SALMON MARINADE

2 fl oz/60 mL Chablis

2 fl oz/60 mL orange juice

2 fl oz/60 mL soy sauce

½ fl oz/15 mL lemon juice

LEMON-HORSERADISH-DILL CRUST

8 oz/227 g freshly toasted bread crumbs (4 cups/960 mL; page 116) or panko

6 oz/170 g unsalted butter, melted, plus as needed to adjust crust (¾ cup/180 mL)

2 oz/57 g finely grated fresh horseradish (¼ cup/60 mL)

1 fl oz/30 mL lemon juice

½ oz/14 g chopped dill (¼ cup/60 mL)

¼ oz/7 g lemon zest (1 tbsp/15 mL or about 1 lemon)

1¾ tsp/5 g kosher salt, plus as needed to adjust seasoning

¾ tsp/2 g coarsely ground black pepper, plus as needed to adjust seasoning

SALMON

4 lb 8 oz/2.04 kg center-cut salmon fillets, skin removed, cut into twelve 6-oz/170-g portions, fresh wild Alaskan preferred

½ fl oz/15 mL canola oil, plus as needed, to cook the salmon

½ oz/14 g unsalted butter (1 tbsp/15 mL), plus as needed, to cook the salmon

1. For the salmon marinade, in a 2-gal/7.68-L zip-close plastic bag set into a 2-qt/1.92-L bowl for support, whisk all the ingredients. *The marinade can be made 3 weeks in advance. Store wrapped in the refrigerator.*

2. For the crust, in a 4-qt/3.84-L bowl combine all the ingredients. Taste and adjust seasoning. *The crust can be made in advance. Store in a plastic bag in the refrigerator for 3 days or in the freezer for 3 months.*

3. To marinate the salmon, place the salmon in the bag and coat with the marinade. Squeeze the air out of the bag and seal. Refrigerate for 1½ to 2 hours, turning occasionally. Remove the salmon from the bag, discard the marinade, pat the salmon dry, and let sit in a single layer at room temperature for 5 minutes. *The salmon can be marinated, then patted dry, 1 day in advance. Store wrapped in the refrigerator. Let sit at room temperature for 10 minutes before proceeding.*

4. To pan roast the salmon, add the oil to a 12-in/30-cm nonstick sauté pan and warm over medium heat, about 1 minute. Add the butter to the pan and heat until melted, about 10 seconds. Adjust the heat to high and heat the pan to hot but not smoking, so when the salmon is placed into the pan there is a loud sizzle, about 20 seconds more. Carefully place about one-third of the salmon fillets skinned side up into the pan ½ in/1.25 cm apart, giving each a gentle press so all of the surface area touches the pan. Cook the salmon undisturbed until the bottom is well browned, about 2 minutes. Flip the salmon over and cook for 1 minute more. Place the salmon skinned side down onto a sheet pan. Repeat with remaining salmon, carefully wiping out the pan with a paper towel and adding oil and butter as needed between batches. Evenly pat the crust on each piece of salmon, forming about a ½-in/1.25-cm-thick crust. *The salmon can be crusted 4 hours in advance. Quickly cool and immediately store wrapped in the refrigerator.*

5. Heat the oven to 425°F/218°C. Roast the salmon until cooked to medium and the center is still translucent and reaches an internal temperature of 140°F/60°C, 6 to 8 minutes, rotating the baking sheets halfway through the roasting time from front to back and top to bottom. Remove from the oven, place on a platter, and loosely tent with aluminum foil. Let the salmon rest for 5 minutes before serving.

Creamy Corn and Edamame Succotash (page 171) makes a great summer pairing, and Charred Brussels Sprouts with Almonds, Grapes, and Pancetta (page 177) makes a perfect fall or winter pairing. Top with Horseradish Gremolata (page 315) for an attractive garnish.

THAI-STYLE SEARED SALMON: Eliminate the Lemon-Horseradish-Dill Crust. Combine 4½ tsp/11 g curry powder, 1 tbsp/6 g chili powder, 1 tbsp/6 g ground coriander, 1 tbsp/6 g ground cumin, 1 tbsp/6 g dry mustard, 1 tbsp/6 g brown sugar, and 1½ tsp/4.5 g kosher salt to make the Thai seasoning. *The Thai seasoning can be made in advance. Store in a sealed container in a cool spot for 3 months.* Prepare the marinade in step 1 and marinate the salmon as instructed. Pat the salmon dry as instructed in step 3, then dredge each piece in the Thai seasoning and evenly coat, shaking off any excess. Cook as instructed in steps 4 and 5. Serve with Tahini Sauce (page 322).

PAN-ROASTED MEDITERRANEAN RED SNAPPER

YIELD: 12 SERVINGS

GARLIC

2 fl oz/60 mL extra-virgin olive oil

1½ oz/43 g sliced garlic (12 cloves)

MARINADE

24 fl oz/720 mL Sauvignon Blanc or dry white wine

4 fl oz/120 mL lemon juice (about 4 lemons)

4 anchovy fillets, oil packed

4 tsp/12 g kosher salt

2 tsp/4 g ground black pepper

½ tsp/1 g red pepper flakes

8 fl oz/240 mL extra-virgin olive oil

¼ oz/7 g coarsely grated lemon zest (1 tbsp/15 mL or about 1 lemon)

FISH

4 lb 8 oz/2 kg red snapper fillets, 1 in/3 cm thick, cut into 12 portions

5 oz/142 g unbleached all-purpose flour (1 cup/240 mL)

1 tbsp/10 g kosher salt

½ tsp/1 g ground black pepper

6 fl oz/180 mL canola oil, plus as needed

3 oz/85 g unsalted butter, plus as needed

MEDITERRANEAN SAUCE

½ oz/14 g flat-leaf parsley, minced (¼ cup/60 mL)

¾ oz/14 g basil chiffonade (6 tbsp/90 mL) or 2 tbsp/30 mL Basil Purée (page 323)

¾ oz/14 g mint chiffonade (6 tbsp/90 mL) or 2 tbsp/30 mL Mint Purée (page 323)

¼ oz/7 g lemon zest (1 tbsp/15 mL or about 1 lemon)

1. For the garlic, in a cold 6-in/15-cm sauté pan, combine the olive oil and garlic. Over low heat, cook the garlic, tossing occasionally, until golden, about 5 minutes. Cool.

2. For the marinade, heat the wine in a 10-in/25-cm sauté pan over medium-low heat, so there are wisps of steam and very tiny bubbles but it is not simmering. Reduce to 8 fl oz/240 mL, about 45 minutes. Cool at room temperature. *The wine can be reduced 3 weeks in advance. Store wrapped in the refrigerator.*

3. Put the cooked garlic and oil, reduced wine, lemon juice, anchovies, salt, black pepper, and red pepper flakes into a blender. Run the motor until smooth, first on the lowest setting for about 30 seconds and then on the highest setting for about 30 seconds. Slowly drizzle in the olive oil with the motor running on the lowest speed. Continue to blend until thick and emulsified, about 30 seconds more. Stir in the lemon zest. *The marinade can be prepared 1 week in advance. Immediately store in a sealed bottle in the refrigerator. Shake to emulsify before using.*

4. For the fish, pour 8 fl oz/240 mL marinade into a 2-gal/7.68-L zip-close plastic bag set into a 2-qt/1.92-L bowl for support. Reserve the remaining uncontaminated marinade (about 14 fl oz/420 mL) for the sauce. Place the fish fillets in the plastic bag, coat with the marinade, and seal. Marinate the fish for 5 minutes.

5. Combine the flour, salt, and pepper in a 2-qt/1.92-L shallow bowl. Remove the fish from the plastic bag, allowing the excess marinade to drip back into bag. Coat 1 fillet at a time with the flour, shaking off any excess. Lay the coated fish on a parchment-lined sheet pan. Repeat with the remaining fish, using parchment paper to separate the layers. Discard all marinade that came into contact with the fish.

6. Heat the oven to 450°F/232°C. In a 12-in/30-cm nonstick oven-safe sauté pan, heat 2 fl oz/60 mL canola oil over medium heat until the oil is very hot but not smoking. It is hot enough when a small piece of fish causes the oil to immediately sizzle. Carefully place enough fish into the oil, skin side down, to fill the pan without touching, about 4 pieces. Gently press on the fish so it remains flat in the pan. Adjust the heat so the oil sizzles but does not smoke or burn. Sear the fish until the skin is golden brown, 2½ to 3 minutes, turn over, add 1 oz/28 g butter to the pan, and carefully swirl the pan so the butter is evenly distributed. Baste the fish with the butter, then place in the oven. Roast until evenly browned, the center is opaque and firm, and it reaches an internal temperature of 140°F/60°C, 3 to 4 minutes. Place the cooked fish on a warm platter tented with aluminum foil. Wipe out the pan, discarding the oil and butter, and repeat with all the fish and the remaining oil and butter.

7. For the Mediterranean sauce, stir the parsley, basil purée, mint purée, and lemon zest into the reserved uncontaminated marinade and spoon over the fish. *The acidity in the marinade oxidizes the herbs very quickly, so the sauce needs to be finished as close to serving as possible.*

What's not to like about the aroma of freshly baking bread wafting from the kitchen? These scratch-made breads and biscuits, buns and muffins, cakes and tarts mix and match for any shape or size to fit the occasion. Brunch crosses the barriers of breakfast and lunch by offering many inexpensive yet irresistible options. Desserts should be thought of as the flavor that people leave with and remember; scratch-made here assures that this tasteful memory will linger.

PAIRINGS
palate + plate

Fruit Salad
Scented with Ginger and Lime

9

BREAD, BRUNCH, *and* DESSERT

PAIRINGS
palate + plate

Dulce de Leche Tartlets

POPOVERS

YIELD: 1 DOZEN POPOVERS

BATTER

16 fl oz/480 mL milk

2 oz/57 g unsalted butter, room temperature
(¼ cup/60 mL)

3 eggs

3 egg whites

10 oz/284 g unbleached all-purpose flour (2 cups/480 mL)

1 tbsp/10 g kosher salt

FOR PANS

1 oz/28 g unsalted butter, room
temperature (2 tbsp/30 mL)

1. For the batter, in a 1½-qt/1.44-L saucepan over
medium heat, warm the milk and butter until the butter
has melted and the milk has bubbles in it, about 6 minutes. Be careful the milk does not scorch and boil over.

**Popovers. 12-cup mini popover
pan by Chicago Metallic Bakeware**
(see Resources, page 347).

2. In a 3-qt/2.88-L bowl, combine the whole eggs and egg whites with an immersion blender until very foamy and about double in volume, about 1 minute (or blend the eggs in a blender bowl). Slowly temper all of the warm milk into the eggs, taking another minute to do so. Add the flour and salt and blend until smooth, about 30 seconds. *The batter can be made 1 day in advance. Store wrapped in the refrigerator.*

3. Position a rack in the bottom third of the oven and heat it to 325°F/163°C. To prepare the pan wells, grease a 12-cup popover pan with the butter. Scale 3 oz/85 g

(generous ⅓ cup/80 mL) batter into each prepared well. Place the pan into the oven and immediately raise the heat to 450°F/232°C. Bake for 20 minutes, then, without opening the door, lower the heat to 350°F/177°C and bake for 20 minutes more. Finally, turn the oven off and let the popovers finish baking for 20 minutes in the cooling oven. Do not open the oven door to check. This change in temperature could cause the popovers to collapse.

CASHEW-STUDDED NAAN

YIELD: 1 DOZEN FLATBREADS

GHEE

8 oz/227 g unsalted butter, melted (1 cup/240 mL)

DOUGH

1 lb 6½ oz/637 g bread flour (4¼ cups plus 1 tbsp/1.04 L), plus bench flour as needed

1½ oz/43 g granulated sugar (3 tbsp/45 mL)

4 tsp/13 g kosher salt

½ oz/14 g instant yeast, also called rapid-rise yeast or highly active yeast (2¼ tsp/11.25 mL) (if using active dry yeast, see page 265)

8 fl oz/240 mL filtered tap water

3 oz/85 g plain yogurt (⅓ cup/80 mL)

2 eggs, beaten

Canola oil as needed to coat plastic wrap, bowl, and grill grates

GARNISH

2½ oz/71 g coarsely chopped cashews or almonds (½ cup/120 mL)

1½ oz/43 g chopped cilantro (¾ cup/80 mL)

⅜ oz/10 g finely minced garlic (1 tbsp/15 mL or 3 cloves)

1 tsp/3 g coarse sea salt

1. For the ghee (clarified and caramelized butter), melt the butter in a 1½-qt/1.44-L saucepan over medium-low heat. Gently simmer until all the moisture in the butter has evaporated, the butter is golden, and the milk solids on the bottom of the pan turn deep brown, about 15 minutes. Immediately pour the butter through a fine-mesh strainer into a 1-qt/960-mL bowl, discarding the browned milk solids. *Ghee can be made 2 weeks in advance. Store wrapped in the refrigerator.*

2. For the dough, combine the flour, sugar, salt, and yeast in a stand mixer fitted with a paddle on medium-low speed, about 10 seconds. Whisk 3 fl oz/90 mL ghee and the water, yogurt, and eggs in a 1-qt/960-mL bowl. Pour the liquid into the flour and mix on low speed until

combined, about 1 minute. Remove the bowl from the mixer, scrape down the sides to incorporate, cover with oiled plastic wrap, and let rest for 20 minutes.

3. Return the dough bowl to the mixer, replacing the paddle with a dough hook, and knead on medium-low speed for 10 minutes, stopping occasionally to move the dough off the hook. When done, the dough should be moist and slightly sticky. Coat a 4-qt/3.84-L bowl with ½ fl oz/15 mL oil. Place the dough into the bowl and turn to coat with oil. Cover with oiled plastic wrap and and allow the dough to rise until doubled in size, 1 to 2 hours at room temperature or 6 hours to 4 days in the refrigerator. Press a finger into the dough center and, if an indentation remains, it is ready. A longer rise in the refrigerator, either at this point or at step 4, will result in a better-developed flavor. *The dough can be made 4 days in advance to this point or after being rolled out in step 5. Store wrapped in the refrigerator.*

4. Place the dough onto a work surface and gently fold down several times. Scale the dough into 12 equal rounds, about 3½ oz/99 g each. Cover the dough pieces with oiled plastic wrap and let rest at room temperature for 20 minutes or refrigerate for 12 hours to 4 days. If it is cold from refrigerator, let the dough come to room temperature for 30 minutes before proceeding. Combine all the garnishes in a 2-cup/480-mL bowl.

5. Turn 1 dough ball out onto the work surface and lightly dust the top of the ball with flour. Press the dough with your fingers to flatten it out to a 6-in/15-cm teardrop. Evenly sprinkle about 1 tbsp/15 mL garnish over the dough and continue walking your fingers over the dough and stretching it to 8 in/20 cm. The garnish should be embedded in the dough so that it does not fall off while cooking. (The dough can also be rolled out with a lightly dusted rolling pin.) Repeat with all the dough and garnish. *The flattened dough rounds can be transferred to a sheet pan dusted with flour and held for 20 minutes.*

6. Position an inverted wok over an open gas flame. Turn the flame to high and heat until a drop of water sizzles immediately when it hits the wok, about 5 minutes, and then lower heat to medium high. (Or heat the grill to high for 10 minutes and then lower to medium high. Clean, then oil, the grates.) Shake the excess flour off a

piece of dough and lay it, garnish side down, onto the wok (or hot grill grates). Adjust the heat so the dough does not burn. Arrange as many pieces of dough on the wok or grill as will fit without touching. Bake until the naan is golden and bubbly, about 2 minutes, then turn over and bake until evenly golden, about 2 minutes more. Remove from the heat and brush the garnish side with ghee. Repeat with the remaining dough and ghee.

CRISPY THIN PIZZA CRUST

YIELD: 1 DOZEN PIZZA ROUNDS
(4 LB 12 OZ/2.15 KG)

1 lb 14 oz/851 g bread flour or high-gluten flour (5¾ cups/1.38 L), plus bench flour as needed

7½ oz/212 g durum semolina (1¼ cups/300 mL)

5 oz/142 g white whole wheat flour (1 cup/240 mL)

1 oz/28 g kosher salt

½ oz/14 g instant yeast, also called rapid-rise yeast or highly active yeast (4½ tsp/22.5 mL) (if using active dry yeast, see page 265)

14 fl oz/420 mL cold filtered tap water

12 fl oz/360 mL cold lager beer

2 fl oz/60 mL vodka

4 fl oz/120 mL extra-virgin olive oil, plus as needed to coat plastic wrap and bowl

1. Combine the bread flour, durum semolina, white whole wheat flour, salt, and yeast in a stand mixer fitted with a paddle on medium-low speed, 10 seconds. Combine the water, beer, vodka, and oil in a 2-qt/1.92-L bowl. Pour the liquid onto the flour, and mix on medium speed until combined, about 1½ minutes. Remove the bowl from the mixer, cover with oiled plastic wrap, and let it rest for 20 minutes.

2. Return the dough to the mixer, replacing the paddle with a dough hook, and knead on medium-low speed for 5 minutes, stopping occasionally to move the dough off the hook. When done, the dough should be moist and stick to the bowl. Coat a 4-qt/3.84-L bowl with 1 tbsp/ 15 mL oil. Place the dough into the bowl and turn to coat with oil. Cover with oiled plastic wrap and allow the dough to rise until doubled in size, 1 to 2 hours at room temperature or 6 hours to 4 days in the refrigerator. Press a finger into the dough center and, if an indentation remains, it is ready. A longer rise in the refrigerator, either at this point or at step 3, will result in a better-developed flavor. *The dough can be made 4 days in advance to this point or after being rolled out in step 3. Store wrapped in the refrigerator.*

3. Place the dough onto the work surface and gently fold down several times. Scale the dough into twelve 6¼-oz/177-g rounds or into the size needed for the recipe. Cover the dough pieces with oiled plastic and let rest at room temperature for 20 minutes or refrigerate for 12 hours to 4 days. If it is cold from refrigerator, let the dough come to room temperature for 30 minutes before proceeding.

4. Turn 1 dough ball out onto the work surface and lightly dust with flour. Press the dough with your fingers to flatten. Continue walking your fingers over the dough and stretch it to a 9-in/23-cm round. Repeat with all the dough. The flattened dough rounds can also be transferred to a sheet pan dusted with durum semolina and held for about 20 minutes.

5. Position a pizza stone in the bottom of the oven and heat to 475°F/246°C. (Or heat the grill to high. Clean, then oil, the grates.) Shake the excess flour off a piece of dough and slide or lay it onto the stone (or grill grates with the temperature lowered to medium-low). Bake until the pizza bottom is barely golden and the top looks dry and set, 3 to 4 minutes, then turn over and bake until evenly baked, 3 to 4 minutes more. Remove from the oven (or grill). *The pizza crust can be prebaked in advance. Store wrapped in the refrigerator for 1 day or in the freezer for 3 months.*

6. Top as desired, leaving a ½-in/1.25-cm crust border ungarnished. Bake on a pizza stone, a wire rack set over a sheet pan, or a parchment-lined sheet pan, or place directly on the grill grates and bake until the edges are golden brown, the bottom is crispy, and the topping is bubbly and melted, 10 to 12 minutes more.

CHEESE STICKS

YIELD: 2 DOZEN PIECES

DOUGH

1 lb 10 oz/737 g bread flour or high-gluten flour (5 cups/1.2 L), plus bench flour as needed

1 tbsp/10 g kosher salt

1 tbsp/13 g granulated sugar

1½ tsp/5 g instant yeast, also called rapid-rise yeast or highly active yeast (see page 265)

16 fl oz/480 mL cold filtered tap water

1½ fl oz/45 mL extra-virgin olive oil, plus as needed to coat plastic wrap and bowl

CHEESE TOPPING

2 fl oz/60 mL extra-virgin olive oil

1½ oz/43 g finely minced garlic (¼ cup/60 mL or 12 cloves)

1½ oz/43 g grated Pecorino Romano (½ cup/120 mL)

2½ oz/71 g shredded low-moisture mozzarella, provolone, or Fontina (½ cup/120 mL)

2 oz/57 g Dijon mustard (¼ cup/60 mL)

½ tsp/1.5 g kosher salt

¼ tsp/0.5 g ground black pepper

¼ tsp/0.5 g red pepper flakes

1. For the dough, combine the flour, salt, sugar, and yeast in a stand mixer fitted with a paddle and mix on medium-low speed for 10 seconds. Combine the water and oil in a 1-qt/960-mL measuring cup. Pour the liquid into the flour, and mix on medium speed until combined, about 1½ minutes. Remove the bowl from the mixer, cover with oiled plastic wrap, and let it rest for 20 minutes.

2. Return the dough to the mixer, replacing the paddle with the dough hook, and knead on medium-low speed for 5 minutes, stopping occasionally to move the dough off the hook. When done, the dough should be moist and stick to the bowl. Coat a 4-qt/3.84-L bowl with 1 tbsp oil. Place the dough into the bowl and turn to coat with oil.

Cover with oiled plastic wrap and allow the dough to rise until doubled in size, 1 to 2 hours at room temperature or 6 hours to 1 day in the refrigerator. Press a finger into the dough's center and, if an indentation remains, it is ready. A longer rise in the refrigerator, either at this point or at step 5, will result in a better-developed flavor. *The dough can be made 4 days in advance. Store wrapped in the refrigerator.*

3. For the cheese topping, in a cold 6-in/15-cm sauté pan combine the oil and garlic. Over low heat, fry the garlic, tossing occasionally, until golden but not browned, about 5 minutes. Pour the oil and garlic into a 1-qt/960-mL bowl and cool at room temperature for 10 minutes. Add the Pecorino Romano, mozzarella, mustard, salt, pepper, and red pepper flakes. Toss, taste, and adjust seasoning. *The cheese topping can be made 1 day in advance. Store wrapped in the refrigerator.*

4. Line 2 half sheet pans with parchment paper. Place the dough onto the work surface and gently fold down several times. Cover the dough with oiled plastic and let rest at room temperature for 20 minutes. Place the dough onto a lightly floured work surface and dust a rolling pin with flour. Roll out to a rectangle measuring 12 by 16 in/30 by 41 cm.

5. Evenly spread the cheese topping over the dough. Fold the dough in half, lining up the long edges so it forms a rectangle measuring 6 by 16 in/15 by 41 cm. Firmly press on the dough, pushing the cheese into the dough. Slice into 24 equal pieces, about ½ by 6 in/1 by 15 cm. With a strip resting on the board, twist it 6 times, then place it on the prepared sheet pan, pressing the ends lightly onto the parchment to anchor and help them keep the twisted shape. Repeat with all the strips, placing them 2 in/5 cm apart on the baking sheets. Cover with oiled plastic wrap, allowing enough give for the dough to rise. Let proof in a warm, draft-free spot until doubled in size, 1 hour, or place in the refrigerator for 6 hours to 1 day. If cold from the refrigerator, let come to room temperature for 15 minutes before baking. *The cheese sticks can be assembled 1 day in advance. Store wrapped in the refrigerator.*

6. Position racks in the top third and bottom third of the oven and heat to 375°F/191°C. Bake until puffy and golden, 18 to 24 minutes, rotating the baking sheets halfway through the baking time from front to back and top to bottom.

GARLIC AND ROSEMARY FOCACCIA: Eliminate the mozzarella and mustard from the cheese topping and add 2 tbsp/30 mL rosemary leaves and 1 tbsp/15 mL thyme leaves. Line 1 sheet pan with parchment and, after rolling the dough out into a rectangle, place it on the pan. Evenly spread on the topping. Cover with plastic and let rise as directed. Just before baking, use your fingertips to gently dimple the surface of the focaccia. Drizzle on 2 tbsp/ 30 mL extra-virgin olive oil. Increase baking time to 30 to 35 minutes, or until the bread is golden and has reached an internal temperature of 190°F/88°C.

INSTANT YEAST VS. ACTIVE DRY YEAST

IF USING ACTIVE DRY YEAST, instead of ½ oz/14 g instant yeast, use ¾ oz/21 g (6¾ tsp/33 mL) active dry yeast. Put water (or milk) in a 1-qt/960-mL microwaveable bowl (or saucepan) and warm in the microwave on high power (or over medium heat) to 110°F/43°C but not more than 125°F/52°C, about 30 to 45 seconds on high power. Dissolve the yeast in the warmed water and let sit for 5 minutes before adding to the flour and continuing with the recipe.

LOUISIANA BISCUITS

YIELD: 2 DOZEN BISCUITS

10 oz/284 g unbleached all-purpose flour (2 cups/480 mL)

4½ oz/128 g cake flour (1 cup/240 mL)

2⅛ oz/60 g granulated sugar (5 tbsp/75 mL)

1 oz/28 g baking powder (5 tsp/25 mL)

1¾ tsp/5 g kosher salt

⅛ tsp/0.25 g Cajun Spice (page 333)

6 oz/170 g cold unsalted butter, cut into ½-in/1.25-cm dice (¾ cup/180 mL)

10 fl oz/300 mL cold fat-free milk or regular milk

1. Line 2 baking sheets with parchment paper. Process both flours and the sugar, baking powder, salt, and Cajun spice in a food processor fitted with a steel blade until mixed, 10 seconds. Evenly scatter the butter over the flour mixture, breaking up any pieces that have clumped together. Pulse the motor until the dough looks like coarse meal, fifteen 3-second on/off pulses, and transfer the mixture to a 2-qt/1.92-L bowl. Pour the milk over the flour and, with a plastic spatula, mix until combined, taking no more than 30 seconds. Work the dough as little as possible. Clumps of butter should still be visible in dough.

2. Place the dough on a lightly floured cold surface and dust the top of the dough and a rolling pin with flour. Gently roll out to an even ½-in/1.25-cm-thick circle and cut into 2-in/5-cm rounds, about 1½ oz/43 g each, reserving the scraps. Push the pastry cutter straight down and pull straight up without twisting the dough for the best rise. Place on baking sheets 2 in/5 cm apart. Combine all scraps and repeat. *The biscuits can be shaped 1 month in advance and frozen immediately. They oxidize in the refrigerator. Store wrapped in the freezer. They bake best without thawing.*

3. Position racks in the top third and bottom third of the oven and heat to 375°F/191°C. Bake until the tops and bottom are golden and the biscuits are set, 25 to 30 minutes.

SOFT DINNER ROLLS

YIELD: 3 DOZEN ROLLS

ROLLS

12 fl oz/360 g milk

3 eggs, room temperature, beaten

1 lb 11½ oz/780 g bread flour (5¼ cups/1.26 L), plus bench flour as needed

3½ oz/99 g granulated sugar (½ cup/120 mL)

½ oz/14 g instant yeast, also called rapid-rise yeast or highly active yeast (4½ tsp/22.5 mL) (if using active dry yeast, see page 265)

4 tsp/13 g kosher salt

4 oz/113 g unsalted butter, cut into ½-in/1.25-cm pats, soft (½ cup/120 mL)

Canola oil as needed to coat plastic wrap and bowl

EGG WASH

1 egg

2 fl oz/60 mL milk

¼ tsp/1 g kosher salt

GARNISHES (OPTIONAL)

1 tsp/3 g coarse smoked sea salt

1 tbsp/10 g poppy seeds

1 tbsp/10 g sesame seeds

1. For the rolls, whisk the milk and eggs in a 1-qt/960-mL bowl. Combine the flour, sugar, yeast, and salt in a stand mixer fitted with a paddle on medium-low speed, 10 seconds. Add the butter and mix on medium-low speed until fine crumbs form, about 1 minute. Pour in the liquid and mix on low speed until combined, about 1½ minutes. Remove the bowl from the mixer, scrape down the sides to incorporate, cover with oiled plastic wrap, and let rest for 20 minutes.

2. Return the dough to the mixer, replacing the paddle with a dough hook, and knead on medium-low speed for 10 minutes, stopping occasionally to move the dough off the hook. When done, the dough should be moist and sticky and stick to the sides and bottom of the bowl. Coat a 4-qt/3.84-L bowl with oil. Place the dough into the bowl and turn to coat with oil. Cover with plastic wrap and allow the dough to rise until doubled in size, 1 to 2 hours, or place in the refrigerator for at least 6 hours and up to to 1 day. Press a finger into the dough center and, if an indentation remains, it is ready. A longer rise, either at this point or at step 3, will result in a better-developed flavor. *The dough can be made 4 days in advance to this point or after being rolled out in step 3. Store wrapped in the refrigerator.*

3. Line 2 half sheet pans with parchment paper. Place the dough onto a work surface and gently fold down several times. Scale the dough into thirty-six 1½-oz/43-g rounds. Cover the dough pieces with oiled plastic wrap and let rest at room temperature for 20 minutes. To form into rolls, cup your palm over each dough round, applying gentle pressure, and roll on an unfloured work surface to create a tight, smooth ball. Repeat with all the dough, placing the rolls on the baking sheet about 2 in/5 cm apart. Cover with oiled plastic wrap, allowing enough give for the dough to rise. Let proof in a warm, draft-free spot until doubled in size, about 1 hour, or place in the refrigerator for 6 hours to 2 days. If cold from the refrigerator, let come to room temperature for 15 minutes before baking. *The rolls can be formed 2 days in advance. Store wrapped in the refrigerator.*

4. Position racks in the top third and bottom third of the oven and heat to 350°F/177°C. For the egg wash, whisk the egg, milk, and salt together. Brush all the rolls with egg wash and sprinkle with the garnishes, if using. Bake until the rolls are golden and have reached an internal temperature of 190°F/88°C, 20 to 25 minutes, rotating the baking sheets halfway through the baking time from front to back and top to bottom. Let set and cool on the pans for 10 minutes before serving.

SOFT BUTTERY DINNER ROLLS: Replace the egg wash with 4 oz/113 g clarified butter. Brush with butter twice before baking and a third time as soon as the rolls are removed from the oven.

SOFT WHOLE WHEAT DINNER ROLLS: Decrease the bread flour to 15 oz/425 g (3 cups/720 mL) and add 12¼ oz/347 g white whole wheat flour (2¾ cups/660 mL).

FRENCH ONION ROLLS: Scale the dough and preshape into two 1 lb 11-oz/765-g rounds. Cover with oiled plastic and let rest at room temperature for 20 minutes. Place 1 dough round onto a lightly floured work surface and dust a rolling pin with flour. Roll out to a rectangle 8 by 16 in/ 20 by 40 cm. Evenly spread ⅓ cup/80 mL Onion Marmalade (⅓ batch; page 326) over the dough, leaving a 1-in/3-cm border on the long side farthest from you. Brush egg wash on that border. Start with the long filling side and roll to form a log, sealing it with the egg wash side. Don't roll the log too tight; there needs to be room for the dough to expand. Pinch the dough to seal the seam. Slice into 18 equal pieces, about ¾ in/2 cm thick. Place the rolls on a parchment-lined sheet pan 2 in/5 cm apart. Repeat with the remaining dough.

MONTAZZOLI BRAIDED BREAKFAST BREAD (TARROLLE)

YIELD: 2 LOAVES (12 SERVINGS EACH)

BREAD

12 fl oz/360 mL milk

3 eggs, room temperature, beaten

2 tsp/10 mL vanilla extract

½ tsp/2.5 mL anise extract

1 lb 11½ oz/780 g bread flour (5¼ cups/1.26 L), plus bench flour as needed

3½ oz/99 g granulated sugar (½ cup/120 mL)

½ oz/14 g instant yeast, also called rapid-rise yeast or highly active yeast (4½ tsp/22.5 mL) (if using active dry yeast, see page 265)

½ oz/14 g anise seed (2 tbsp/30 mL)

4 tsp/12 g kosher salt

4 oz/113 g unsalted butter, cut into ½-in/1.25-cm pats, soft (½ cup/120 mL)

Canola oil as needed to coat plastic wrap and bowl

EGG WASH

1 egg

2 fl oz/60 mL milk

Pinch kosher salt

GLAZE

1½ oz/43 g milk (3 tbsp/45 mL), plus as needed to adjust glaze

1 oz/28 g unsalted butter (2 tbsp/30 mL)

8 oz/227 g confectioners' sugar (2 cups/480 mL)

1 tsp/5 mL vanilla extract

Pinch kosher salt

1. For the bread, whisk the milk, eggs, vanilla extract, and anise extract in a 1-qt/960-mL bowl. Combine the flour, sugar, yeast, anise seed, and salt in a stand mixer fitted with a paddle on medium-low speed for 10 seconds.

Add the butter and mix on medium-low speed until fine crumbs form, 1 minute. Pour in the liquid and mix on low speed until combined, 1 minute. Remove the bowl from the mixer, scrape down the sides to incorporate, cover with oiled plastic wrap, and let the dough rest for 20 minutes.

2. Return the dough to the mixer, replacing the paddle with a dough hook, and knead on medium-low speed for 10 minutes, stopping occasionally to move the dough off the hook. When done, the dough should still be moist and sticky and stick to the sides and bottom of the bowl. Grease a 4-qt/3.84-L bowl with oil. Place the dough into the bowl and turn to coat it with oil. Cover with oiled plastic wrap and allow the dough to rise until doubled in size, 1 to 2 hours, or place in the refrigerator 12 hours to 2 days. Press a finger into the dough center and, if an indentation remains, it is ready. A longer rise, either at this point or at step 4, will result in a better-developed flavor. *The dough can be made 4 days in advance to this point or after being rolled out in step 3. Store wrapped in the refrigerator.*

3. Line 2 half sheet pans with parchment paper. Place the dough onto the work surface and gently fold down several times. Scale the dough into six 9-oz/255-g oblong pieces. Cover the dough pieces with oiled plastic wrap and let rest at room temperature for 20 minutes. Starting at the center of one dough piece, gently roll outward with your fingers on an unfloured surface into a 16-in/40-cm rope. Repeat with all of the dough. Lightly dust each rope with flour. Lay 3 ropes vertically parallel to each other. Start from the middle and braid toward you until the end is reached. Pinch the ends together. Turn the braid around and flip over. Repeat the braiding process and place onto the prepared baking sheet. Repeat with the other 3 ropes to make a second loaf. Cover both with oiled plastic wrap, allowing enough give for the dough to rise. Let proof in a warm, draft-free spot until doubled in size, 1 to 1½ hours, or place in the refrigerator for 12 hours to 2 days. If cold from the refrigerator, let come to room temperature for 15 minutes before baking.

4. Position racks in the top third and bottom third of the oven and heat to 375°F/191°C. For the egg wash, whisk the egg, milk, and salt together. Brush both loaves with egg wash. Bake until the loaves are golden brown and have reached an internal temperature of 190°F/88°C, 45 to 50 minutes, rotating the baking sheets halfway through the baking time from front to back and top to bottom. If the bread gets too dark before it is fully baked, loosely tent with aluminum foil. Let set and cool on the pan for 5 minutes.

5. For the glaze, put the milk and butter in a 1-qt/960-mL microwaveable bowl and warm in the microwave until the butter is melted, 30 seconds on high power. Sift the confectioners' sugar into the milk and add the vanilla and salt. Whisk until completely smooth. If the glaze is too thick to drizzle, add milk, 1 teaspoon at a time.

6. Move the breads to a wire rack set on baking sheet. Evenly drizzle the glaze over the top of the hot breads. Cool the breads and allow the glaze to set for 30 minutes before slicing.

WHOLE WHEAT MONTAZZOLI BREAKFAST BREAD (TARROLLE): Decrease the bread flour to 14¼ oz/404 g (2¾ cups/660 mL) and add 11¼ oz/318 g white whole wheat flour (2½ cups/600 mL).

MONTAZZOLI BREAKFAST BUNS: Yield: 3 dozen buns. Scale the dough into thirty-six 1½-oz/43-g rounds. To form into buns, cup your palm over the dough, applying gentle pressure, and roll on an unfloured work surface to create a tight, smooth ball. Repeat with all the dough, placing the buns on a baking sheet about 2 in/5 cm apart. After proofing, score each with an X in the center. Bake until golden brown, 20 to 25 minutes.

FRUITY YOGURT SMOOTHIE

YIELD: 2 SERVINGS

6 oz/170 g peeled, pitted, hulled, and/or chopped fruit, such as apples, blackberries, blueberries, cantaloupe, honeydew, kiwi, mangos, nectarines, peaches, pears, pineapple, raspberries, seedless grapes, strawberries, or watermelon (1½ to 2 cups/360 to 480 mL)

2 oz/57 g ripe banana, (about ½ banana)

2 fl oz/60 mL milk

4 oz/113 g plain yogurt, Greek preferred (about ½ cup/120 mL)

1½ oz/43 g honey (2 tbsp/30 mL), plus as needed to adjust seasoning

½ fl oz/15 mL lime juice (about 1 lime), plus as needed to adjust seasoning

¼ tsp/1.25 mL vanilla extract

2 cups/480 mL ice cubes, plus as needed to adjust viscosity

1. Put the fruit, banana, milk, yogurt, honey, lime juice, and vanilla into a blender. Run the motor until smooth, first on the lowest setting for about 30 seconds and then on the highest setting for about 30 seconds.

2. Add the ice cubes and blend until smooth, about 30 seconds. Taste and adjust seasoning.

MANGO-STUFFED FRENCH TOAST WITH COCONUT CRUNCH AND MAPLE BUTTER

YIELD: 3 DOZEN PIECES (12 TO 18 SERVINGS)

36 slices brioche, firm white bread, or Texas toast, ½ in/1.25 cm thick, crusts removed

CUSTARD

48 fl oz/1.44 L light cream or half-and-half

8 eggs, beaten

4½ tsp/22.5 mL vanilla extract

10½ oz/298 g granulated sugar (1½ cups/360 mL)

4½ tsp/9 g ground cinnamon

¾ tsp/2 g kosher salt

¼ tsp/0.5 g ground nutmeg

CREAM CHEESE STUFFING

1 lb 8 oz/680 g cream cheese (3 cups/720 mL)

5¼ oz/149 g granulated sugar (¾ cup/180 mL)

¾ tsp/2 g kosher salt

3 eggs, beaten

4½ tsp/22.5 mL vanilla extract

1 lb 14 oz/851 g diced mango (6 cups or about 3 mangos)

MAPLE BUTTER

8 fl oz/240 mL maple syrup

2 fl oz/60 mL Calvados

2 oz/57 g unsalted butter (¼ cup/60 mL)

COCONUT CRUNCH

2 oz/57 g cornflakes, crushed (2 cups/480 mL)

4 oz/113 g toasted sweetened coconut (1 cup/240 mL; page 114)

1. Grease 2 half hotel pans or equivalent size baking pans and dust with flour, tapping the pans to remove any excess flour. Cover the bottom of each baking pan with 9 slices of bread, cutting the bread so it does not overlap but fits snugly in a single layer. Butter one side of a piece of parchment paper large enough to line the top of the pan and set aside.

2. For the custard, whisk all the ingredients in a 2-qt/1.92-L bowl until combined. Pour about one-quarter of the custard (2 cups/480 mL) evenly over the bread in each baking pan.

3. For the cream cheese filling, mix the cream cheese on medium speed in the bowl of a stand mixer fitted with a paddle attachment until soft and fluffy, scraping down the sides and bottom of the bowl, about 1 minute. Pour in the sugar and salt and continue beating until completely smooth, about 1 minute, scraping down the sides and

bottom of the bowl and paddle several times. It is critical that no lumps be in the batter at this point, as they will not bake out. Reduce the speed to low and beat in the egg and vanilla extract until completely combined, about 1 minute.

4. Evenly divide the cream cheese filling between the pans (2 cups/240 mL) and spread it over the bread. Divide the mango (3 cups/360 mL) evenly atop the cream cheese. Top both pans with another layer of bread, just like the bottom layer, so it fits snugly over the top of the mango. Finish by evenly pouring the remaining custard over each pan. Line the top of the French toast with the parchment paper, buttered side touching the bread, and seal with aluminum foil. Let set wrapped in the refrigerator for at least 12 hours. *The stuffed French toast can be prepared 2 days in advance. Store wrapped in the refrigerator.*

5. For the maple butter, warm the maple syrup, Calvados, and butter over low heat until the butter melts. Stir until incorporated. *The maple butter can be prepared 3 weeks in advance. Store wrapped in the refrigerator and reheat before serving.*

6. For the coconut crunch, combine the cornflakes and coconut in a 1-qt/960-mL bowl. *The coconut crunch can be prepared 3 weeks in advance. Store wrapped at room temperature.*

7. Position a rack in the middle of the oven and heat to 350°F/177°C. Bake the French toast until it puffs up in the middle, 45 to 60 minutes. Remove the foil and bake until the edges and top start to brown, about 10 minutes more. Let the French toast set at room temperature tented with foil for 15 minutes. Garnish with the coconut crunch and serve with the maple butter.

———

This stuffed French toast is terrific stuffed with Double-Cinnamon Apples (page 302), Vanilla-Scented Pears (page 302), and with many seasonal fruits, including blueberries and pineapple.

CHOCOLATE LOVERS' CAKE

YIELD: TWO 10-IN/25-CM ROUND LAYER CAKES

10 oz/284 g unsalted butter, room temperature, plus as needed

10 oz/284 g unbleached all-purpose flour, plus as needed

2¼ oz/64 g Dutch-process cocoa powder (¾ cup/180 mL)

1 tsp/3 g fine sea salt

½ tsp/.5 g baking powder

½ tsp/2 g baking soda

15¾ oz/446 g granulated sugar (2¼ cups/540 mL)

2 tsp/10 mL vanilla extract

4 eggs, room temperature

8 oz/227 g sour cream, room temperature (1 cup/240 mL)

1. Line two 10-in/25-cm round cake pan bottoms with parchment paper. Butter and flour the pans. Sift the flour, cocoa powder, salt, baking powder, and baking soda together.

2. Beat the butter in the bowl of a stand mixer fitted with a paddle attachment on medium speed until it is soft and fluffy, about 30 seconds. Sprinkle in the sugar and beat until fluffy and pale yellow, about 3 minutes. Beat in the vanilla. Add the eggs one at a time and mix until fully incorporated, scraping down the bowl several times. Reduce the speed to low and alternate adding the sour cream, then the flour mixture, each in 3 additions, scraping down the bowl several times, until just mixed.

3. Scale 1 lb 10½ oz/751 g batter into each prepared pan. Gently tap the pans on the counter to remove air pockets. Bake in a 350°F/177°C oven until the center puffs and a toothpick inserted comes out clean, 35 to 45 minutes. Halfway through, rotate the pans from front to back and top to bottom. Cool the cakes in the pans for 15 minutes, then remove from the pans and transfer to wire racks to cool completely, about 1 hour. The cakes are best served at room temperature. *The cakes can be prepared in advance. Store wrapped in plastic wrap at room temperature for 1 day, in the refrigerator for 2 days, or in the freezer for 3 months. Bring back to room temperature to serve.*

Chocolate Lovers' Cake with Raspberry Coulis (page 305), **Bittersweet Chocolate Ganache Icing** (page 304), **and toasted hazelnuts. Square aluminum cake stand by Willow Group, Ltd** (see Resources, page 347).

BANANA SPICE CAKE

YIELD: ONE 10-IN/25-CM BUNDT CAKE OR
TWO 10-IN/25-CM ROUND LAYER CAKES OR
36 CUPCAKES OR 72 MINI CUPCAKES

8 oz/227 g unsalted butter, room temperature, plus as needed for preparing pans (1 cup/240 mL)

15 oz/425 g unbleached all-purpose flour (3 cups/720 mL), plus as needed for preparing pans

2 tsp/10 g baking soda

1 tsp/4 g baking powder

2 tsp/4 g ground cinnamon

1 tsp/2 g ground ginger

1 tsp/3 g kosher salt

½ tsp/1 g ground nutmeg

½ tsp/1 g ground allspice

12 oz/340 g very ripe mashed bananas (1½ cups/360 mL or about 3 bananas)

8 fl oz/240 mL buttermilk, room temperature (1 cup/240 mL)

2 fl oz/60 mL light rum

7 oz/198 g dark brown sugar (1 cup/240 mL)

7 oz/198 g granulated sugar (1 cup/240 mL)

2 tsp/10 mL vanilla extract

4 eggs, room temperature

1. Position a rack in the middle of the oven and heat it to 350°F/177°C. Line the cake pan bottom(s) or wells with parchment paper. Butter and flour the pan(s). Sift the flour, baking soda, baking powder, cinnamon, ginger, salt, nutmeg, and allspice together in a 2-qt/1.92-L bowl. Whisk until evenly combined. Purée the bananas, buttermilk, and rum with an immersion blender in a 1-qt/960-mL bowl (or in a blender) until smooth.

2. Whip the butter in the bowl of a stand mixer fitted with a paddle attachment on medium speed until soft and fluffy, about 1½ minutes. Slowly sprinkle in both sugars while beating, about 1 minute. Continue to beat until

creamed and pale brown, about 3 minutes more. Beat in the vanilla, then add the eggs one at a time and mix until fully incorporated, 20 seconds per addition, scraping down the bowl several times. Reduce the speed to low and alternately add the flour mixture, then the banana mixture, in 3 additions each, scraping down the bowl several times, until just mixed, about 1 minute total.

3. *For Bundt cake:* Pour the batter into the cake pan. Gently tap on the counter several times to remove air pockets. Bake until a toothpick inserted in the center comes out clean, 50 to 60 minutes. Cool the cake in the pan set on a wire rack for 10 minutes, remove from the pan, then transfer back to the wire rack to cool completely.

For two 10-in/25-cm cakes: Scale 2 lb 3 oz/992 g of batter into each of the prepared cake pans. Gently tap on the counter several times to remove air pockets. Bake until a toothpick inserted in the center comes out clean, 30 to 35 minutes. Cool the cakes in the pans set on a wire rack for 10 minutes, remove the cakes from the pans, then transfer back to the wire rack to cool completely.

For cupcakes: Evenly distribute the batter into 36 muffin wells, 1⅞ oz/53 g per well. Gently tap the pan on the counter several times to remove air pockets. Each well should be about three-quarters filled. Bake until a toothpick inserted in the center comes out clean, 23 to 26 minutes. Cool the cupcakes in the pans set on a wire rack for 5 minutes, remove from the pans, then transfer back to the wire rack to cool completely.

For mini cupcakes: Evenly distribute the batter into 72 mini muffin wells, about ⅞ oz/25 g per well. Gently tap the pan on the counter several times to remove air pockets. Each well should be about three-quarters filled. Bake until a toothpick inserted in the center comes out clean, 15 to 17 minutes. Cool the cupcakes in the pans set on a wire rack for 5 minutes, remove from the pans, then transfer back to a wire rack to cool completely. *The cake(s)/cupcakes can be prepared in advance. Store wrapped in plastic at room temperature for 1 day, in the refrigerator for 2 days, or in the freezer for 3 months. Bring back to room temperature before serving.*

BANANA-MACADAMIA CAKE: Fold 2½ oz/71 g finely chopped macadamia nuts (½ cup/120 mL) into the batter before filling the pan(s).

BANANA–CHOCOLATE CHIP CAKE: Fold 6 oz/170 g 60% cacao bittersweet chocolate chips (1 cup/240 mL) into the batter before filling the pan(s).

MONTAZZOLI CHIFFON CAKE

YIELD: ONE 10-IN/25-CM TUBE CAKE OR
TWO 10-IN/25-CM ROUND LAYER CAKES

CAKE BATTER BASE

6 fl oz/180 mL water

4 fl oz/120 mL canola oil

2 tsp/10 mL vanilla extract

1 tsp/5 mL almond extract

10 oz/284 g unbleached all-purpose flour (2 cups/480 mL)

2 tsp/8 g baking powder

½ tsp/1.5 g fine sea salt

8 egg yolks

7 oz/198 g granulated sugar (1 cup/240 mL)

MERINGUE

3½ oz/99 g granulated sugar (½ cup/120 mL)

½ tsp/2 g cream of tartar

¼ tsp/0.75 g fine sea salt

8 egg whites

1. Position a rack in the middle of the oven and heat it to 350°F/177°C. For the cake batter base, in a 1-qt/960-mL bowl, combine the water, oil, vanilla, and almond extract. In a 2-qt/1.92-L bowl, sift the flour, baking powder, and salt together.

2. In the bowl of a stand mixer fitted with a whisk attachment, whip the egg yolks on medium-high speed until combined, about 30 seconds. While whipping, slowly sprinkle in the sugar 1 tbsp/15 mL at a time. This will take about 2 minutes. Continue to whip until the yolks reach the ribbon stage, about 1 minute more, scraping down the sides several times. Add the water and oil mixture to the yolk mixture and continue to whip on medium-high speed until completely combined, 1 minute. Gently add the flour mixture and whip on medium speed, scraping down the sides several times, until the batter is smooth, about 1 minute more.

3. For the meringue, in a 1-qt/960-mL bowl, combine the sugar, cream of tartar, and salt. In the bowl of a stand mixer fitted with a whisk attachment, mix the egg whites on medium speed until frothy, about 1 minute. While whipping, slowly sprinkle in the sugar mixture 1 tbsp/15 mL at a time. This will take about 2 minutes. Increase the speed to medium-high and whip the whites until medium glossy peaks form, about 2 minutes more. The finished whites will have peaks that stay in place and look like marshmallow. With a large plastic spatula, gently fold one-third of the egg whites into the cake batter base. Then gently fold in the remaining whites.

4. Pour the batter into an ungreased (not nonstick) 2-piece 10-in/25-cm round tube pan, or divide it evenly into 2 ungreased 10-in/25-cm round cake pans. Bake until a toothpick inserted in the center comes out clean and the cake's center springs back, 55 to 65 minutes for the 10-in/25-cm tube pan or 35 to 45 minutes for the 10-in/25-cm round layers. Immediately invert the tube over a bottle or invert the layers over a cooling rack and cool completely, about 1 hour. Run a flexible knife around the edge and bottom of the cake to loosen it from the pan. *The cake can be made in advance. Store wrapped at room temperature for 1 day, in the refrigerator for 2 days, or in the freezer for 1 month.*

CHOCOLATE TIRAMISÙ CAKE

YIELD: ONE 10-IN/25-CM CAKE

TIRAMISÙ FILLING

4 fl oz/120 mL Vanilla Bean Pastry Crème (page 307)

4 fl oz/120 mL mascarpone

2 oz/57 g confectioners' sugar (½ cup/120 mL)

1 tbsp/15 mL Grand Marnier

1 tbsp/15 mL brandy

ESPRESSO SYRUP

½ cup/120 mL hot espresso

1 tsp/4 g granulated sugar

1 tbsp/15 mL Grand Marnier

CAKE ASSEMBLY

1 batch Montazzoli Chocolate Chiffon Cake, made into two 10-in/25-cm round cake layers (page 277)

2 batches Chocolate Whipped Cream Icing, freshly prepared (page 305)

GARNISHES (OPTIONAL)

Chocolate curls, as needed

Cocoa powder, as needed

Chocolate-covered espresso beans, as needed

1. For the tiramisù filling, beat the pastry crème, mascarpone, confectioners' sugar, Grand Marnier, and brandy in the bowl of a stand mixer fitted with a paddle attachment on medium-high speed until completely combined and thick, about 1 minute. *The tiramisù filling can be prepared in advance. Store wrapped in the refrigerator for 3 days.*

2. For the espresso syrup, stir the espresso and sugar together to dissolve the sugar. Cool at room temperature for 10 minutes. Stir in the Grand Marnier. *The espresso syrup can be prepared in advance. Store wrapped in the refrigerator for 3 days.*

3. To assemble the cake, place one chiffon cake layer on a cardboard round. Moisten with half the espresso syrup. Evenly spread the tiramisù filling over the layer. Top with the second layer of cake and moisten it with the remaining espresso syrup. Reserve 8 oz/227 g icing to decorate the cake. Coat the top and sides of the cake with the remaining whipped cream icing. Decorate the cake with the reserved whipped cream icing and the garnishes, if using.

MINI TIRAMISÙ: Yield: 24 servings. Cut the moistened cake into ½-in/1.25-cm dice. Evenly divide the cake between twenty-four 4 fl-oz/120-mL martini glasses. Evenly divide the tiramisù filling between the glasses (about 1 tbsp/15 mL each) and spread to coat the top of the cake cubes. Evenly divide the whipped cream between the glasses (about 2 tbsp/30 mL each) and spread to make a flat top. Decorate with the optional garnishes.

Mini Tiramisù. Temptationz Tini-Martini glasses by Fortessa
Tableware (see Resources, page 347).

New York Cheesecake with Pecan Crust with Cherries in Blueberry Sauce (page 305), Lemon Curd (page 306), and Vanilla Bean Chantilly Cream (page 305). Tavola plates by Fortessa Tableware (see Resources, page 347).

NEW YORK CHEESECAKE WITH PECAN CRUST

YIELD: TWO 8-IN/20-CM CHEESECAKES

CRUST

11 oz/312 g Sugar Cookies, broken into
1-in/3-cm pieces (page 295)

4 oz/113 g raw pecans (1 cup/240 mL)

3½ oz/99 g granulated sugar (½ cup/120 mL)

2 oz/57 g unsalted butter, melted (¼ cup/60 mL),
plus soft butter as needed for preparing pans

CHEESECAKE FILLING

2 lb 8 oz/1.13 kg block cream cheese (not whipped
or spreadable), room temperature (5 cups/1.2 L)

10½ oz/297 g granulated sugar (1½ cups/360 mL)

½ tsp/1.5 g kosher salt

2 tsp/10 mL vanilla extract

¼ tsp/1.25 mL almond extract

6 eggs, room temperature (10½ oz/297 g)

1 egg yolk, room temperature (¾ oz/21 g)

8 oz/227 g sour cream, room temperature (1 cup/240 mL)

MAPLE TOPPING

8 oz/227 g sour cream, room temperature (1 cup/240 mL)

2¾ oz/78 g maple syrup (¼ cup/60 mL)

1 tsp/4 g granulated sugar

½ tsp/2.5 mL vanilla extract

1. Position a rack in the middle of the oven and heat to 350°F/177°C. Grease two 8-in/20-cm round springform pans. Wrap each pan with an 18-in/46-cm square piece of heavy aluminum foil. Sit each pan on the center of the foil and pull it up the sides of the pan as tightly as possible and crimp over the rim so it leans in slightly, completely sealing the pan. Heat water for a water bath and line a roasting pan with a kitchen towel.

2. For the crust, put the cookies, pecans, and sugar into a food processor fitted with a steel blade. Pulse until finely chopped, ten 2-second on/off pulses. Add the butter and process until combined, scraping down the side of

the bowl once. Scale 10¼ oz/290 g cookie crust into each pan and press the crumbs into the bottom and halfway up the sides into a compact crust. Bake the crusts until golden, about 10 minutes. *The crust can be prepared in advance. Store wrapped in the refrigerator for 2 days or in the freezer for 1 month.*

3. For the cheesecake filling, beat the cream cheese on medium speed with a stand mixer fitted with a paddle attachment until soft and fluffy, scraping down the sides and bottom of the bowl and paddle twice, about 1 minute. Pour in the sugar and salt and continue beating until completely smooth, scraping down the sides and bottom of the bowl and paddle several times, beating for 3 minutes. It is critical that no lumps be in the batter at this point, as they will not bake out. Reduce the speed to low and beat in the vanilla extract and almond extract. Add the eggs and egg yolk, one at a time, and then the sour cream, and mix until fully incorporated, 20 seconds after each addition, scraping down the bowl several times. Divide the batter between the pans by scaling 2 lb 3 oz/992 g batter into each.

4. Place the pans into the roasting pan and then place the roasting pan in the oven. Fill the roasting pan with hot water so it goes halfway up the sides of the cheesecake pans. Bake for 10 minutes, then lower the temperature to 325°F/163°C and bake for 50 minutes more. The cheesecakes will still be jiggly in the center.

5. For the maple topping, combine all the ingredients in a 1-qt/960-mL bowl. Divide the topping by scaling 5⅜ oz/152 g maple topping onto each cheesecake, evenly distribute, and continue to bake for 10 minutes. Then, without opening the oven door, turn off the oven and leave the cheesecakes in the cooling oven for 1 hour.

6. Remove the cheesecakes from the water bath, remove the foil, and transfer to wire racks to cool completely in the pans at room temperature for 2 hours. Wrap the cheesecakes in the pans and refrigerate for 12 hours to set completely before serving. *The cakes can be prepared in advance. Store wrapped in the refrigerator for 1 week or in the freezer for 1 month.*

7. To unmold, carefully pass the side and bottom of each cheesecake pan over a low gas flame for 30 seconds. Slide a knife around the sides of the cheesecake and open the pan's clasp.

SOUR CREAM AND WALNUT COFFEE CAKE

YIELD: ONE 9 BY 13-IN/22 BY 33-CM CAKE OR
36 MUFFINS OR 72 MINI MUFFINS

STREUSEL FILLING AND TOPPING

4 oz/113 g toasted chopped walnuts
(1 cup/240 mL; page 114)

4⅔ oz/131 g dark brown sugar (⅔ cup/160 mL)

4⅔ oz/131 g granulated sugar (⅔ cup/160 mL)

2 tsp/6 g ground cinnamon

½ tsp/1 g ground nutmeg

¼ tsp/1 g kosher salt

3¼ oz/92 g unbleached all-purpose flour (⅔ cup/160 mL)

2½ oz/70 g rolled oats (⅔ cup/160 mL)

4 oz/113 g unsalted butter, room
temperature (½ cup/120 mL)

½ tsp/2.5 mL vanilla extract

SOUR CREAM CAKE

10 oz/284 g unsalted butter, room temperature (1¼ cups/
300 mL), plus more as needed for the pan

15 oz/425 g unbleached all-purpose flour (3 cups/720 mL),
plus more as needed for the pan

1½ tsp/6 g baking powder

1 tsp/5 g baking soda

1 tsp/3 g kosher salt

4 eggs, room temperature

12 oz/340 g sour cream, room
temperature (1½ cups/360 mL)

10½ oz/298 g granulated sugar (1½ cups/360 mL)

2 tsp/10 mL vanilla extract

GLAZE

4 oz/113 g confectioners' sugar (1 cup/240 mL)

2 fl oz/60 mL cream, plus as needed to adjust viscosity

¼ tsp/1.25 mL vanilla extract

Pinch kosher salt

1. For the streusel filling and topping, combine the walnuts, brown sugar, granulated sugar, cinnamon, nutmeg, and salt in a 1-qt/960-mL bowl. Set aside 5½ oz/155 g (1 cup/240 mL) for the streusel filling. *The streusel filling can be mixed in advance. Store in a plastic bag in the refrigerator for 3 days or in the freezer for 3 months.*

2. For the streusel topping, add the flour and oats to the remaining streusel and mix until combined. Whip the butter in the bowl of a stand mixer fitted with a paddle attachment on medium speed until soft and fluffy, about 1½ minutes, scraping down the bowl once. Add the vanilla and combine thoroughly, about 10 seconds. Add the flour-oatmeal mixture and mix until it becomes clumpy, about 1 minute, scraping down the bowl once. *The streusel topping can be mixed in advance. Store in a plastic bag at room temperature for 3 days, in the refrigerator for 3 weeks, or in the freezer for 3 months.*

3. Position a rack in middle of oven and heat to 350°F/177°C. Line the bottom of a cake pan measuring 9 by 13 in/23 by 33 cm or muffin pan wells with parchment paper. Butter and flour the pan(s). Sift the flour, baking powder, baking soda, and salt into a 2-qt/1.92-L bowl. Beat the eggs in a 1-qt/960-mL bowl, then add the sour cream and whisk until combined.

4. Whip the butter in the bowl of a stand mixer fitted with a metal paddle attachment on medium speed until soft and fluffy, about 1½ minutes. While whipping, slowly sprinkle in the granulated sugar and cream until pale yellow, about 3 minutes. Beat in the vanilla. Reduce the speed to low and alternately add the egg mixture and the flour mixture in 3 additions, starting with the egg mixture and ending with the flour mixture, scraping down the bowl several times.

5. *For coffee cake:* Scale half of the batter (1 lb 11½ oz/779 g) into the cake pan. Evenly cover with the streusel filling and then with the remaining batter. Gently tap the pan on the counter several times to remove possible air pockets. Insert a long skewer into the batter, touching the bottom of the pan. Move the skewer in a zigzag pattern, marbling the streusel into the batter. Break the streusel topping into crumbles and evenly distribute onto the top of the batter. Bake until a toothpick inserted in the center

comes out clean, 55 to 65 minutes. Cool in the pan for 15 minutes, remove from the pan, then transfer to a wire rack and cool completely, about 1 hour.

For muffins: Evenly distribute half of batter into 36 wells, about ¾ oz/21 g per well. Evenly distribute all streusel filling on top of batter, about ⅛ oz/3 g or 1 tsp per well. Evenly distribute remaining batter on top of streusel filling, about ¾ oz/21 g per well. Gently tap pan on counter several times to remove possible air pockets. Insert a skewer into batter, touching bottom of pan. Move skewer in zigzag pattern, marbling streusel into batter. Evenly distribute all streusel topping onto tops of muffins, about ⅝ oz/17 g or 1 heaping tbsp per well. Well should be about three-quarters filled. Bake until a toothpick inserted in center comes out clean, 25 to 30 minutes. Cool in pan for 10 minutes, remove from pan, then transfer to a wire rack and cool completely, about 30 minutes.

For mini muffins: Evenly distribute half of batter into 72 wells, about ⅜ oz/10 g per well. Evenly distribute all streusel filling on top of batter, about ½ teaspoon per well. Evenly distribute remaining batter on top of streusel filling, about ⅜ oz/10 g per well. Gently tap pan on counter several times to remove possible air pockets. Insert a toothpick into batter, touching bottom of pan. Move toothpick in zigzag pattern, marbling streusel into batter. Evenly distribute all streusel topping onto tops of muffins, about ¼ oz/7 g or 1 heaping tsp per well. Well should be about three-quarters filled. Bake until a toothpick inserted in center comes out clean, 15 to 20 minutes. Cool in pan for 10 minutes, remove from pan, then transfer to a wire rack and cool completely, about 30 minutes.

6. For the glaze, sift the confectioners' sugar into a 1-qt/960-mL bowl and add the cream, vanilla, and salt. Whisk until completely smooth. If there are any lumps, pour through a fine-mesh strainer. If the glaze is too thick to drizzle, add more cream, a teaspoon at a time.

7. Place a baking sheet under a wire rack. Evenly drizzle the glaze over the top of the cooled cake or muffins. *The coffee cake and muffins can be made in advance. Store wrapped at room temperature for 1 day, in the refrigerator for 3 days, or in the freezer for 3 months. They are best served at room temperature.*

VANILLA CAKE

YIELD: TWO 10-IN/25-CM ROUND LAYER CAKES

Unsalted butter for preparing pan

12½ oz/354 g unbleached all-purpose flour (2½ cups/ 600 mL), plus as needed for dusting pans

2¼ tsp/9 g baking powder

¾ tsp/2 g fine sea salt

4 eggs, room temperature

14 oz/397 g granulated sugar (2 cups/480 mL)

8 fl oz/240 mL canola oil

8 fl oz/240 mL milk, room temperature

1½ tsp/7.5 mL vanilla extract

½ tsp/2.5 mL almond extract

1. Position a rack in the middle of the oven and heat it to 350°F/177°C. Line two 10-in/25-cm round cake pan bottoms with parchment paper. Butter and flour the pans.

2. Sift the flour, baking powder, and salt together in a 4-qt/3.84-L bowl.

3. Beat the eggs in the bowl of a stand mixer fitted with a paddle attachment on medium high speed until combined, 30 seconds. While beating, slowly sprinkle in the sugar, taking 2 minutes. Continue to beat until the mixture reaches ribbon stage, about 1 minute more, scraping down the sides occasionally to ensure that the ingredients are evenly incorporated. Add the oil and beat on medium-high speed until completely combined, about 1 minute. Add the milk, vanilla, and almond extract, and beat on medium-high speed until completely combined, about 1 minute more. Scrape down the bowl between each addition. Reduce the speed to low and sprinkle in the flour mixture in 4 additions, scraping down the bowl several times. Mix until smooth, about 2 minutes total. If necessary, strain the batter through a fine-mesh strainer to remove any flour lumps.

4. Scale 1 lb 9 oz/709 g batter into each prepared pan. Gently tap the pans on the counter several times to remove possible air pockets. Bake until the center of each cake puffs and a toothpick inserted in the center comes

out clean, 35 to 45 minutes. Cool the cakes in the pans for 15 minutes, remove from the pans, then transfer to wire racks to cool completely, 1 hour. *The cake can be prepared in advance. Store wrapped in plastic at room temperature for 1 day, in the refrigerator for 2 days, or in the freezer for 3 months. Bring to room temperature before serving.*

For a moist marble cake, swirl Vanilla Cake batter with Chocolate Lovers' Cake batter.

CINNAMON CHURROS

YIELD: 4 DOZEN CHURROS

CHURRO PÂTE À CHOUX

8 fl oz/240 mL water

2 oz/57 g unsalted butter, cut into ½-in/1.25-cm pats (¼ cup/60 mL)

2 tbsp/24 g granulated sugar

½ tsp/1.5 g kosher salt

5¼ oz/149 g bread flour (1 cup/240 mL)

2 eggs plus enough egg whites to total 5 oz/150 mL

½ tsp/2.5 mL vanilla extract

CINNAMON SUGAR

3½ oz/99 g granulated sugar (½ cup/120 mL)

1 tbsp/7 g ground cinnamon

¼ tsp/0.5 g ground nutmeg

Pinch kosher salt

32 fl oz/960 mL extra-virgin olive oil, Spanish preferred, plus as needed, to fry churros

1. For the pâte à choux, bring the water, butter, sugar, and salt to a simmer over medium-high heat in a 1½-qt/1.44-L saucepan and cook until the butter is melted. Remove from the heat and pour the flour all at once into the water mixture. Vigorously stir with a wooden spoon to form a smooth, thick paste. Put back over medium heat and cook, stirring constantly, until a film develops on the bottom of the pan and the paste becomes shiny, about 2 minutes. You will hear a faint sizzle on the bottom of the pan, but it should not burn.

2. Place the paste in the bowl of a stand mixer fitted with a paddle attachment and beat on low speed for 1 minute to cool. Add the eggs, one at a time, and mix on low speed until fully incorporated and paste comes back together, scraping down the bowl as necessary. Add the vanilla and mix on low speed until fully incorporated. The pâte à choux should be smooth and shiny and the consistency of toothpaste. *The pâte à choux can be made 24 hours in advance. Immediately store wrapped in the refrigerator.*

3. For the cinnamon sugar, combine all the ingredients in a 2-qt/1.92-L shallow bowl. *The cinnamon sugar can be made 3 months in advance. Store wrapped in a plastic bag at room temperature.*

4. Fit a pastry bag with a No. 4 star piping tip and fill with the pâte à choux. Fill a 12-in/30-cm sautoir with enough oil to go one-quarter of the way up the side of the pan. Over medium heat, heat the oil to 325°F/163°C, 8 minutes. It is hot enough when a small mound of pâte à choux causes the oil to immediately sizzle but takes 1 minute to begin browning. Pipe six to eight 4-in/10-cm logs, about ½ oz/14 g each, into the oil without them touching. Adjust the heat so the oil does not smoke or burn. Deep-fry until the churros are cooked through, uniformly golden, and puffed, 6 to 7 minutes, turning several times. Test one to be sure the center is cooked.

5. Place the cooked churros on a cooling rack lined with paper towels to blot the oil. While hot, evenly coat with the cinnamon sugar, shaking off any excess. Repeat with all the choux. *The churros can be made 4 hours in advance. Rewarm on a sheet pan in a single layer in a 350°F/177°C oven until hot, 5 to 10 minutes.*

To make the churros more uniform, pipe the choux onto 5 by 1½-in/13 by 4-cm strips of parchment paper. Carefully lower the parchment into the hot oil. Once the choux releases from the paper, remove the paper and finish as above.

Cinnamon Churros with Bittersweet Chocolate Sauce (page 304), Dulce de Leche (page 303), and Candied Pecans (page 331). Plate and bowl by Fortessa Tableware (see Resources, page 347).

Cream Puffs. Kyoto 9-square taster by **Fortessa Tableware** (see Resources, page 347).

CREAM PUFFS

YIELD: 2 DOZEN CREAM PUFFS

PÂTE À CHOUX

8 fl oz/240 mL water

4 oz/113 g unsalted butter, cut into
½-in/1.25-cm pats (½ cup/120 mL)

1 tbsp/12 g granulated sugar

½ tsp/1.5 g kosher salt

5¼ oz/149 g bread flour (1 cup/240 mL)

3 eggs plus enough egg whites to total 8 oz/240 mL

½ tsp/2.5 mL vanilla extract

CREAM PUFFS

2 egg yolks

1 fl oz/30 mL milk

24 fl oz/720 mL Vanilla Bean Mousse (page 307)

4 oz/113 g confectioners' sugar (½ cup/120 mL)

1. For the pâte à choux, bring the water, butter, sugar, and salt to a simmer over medium-high heat in a 1½-qt/1.44-L saucepan and cook until the butter is melted. Remove from the heat and pour the flour all at once into the water mixture. Vigorously stir with a wooden spoon to form a smooth, thick paste. Put back over medium heat and cook, stirring constantly, until a film develops on the bottom of the pan and the paste becomes shiny, about 2 minutes. You will hear a faint sizzle on the bottom of the pan, but it should not burn.

2. Place the paste in the bowl of a stand mixer fitted with a paddle attachment and beat on low speed for 1 minute to cool. Add the eggs, one at a time, and mix on low speed until fully incorporated and the paste comes back together, about 20 seconds after each addition, scraping down the bowl as necessary. Add the vanilla and mix on low speed until fully incorporated. The pâte à choux should be smooth and shiny and the consistency of toothpaste. If it is too dry, mix in another egg white. *The pâte à choux can be made 24 hours in advance. Immediately store wrapped in the refrigerator.*

3. For the cream puffs, position a rack in the middle of the oven and heat to 375°F/191°C. Line 2 sheet pans with parchment paper. Mix the egg yolks and milk in a 2-cup/480-mL bowl until combined to form an egg wash. Fill a pastry bag fitted with a No. 5 plain piping tip with pâte à choux.

4. Pipe the dough onto the sheet pans in even 1-oz/28-g mounds, 1½ in/4 cm in diameter and about 3 in/8 cm apart. Lightly brush with the egg wash, smoothing out any bumps. Place the pans in the oven and immediately raise the temperature to 450°F/232°C. Bake for 15 minutes, then, without opening the oven door, lower the temperature to 350°F/177°C and bake for 30 minutes more. Finally, turn the oven off and let the cream puffs finish baking for 20 minutes in the cooling oven. Do not open the oven door to check. This sudden change in temperature can cause the cream puffs to collapse.

5. As soon as they are removed from the oven, make a small slit in each one to allow steam to escape. They should be deep golden puffs, firm to the touch. Cool on the sheet pan. *The cream puff shells can be prepared in advance. Store wrapped in the refrigerator for 1 day or in the freezer for 1 month. If necessary, re-crisp in a 350°F/177°C oven, 4 to 5 minutes.*

6. Slice the top third off of each cream puff. Pipe about 1 fl oz/30 mL mousse into the base with a No. 5 plain piping tip, leaving a small mound on the top that will fill the cavity of the top when it is placed back on without oozing out. Place the top of each pastry onto the cream. Lightly dust the top with confectioners' sugar. *The cream puffs can be filled in advance. Store wrapped in the refrigerator for 6 hours.*

If a scale is unavailable, measure exactly the same volume of water, flour, and eggs (whole eggs and whites combined) by using the same 1-cup dry measure.

The cream puffs are also delicious drizzled with Bittersweet Chocolate Sauce (page 304), Chocolate Glaze (page 304) and/or Dulce de Leche (page 303).

CHOCOLATE–PEANUT BUTTER BONBONS

YIELD: 10 ½ DOZEN BONBONS

10 oz/284 g unsalted butter, cut into ½-in/1.25-cm pats (1¼ cups/300 mL), plus as needed to adjust consistency

9 oz/255 g creamy peanut butter (1 cup/240 mL)

1 tsp/5 mL vanilla extract

½ tsp/1.5 g kosher salt

8 oz/227 g toasted pecan pieces, finely chopped (2 cups/480 mL; page 114)

1 lb/454 g confectioners' sugar (4 cups/960 mL)

7½ oz/213 g graham cracker crumbs (2 cups/480 mL)

4 oz/113 g shredded sweetened coconut (1 cup/240 mL lightly packed)

1 batch Chocolate Glaze, melted (page 304)

1. In a 4-qt/3.84-L saucepan over low heat, melt the butter. Remove from the heat and stir in the peanut butter, vanilla, and salt until completely smooth. Add the pecans, confectioners' sugar, graham cracker crumbs, and coconut. Stir until completely combined. The peanut butter filling will look crumbly but should hold together when pressed. If it does not, add more melted butter, a tablespoon at a time, until it does. Roll all the peanut butter filling into ¼-oz/7-g (1-tsp/5-mL) tightly packed balls. Place on baking sheets (the balls can touch), wrap with plastic wrap, and chill in the refrigerator until firm, about 1 hour or up to 1 day.

2. Dip each chilled ball into the chocolate glaze, taking it out with a dipping fork. Hold it over the glaze to allow the excess to drip back into the glaze and place the dipped bonbons on a rack, ¼ in/6 mm apart. Allow to set at room temperature for 5 minutes. Refrigerate for 1 hour to set. Serve at room temperature. *The bonbons can be made in advance. Store wrapped in the refrigerator for 3 days or in the freezer for 3 months.*

Keep the bonbons small so that there is a high ratio of chocolate to filling. They are most delicious when they can be eaten in one bite.

CREAM CHEESE SOUFFLÉ FILLING

YIELD: 2 QT/1.92 L

2 tbsp/30 mL unsalted butter

Granulated sugar for preparing pans

CREAM CHEESE SOUFFLÉ BASE

2 lb 8 oz/1.13 kg block cream cheese (not whipped or spreadable), room temperature (5 cups/1.2 L)

5 egg yolks

4 fl oz/120 mL sour cream, room temperature

1 tsp/5 mL vanilla extract

1 tsp/5 mL almond extract

½ tsp/1.5 g kosher salt

MERINGUE

5 egg whites

3½ oz/99 g granulated sugar (½ cup/120 mL)

¼ tsp/1 g kosher salt

1. Position a rack in the middle of the oven and heat it to 350°F/177°C. Liberally brush a 2-qt/1.92-L soufflé dish with the butter. Lightly coat the interior of the dish with sugar.

2. For the cream cheese soufflé base, beat the cream cheese on medium speed in the bowl of a stand mixer fitted with a paddle attachment until soft and fluffy, scraping down the sides and bottom of the bowl and paddle twice, taking 1 minute. Add the egg yolks, one at a time, and then the sour cream, and mix until fully incorporated, 20 seconds after each addition, scraping down the bowl several times. Add the vanilla, almond extract, and salt and continue beating until completely smooth, scraping down the sides and bottom of the bowl and paddle several times, beating for 1 minute. It is critical that no lumps be in the batter at this point, as they will not bake out.

3. For the meringue, in the bowl of a stand mixer fitted with a whisk attachment, mix the egg whites on medium

speed until frothy, about 1 minute. While whipping, slowly sprinkle in the sugar a tablespoon at a time and then the salt. This will take about 2 minutes. Increase the speed to medium-high and whip the whites until medium glossy peaks form, about 2 minutes more. The finished whites will have peaks that stay in place and look like marshmallow. With a large plastic spatula, gently fold one-third of the egg whites into the cream cheese soufflé base. Then gently fold in the remaining whites.

4. Pour the batter into the prepared soufflé dish. Wipe the rim carefully to remove any batter. Gently tap the soufflé dish on the counter to settle the batter. Bake until the center of the soufflé is puffy and a toothpick inserted in the center comes out clean, 55 to 65 minutes.

CRÊPES STUFFED WITH CREAM CHEESE SOUFFLÉ:
For traditionally rolled crêpes, place 2 oz/57 g Cream Cheese Soufflé Filling on the lower third of a crêpe. Fold the bottom of the crêpe over the filling and roll it up to form a cylinder. Place onto a baking tray seam side down. Repeat with all the filling and crêpes. Warm in a 350°F/177°C oven for 8 to 10 minutes (yield: 3 dozen crêpes).

BLINTZES STUFFED WITH CREAM CHEESE SOUFFLÉ:
For blintzes, place 1 oz/28 g Cream Cheese Soufflé in the middle of a crêpe. Fold the left then right side of the crêpe over the filling and then roll it up from top to bottom to form a blintz. Place onto a baking tray seam side down. Repeat with all the filling and crêpes. Warm in a 350°F/177°C oven for 8 to 10 minutes (yield: 6 dozen blintzes).

The stuffed crêpes can be assembled in advance. They can be stacked 2 layers high with 2 pieces of waxed paper between layers. Store wrapped in the refrigerator for 2 days or in the freezer for 3 months.

CRÊPES

YIELD: 7 DOZEN 7-IN/18-CM CRÊPES

1 lb/454 g unsalted butter (2 cups/480 mL)

12 eggs

40 fl oz/1.2 L cold whole milk, plus as needed to adjust batter

24 fl oz/720 mL water

1 lb 14 oz/851 g unbleached all-purpose flour (6 cups/1.44 L)

4 tsp/13 g kosher salt

1. Melt the butter over medium-low heat in a 1½-qt/1.44-L saucepan. Gently simmer until the moisture in the butter has evaporated and the milk solids on the bottom of the pan turn golden, about 10 minutes. Pour the butter through a very-fine-mesh strainer into another 1½-qt/1.44-L saucepan, discarding the milk solids.

2. Combine the eggs, milk, water, flour, and salt in a 6-qt/5.76-L bowl with an immersion blender (or in a blender) until smooth, about 1 minute. Add 6 fl oz/180 mL melted butter and blend until combined, about 30 seconds. Cover the batter and immediately refrigerate for at least 1 hour or overnight. Blend again before proceeding. *The batter can be prepared 2 days in advance. Store wrapped in the refrigerator.*

3. Heat a 7-in/18-cm nonstick pan over medium heat for 30 seconds. Brush it with melted butter and heat until hot but not smoking, about 30 seconds more, so when the batter hits the pan it sizzles. Ladle 1¼ fl oz/37.5 mL batter into one side of the pan, then tilt and swirl the pan to evenly coat with the batter. If the batter is too thick to coat the entire bottom of the pan, thin out the remaining batter in the bowl by whisking in enough milk, ¼ cup/60 mL at a time, until it does. Cook the crêpe until the top is dry and the edges and bottom are lightly browned, about 1 minute. Place the crêpe on a baking sheet. Repeat, stacking the crêpes with waxed paper sheets between each. *The crêpes can be prepared in advance. Stack the cooled crêpes in batches of 24 with waxed paper sheets between the layers. Store wrapped in the refrigerator for 2 days or in the freezer for 1 month.*

The pan must be hot before the batter is added so that the batter "sticks" to the pan when you swirl it to cover the bottom. If it's not hot, the batter will not spread out evenly. Reheat the pan for 20 seconds before adding cold batter.

For quick production, line up 4 to 6 nonstick pans in assembly line fashion.

Browning the inside of the crêpe is not necessary, as it is already cooked and doing so does not add noticeable flavor. This saves about 25 percent of the production time. Place the filling on the side that was not browned, and fold/roll so the browned side is up.

SAVORY CRÊPES: Blend an additional 1 tsp/5 mL salt and 2 oz/57 g chopped herbs into the batter.

SWEET CRÊPES: Blend 3½ oz/99 g granulated sugar and 1 tbsp/15 mL vanilla extract into the batter.

DULCE DE LECHE TARTLETS

YIELD: 6 DOZEN TARTLETS

18 fl oz/540 mL Dulce de Leche (page 303)

6 dozen Shortbread Tartlet Shells, cooled for at least 1 hour (page 309)

9 oz/255 g Chocolate Glaze (page 304)

72 toasted almond slivers (page 114) or 1 tsp/4 g coarse smoked sea salt

1. Fit a pastry bag with a No. 3 plain piping tip and fill with the dulce de leche. Pipe about ¼ oz/7 g (1 heaping tsp/5 ml) dulce de leche into each tartlet shell so it fills the cavity but is ⅛ in/3 mm below the top of the crust.

2. Spoon about ⅛ oz/3 g (scant ½ tsp/2.5 mL) chocolate glaze onto the dulce de leche in each tart, covering the top without allowing the glaze to ooze out. Garnish each tartlet with 1 almond sliver or a pinch of sea salt. *The tartlets can be assembled 6 hours in advance.*

LEMON, LIME, OR ORANGE MERINGUE TARTLETS

YIELD: 6 DOZEN TARTLETS

18 fl oz/540 mL Lemon Curd, Lime Curd, or Orange Curd, freshly made (pages 306–307)

1 batch Italian Meringue, freshly made (page 306)

6 dozen Shortbread Tartlet Shells, cooled for at least 1 hour (page 309)

1. Fit a pastry bag with a No. 3 plain piping tip and fill with the curd. Fill another pastry bag fitted with a No. 3 star piping tip with the meringue.

2. Pipe about ¼ oz/7 g curd (1 heaping tsp) into each tartlet shell so it fills the cavity and is level with the top of the crust without oozing out. Pipe about ¼ oz/7 g (1 heaping tbsp/15 mL) meringue in a rosette to cover the top of the curd on each tartlet. Brown the meringue using a torch or salamander. *The tartlets can be assembled 6 hours in advance. Store wrapped in the refrigerator.*

Lemon, Lime, and Orange Meringue Tartlets

RASPBERRY-PECAN THUMBPRINT COOKIES

YIELD: 4 DOZEN COOKIES

1 lb 14 oz/851 g unbleached all-purpose flour (6 cups/1.44 L)

1½ tsp/5 g kosher salt

½ tsp/2 g baking soda

1 lb 2 oz/510 g unsalted butter, cut into ½-in/1.25-cm pats, room temperature (2¼ cups/540 mL)

9¼ oz/262 g granulated sugar (1⅓ cups/300 mL)

1 tbsp/15 mL vanilla extract

¼ tsp/1 mL almond extract

3 eggs, room temperature

8 oz/227 g chopped pecans (2 cups/480 mL)

4 fl oz/120 mL seedless raspberry jam

1. Sift the flour, salt, and baking soda into a 1-qt/960-mL bowl.

2. Whip the butter in the bowl of a stand mixer fitted with a paddle attachment on medium speed until soft and fluffy, 1½ minutes. Slowly sprinkle in the sugar while beating, taking about 1 minute. Continue to beat until creamed and pale yellow, 3 minutes more. Beat in the vanilla and almond extract and then the eggs one at a time and mix until fully incorporated, 20 seconds per addition, scraping down the bowl several times. Reduce the speed to low, add the nuts, and mix until combined, about 30 seconds. Add the flour mixture 1 cup/240 mL at a time, scraping down the bowl several times, until just mixed, about 1 minute total. Wrap the bowl in plastic wrap and chill in the refrigerator for at least 1 day or up to 3 days. *The cookie dough can be made in advance. Store it wrapped in the refrigerator for 3 days or in the freezer for 3 months. Thaw in the refrigerator before proceeding.*

3. Position the racks in the top third and bottom third of the oven and heat it to 350°F/177°C. Line baking sheets with parchment paper. Scale the cookie dough into 1½-oz/43-g mounds and roll into balls. Place the balls on the baking sheets 3 in/8 cm apart. With the end of a wooden spoon, press a small well in the center of each ball of dough. Fill each well with ½ tsp/2.5 mL raspberry jam.

4. Bake until the cookies are set and the edges and bottoms are barely golden, 12 to 14 minutes, rotating the baking sheets halfway through the baking time from front to back and top to bottom. Remove from the oven and let the cookies set on the baking sheets for 5 minutes, and then cool on wire racks. *The cookies can be baked in advance. Store wrapped at room temperature for 3 days or in the freezer for 3 months.*

RUSSIAN TEA CAKES: Do not press a well into the center of each cookie; bake them in the shape of balls. After they are baked, cool for 3 minutes then roll the cookies in 1 cup/240 mL confectioner's sugar. Cool completely and then roll again in confectioner's sugar. *The cookies can be baked in advance. Store wrapped at room temperature for 3 days or in the freezer for 3 months.*

SOFT CHOCOLATE CHUNK COOKIES

YIELD: 4 DOZEN COOKIES

1 lb 7⅓ oz/660 g unbleached all-purpose flour (4⅔ cups/1.12 L)

4¼ tsp/14 g kosher salt

2 tsp/8 g baking soda

4 eggs, room temperature

1 tbsp/15 mL vanilla extract

1 lb/454 g unsalted butter, cut into ½-in/1.25-cm pats, room temperature (2 cups/480 mL)

10½ oz/297 g dark brown sugar, packed (1½ cups/360 mL)

7 oz/198 g granulated sugar (1 cup/240 mL)

1 lb 8 oz/680 g 60% cacao bittersweet chocolate chips (4 cups/960 mL)

1. Sift the flour, salt, and baking soda into a 1-qt/960-mL bowl. Whisk the eggs and vanilla in another 1-qt/960-mL bowl until blended.

2. Mix the butter, brown sugar, and granulated sugar in the bowl of a stand mixer fitted with a paddle attachment on low speed until it is completely combined and smooth, about 1 minute, scraping down the bowl and beater several times. Don't overbeat. Slowly add the egg mixture to the sugar mixture, 1 tbsp/15 mL at a time, taking about 1 minute. Scrape the bowl and beater several times. Slowly add the flour, scraping the bowl and beater several times, taking about 1 minute. Fold the chocolate chips into the dough with a plastic spatula to evenly distribute. Wrap the bowl in plastic wrap and chill in the refrigerator for at least 1 day or up to 3 days. *The cookie dough can be made in advance. Store it wrapped in the refrigerator for 3 days or in the freezer for 3 months. Thaw in the refrigerator before proceeding.*

3. Position racks in the top third and bottom third of the oven and heat to 325°F/163°C. Line baking sheets with parchment paper. Scale the cookie dough into 2⅓-oz/66-g mounds (scant ¼ cup) on the baking sheets 3 in/8 cm apart. Bake until the cookies are set and the edges and bottoms are barely golden, 12 to 14 minutes, rotating the baking sheets halfway through the baking time from front to back and top to bottom. Remove from the oven and let the cookies set on the baking sheets for 5 minutes, and then cool on wire racks. *The cookies can be baked in advance. Store wrapped at room temperature for 3 days or in the freezer for 3 months.*

For cookies with more texture and richness, add 12 oz/340 g toasted chopped nuts, such as walnuts, pecans, almonds, or hazelnuts (see page 114; 3⅓ cups/800 mL) to the batter when the chocolate is added.

Soft Chocolate Chunk Cookies (back, page 293), **Russian Tea Cakes** (back center, page 292),
Raspberry-Pecan Thumbprint Cookies (front center, page 292), **and Sugar Cookies** (front).
Stainless-steel oval hammered bowls by American Metalcraft (see Resources, page 347).

SUGAR COOKIES

YIELD: 3 DOZEN COOKIES

1 egg

1 tsp/5 mL vanilla extract

7 oz/198 g granulated sugar (1 cup/240 mL)

10 oz/284 g unbleached all-purpose flour (2 cups/480 mL)

½ tsp/2 g baking powder

¼ tsp/1 g baking soda

¼ tsp/0.75 g fine sea salt

6 oz/170 g cold unsalted butter, cut into ½-in/1.25-cm dice (¾ cup/180 mL)

TOPPING

1¾ oz/51 g turbinado sugar (¼ cup/60 mL)

1. Beat the egg and vanilla in a 2-cup/480-mL bowl until blended. Grind the sugar in a food processor fitted with a steel blade until it is a fine powder, about 30 seconds. Add the flour, baking powder, baking soda, and salt and run the motor until mixed, 10 seconds.

2. Evenly scatter the butter over the flour mixture, breaking up any pieces that have clumped together. Pulse the motor until the dough looks like coarse meal, fifteen 2-second on/off pulses. Pour the egg mixture over the flour and pulse the motor until it is evenly distributed and a dough forms, twelve 4-second on/off pulses. The dough should not be a cohesive ball but should be crumbles that are pushed up to the side of the bowl and stick together when pinched.

3. Pour the dough out onto a lightly floured cold surface. Press it together to form a ball. *The cookie dough can be made in advance. Store it wrapped in the refrigerator for 2 days or in the freezer for 3 months. Thaw in the refrigerator before proceeding.*

4. Position racks in the top third and bottom third of the oven and heat to 350°F/177°C. Line 3 baking sheets with parchment paper. Scale the cookie dough into ⅝-oz/18-g balls (1 tbsp/15 mL). If coating the cookies with topping, place each ball into the sugar topping and flatten so the sugar sticks to one side, letting any excess fall back into the bowl. Repeat with all the dough. Place the balls on the baking sheets, giving each a gentle press to flatten into a disk, placing them 3 in/8 cm apart. If coated with sugar, place sugar side up. Bake until the edges and bottoms are light golden, 14 to 16 minutes, rotating the baking sheets halfway through the baking time from front to back and top to bottom. Let the cookies set for 5 minutes on the baking sheets, and then cool on wire racks. *The cookies can be baked in advance. Store them wrapped at room temperature for 2 days, in the refrigerator for 1 week, or in the freezer for 3 months.*

To save time if grinding the cookies into crumbs: Form the dough into about a 12-in/30-cm log, 1½ in/4 cm in diameter. Cut the log into 36 disks. The sugar coating is not necessary for the crumbs. Bake according to the directions.

CINNAMON COOKIES: As and alternative topping, combine 1¾ oz/51 g granulated sugar (¼ cup/60 mL), 1½ tsp/3 mL ground cinnamon and ⅛ tsp/0.25 g ground nutmeg.

PIZZELLES

YIELD: 7 DOZEN PIZZELLES

12 oz/340 g unsalted butter (1½ cups/360 mL)

8 eggs (14 oz/397 g)

12¼ oz/347 g granulated sugar (1¾ cups/420 mL)

¾ tsp/2 g fine sea salt

1 lb ¼ oz/460 g unbleached all-purpose flour (3¼ cups/780 mL)

2 tsp/10 mL vanilla extract

½ oz/14 g anise seed (2 tbsp/30 mL)

2 oz/57 g confectioners' sugar (½ cup/120 mL)

1. Melt the butter over medium-low heat in a 1½-qt/1.44-L saucepan. Cool at room temperature for 10 minutes.

2. Combine the eggs, sugar, salt, and flour in a stand mixer fitted with a whisk attachment on medium-high speed until blended and foamy, about 2 minutes. Drizzle in the cooled butter and the vanilla and mix until thick and light yellow, about 2 minutes, scraping the bowl a couple of times. Remove the bowl from the stand and sift the flour over the top. Add the anise seed. Return to the stand mixer base and combine on low speed, about 30 seconds, scraping the bowl twice. The batter should be smooth and shiny, the consistency of toothpaste. Cover the top of the bowl with plastic wrap and let the batter rest at room temperature for 1 hour or in the refrigerator for up to 1 day. If chilled, let it sit at room temperature for 1 hour before continuing. *The batter can be prepared 1 day in advance. Store wrapped in the refrigerator.*

3. Preheat a pizzelle iron until hot, about 10 minutes. Just before making the first batch, lightly spray the iron with vegetable spray. Fill a pastry bag fitted with a No. 5 plain piping tip with batter. Pipe 1 level tbsp/15 mL (⅝ oz/18 g) of batter in the center of the pizzelle maker design. Close the cover, press down firmly so the top locks in place, and bake until the steam starts to subside and the pizzelle is golden, about 20 seconds. To remove the pizzelle, slide a small offset spatula under the pizzelle and lift it off. Cool flat on a wire rack. Repeat with all the batter. *The pizzelles can be prepared in advance. Stack in batches of 12 with a waxed paper sheet between each layer. Store wrapped at room temperature for 2 weeks or in the freezer for 3 months.*

4. Just before serving, lightly dust the pizzelles with confectioners' sugar.

Vanilla-Scented Pear Strudel

VANILLA-SCENTED PEAR STRUDEL

YIELD: 12 SERVINGS

½ batch Sugar Cookies, broken into small pieces (11 oz/312 g; page 295)

6¼ oz/177 g toasted pecan pieces (1¼ cups/300 mL; page 114)

1 lb/454 g phyllo dough, thawed in refrigerator

8 oz/227 g unsalted butter, melted (1 cup/240 mL), plus as needed

1 batch cold Vanilla-Scented Pears, 3 lb/1.36 kg with cornstarch increased to 3 tbsp/21 mL (page 302)

1. Put the cookies and pecans into a food processor fitted with a steel blade and pulse the motor until finely chopped, ten 4-second on/off pulses. *The cookie crumbs can be prepared in advance. Store wrapped at in the refrigerator for 3 days or in the freezer for 3 months.*

2. Open and unfold the phyllo, place on the work surface, and immediately cover completely with a dry kitchen towel topped with a damp kitchen towel. Line a sheet pan with parchment paper.

3. Place a sheet of parchment paper, slightly larger than the phyllo, with the long side toward you on an adjacent work surface. Place 2 sheets of phyllo, one on top of the other, on the parchment paper in the same direction. Brush the top layer with a thin, even coat of butter. Sprinkle with 2¾ oz/77 g (scant ½ cup/120 mL) cookie crumbs. Repeat until there are 3 layers of cookie crumbs between 5 phyllo layers.

4. Scale 1 lb 8 oz/680 g (half) of the vanilla-scented pears about 4 in/10 cm in from and parallel to the long end of the phyllo closest to you, forming a cylinder of filling. Using the parchment paper as an aid, fold the edge over the filling and roll to enclose the pear filling and form a strudel. Lift the parchment under the strudel and roll the strudel onto the sheet pan seam side down. Coat the strudel with butter. Make 11 evenly spaced ½-in/1.25-cm-deep scores on top of the strudel, about every 1⅜ in/3 cm, and top with 2 tbsp/30 mL cookie crumbs. Repeat with the remaining phyllo, cookie crumbs, butter, and filling to make a second strudel. Place it on same

sheet pan parallel to and 2 in/5 cm away from the first strudel. Chill the strudels for 30 minutes before baking. *The unbaked strudels can be made in advance. Immediately store wrapped in the refrigerator for 2 days or in the freezer for 3 months. The strudel does not have to be thawed before baking.*

5. Position a rack in the middle of the oven and heat to 350°F/177°C. Bake until deep golden, about 45 minutes, rotating the baking sheet halfway through the baking time from front to back. Cool on the baking sheet. *The strudels can be baked in advance. Cool completely for 2 hours at room temperature and refrigerate wrapped for 2 days. Reheat at 350°F/177°C until the phyllo is crispy, about 20 minutes.*

For the best results, thaw phyllo in the refrigerator overnight. If time is of the essence, take the phyllo out of the box, but leave it in the sealed plastic and thaw it in a warm spot. Don't be tempted to rush this in the microwave. It does not work.

Phyllo must be as fresh as possible. If it appears dried out and breaks up when you try to separate it, it is old phyllo (and not your technique) that needs to be discarded.

Always keep phyllo covered when not in use.

Scoring the strudel before it bakes makes it much easier and neater to slice after it is baked.

MINI PHYLLO TURNOVERS: Replace the medium-dice pears or apples with same amount of pears or apples brunoise. Decrease the layers to 1 cookie crumb layer between 2 phyllo layers. Cut the phyllo from top to bottom into 6 even strips about 2¾ in/7 cm wide. Place 1 tsp/5 mL filling on the side of the strip closest to you and fold like a flag: Fold the bottom right corner of the strip diagonally to the left side of strip to create a triangle encasing the filling. Fold bottom left point up, aligning it with the left side of the dough. Fold the bottom left corner diagonally to the right side of the strip and then fold the bottom right point up, aligning it with the right side of the dough. Repeat to the end of the strip, completely enclosing the filling. Brush with butter, seal the seam, and place on the sheet pan. Repeat with all the filling and phyllo, placing the turnovers on the pans 1 in/3 cm apart and in a single layer. Chill the turnovers for at least 30 minutes and up to 24 hours before baking. Decrease the baking time to 15 to 20 minutes.

ZINFANDEL-POACHED PEARS WITH CHOCOLATE AND TOASTED ALMONDS

YIELD: 12 SERVINGS

ZINFANDEL-POACHED PEARS

64 fl oz/1.92 L Zinfandel or dry red wine

1 qt/960 mL water

1 lb 12 oz/793 g granulated sugar (4 cups/960 mL)

1 oz/28 g lemon peel (4 tbsp/60 mL or about 4 lemons)

12 cloves

8 black peppercorns

3 cinnamon sticks

1 vanilla bean, split in half lengthwise,
or 1 tbsp/15 mL vanilla extract

12 peeled, cored firm Bosc pears, stems
intact, tossed with 3 fl oz/90 mL lemon juice
(about 3 lemons) to prevent oxidizing

CHOCOLATE-ZINFANDEL GANACHE

8 fl oz/240 mL Zinfandel or dry red wine

2 tbsp/24 g granulated sugar

9 oz/255 mL bittersweet chocolate, finely
chopped (1½ cups/360 mL)

1 oz/28 g unsalted butter, room
temperature (2 tbsp/30 mL)

¼ tsp/1 mL vanilla extract

Pinch kosher salt

GARNISH

5 oz/142 g chopped toasted almonds
(1 cup/240 mL; page 114)

1. For the poached pears, put the wine, water, sugar, lemon peel, cloves, peppercorns, and cinnamon sticks into a wide-mouth 12-qt/11.52-L stock pan. Scrape the seeds from the vanilla bean, place the seeds and pod into the liquid, and whisk until combined. Cook over medium heat until the sugar melts and the liquid comes to a simmer, about 10 minutes. Place the pears and the lemon

juice into the pot. Cover the pears with parchment paper touching them and place a lid, a little bit smaller than the pot circumference, on the parchment to hold the pears under the liquid. Simmer the pears until fork-tender, 20 to 30 minutes, depending on the ripeness of the pears. Remove from the heat and cool at room temperature for 1 hour. Then cool in the refrigerator for 1 hour. *The pears can be poached 1 week in advance. Store wrapped in the refrigerator in the poaching liquid. The poaching liquid can be used to poach a second batch of pears.*

2. In a 2-qt/1.92-L saucepan, reduce 4 cups/960 mL of the poaching liquid over medium-low heat until the liquid is syrupy, about 30 minutes. *The sauce can be reduced 1 week in advance. Store wrapped in the refrigerator.*

3. For the ganache, put the wine and sugar into a 2-qt/1.92-L saucepan and whisk until combined. Cook over medium-low heat so there are wisps of steam and very tiny bubbles, but it is not simmering. Cook until the sugar melts and the wine reduces by one-quarter of its original volume or ¾ cup/180 mL, about 10 minutes. Remove from the heat, add the chocolate, cover, and let stand for 1 minute. Whisk the chocolate until smooth. Whisk in the butter, vanilla, and salt. *The ganache can be made 3 days in advance. Store wrapped in the refrigerator. Melt in a bowl set over hot water.*

4. Place the nuts into a flat-bottomed 2-cup/480-mL bowl. Remove the chilled pears from the liquid and pat dry with paper towels. Dip the bottom 2 inches of each pear into the chocolate and then roll the chocolate-coated part in the nuts. Place on a cooling rack until set, 10 minutes. Serve with the reduced sauce.

The Zinfandel-Poached Pears (without the Chocolate-Zinfandel Ganache) are delicious on an arugula salad salad tossed with bacon lardons, toasted walnuts (page 114), stilton cheese, and Balsamic Vinaigrette (page 329).

Zinfandel-Poached Pears with Chocolate and Toasted Almonds. Rectangular glass platter by Willow Group, Ltd. (see Resources, page 347).

VANILLA-SCENTED PEARS

YIELD: 3 LB/1.36 KG

---

3 oz/85 g unsalted butter (6 tbsp/90 mL)

3 lb/1.36 kg peeled, cored Bosc or Bartlett pears, cut into ½-in/1.25-cm cubes (see Note), tossed with 2 fl oz/60 mL lemon juice to prevent oxidizing

1 vanilla bean, split in half lengthwise, or 1 tbsp/15 mL vanilla extract

5¼ oz/148 g granulated sugar (¾ cup/180 mL), plus as needed to adjust seasoning

1 tbsp/15 mL cornstarch

⅛ oz/3 g lemon zest (1½ tsp/7.5 mL or about ½ lemon)

½ tsp/0.5 g ground cinnamon

¼ tsp/1 g kosher salt

⅛ tsp/0.25 g ground nutmeg

1. Melt the butter in a 12-in/30-cm sauté pan over medium heat. Lift the pears out of the bowl and transfer to the sauté pan, discarding the lemon juice. Scrape the seeds from the vanilla bean and place the seeds and pod into the sauté pan with the pears. (If substituting vanilla extract, add it after the pears are removed from the heat.) Cook, tossing occasionally, until most of the liquid has evaporated and the pears are tender, about 20 minutes. If all of the liquid has evaporated and the pears are not tender enough, add ½ cup/120 mL water, or more as necessary, and continue to cook until the pears are tender and the water has evaporated.

2. Whisk the sugar, cornstarch, lemon zest, cinnamon, salt, and nutmeg into a 1-qt/960-mL bowl. Sprinkle the mixture onto the pears and simmer until a thick sauce forms, 5 minutes. It is done when the butter starts to separate from the sauce. Remove from the heat. Remove the vanilla bean. (If substituting vanilla extract, add it now.) Taste and adjust the sugar as necessary. *The pears can be prepared in advance. Rapidly cool, then immediately store wrapped in the refrigerator for 3 days or in the freezer for 3 months.*

To prepare the pears, peel each pear. Cut it in half lengthwise from blossom end to stem. With a melon baller, remove the core, stem, and blossom end. Slice the pear in half again lengthwise, from blossom end to stem, and then slice crosswise into ½-in/1.25-cm chunks.

To juice lemons: Room temperature lemons release more juice; 10 seconds in the microwave helps. Roll the lemon on a hard surface while applying pressure. This breaks the membranes holding the juice. Then squeeze with a juicer.

The lemon juice not only adds flavor to this recipe but also keeps the pears from oxidizing or turning brown and should be added immediately after peeling the pears.

To zest the citrus, use a Microplane to remove only the thin yellow rind, avoiding the bitter white pith beneath. If you don't have one, use a swivel-blade peeler with gentle pressure and finely mince the zest with a chef's knife.

DOUBLE-CINNAMON APPLES: Replace the pears with peeled, cored, medium-diced Golden Delicious, Honeycrisp, and Granny Smith apples (12 to 14 apples total). Increase the cinnamon to 1½ tsp/1.5 g and the nutmeg to ¼ tsp/0.5 g.

DOUBLE-CINNAMON APPLE SAUCE: Place the cooked apples into a food processor and process until the desired consistency is achieved.

DULCE DE LECHE

YIELD: 32 FL OZ/946 ML

Three 14-oz/397-g cans sweetened condensed milk

1½ fl oz/45 mL light rum

1½ tsp/7.5 mL vanilla extract

Pinch kosher salt

1. Peel the labels off of the cans and open them, leaving the tops of the cans resting on the milk. Put a 6-in/15-cm heavy aluminum foil square over the top of each can, pushing down on the center of the foil and running your fingers around the inner and outer rim, so the can is sealed as tightly as possible. Put the cans into a 3-qt/2.83-L saucepan and fill with hot tap water, leaving ½ in/1.25 cm of can above the waterline. Cover the saucepan with a lid. Bring the water to a boil over high heat, then reduce the heat to medium-low and simmer until the condensed milk forms a deep golden brown pudding thick enough for a fork to stand up in on its own, 3 to 3 ½ hours. It is critical to maintain the water level.

2. Carefully remove the cans from the pot and, when cool enough to handle, pour the Dulce de Leche into the bowl of a food processor fitted with a steel blade. It must be done while still hot. Add the rum, vanilla, and salt and process until smooth, scraping down the bowl once, about 20 seconds. Transfer to a 1-qt/960-mL bowl and cool to room temperature. Rapidly cool, then immediately store wrapped in the refrigerator for 4 hours to thicken. *The dulce de leche can be prepared 2 weeks in advance. Keep wrapped in the refrigerator.*

The Dulce de Leche is excellent drizzled on Chocolate Lovers' Cake (page 174), Cream Puffs (page 187), or New York Cheesecake with Pecan Crust (page 281), as a filling for Montazzoli Chiffon Cake (page 277) or Vanilla Cake (page 283), and as a dip for Cinnamon Churros (page 384).

BROWN SUGAR GLAZE

YIELD: 32 FL OZ/960 ML

7 oz/198 g dark brown sugar (1 cup/240 mL)

4 oz/113 g unsalted butter (½ cup/120 mL)

2 fl oz/60 mL light rum

8 oz/227 g block cream cheese, not whipped or spreadable (1 cup/240 mL)

8 oz/227 g confectioners' sugar (2 cups/480 mL)

1 tsp/5 mL vanilla extract

½ tsp/1.5 g salt

1. Bring the brown sugar, butter, and rum to a simmer in a 1½-qt/1.44-L saucepan over medium heat, stirring constantly for 5 minutes. Adjust the heat to low and gently simmer until the mixture is reduced to a thick syrup and reaches the thread stage, 220°F/104°C, about 4 minutes. Cool for 10 minutes over an ice bath.

2. Whip the cream cheese in the bowl of a stand mixer fitted with a paddle attachment on medium speed until smooth, 1 minute. Scrape down the bowl whenever necessary. Add the confectioners' sugar, vanilla, and salt and beat until smooth, 1 minute. Add the cooled brown sugar syrup and beat until smooth, 1 minute more. Refrigerate for 2 hours to thicken. *The glaze can be prepared in advance. Store wrapped in the refrigerator for 2 weeks. Gently warm over a double boiler, stirring until smooth.*

BITTERSWEET CHOCOLATE SAUCE

YIELD: 1 LB 8 OZ/680 G (ABOUT 3 CUPS/720 ML)

12 fl oz/360 mL heavy cream

½ tsp/1 g instant espresso powder

½ tsp/1.5 g kosher salt

1 tsp/5 mL vanilla extract

12 oz/340 g bittersweet chocolate, at least 70% cacao, finely chopped (2 cups/480 mL)

Put the cream, instant espresso powder, and salt into a 2 qt/1.92-L saucepan. Over medium heat, bring to a simmer. Remove from the heat and add the chocolate. Cover the pot and let stand undisturbed for 2 minutes. Add the vanilla and stir until the cream is fully incorporated and the mixture is completely smooth. Taste and adjust seasoning as needed. *The sauce can be prepared in advance. Store wrapped in the refrigerator for 2 weeks. Gently warm over a double boiler, stirring until smooth.*

BITTERSWEET CHOCOLATE GANACHE ICING: Cool the chocolate sauce at room temperature for 30 minutes. Cover and chill until firm but still pliable, 20 to 30 minutes. Place in a stand mixer fitted with a paddle attachment and beat until thick and spreadable, 2 to 3 minutes.

CHOCOLATE GLAZE

YIELD: 1 LB 2½ OZ/525 G
(ABOUT 2¼ CUPS/540 ML)

8 oz/227 g unsalted butter, cut into ½-in/1.25-cm pats (1 cup/240 mL)

9 oz/255 g bittersweet chocolate, at least 70% cacao, finely chopped (1½ cups/360 mL)

1½ oz/43 g honey (2 tbsp/30 mL)

1. Melt the butter in a 1-qt/960-mL microwaveable bowl on high power, 1 minute (or in a pot over medium heat).

2. Remove the bowl from the microwave and add the chocolate and honey. Let stand for 1 minute; the heat from the butter should melt the chocolate. Stir until melted. If necessary, microwave on medium power for 20-second intervals until all the chocolate is melted. *The glaze can be prepared in advance. Store wrapped in the refrigerator for 3 weeks. Gently warm in a microwave on low power for 30-second intervals, stirring in between until smooth (or warm over a double boiler).*

WHIPPED CREAM ICING

YIELD: 32 FL OZ/960 ML

1½ fl oz/45 mL cold water

⅛ oz/3 g gelatin powder (1 tsp/5 mL)

1½ fl oz/45 mL boiling water

16 fl oz/480 mL very cold heavy cream, 40% fat content

1¾ oz/51 g superfine sugar (¼ cup/60 mL), or granulated sugar ground in food processor fitted with steel blade until it is a fine powder, about 30 seconds

¾ tsp/3 mL vanilla extract

1. Place the cold water into the bowl of a stand mixer, sprinkle on the gelatin, and bloom until melted, 2 minutes. Add the boiling water and stir until dissolved. Cool for 2 minutes.

2. Start whipping on medium speed in the stand mixer fitted with a whisk attachment; while whipping, add the heavy cream. Slowly sprinkle in the sugar a tablespoon at a time, 1 minute. Add the vanilla. Increase the speed to high and whip until firm peaks form, 3 to 4 minutes more, being careful not to overwhip into butter. The finished cream will have peaks that stay in place and look like marshmallow. Immediately spread or pipe the icing.

VANILLA BEAN WHIPPED CREAM ICING: Replace the vanilla extract with the seeds from half a vanilla bean.

VANILLA BEAN CHANTILLY CREAM: When adding the heavy cream, also add 2 oz /57 g sour cream (¼ cup/ 60 mL). Increase the sugar to 3½ oz/99 g (½ cup/120 mL). Replace the vanilla extract with the seeds from half a vanilla bean and add 2 tsp/10 mL brandy and 2 tsp/10 mL Grand Marnier.

CHOCOLATE WHIPPED CREAM ICING: Add ¼ tsp/ 0.5 g instant espresso coffee to the hot water. Increase the sugar to 3½ oz/99 g (½ cup/120 mL) and combine with 2 tbsp/14 g Dutch-process cocoa powder in a food processor fitted with a steel blade, and process for 30 seconds.

RASPBERRY COULIS

YIELD: 32 FL OZ/960 ML

2 lb/907 g raspberries

1 lb/454 g granulated sugar, plus as needed to adjust seasoning

2 fl oz/60 mL lemon juice (about 2 lemons), plus as needed to adjust seasoning.

1. Put all the ingredients into a wide-mouth 4-qt/3.84-L saucepan. Cook over medium heat, stirring, until the sugar has dissolved, 10 to 15 minutes.

2. Strain through a fine-mesh strainer, discarding any seeds. Taste and adjust the seasoning. *The coulis can be made in advance. Store wrapped in the refrigerator for 3 days or in the freezer for 3 months.*

STRAWBERRIES IN BLUEBERRY SAUCE

YIELD: 32 FL OZ/960 ML

1 lb 8 oz/680 g blueberries (3½ cups/840 mL)

7 oz/198 g granulated sugar (1 cup/360 mL), plus as needed to adjust seasoning

4 fl oz/20 mL water

1 fl oz/30 mL lemon juice (about 1 lemon)

14 oz/397 g sliced strawberries (2 cups/480 mL)

1. Combine the blueberries, sugar, water, and lemon juice in a 1½-qt/1.44-L saucepan. Bring the mixture to a boil over medium heat. Reduce the heat to low and simmer, stirring occasionally, until the blueberries form a thick sauce, 10 to 15 minutes. Taste and adjust the sugar. Cool completely, about 30 minutes. *The sauce can be cooked 3 days in advance, but do not add the strawberries until just before serving. Immediately store wrapped in the refrigerator.*

2. Stir in the strawberries just before serving. Taste and adjust seasoning.

CHERRIES IN BLUEBERRY SAUCE: Replace the strawberries with an equal amount of pitted cherries.

ITALIAN MERINGUE

YIELD: 1 LB 8¼ OZ/687 G

SUGAR SYRUP

7 oz/198 g granulated sugar (1 cup/240 mL)

6 oz/170 g water (¾ cup/180 mL)

MERINGUE

6 pasteurized egg whites, room temperature

⅛ tsp/0.25 g kosher salt

3½ oz/99 g granulated sugar (½ cup/120 mL)

1 tsp/5 mL vanilla extract

1. For the sugar syrup, put the sugar and water into 1½-qt/1.44-L saucepan and bring to a boil over medium-high heat, stirring to dissolve the sugar. Once it comes to a boil, stop stirring and cook until it reaches the soft ball stage (240°F/115°C).

2. For the meringue, while the sugar syrup is cooking, whip the egg whites and salt in the bowl of a stand mixer fitted with a whisk attachment on medium speed until frothy, about 1 minute. While whipping, slowly sprinkle in the sugar 1 tbsp/15 mL at a time, about 2 minutes. Increase the speed to medium-high and whip the whites until medium glossy peaks form, about 2 minutes more. Lower the speed to medium and slowly and carefully drizzle the sugar syrup directly onto the meringue in a steady stream, scraping down the sides once, about 1 minute. Increase the speed to medium-high and whip until stiff peaks form, 3 to 4 minutes. Lower the speed to medium, add the vanilla, and whip until combined and the meringue has cooled, scraping down the sides once, about 3 minutes more. Italian Meringue is best piped within 2 hours.

LEMON CURD

YIELD: 32 FL OZ/960 ML

7 oz/198 g unsalted butter, cut into ½-in/1.25-cm dice (14 tbsp/210 mL)

12¼ oz/354 g granulated sugar (1¾ cups/420 mL)

⅛ tsp/0.25 g kosher salt

4 eggs

6 egg yolks

8 fl oz/240 mL lemon juice (about 8 lemons)

½ oz/14 g lemon zest (2 tbsp/30 mL or about 2 lemons)

1 oz/28 g heavy cream (2 tbsp/30 mL)

1. Put 1 oz/28 g butter (2 tbsp/30 mL) into a 1½-qt/1.44-L bowl and place a fine-mesh strainer over the bowl.

2. Melt 6 oz/170 g butter (1½ cups/360 mL) in a 3-qt/2.88-L saucepan over low heat. Remove the pan from the heat and add the sugar and salt. Mix together with an immersion blender, about 20 seconds. Add the eggs and the egg yolks, one at a time, and blend until fully incorporated, 10 seconds after each addition. Add the lemon juice and blend until combined. Stir in the lemon zest.

3. Cook over medium heat, stirring constantly, until the curd is nappé, or thick enough to coat the back of a spoon, and it reaches 180°F/82°C on an instant-read thermometer. It will start to steam slightly when it is almost done. Before it starts to bubble, remove from the heat, strain into the bowl with the butter, and add the cream.

4. Stir until the butter is melted and the cream is incorporated. Cool over an ice bath for 30 minutes. Stir occasionally so it cools evenly. Wrap with plastic pressed onto the surface area, completely sealing it to prevent a skin from forming, and immediately refrigerate for 4 hours to thicken before serving. *The curd can be prepared 1 week in advance. Store wrapped in the refrigerator with plastic pressed onto the surface area, completely sealing it to prevent a skin from forming.*

LIME CURD: Replace the lemon juice and zest with lime juice and zest.

ORANGE CURD: Replace the lemon juice and zest with orange juice and zest. Reduce the sugar to 8 ¾ oz/248 g (1¼ cups/300 mL).

VANILLA BEAN PASTRY CRÈME

YIELD: 1 QT/960 ML

24 fl oz/720 mL heavy cream

½ vanilla bean

6 oz/170 g egg yolks, room temperature (8 yolks)

5¼ oz/149 g granulated sugar (¾ cup/180 mL)

½ tsp/2 g kosher salt

3¾ oz/106 g unbleached all-purpose flour (¾ cup/180 mL)

1. Pour the cream into a 4-qt/3.84-L saucepan. Scrape the seeds from the vanilla bean and place the seeds and pod into the cream. Over medium heat, bring the cream to a simmer. Turn off the heat and let the vanilla bean steep in the cream while whipping the egg yolks.

2. Beat the egg yolks in the bowl of a stand mixer fitted with a whisk attachment on medium speed until combined, about 30 seconds. Sprinkle in the sugar and salt and beat until fluffy and pale yellow and the mixture reaches the ribbon stage, about 3 minutes, scraping down the bowl several times. Sprinkle in the flour and beat until fully combined and thick, about 1 minute more, scraping down the bowl.

3. Bring the cream back to a simmer. With the stand mixer on low speed, slowly and carefully pour all of the cream into the egg yolks. Pour all of mixture back into the saucepan and cook over medium heat, stirring constantly with a flat-bottomed wooden spoon, until thick and the pastry crème starts to bubble, about 10 minutes, taking care that the bottom does not scorch. When the pastry crème starts to bubble, it will separate or break, but this is not a problem. Remove from the heat. Pour into a clean stand mixer bowl. Cool over an ice bath for 30 minutes. Stir occasionally so it cools evenly.

4. Remove the vanilla pod. Beat the cooled pastry crème with a paddle attachment on medium-high speed until completely combined, thick, fluffy, and a pale yellow, about 1 minute. *The pastry crème can be prepared in advance. Store wrapped in the refrigerator for 3 days or in the freezer for 3 months. It may need to be whipped with a paddle attachment again before using.*

VANILLA BEAN MOUSSE: Gently fold 16 fl oz/480 mL whipped cream into Vanilla Bean Pastry Crème until combined.

CHOCOLATE PASTRY CRÈME: While heating the cream in step 1, whisk in 1⅛ oz/32 g unsweetened cocoa powder (½ cup/120 mL) and ¼ tsp/0.5 g instant espresso powder.

CHOCOLATE MOUSSE: Gently fold 16 fl oz/480 mL whipped cream into Chocolate Pastry Crème until combined.

MOCHA PASTRY CRÈME: While heating the cream in step 1, whisk in 1⅛ oz/32 g unsweetened cocoa powder (½ cup/120 mL) and 1 tsp/2 g instant espresso powder.

MOCHA MOUSSE: Gently fold 16 fl oz/480 mL whipped cream into Mocha Pastry Crème until combined.

PUMPKIN PASTRY CRÈME: While heating the cream in step 1, whisk in 4 oz/113 g pumpkin purée (½ cup/120 mL) and ½ tsp/3 g ground cinnamon, ¼ tsp/1 g ground ginger, ¼ tsp/0.5 g ground nutmeg, and ¼ tsp/0.5 g kosher salt.

PUMPKIN MOUSSE: Gently fold 16 fl oz/480 mL whipped cream into Pumpkin Pastry Crème until combined.

LAGER PASTRY DOUGH

YIELD: 1 LB 10 OZ/737 G

12½ oz/354 g unbleached all-purpose
flour (2½ cups/600 mL)

½ oz/14 g granulated sugar (1 tbsp/15 mL)

¼ oz/7 g kosher salt (2 tsp/10 mL)

8 oz/227 g unsalted butter, cut into ½-in/1.25-cm dice,
chilled in freezer for 10 minutes (1 cup/240 mL)

6 fl oz/180 mL cold lager beer, plus
as needed to adjust dough

1. Put the flour, sugar, and salt in a food processor fitted with a steel blade and process until combined, about 10 seconds. Place the food processor bowl, blade, and contents in the freezer for 10 minutes.

2. Evenly scatter the butter over the flour mixture, breaking up any pieces that have clumped together. Pulse the motor until the dough looks like coarse meal and there are some butter pieces the size of small peas, about twelve 2-second on/off pulses.

3. Pour the flour mixture into a 4-qt/3.84-L bowl. Pour the beer over the flour and mix with a plastic spatula until barely combined, about 30 seconds. The dough should not be a cohesive ball. Don't overwork the dough. Doing so will develop the flour's gluten strands, which can make the crust tough.

4. Pour the dough out onto a lightly floured cold surface. Fold the dough over with a bench scraper and press together with a rolling pin, touching it as little as possible with your hands. Repeat 5 or 6 times, until it starts to come together like a dough, but butter pieces should still be evident and the dough should be a little crumbly. If it does not come together at all, add beer 1 tbsp/15 mL at a time until it does. Form the dough into a 1-in/2.5-cm-thick disk.

5. Wrap the disk in plastic wrap and chill in the refrigerator for 1 hour or up to 2 days. This allows the butter to firm up, the moisture to absorb evenly into the flour, and the dough to relax for easier rolling and less shrinkage

when baked. Roll out according to the recipe. See page 110 for tips on rolling dough. *The pastry crust can be made in advance. Immediately store wrapped in a disk or rolled out according to the recipe and stored in the refrigerator for 2 days or in the freezer for 3 months.*

MAKING PIE DOUGH

ACHIEVING FLAKY PIE DOUGH can be daunting, yet it is actually simple when made with cold flour, cold butter, and cold beer. The key, the cold temperature, is crucial because it is this coldness that allows the ingredients to combine yet remain independent and separate. Unlike cookie dough—where room temperature ingredients are creamed together, causing the butter, which is actually 15 to 20 percent water, to melt into and mix with the starch in the flour—pie dough is never creamed together. It is best made by flaking cold butter into cold flour. This separation of butter and flour, when baked, causes the steam that is released from the water in the butter to expand the unset dough into flaky layers. If the butter is warm and melted into the flour, this steam release can't happen and flaky layers can't and won't form.

Not only do you need to start with cold ingredients, but the dough should also be made cold, chilled, rolled out cold, chilled in the freezer, and put cold/frozen into a very hot oven. Another factor affecting the success of this dough is the beer. It adds a subtle yet rich flavor and its alcohol tenderizes the dough. Because alcohol evaporates more quickly than water, you can use a little more of it, making the dough more pliable.

SHORTBREAD TARTLET SHELLS

YIELD: 6 DOZEN TARTLET SHELLS

(2 LB 2½ OZ/978 G)

7 oz/198 g granulated sugar (1 cup/240 mL)

10 oz/284 g unbleached all-purpose flour (2 cups/480 mL), plus bench flour as needed

4 oz/113 g cornstarch (1 cup/240 mL)

½ tsp/2 g baking powder

¼ tsp/1 g kosher salt

8 oz/227 g unsalted butter, cut into ½-in/1.25-cm dice, chilled in freezer for 10 minutes (1 cup/240 mL)

3 oz/85 g cream cheese, cut into ½-in/1.25-cm dice, chilled in freezer for 10 minutes (6 tbsp/90 mL)

4 egg yolks

1 tbsp/15 mL vanilla extract

1. Grind the sugar in a food processor fitted with a steel blade until it is a fine powder, 30 seconds. Add the flour, cornstarch, baking powder, and salt and run the motor until mixed, 10 seconds. Evenly scatter the butter and cream cheese over the flour mixture, breaking up any pieces that have clumped together. Pulse the motor until the dough looks like coarse meal, fifteen 2-second on/off pulses.

2. Beat the egg yolks and vanilla in a 2-cup/480-mL bowl until blended. Pour the egg mixture over the flour and pulse the motor until it is evenly distributed and a dough forms, about twelve 4-second on/off pulses. The dough should not be a cohesive ball but should be crumbles that are pushed up the side of the bowl and stick together when pinched. Pour the dough out onto an unfloured work surface and press it together to form a ball.

3. Divide the dough into thirds, pat each into a flat 1-in/3-cm-thick disk, and wrap in plastic wrap. Refrigerate for 30 minutes. *The tartlet dough can be made in advance. Immediately store wrapped in the refrigerator for 2 days or in the freezer for 3 months. Thaw in the refrigerator before rolling out.*

4. Position racks in the top third and bottom third of the oven and heat to 375°F/191°C. Take 1 disk at a time out of the refrigerator, place it on a lightly floured cold surface, and dust the top of the dough and a rolling pin with flour. Roll the dough out to an even ⅛-in/3-mm-thick circle. Cut into 2½-in/6-cm rounds, ⅜ oz/10 g each, reserving scraps in the refrigerator. Press 1 round into each well of a mini muffin pan. Dock the dough by lightly pricking it with a fork or dough docker several times so it does not form blisters as it bakes. Place the pan in the freezer until the dough is firm before baking, at least 10 minutes. See page 110 for tips on rolling dough. *The tartlet shells can be rolled out and frozen in advance. Freeze in the mini muffin wells for at least 30 minutes. Quickly remove from the wells and stack them with 2 waxed paper sheets between each layer. Work quickly so they do not thaw.*

5. Bake until the edges and bottoms are a very light golden, about 12 minutes, rotating the pans halfway through the baking time from front to back and top to bottom. Let the tartlets set for 1 to 1½ minutes in the pans, then gently place a flat tray over the wells and invert the pans so the tartlets come out. They are difficult to remove from the wells when cooled. Cool the tartlets on a wire rack. *The tartlet shells can be baked in advance. Cool completely. Stack them with 2 waxed paper sheets between each layer. Store wrapped in the refrigerator for 2 days or in the freezer for 3 months.*

Flavor profiles and ingredients, recipes and ratios course through our minds, meshing and coalescing into a mass of possibilities. For the buffet, it is these basic building blocks—the sauces, salsas, relishes, and vinaigrettes—that add the finishing touch to the menu. These components elevate a good meal into a great event; they bring zest and zing and are the way to garnish with functionality. Many have inexpensive ingredients or use parts that would otherwise go to waste. Our Cajun Spice, used in many recipes, has been respectfully adapted from Chef Paul Prudhomme's original Louisiana Kitchen blend.

10

SAUCES, DRESSINGS, *and* CONDIMENTS

HERBED TOMATO SAUCE

YIELD: 1 GAL/3.84 L

6½ fl oz/195 mL extra-virgin olive oil

1 lb 2 oz/510 g finely chopped onions (4 cups/960 mL)

1 tbsp/10 g kosher salt, plus as needed to adjust seasoning

1 oz/28 g chopped garlic (8 tsp/40 mL or 8 cloves)

½ tsp/1 g dried oregano

¼ tsp/0.5 g red pepper flakes

8 fl oz/240 mL Burgundy or dry red wine

½ tsp/2 g granulated sugar, plus as needed to adjust seasoning

8 lb 12 oz/3.97 kg canned peeled whole plum tomatoes in tomato juice, no salt added

4 flat-leaf parsley stems

2 bay leaves

1 carrot

½ oz/14 g Pecorino Romano or Parmigiano-Reggiano cheese rinds

1½ oz/43 g grated Pecorino Romano (½ cup/120 mL)

½ oz/14 g basil chiffonade (¼ cup/60 mL) or 4 tsp/20 mL Basil Purée (page 323)

½ oz/14 g chopped flat-leaf parsley (¼ cup/60 mL)

½ tsp/1 g ground black pepper, plus as needed to adjust seasoning

1. Warm an 8-qt/7.68-L stockpot over medium-high heat, about 1 minute. Add 2 fl oz/60 mL oil to the pan, and heat to hot but not smoking, about 10 seconds. Add the onions and salt (reduce the salt to 1 tsp/3 g if using tomatoes with salt). Adjust the heat to medium-low and cook, stirring occasionally until soft and translucent, about 20 minutes. If the onions start to brown, add 1 fl oz/30 mL water to the pan and cook until the liquid evaporates. Move the onions to one side of the pot. Add ½ fl oz/15 mL oil and the garlic, oregano, and red pepper flakes to the empty space and cook until fragrant, about 1 minute. Combine and cook until the onions are golden, about 10 minutes more. Add the wine and sugar,

incorporating the onion into the liquid, and simmer until almost completely reduced, about 20 minutes.

2. Pass the tomatoes through a food mill fitted with a coarse disk into an 8-qt/7.68-L bowl and discard the tough pulp. Rinse the cans out with 8 fl oz/240 mL water and add the water to the tomatoes. Add the plum tomatoes, parsley stems, bay leaves, carrot, and cheese rinds to the onions. Simmer until the sauce is reduced by one-quarter and thickened, about 1½ hours. Stir frequently, especially at the beginning, with a flat-sided wooden spoon. The tomato pulp can stick to the bottom of the pan and burn, completely ruining the sauce.

3. Remove the pot from the heat. Remove the parsley stems, bay leaves, carrot, and cheese rind. Stir in the remaining 3 fl oz/120 mL olive oil and the grated cheese, basil, parsley, and black pepper. Taste and adjust seasoning. *The tomato sauce can be prepared in advance. Store wrapped in the refrigerator for 3 days or in the freezer for 3 months. Thaw in the refrigerator or on medium-low heat. Stir frequently with a flat-sided wooden spoon to check that the tomato pulp is not sticking to the bottom of the pan.*

CREAMY VODKA SAUCE: In a 6-qt/5.76-L stockpot, simmer ½ cup/120 mL vodka and ½ tsp/1 g red pepper flakes over medium-high heat until reduced by half, about 1 minute. Add 3 qt/2.88 L Herbed Tomato Sauce and 1 qt/960 mL heavy cream. Simmer for 10 minutes. Remove from the heat and add 2 oz/57 g grated Pecorino Romano (1 cup/240 mL).

ARTICHOKE, CAPER, AND LEMON SAUCE

YIELD: 2 QT/1.92 L

2 fl oz/60 mL extra-virgin olive oil

5 oz/142 g minced shallots

½ tsp/1 g kosher salt, plus as needed to adjust seasoning

¾ oz/21 g minced garlic (2 tbsp/30 mL or 6 cloves)

¼ tsp/1 g red pepper flakes

2 lb 4 oz/1.02 kg artichoke hearts, cut into ½-in/1.25-cm slices and tossed in a bowl with 4 fl oz/120 mL lemon juice to prevent oxidizing

1 oz/28 g unbleached all-purpose flour (3 tbsp/45 mL)

8 fl oz/240 mL dry white wine

24 fl oz/720 mL fortified chicken stock (see Note)

½ oz/ 14 g Dijon mustard (1 tbsp/15 mL)

3 oz/85 g nonpareil capers, rinsed (½ cup/120 mL)

2 tsp/8 g coarsely grated lemon zest (about ⅔ lemon)

Ground black pepper, as needed to adjust seasoning

GARNISH

1 oz/28 g minced parsley (½ cup/120 mL)

1. Heat a 4-qt/3.84-L wide-mouth saucepan over medium heat until it begins to get hot, about 1 minute. Add 1½ oz/45 mL oil to the pan, and heat until hot but not smoking, 10 seconds. Add the shallots and salt, adjust the heat to low, and cook until golden, about 15 minutes. Move the shallots to one side of pan. Add the remaining ½ fl oz/15 mL oil, the garlic, and red pepper flakes to the empty space and cook for 1 minute.

2. Lift the artichoke hearts out of the bowl, reserving the lemon juice, and add them to the pan with the shallots. Cook, tossing occasionally, until golden, about 10 minutes. Add the flour, stir until smooth, and cook for 1 minute. Add the wine and reserved lemon juice, scraping the fond from the bottom of the pan, then adjust the heat to low and simmer until reduced by half, 5 to 10 minutes. Add the fortified chicken stock. Whisk in the mustard.

3. Add the shallots and artichoke hearts, capers, and lemon zest. Simmer for 10 to 20 minutes, until it reaches the proper flavor and consistency. Taste and adjust seasoning. *The sauce can be made 3 days in advance. Cool rapidly and immediately store wrapped in the refrigerator.*

4. Just before serving, add the parsley. Taste and adjust seasoning.

For maximum flavor, fortify the chicken stock before making the sauce. Simmer 48 fl oz/1.44 L chicken stock with 2 lb 4 oz/1.02 kg chicken trimmings and bones, 2 carrots, 2 stalks celery, 1 coarsely chopped Spanish onion, 2 flat-leaf parsley stems, 10 cracked black peppercorns, and 1 bay leaf for about 1 hour. Strain the stock, discarding all solids, and it is ready to use.

LEMON SAUCE: Eliminate the artichoke hearts and capers.

TURKEY GRAVY: Eliminate the artichoke hearts and lemon juice. Replace the chicken stock with turkey stock. Eliminate the capers and lemon zest.

GREEN APPLE–GINGER SALSA

YIELD: 32 FL OZ/960 ML

8 oz/227 g peeled and cored Granny Smith apple or Asian pear or peeled jícama, minced (2 cups/480 mL)

4½ oz/128 g peeled and seeded English cucumber, minced (1 cup/240 mL)

½ oz/14 g finely minced ginger (1 tbsp/15 mL)

2 fl oz/60 mL canola oil

2 fl oz/60 mL mirin

1 fl oz/30 mL lime juice (about 2 limes)

1 fl oz/30 mL rice wine vinegar

½ tsp/2 mL Tabasco sauce

1 tsp/3 g kosher salt, plus as needed to adjust seasoning

¼ tsp/0.5 g ground black pepper

4½ oz/128 g red onion, minced (1 cup/240 mL)

½ oz/14 g chopped cilantro or flat-leaf parsley (¼ cup/60 mL)

1. Combine the apples, cucumber, ginger, oil, mirin, lime juice, vinegar, Tabasco, salt, and pepper in a 2-qt/1.92-L bowl. Taste and adjust seasoning. *The salsa can be made in advance. Rapidly chill and immediately store wrapped in the refrigerator for 2 days.*

2. Just before serving, garnish with the red onion and cilantro. (Add the red onion just before serving, because it can bleed into the salsa, turning it pink.) Taste and adjust seasoning.

ORANGE-HORSERADISH SALSA

YIELD: 32 FL OZ/960 ML

32 fl oz/960 mL orange marmalade (2 lb 4 oz/1.02 kg)

4 oz/113 g finely grated fresh horseradish or drained prepared horseradish (½ cup/120 mL)

½ tsp/1 g cayenne, plus as needed to adjust seasoning

¼ tsp/1 g kosher salt, plus as needed to adjust seasoning

Place all the ingredients in a 2-qt/1.92-L bowl and combine. Taste and adjust seasoning.

HORSERADISH GREMOLATA

YIELD: 20 FL OZ/600 ML

8 oz/227 g finely grated fresh horseradish or drained prepared horseradish (1 cup/240 mL)

½ fl oz/15 mL lemon juice

1 oz/28 g coarse lemon zest (¼ cup/60 mL or about 4 lemons)

½ tsp/1.5 g kosher salt, plus as needed to adjust seasoning

¼ tsp/0.5 g ground black pepper, plus as needed to adjust seasoning

2 oz/57 g chopped flat-leaf parsley (1 cup/240 mL)

1 oz/28 g minced chives (½ cup/120 mL)

1. Combine the horseradish, lemon juice, lemon zest, salt, and pepper in a 1-qt/960-mL bowl. *The horseradish gremolata can be prepared 1 week in advance. Store wrapped in the refrigerator.*

2. Add the parsley and chives to the gremolata just before serving.

PICO DE GALLO

YIELD: 32 FL OZ/960 ML

1 lb 8 oz/680 g diced plum tomatoes (5¾ cups/1.38 L or about 8 tomatoes)

2¼ oz/64 g finely minced red onion (½ cup/120 mL)

2 fl oz/60 mL lime juice (about 4 limes)

½ oz/14 g finely minced jalapeño (2 tsp/10 mL)

¼ oz/7 g garlic paste (2 tsp/10 mL or 2 cloves) made with ¼ tsp/0.5 g kosher salt

¾ tsp/2 g kosher salt, plus as needed to adjust seasoning

½ tsp/1 g ground black pepper, plus as needed to adjust seasoning

¼ tsp/1 g Cajun Spice (page 333), plus as needed to adjust seasoning

1 oz/28 g chopped cilantro (½ cup/120 mL)

1. In a 2-qt/1.92-L/ bowl, combine the tomatoes, onion, lime juice, jalapeño, garlic paste, salt, pepper, and Cajun spice. Taste and adjust seasoning. *The pico de gallo can be prepared 4 hours in advance. Store wrapped in the refrigerator.*

2. Add the cilantro just before serving. Taste and adjust seasoning.

ROMA SALSA

YIELD: 32 FL OZ/960 ML

1 lb 8 oz/680 g plum tomatoes or grape tomatoes
(5¾ cups/1.38 L or about 8 plum tomatoes)

1½ fl oz/45 mL olive oil, Italian preferred

6¼ oz/178 g minced shallots (1¼ cups/300 mL)

2 tsp/6 g kosher salt, plus as needed to adjust seasoning

½ oz/14 g finely minced garlic (4 tsp/20 mL or 4 cloves)

2 tsp/10 mL balsamic vinegar, plus as
needed to adjust seasoning

4 tsp/20 mL lime juice, plus as needed to adjust seasoning

1½ fl oz/45 mL extra-virgin olive oil, Italian preferred

1½ oz/43 g grated Pecorino Romano (½ cup/120 mL)

¼ tsp/0.5 g ground black pepper, plus
as needed to adjust seasoning

GARNISHES

3 oz/85 g pitted and chopped oil-cured
Gaeta olives (½ cup/120 mL)

3 fl oz/90 mL nonpareil capers, rinsed (½ cup/120 mL)

2½ oz/71 g roasted red or green pepper (½ cup/120 mL
or about ½ pepper; page 123)

¾ oz/21 g basil chiffonade (6 tbsp/90 mL) or
2 tbsp/30 mL Basil Purée (page 323)

½ oz/14 g minced chives (¼ cup/60 mL)

1. If using plum tomatoes, roast the tomatoes over an open gas flame or under a hot broiler, turning every 10 seconds, until the skin starts to blister. Cool at room temperature for 10 minutes. Peel off and discard the skin. Chop the tomatoes into fine dice, keeping all seeds and juice with tomatoes, and place in a colander set over a 2-qt/1.92-L bowl. If using grape tomatoes, slice each into 6 to 8 pieces and set aside in a small bowl, as they don't have much juice.

2. Heat a 10-in/25-cm sauté pan over medium heat, about 1 minute. Add 1 fl oz/30 mL olive oil to the pan, and heat until hot but not smoking, about 10 seconds. Add the shallots and salt, adjust the heat to medium-low, and cook until translucent and tender, occasionally checking that the bottom is not burning, 20 minutes. If the shallots start to brown, add ½ fl oz/15 mL water. Move the shallots to one side of the pan. Add the remaining ½ fl oz/15 mL olive oil and the garlic to the empty space and cook for 1 minute. Combine and cook until the shallots are golden, about 5 minutes. Add the juice from the tomatoes, the vinegar, and lime juice and cook until completely reduced, about 5 minutes more. Put back into the bowl and cool at room temperature for 10 minutes. Add the tomatoes, extra-virgin olive oil, cheese, and black pepper. Add the garnish(es) . *The salsa can be prepared up to 6 hours in advance. Do not toss, but rather leave the ingredients layered. Store wrapped in the refrigerator.*

3. Add the basil and chives. Toss, taste, and adjust seasoning.

CRANBERRY-BOURBON RELISH

YIELD: 32 FL OZ/960 ML

1 lb/ 454 g cranberries (1 qt/960 mL)

5¼ oz/149 g brown sugar (¾ cup/180 mL), plus as needed to adjust sweetness

6 fl oz/180 mL orange juice (about 3 oranges)

2 fl oz/60 mL bourbon

½ tsp/2.5 mL lemon juice

⅛ oz/4 g finely grated lemon zest (1½ tsp/7.5 mL or about ½ lemon)

⅛ oz/4 g finely grated orange zest (1½ tsp/7.5 mL or about ¼ orange)

4 oz/113 g orange suprêmes (½ cup/120 mL or about 1 orange)

Bring the cranberries, brown sugar, orange juice, and bourbon to a simmer in a 4-qt/3.84-L wide-mouth sauce-pan over medium heat. Reduce the heat to medium-low and simmer until the berries burst and the liquid is reduced and thickened, 15 to 20 minutes. Add the lemon juice, lemon zest, and orange zest. Taste and adjust the sweetness. Very gently fold in the orange suprêmes. Cool. *The cranberry relish can be prepared in advance. Store wrapped in the refrigerator for 2 weeks or in the freezer for 3 months.*

ROSEMARY-SCENTED HONEY

YIELD: 16 FL OZ/480 ML

1 lb/454 g honey (1¼ cups/ mL)

5 fl oz/150 mL lemon juice

½ oz/14 g minced rosemary (5 tbsp/75 mL)

1¼ tsp/2.5 g mL butcher-grind coarse black pepper

½ tsp/2 g kosher salt

Whisk the honey, lemon juice, rosemary, peppercorns, and salt in a 1½-qt/1.44-L saucepan until combined. Reduce over medium-low heat to a thick syrup, 15 to 20 minutes. It should look as though all the liquid has evaporated, leaving soft popping air bubbles. Cool for 15 minutes. *The honey can be made 1 month in advance. Store wrapped in the refrigerator. If it becomes too thick, set in a bowl of warm water or microwave on low power for 30 seconds at a time until it thins out.*

BALSAMIC MOLASSES

YIELD: 8 FL OZ/236 ML

30 fl oz/900 mL balsamic vinegar

2 fl oz/60 mL molasses

5 cracked black peppercorns

1 bay leaf

½ oz/14 g unsalted butter, cut into
¼-in/6-mm pats (1 tbsp/15 mL)

Put the vinegar and molasses into a wide-mouth 4-qt/3.84-L saucepan and whisk until combined. Add the peppercorns and bay leaf. Cook over medium-low heat, so there are wisps of steam and very tiny bubbles, but it is not simmering. Reduce to one-quarter of its original volume or 1 cup/240 mL, about 1 hour. It should be thick and syrupy. Be careful, because the vinegar fumes can be strong. Remove from the heat and whisk in the butter. Strain, discarding the peppercorns and bay leaf. *The molasses can be made 1 month in advance. Store wrapped in the refrigerator.*

QUINCE GASTRIQUE

YIELD: 32 FL OZ/960 ML

1 lb 8 oz/680 g quince paste (3 cups/720 mL)

3 fl oz/90 mL sherry vinegar

5 fl oz/150 mL hot water, plus as
needed to adjust consistency

Put all the ingredients into a blender. Run the motor until smooth, first on the lowest setting for 30 seconds and then on the highest setting for 30 seconds. If necessary, adjust the consistency with more water. *The gastrique can be made 1 month in advance. Store in a sealed bottle in the refrigerator.*

RÉMOULADE

YIELD: 32 FL OZ/960 ML

2 oz/57 g nonpareil capers (⅓ cup/80 mL)

3 small anchovy fillets

Milk, as needed for anchovies

1 lb 8 oz/680 g mayonnaise (3 cups/720 mL)

1 oz/28 g ketchup (2 tbsp/30 mL)

1 fl oz/30 mL lemon juice

½ oz/14 g Dijon mustard (1 tbsp/15 mL)

1 tsp/3 g Cajun Spice (page 333)

1 tsp/5 mL Tabasco sauce

½ tsp/1 g ground black pepper, plus
as needed to adjust seasoning

2 oz/57 g cornichons, chopped (⅓ cup/80 mL)

½ oz/14 g chopped chervil or flat-
leaf parsley (¼ cup/60 mL)

½ oz/14 g chopped chives (¼ cup/60 mL)

⅛ oz/4 g chopped tarragon (1 tbsp/15 mL)

1. If the capers are salt-cured, soak in 2 cups cold water for 30 minutes. Drain and repeat. If the capers are in vinegar brine, drain, taste, and if too salty soak in 2 cups cold water for 5 minutes and then drain. If the anchovies are salt-cured, soak, refrigerated, in 1 cup/240 mL cold milk for 30 minutes. Drain and repeat. If the anchovies are in oil, drain the oil, soak in ¼ cup/60 mL cold milk for 5 minutes, and then drain, discarding milk.

2. Place the anchovies, mayonnaise, ketchup, lemon juice, mustard, Cajun Spice, Tabasco, and pepper in the bowl of a food processor fitted with the metal blade. Run the motor until combined, scraping down the bowl once, about 20 seconds. Add the capers, cornichons, chervil, chives, and tarragon and pulse the motor until the cornichons are finely chopped, about ten 2-second on/off pulses. Taste and adjust the seasoning. *The rémoulade can be made 3 days in advance. Immediately store wrapped in the refrigerator.*

ARUGULA-CUCUMBER-SPINACH TZATZIKI

YIELD: 48 FL OZ/1.44 L

1 lb/454 g peeled and seeded English cucumber,
chopped (3½ cups/840 mL or about 1½ cucumbers)

6 oz/170 g arugula (2 cups/480 mL)

6 oz/170 g spinach, squeezed dry (2 cups/480 mL)

12 oz/340 g plain Greek yogurt, full-fat
preferred (about 1½ cups/360 mL)

3 oz/85 g Dijon mustard (6 tbsp/90 mL)

1¼ oz/35 g minced shallot (¼ cup/60 mL or
about 1 shallot)

½ fl oz/15 mL lemon juice (about ½ lemon),
plus as needed to adjust seasoning

⅛ oz/4 g garlic paste (1 tsp/5 mL or 1 clove)
made with ¼ tsp/1 g kosher salt

1 tsp/3 g kosher salt, plus as needed to adjust seasoning

½ tsp/1 g finely ground black pepper, plus
as needed to adjust seasoning

Put all the ingredients into a blender. Run the motor until smooth, first on the lowest setting for about 30 seconds and then on the highest setting for about 30 seconds. Taste and adjust seasoning. *The tzatziki can be blended 3 days in advance. Immediately store wrapped in the refrigerator.*

PEANUT SAUCE

YIELD: 32 FL OZ/960 ML

13½ oz/385 g chunky peanut butter (1½ cups/360 mL)

12 fl oz/360 mL coconut milk

6 fl oz/180 mL soy sauce

1¾ oz/51 g dark brown sugar (¼ cup/60 mL firmly packed), plus as needed to adjust sweetness

1½ fl oz/45 mL lime juice

½ oz/14 g finely minced jalapeño (2 tsp/10 mL or about ½ jalapeño), plus as needed to adjust seasoning

½ oz/14 g garlic paste (4 tsp/20 mL or 4 cloves) made with ¼ tsp/1 g kosher salt

Whisk all the ingredients together in a 4-qt/3.84-L bowl. Taste and adjust seasoning. *The sauce can be prepared 1 week in advance. Store in a sealed bottle in the refrigerator. Shake to emulsify before using.*

GORGONZOLA, BACON, AND TOASTED WALNUT CRÈME

YIELD: 32 FL OZ/960 ML

1½ oz/43 g cooked thick-sliced bacon that was cut into ¼-in/6-mm pieces before cooking (½ cup/120 mL)

16 fl oz/480 mL heavy cream

4 oz/113 g crumbled Gorgonzola (1 cup/240 mL)

4 oz/113 g toasted walnuts (½ cup/120 mL; page 114)

¼ tsp/0.5 g cayenne, plus as needed to adjust seasoning

Kosher salt, as needed to adjust seasoning

Ground black pepper, as needed to adjust seasoning

Heat a 2-qt/1.92-L saucepan over medium heat , about 1 minute. Add the bacon and heavy cream and simmer until thickened, 10 minutes. Turn off the heat and stir in the cheese, walnuts, and cayenne. Taste and adjust seasoning.

Serve blanched green beans tossed in warm Gorgonzola, Bacon, and Toasted Walnut Crème.

GORGONZOLA CRÈME: Eliminate the bacon and walnuts. Increase the Gorgonzola to 8 oz/227 g (1 cup/240 mL).

HORSERADISH CRÈME

YIELD: 32 FL OZ/960 ML

1 lb/454 g mayonnaise (2 cups/480 mL)

16 fl oz/480 mL sour cream

2 oz/57 g g finely grated fresh horseradish or drained prepared horseradish (¼ cup/60 mL), plus as needed to adjust seasoning

¼ tsp/0.5 g cayenne, plus as needed to adjust seasoning

Kosher salt, as needed to adjust seasoning

Ground black pepper, as needed to adjust seasoning

Place the mayonnaise, sour cream, horseradish, and cayenne in a 2-qt/1.92-L bowl and combine. If a smoother texture is desired, blend with an immersion blender. Taste and adjust seasoning. *The horseradish crème can be made 3 days in advance. Store wrapped in the refrigerator.*

GUACAMOLE

YIELD: 32 FL OZ/960 ML

6 Hass avocados, halved, pitted, flesh scored into a dice, and scooped out

4¼ oz/120 g diced plum tomatoes (1 cup/240 mL)

2½ oz/71 g diced yellow or red pepper (½ cup/120 mL or about ½ pepper)

2¼ oz/57 g minced red onion (½ cup/120 mL)

½ oz/14 g finely minced jalapeño (2 tsp/10 mL or about ½ jalapeño)

¼ oz/7 g garlic paste (2 tsp/10 mL or 2 cloves) made with ¼ tsp/1 g kosher salt

¼ oz/7 g chopped cilantro (2 tbsp/20 mL)

3 oz/85 g sour cream (6 tbsp/90 mL)

1 fl oz/30 mL lime juice

1½ tsp/5 g kosher salt, plus as needed to adjust seasoning

½ tsp/1.5 g Cajun Spice (page 333)

¼ tsp/0.5 g ground black pepper

In a 2-qt/1.92-L bowl, combine all the ingredients. Taste and adjust seasoning. *All of the ingredients except for the avocado can be layered in the bowl 1 day in advance. The avocado can be added 4 hours in advance. Immediately store wrapped in the refrigerator with plastic pressed onto the surface area, completely sealing it, to prevent oxidation.*

AVOCADO-PEACH GUACAMOLE: Add 5 oz/142 g peeled, pitted, and diced peaches (1 cup or about 1 peach).

AVOCADO-MANGO GUACAMOLE: Add 5 oz/142 g peeled, pitted, and diced mango (1 cup or about ½ mango).

ROMESCO

YIELD: 32 FL OZ/960 ML

1 lb 2 oz/510 g plum tomatoes, halved (4½ cups/1.08 L or about 6 tomatoes)

2 fl oz/60 mL olive oil

2 fl oz/60 mL sherry vinegar

3¾ oz/106 g minced shallots (¾ cup/180 mL)

¾ oz/21 g minced garlic (2 tbsp/30 mL or 6 cloves)

2 tsp/6 g kosher salt, plus as needed to adjust seasoning

½ tsp/1 g ground black pepper

½ tsp/2 g hot smoked Spanish paprika, plus as needed to adjust seasoning

¼ tsp/1 g granulated sugar

1 pinch red pepper flakes

4 roasted red peppers (2 lb/908 g; page 123)

1 roasted jalapeño (¾ oz/21 g)

8 oz/227 g toasted hazelnuts, skinned and chopped (1½ cups/360 mL; page 114)

8 oz/227 g toasted Marcona almonds, chopped (1¾ cups/420 mL; page 114)

2 oz/57 g baguette, cubed and toasted

6 fl oz/180 mL extra-virgin olive oil, Spanish preferred, plus as needed to adjust viscosity

1. Slice the tomatoes in half lengthwise, put into a 2-qt/1.92-L bowl, and combine with the olive oil, vinegar, shallots, garlic, salt, black pepper, paprika, sugar, and red pepper flakes. Pour the seasoned tomatoes onto a sheet pan and evenly distribute. Bake the tomatoes for 20 minutes, then lower the heat to 300°F/149°C and continue to bake until they shrivel and caramelize, about 2 hours more. Turn the oven off and leave the tomatoes in the cooling oven for 1 hour. *The roasted tomatoes can be prepared 1 week in advance. Immediately store wrapped in the refrigerator.*

2. Put the roasted tomatoes, the roasted red peppers and jalapeño, both toasted nuts, and the baguette into a food processor. Pulse the motor until the ingredients are minced but not puréed, fifteen 2-second on/off pulses.

Drizzle in the extra-virgin olive oil with the motor running to form a thick paste, taking about 45 seconds, scraping down the bowl a few times. It should still have a nutty texture. Add more extra-virgin olive oil as needed to adjust the viscosity and flavor. Taste and adjust seasoning. *The romesco can be prepared 3 days in advance. In fact, it tastes better the next day. Store in the refrigerator.*

TAHINI SAUCE

YIELD: 48 FL OZ/1.44 L

8 fl oz/240 mL soy sauce

8 fl oz /240 mL water

4 fl oz/120 mL tahini paste

2 fl oz/60 mL mirin

2 fl oz/60 mL rice wine vinegar

2 fl oz/60 mL Thai chili paste

1½ fl oz/45 mL lime juice (about 3 limes)

7 oz/210 g dark brown sugar (1 cup/240 mL firmly packed)

½ oz/14 g minced garlic (4 tsp/20 mL or 4 cloves)

8 fl oz/240 mL canola oil

8 fl oz/240 mL sesame oil

2 oz/57 g chopped cilantro, flat-leaf parsley, or chives (1 cup/240 mL)

1. Put the soy sauce, water, tahini paste, mirin, vinegar, chili paste, lime juice, brown sugar, and garlic into a blender. Run the motor until smooth, first on the lowest setting for 30 seconds and then on the highest setting for 30 seconds.

2. Slowly drizzle in both oils with the motor running on the lowest speed, taking about 1 minute. Continue to blend until thick and emulsified, 30 seconds more. If necessary, adjust the consistency with water. Taste and adjust seasoning. *The tahini sauce can be prepared 3 weeks in advance. Store in a sealed bottle in the refrigerator. Shake to emulsify before using.*

3. Whisk in the cilantro just before serving.

MACADAMIA-PIGNOLI PESTO

YIELD: 32 FL OZ/960 ML

---

1 oz/28 g garlic cloves (8 cloves)

1 tbsp plus 2 tsp/16 g kosher salt, plus
as needed to adjust seasoning

8 oz/227 g basil leaves (6 cups/1.44 L loosely packed)

12 oz/340 g extra-virgin olive oil (1½ cups/360 mL),
plus as needed to adjust viscosity and flavor

5 oz/142 g toasted macadamia nuts
(1 cup/240 mL; see page 114)

5 oz/142 g toasted pine nuts (1 cup/240 mL; page 114)

1 tsp/2 g ground black pepper, plus as
needed to adjust seasoning

4 oz/113 g grated Parmigiano-Reggiano (1⅓ cups/320 mL)

4 oz/113 g grated Pecorino Romano (1⅓ cups/320 mL)

1. Bring a 3-qt/2.88-L saucepan filled with cold water to a boil. Add the garlic and 1 tbsp/10 g salt. Cover. As soon as the water returns to a boil, add the basil. As soon as the basil becomes vibrant green, 15 seconds, remove the basil and garlic and shock in an ice-water bath. Drain and squeeze basil dry.

2. Drop 1 blanched garlic clove at a time into a food processor fitted with a steel blade with the motor running and process until finely chopped, about 10 seconds for each clove. Turn the motor off and add basil, the remaining 2 tsp/6 g salt, and 4 fl oz/120 mL olive oil. Pulse the motor until the basil is puréed, about fifteen 3-second on/off pulses. *The basil purée can be prepared in advance. Store wrapped in the refrigerator for 3 days or in the freezer for 3 months with plastic gently pressed onto the surface area, completely sealing it to prevent oxidation.*

3. Add both nuts and pulse the motor again until they are finely chopped, about fifteen 3-second on/off pulses. Drizzle in the remaining 8 fl oz/240 mL olive oil with the motor running to form a thick paste, taking about 30 seconds. Add the cheeses and pulse the motor until combined, scraping down the bowl a few times. Add more oil

as needed to adjust the viscosity and flavor. Taste and adjust seasoning. *The pesto can be prepared in advance. Immediately store wrapped in the refrigerator for 3 days with plastic gently pressed onto the surface area, completely sealing it, to prevent oxidation.*

PISTACHIO PESTO: Replace the macadamia nuts and pine nuts with 12 oz/340 g pistachio nuts (2½ cups/600 mL). Increase the kosher salt added to the food processor to 1 tbsp/10 g. Eliminate the Parmigiano-Reggiano and Pecorino Romano.

BASIL PURÉE: Yield: 10 fl oz/300 mL. Follow steps 1 and 2 of the method to make the basil purée.

MINT PURÉE: Yield: 10 fl oz/300 mL. Omit the nuts, garlic, pepper, and cheeses. Replace the basil leaves with an equal amount of mint leaves. Decrease the oil to 4 fl oz/120 mL. *Mint Purée can be prepared in advance. Store, wrapped, in the refrigerator for 3 days or in the freezer for 3 months with plastic gently pressed onto the surface area, completely sealing it to prevent oxidation.*

BASIL OIL: Yield: 16 fl oz/480 mL. Omit the nuts, salt, pepper, and cheeses. Decrease the basil to 3 oz/85 g (2¼ loosely packed cups/540 mL). Add 1 oz/28 g flat-leaf parsley (½ cup/120 mL) and blanch with the basil. Increase the oil to 16 fl oz/480 mL. Purée in a blender. Strain the oil through a fine-mesh strainer lined with a coffee filter. *Basil Oil can be prepared in advance. Store wrapped in the refrigerator for 3 weeks.*

CHIVE OIL: Yield: 16 fl oz/480 mL. Omit the nuts, salt, pepper, and cheeses. Replace the basil with 3 oz/85 g chives and 4 oz/28 g flat-leaf parsley and blanch as directed. Increase the oil to 16 fl oz/480 mL. Purée in a blender. Strain the oil through a fine-mesh strainer lined with a coffee filter. *Chive Oil can be prepared in advance. Store wrapped in the refrigerator for 3 weeks.*

SUN-DRIED TOMATO PESTO

YIELD: 32 FL OZ/960 ML

GARLIC CONFIT

2 fl oz/60 mL extra-virgin olive oil

1 oz/28 g garlic cloves (8 cloves)

PESTO

11¼ oz/318 g dry-packed sun-dried tomatoes (2½ cups/600 mL packed)

6 fl oz/180 mL extra-virgin olive oil

3 oz/85 g grated Pecorino Romano (1 cup/240 mL)

1 oz/28 g basil chiffonade (½ cup/120 mL) or 8 tsp/40 mL Basil Purée (page 323)

1 tbsp/14 g granulated sugar, plus as needed to adjust seasoning

½ tsp/1.5 g kosher salt, plus as needed to adjust seasoning

½ tsp/1 g ground black pepper, plus as needed to adjust seasoning

1. For the garlic confit, put the oil and garlic into a 1½-qt/1.44-L saucepan. Cover with a tight-fitting lid and cook over very low heat until soft and golden but not browned, 10 to 15 minutes. Cool to room temperature.

2. For the pesto, bring 3 cups of water to a boil. Simmer the sun-dried tomatoes for 1 minute. Cover the saucepan, remove the pan from the heat, and rehydrate the tomatoes until they become plump and juicy, about 20 minutes. Remove the lid and let cool. Drain the tomatoes, reserving 2 fl oz/60 mL liquid.

3. Place the sun-dried tomatoes, 2 fl oz/60 mL reserved cooking liquid, and the garlic confit and the oil it was cooked in into a food processor fitted with a steel blade. Run the motor until almost smooth, scraping down the side of the bowl. Add the extra-virgin olive oil, cheese, basil, sugar, salt, and pepper. Run the motor until thoroughly combined and smooth. Taste and adjust seasoning. *The pesto can be made in advance. Immediately store wrapped in the refrigerator for 3 days or in the freezer for 3 months.*

RED PEPPER ROUILLE

YIELD: 32 FL OZ/960 ML

¼ tsp/0.5 g saffron threads

½ tsp/2 mL hot water

1 lb/454 g mayonnaise (2 cups/480 mL)

9 oz/255 g roasted red peppers, chopped (1⅓ cups/320 mL or about 4 peppers; page 123)

4 fl oz/120 mL extra-virgin olive oil

½ fl oz/15 mL lemon juice

½ oz/14 g garlic paste (4 tsp/20 mL or 4 cloves) made with ¼ tsp/0.75 g kosher salt

1 tsp/2 g cayenne

1. Toast the saffron in a 6-in/15-cm sauté pan over low heat for 15 to 30 seconds while continually moving the pan over the flame until the saffron is fragrant. Immediately put the saffron into a bowl and add the hot water. Bloom or steep the saffron for 2 minutes.

2. Put the saffron and all the other ingredients into a blender. Run the motor until smooth, first on the lowest setting for about 30 seconds and then on the highest setting for about 30 seconds. Taste and adjust seasoning. *The rouille can be blended 3 days in advance. Immediately store wrapped in the refrigerator.*

SUN-DRIED TOMATO JAM

YIELD: 32 FL OZ/960 ML

4½ fl oz/135 mL extra-virgin olive oil, plus
as needed to adjust seasoning

9 oz/255 g finely chopped onion (2 cups/480 mL)

1 tsp/3 g kosher salt, plus as needed to adjust seasoning

½ oz/14 g chopped garlic (4 tsp/20 mL or 4 cloves)

1 pinch red pepper flakes

1 tbsp/6 g dried porcini mushroom powder (see Note)

1 lb 12 oz/793 g canned peeled whole plum tomatoes
in tomato juice, no salt added (about 6½ cups/1.56 L)

4½ oz/128 g dry-packed sun-dried tomatoes,
cut into julienne (1 cup/240 mL packed)

¼ oz/7 g basil chiffonade (2 tbsp/30 mL)
or 2 tsp Basil Purée (page 323)

¼ tsp/0.5 g ground black pepper, plus
as needed to adjust seasoning

1. Warm a 3-qt/2.88-L saucepan over medium-high heat, about 1 minute. Add 1 fl oz/30 mL oil to the pan and heat to hot but not smoking, about 10 seconds. Add the onions and salt (reduce the salt to ½ tsp/1.5 g if using tomatoes with salt). Lower the heat to medium-low and cook, stirring occasionally, until soft and translucent, about 20 minutes. If the onions start to brown, add 2 fl oz/60 mL water to the pan and cook until the liquid evaporates. Move the onions to one side of the pan. Add ½ fl oz/15 mL oil, the garlic, and the red pepper flakes to the empty space and cook until fragrant, about 1 minute. Add the dried mushroom powder. Combine and cook until the onions are golden, about 10 minutes more.

2. Pass the tomatoes through a food mill fitted with a coarse disk into a 2-qt/1.92-L bowl and discard the tough pulp. Rinse the cans out with 2 fl oz/60 mL water and add to the tomatoes. Add the plum tomatoes and sun-dried tomatoes to the onions. Simmer until the tomatoes are reduced by one-quarter and thickened, about 30 minutes. Stir frequently, especially at the beginning, with a flat-sided wooden spoon. The tomato pulp can stick to the bottom of the pan and burn, completely ruining the sauce.

3. Remove the pot from the heat. Stir in the remaining 3 fl oz/90 mL olive oil, the basil, and the black pepper. Adjust the consistency with an immersion blender. Taste and adjust seasoning. *The sun-dried tomato jam can be prepared in advance. Rapidly cool, then immediately store wrapped in the refrigerator for 3 days or in the freezer for 3 months.*

To make dried porcini mushroom powder, grind dried porcini mushrooms in a spice grinder until they are reduced to fine dust. Sift the dust through a fine-mesh strainer.

FIG-ONION JAM

YIELD: 32 FL OZ/960 ML

6 fl oz/180 mL extra-virgin olive oil

3 lb 12 oz/1.7 kg red onions, cut into julienne
(14 cups/3.36 L or about 7 large onions)

1½ tsp/5 g kosher salt, plus as needed to adjust seasoning

1 lb 12 oz/794 g dried figs or 2 lb 4 oz/1.25 kg fresh
figs, stems removed, cut into medium dice

8 fl oz/240 mL balsamic vinegar

7 oz/198 g brown sugar (1 cup/240 mL firmly
packed), plus as needed to adjust seasoning

¼ tsp/0.5 g ground black pepper, plus
as needed to adjust seasoning

1. Heat a 10-in/25-cm sautoir over medium heat, about
1 minute. Add the oil to the pan and heat until hot but
not smoking, about 10 seconds. Add the onions and salt
and toss together. Adjust the heat to very low, cover, and
cook the onions until their liquid is released and evaporates, stirring occasionally and checking that the bottom
is not burning, about 1½ hours. If there is not enough
liquid released from the onions to cook for this length of
time without burning, add 2 fl oz/60 mL water and cook
until all of the liquid evaporates.

2. Add the figs, vinegar, and sugar and continue cooking
uncovered over low heat until all of the liquid has evaporated and the mixture looks caramelized and jammy,
about 45 minutes more. Stir frequently to make sure the
bottom is not burning. Remove from the heat. Add the
pepper. Toss, taste, and adjust seasoning. *The fig-onion
jam can be prepared in advance. Rapidly cool, then immediately store wrapped in the refrigerator for 3 days or in the
freezer for 3 months.*

ONION MARMALADE

MAKES 8 FL OZ/240 ML

1 fl oz/30 mL extra-virgin olive oil

1 oz/28 g unsalted butter (2 tbsp/30 mL)

2 lb 8 oz/1.13 kg Spanish onions, cut into julienne
(10 cups/2.4 L or about 5 large onions)

¼ oz/7 g garlic cloves (1 tbsp/15 mL or 3 cloves)

Bouquet garni (consisting of 2 flat-leaf parsley stems,
2 leek leaves, 1 thyme sprig, and 1 bay leaf)

¾ tsp/2 g kosher salt, plus as needed to adjust seasoning

1 fl oz/30 mL Chablis or unoaked Chardonnay

2 tsp/10 mL Cognac or brandy

¼ tsp/0.5 g ground black pepper, plus
as needed to adjust seasoning

1. Heat a 10-in/25-cm sautoir over medium heat, about
1 minute. Add the oil and the butter to the pan and heat
until hot but not smoking, about 10 seconds. Add the
onions, garlic, bouquet garni, and salt and toss together.
Adjust the heat to very low, cover, and cook the onions
until their liquid is released and evaporates, stirring occasionally and checking that the bottom is not burning,
about 1½ hours. If there is not enough liquid released
from the onions to cook for this length of time without
burning, add 2 fl oz/60 mL water and cook until all of the
liquid evaporates.

2. Add the wine and continue cooking uncovered over
low heat until all of the liquid has evaporated and the
onions look caramelized and jammy, about 45 minutes
more. Remove from the heat. Remove the bouquet garni.
Add the Cognac and pepper. Toss, taste, and adjust seasoning. *The onions can be prepared 3 days in advance.
Rapidly cool, then immediately store wrapped in the
refrigerator.*

FIRE-ROASTED RED PEPPER COULIS

YIELD: 32 FL OZ/960 ML

4 fl oz/120 mL olive oil

2½ oz/71 g chopped shallots (½ cup/120 mL)

½ oz/14 g chopped garlic (4 tsp/20 mL or 4 cloves)

12 fl oz/360 mL dry white wine

12 fl oz/360 mL chicken stock, plus
as needed to adjust viscosity

2 lb 4 oz/1.25 kg roasted red peppers
(8 or 9 peppers; page 123)

1 fl oz/30 mL lemon juice, plus as
needed to adjust seasoning

4 tsp/12 g kosher salt, plus as needed to adjust seasoning

1 tsp/2 g ground black pepper, plus as
needed to adjust seasoning

1 tsp/4 g hot smoked Spanish paprika

1. Warm a 12-in/30-cm sautoir over medium heat, about 1 minute. Add 1 fl oz/30 mL oil to coat the pan and heat to hot but not smoking, about 10 seconds. Add the shallots and garlic and cook until fragrant, about 1 minute. Add the wine, lower the heat to medium-low, and reduce the wine to one-third its original volume, or 4 oz/120 mL, about 30 minutes. Add the stock and roasted peppers and reduce the liquid to half its original volume, or 8 oz/240 mL. Cool at room temperature for 20 minutes.

2. Put the reduction, the remaining 3 fl oz/90 mL olive oil, and the lemon juice, salt, black pepper, and paprika into a blender. Run the motor until smooth, scraping down the sides, 2 minutes. Add more stock, if needed, to adjust the viscosity. Taste and adjust seasoning. Strain through a medium-mesh strainer, discarding any solids. *The coulis can be prepared 1 week in advance. Immediately store wrapped in the refrigerator.*

CAUTION: Never fill the blender more than one-quarter full with hot liquid. The steam can cause the hot soup to spray you when the blender is turned on.

HONEY MUSTARD

YIELD: 32 FL OZ/960 ML

1 lb 8 oz/680 g mayonnaise (3 cups/720 mL)

6 oz/170 g Dijon mustard (¾ cup/180 mL)

9 oz/255 g honey (¾ cup/180 mL)

2 oz/57 g finely grated fresh horseradish or
drained prepared horseradish (¼ cup/60 mL)

⅛ tsp/0.25 g cayenne, plus as needed to adjust seasoning

Kosher salt, as needed to adjust seasoning

Place all of the ingredients in a 2-qt/1.92-L bowl and combine with an immersion blender. Taste and adjust seasoning. *The honey mustard can be made 2 days in advance. Immediately store wrapped in the refrigerator.*

To make preparation easier, all ingredients are by weight; simply place the bowl on a scale but don't forget to use the tare feature.

FIG–MARCONA ALMOND VINAIGRETTE

YIELD: 32 FL OZ/960 ML

WINE REDUCTION

6 fl oz/180 mL Zinfandel

GARLIC AND SHALLOT CONFIT

2 fl oz/60 mL extra-virgin olive oil

1½ oz/43 g shallots, peeled, split in half (about 3 shallots)

½ oz/14 g garlic cloves (4 cloves)

VINAIGRETTE

4 oz/113 g chopped dried figs (½ cup/120 mL packed)

8 fl oz/240 mL water

2 fl oz/60 mL sherry vinegar

1 fl oz/30 mL lemon juice

2 tsp/10 mL honey, plus as needed to adjust seasoning

¼ fl oz/7.5 mL Tabasco sauce, plus as
needed to adjust seasoning

4 tsp/12 g kosher salt, plus as needed to adjust seasoning

¾ tsp/1.5 g ground black pepper, plus
as needed to adjust seasoning

8 fl oz/240 mL extra-virgin olive oil

6 fl oz/180 mL almond oil or mild-flavored olive oil

2½ oz/71 g toasted Marcona almonds
(½ cup/120 mL; page 114)

1. For the wine reduction, heat the Zinfandel in a
10-in/25-cm sauté pan over medium-low heat, so there
are wisps of steam and very tiny bubbles, but it is not simmering. Reduce to 2 fl oz/60 mL, about 15 minutes. Cool.
*The wine can be reduced 3 weeks in advance. Immediately
store wrapped in the refrigerator.*

2. For the garlic and shallot confit, put the olive oil, shallots, and garlic into a 1½-qt/1.44-L saucepan. Cover with
a tight-fitting lid and cook over very low heat until soft
and golden but not browned, about 15 minutes. Cool to
room temperature.

3. For the vinaigrette, put the reduced Zinfandel, the
garlic and shallot confit and the oil it was cooked in, and
the dried figs, water, vinegar, lemon juice, honey, Tabasco,
salt, and pepper into a food processor. Run the motor
until the mixture is smooth, about 1 minute.

4. Slowly drizzle in the olive oil and the almond oil with
the motor running, about 1 minute. Continue to blend
until thick and emulsified, about 30 seconds more. Adjust
the viscosity with water. Add the almonds and pulse the
motor until the almonds are finely chopped but not
puréed, about five 2-second on/off pulses. Taste and
adjust seasoning. *The vinaigrette can be prepared 1 week in
advance. Immediately store in a sealed bottle in the refrigerator. Shake to emulsify before using.*

GARLIC CONFIT VINAIGRETTE

YIELD: 32 FL OZ/960 ML

GARLIC CONFIT

4 fl oz/120 mL extra-virgin olive oil

8 oz/227 g shallots, peeled, halved (about 8 shallots)

2 oz/57 g garlic cloves (16 cloves)

VINAIGRETTE

4 fl oz/120 mL champagne vinegar

2 fl oz/60 mL lemon juice

1½ oz/43 g Dijon mustard (3 tbsp/45 mL)

1½ tsp/7.5 mL honey

5½ tsp/16 g kosher salt, plus as needed to adjust seasoning

2 tsp/4 g ground black pepper, plus as needed to adjust seasoning

14 fl oz/420 mL extra-virgin olive oil

1. For the garlic confit, heat the oil, shallots, and garlic in a 1½-qt/1.44-L saucepan. Cover with a tight-fitting lid and cook over very low heat until soft and golden but not browned, about 30 minutes. Cool to room temperature, 15 minutes.

2. For the vinaigrette, put the contents of the pan and the vinegar, lemon juice, mustard, honey, salt, and pepper into a blender. Run the motor until smooth, first on the lowest setting for 30 seconds and then on the highest setting for 30 seconds.

3. Slowly drizzle in the olive oil with the motor running on the lowest speed, taking about 1 minute. Continue to blend until thick and emulsified, 30 seconds more. If necessary, adjust the consistency with water. Taste and adjust seasoning. *The vinaigrette can be prepared 3 weeks in advance. Store in a sealed bottle in the refrigerator. Shake to emulsify before using.*

BALSAMIC VINAIGRETTE: Replace the champagne vinegar with balsamic vinegar and the lemon juice with red wine vinegar. Eliminate the honey.

WHITE BALSAMIC VINAIGRETTE: Decrease the champagne vinegar to 2 fl oz/60 mL and replace the lemon juice with 4 fl oz/120 mL white balsamic vinegar. Eliminate the honey.

BASIL VINAIGRETTE: Replace the champagne vinegar with balsamic vinegar and the lemon juice with red wine vinegar. Eliminate the honey. Up to 4 hours before serving, add 1½ oz/43 g chopped basil leaves to the vinaigrette and process in the blender until the basil is evenly incorporated, about 15 seconds. (Or decrease the salt to 5 tsp/15 g and add 2 tbsp/24 mL Basil Purée, page 323).

CHABLIS VINAIGRETTE: Heat 16 fl oz/480 mL Chablis in a 10-in/25-cm sauté pan over medium-low heat, so there are wisps of steam and very tiny bubbles, but it is not simmering. Reduce to 4 fl oz/120 mL, about 45 minutes. Cool. Replace the champagne vinegar with the reduced Chablis.

LEMON AND FENNEL SEED VINAIGRETTE

YIELD: 32 FL OZ/960 ML

9 fl oz/270 mL lemon juice (about 9 lemons)

3 fl oz/90 mL champagne vinegar or white wine vinegar

1½ oz/43 g Dijon mustard (3 tbsp/45 mL)

2½ oz/71 g minced shallots (½ cup/120 mL)

½ oz/14 g minced garlic (4 tsp/20 mL or 4 cloves)

4 tsp/12 g kosher salt, plus as needed to adjust seasoning

1 tbsp/7 g crushed fennel seed

¾ tsp/1.5 g red pepper flakes, plus as needed to adjust seasoning

½ tsp/1 g ground black pepper, plus as needed to adjust seasoning

18 fl oz/540 mL olive oil

Whisk the lemon juice, vinegar, mustard, shallots, garlic, salt, fennel seeds, red pepper flakes, and black pepper in a 2-qt/1.92-L bowl until combined. Slowly drizzle in the oil while whisking and continue to whisk until emulsified. Taste and adjust seasoning. *The vinaigrette can be prepared 1 week in advance. Store in a sealed bottle in the refrigerator. Shake to emulsify before using.*

LIME-HONEY VINAIGRETTE

YIELD: 32 FL OZ/960 ML

18 fl oz/540 mL grapeseed oil or mild extra virgin olive oil

9 fl oz/270 mL lime juice

4 oz/128 g honey (6 tbsp/90 mL)

2 tbsp/12 g coarsely ground black pepper, plus as needed to adjust seasoning

1 tbsp/10 g kosher salt, plus as needed to adjust seasoning

In a 1-qt/960-mL container with a lid, combine all the ingredients. Shake vigorously to emulsify. Taste and adjust seasoning. *The vinaigrette can be prepared 1 week in advance. Store in the refrigerator. Shake to emulsify before using.*

Room-temperature citrus is easier to squeeze. Warm for 10 seconds in the microwave if needed to bring the fruit to room temperature. Before squeezing, roll the fruit on a hard surface while applying pressure to break the membranes holding the juice.

GEORGIA PEANUT DRESSING

YIELD: 32 FL OZ/960 ML

6 fl oz/180 mL malt vinegar

2¼ oz/64 g peanut butter (¼ cup/60 mL)

4 oz/128 g honey (6 tbsp/90 mL)

1 tsp/5 mL Tabasco sauce

½ oz/14 g minced garlic (4 tsp/20 mL or 4 cloves)

2 tsp/6 g kosher salt, plus as needed to adjust seasoning

1 tsp/2 g ground black pepper

12 fl oz/360 mL peanut oil

6 fl oz/180 mL canola oil

¼ oz/7 g minced cilantro or tarragon (2 tbsp/30 mL)

¼ oz/7 g minced chives (2 tbsp/30 mL)

¼ oz/7 g minced flat-leaf parsley (2 tbsp/30 mL)

1. Put the vinegar, peanut butter, honey, Tabasco, garlic, salt, and pepper into a blender. Run the motor until smooth, first on the lowest setting for 30 seconds and then on the highest setting for 30 seconds.

2. Slowly drizzle in the peanut oil and canola oil with the motor running on the lowest speed, taking about 1 minute. Continue to blend until thick and emulsified, 30 seconds more. If necessary, adjust the consistency with water. Taste and adjust seasoning. *The vinaigrette can be prepared 1 week in advance. Store in a sealed bottle in the refrigerator. Shake to emulsify before using.*

3. Just before serving, whisk in the cilantro, chives, and parsley.

CANDIED PECANS

YIELD: 1 LB/454 G

1 egg white

½ fl oz/15 mL water

1 lb/454 g raw pecans (4 cups/960 mL)

3½ oz/99 g granulated sugar (½ cup/120 mL)

½ tsp/1.5 g kosher salt

1½ tsp/3 g ground ginger

1 tsp/2 g ground cinnamon

½ tsp/1 g ground cardamom

½ tsp/1 g ground allspice

½ tsp/1 g ground coriander

¼ tsp/0.5 g cayenne

1. Position a rack in the middle of the oven and heat to 300°F/149°C. Whisk the egg white and water in a 2-qt/1.92-L bowl until combined. Add the pecans and toss to evenly coat.

2. Grind the sugar, salt, ginger, cinnamon, cardamom, allspice, coriander, and cayenne in a food processor fitted with a steel blade until it is a fine powder, about 30 seconds. Pour over the nuts and toss until evenly coated.

3. Distribute the pecans on a sheet pan. Toast in the oven, tossing several times, for 20 minutes. Lower the heat to 250°F/121°C and bake, tossing occasionally, until fragrant and golden, 15 to 20 minutes more. Cool completely. *The pecans can be made 2 weeks in advance. Store in a plastic bag at room temperature.*

CHILI-ROASTED PEANUTS

YIELD: 1 LB/454 G

1 tbsp/10 g salt

1½ tsp/3 g chili powder

1 tsp/2 g ground cumin

½ tsp/1 g ground white pepper

½ tsp/1 g dried oregano

1 lb/454 g raw unsalted peanuts

1 oz/28 g unsalted butter, melted (2 tbsp/30 mL)

1. Position racks in the top third and bottom third of the oven and heat to 350°F/177°C. In a 1-qt/960-mL cup bowl, combine the salt, chili powder, cumin, pepper, and oregano.

2. Distribute the peanuts on a sheet pan and toss with the butter. Toast in the oven, tossing several times, until fragrant and golden, 9 to 14 minutes. Immediately pour the nuts into the spices and toss to evenly combine. Cool. *The nuts can be toasted in advance. Store in a plastic bag at room temperature for 3 days, in the refrigerator for 3 weeks, or in the freezer for 3 months.*

PICKLED RED ONIONS

YIELD: 32 FL OZ/960 ML

1 lb 2 oz/510 g thinly sliced red onions (4 cups/ 960 mL or about 4 medium onions)

1 tbsp plus 1½ tsp/15 g kosher salt

12 fl oz/360 mL red wine vinegar

4 fl oz/120 mL water

1¾ oz/51 g granulated sugar (¼ cup/60 mL)

1 tsp/1 g ground black pepper

½ tsp/1 g dried oregano

1 pinch red pepper flakes

1 bay leaf

1. Bring a 3-qt/2.88-L saucepot filled three-quarters with water to a boil. Add the onions and 1 tbsp/10 g kosher salt and boil for 1 minute. Drain, discarding the water.

2. Bring the vinegar, water, sugar, black pepper, oregano, red pepper flakes, and bay leaf and the remaining 1½ tsp/5 g salt to a boil in a nonreactive 4-qt/3.84-L saucepan and simmer for 5 minutes. Remove from the heat and immediately add the warm onions. Cool to room temperature, 1 hour.

3. Refrigerate the onions submerged in the pickling solution for at least 6 hours. Drain completely before serving. *The onions can be made 3 weeks in advance. Store wrapped in the refrigerator in the pickling solution.*

CRISPY CAPERS AND PARSLEY PLUCHES

YIELD: 12 SERVINGS

4½ oz/128 g nonpareil capers, rinsed (¾ cup/180 mL)

4 fl oz/120 mL olive oil

½ oz/14 g flat-leaf parsley pluches or the whole leaves removed from stems (¼ cup/60 mL)

1. If the capers are salt-cured, soak in 2 cups/480 mL cold water for 30 minutes. Drain and repeat. If the capers are in vinegar brine, drain, taste, and if too salty, soak in 2 cups/480 mL cold water for 5 minutes and then drain. Blot the capers dry on paper towels, pressing gently to remove as much water as possible. Repeat until the paper towels remain dry.

2. Put the oil into a 1½-qt/1.44-L saucepan over medium heat to warm, about 2 minutes. Carefully add 1½ oz/43 g capers (¼ cup/60 mL) and fry until the capers open and are golden and crispy, about 3 minutes. Be careful, because any moisture in the capers can cause the oil to splatter. The sizzle in the oil will decrease when the capers are almost done. With a slotted spoon, remove the capers and drain on paper towels. Repeat with the remaining capers, cooling the oil in between.

3. Before adding the parsley, cool the oil at room temperature for 5 minutes. Then add half of the parsley, put over medium heat, and fry until vibrant green and crispy, 20 to 30 seconds. With a slotted spoon, remove the parsley and drain on paper towels. Repeat with the remaining parsley, cooling the oil in between. *The fried capers and parsley pluches can be made 4 hours in advance. Store uncovered at room temperature.*

CAJUN SPICE

YIELD: ½ CUP/120 ML

2 tbsp/12 g onion powder

2 tbsp/12 g sweet paprika

1 tbsp/6 g garlic powder

1 tbsp/6 g ground black pepper

1 tbsp/6 g cayenne

1 tbsp/6 g ground white pepper

1½ tsp/3 g dry mustard

1½ tsp/3 g dried thyme

1½ tsp/3 g dried oregano

Combine all the ingredients in a 1-qt/960-mL container with a lid. *The spice mixture can be prepared up to 6 months in advance. Store sealed in a dark, cool, dry place.*

Dried herbs and spices don't go bad, but over time lose their intended flavor, making a dish taste muddy. Rub a little between your fingers and check the aroma, color, and taste. If these are not intense and characteristic of that spice or dried herb, it's probably time to replace it. Store herbs and spices in airtight containers in a dark, cool, dry place. Although it is convenient to keep them next to the stove, this will dramatically shorten their longevity. A conservative rule is that dried herbs and ground spices keep for 6 months to 1 year and whole spices keep for 1 to 2 years.

CROSTINI AND CROUTONS

YIELD: 12 SERVINGS

2 fl oz/60 mL extra-virgin olive oil

¼ tsp/1 g Cajun Spice (page 333)

¼ tsp/0.5 g kosher salt

12 baguette slices, sliced ½ in/1.25 cm thick on the diagonal or 6 oz/170 g ciabatta, cut into ½-in/1.25-cm dice (3½ cups/840 mL)

1. Position the oven racks in the top third and bottom third of the oven and heat to 350°F/177°C. In a 1-qt/960-mL bowl, whisk the oil, cajun spice, and salt until combined.

2. For crostini, paint a thin coating of seasoned oil on both sides of each bread slice and place them on a sheet pan in a single layer. For croutons, toss the bread cubes with the seasoned oil and place on a sheet pan in a single layer.

3. Toast the bread in the oven until crunchy and golden, 15 to 20 minutes, turning/tossing them halfway through. For extra-crunchy crostini or croutons, after 15 minutes, lower the oven temperature to 225°F/107°C and bake for 20 minutes more. Cool to room temperature. *The crostini or croutons can be toasted in advance. Store in a plastic bag at room temperature for 3 days. Re-crisp in 350°F/177°C oven for 5 to 10 minutes, if necessary.*

ON-SITE BUFFET PLANNING WORKSHEET

Client Name: _____ Date of event: _____

Occasion: _____ Time: _____

Venue: _____ Invited: adults _____ kids _____ Guaranteed: _____

Phone: home _____ cell _____ email _____

Billing address: _____

Special instructions: _____

_____

Notes/time line: _____

_____

_____

_____

_____

_____

_____

_____

_____

_____

How many buffet lines: _____ Stations: _____

Flowers: _____ Entertainment: _____

Party planner: _____ Rental Company: _____

Today's date: _____ Initials: _____ Contract Sent: _____ Initials: _____

Deposit Received: _____ Initials: _____

Blank On-Site Buffet Planning Worksheet

APPENDIX B

CATERING MENU

sandwich + salad buffet

select two sandwiches

buttermilk grilled chicken

chicken milanese

chicken pecorino

eggplant parmigianina

meatballs

grilled + roasted vegetables with fresh mozzarella

grilled skirt steak

honey lacquered dark beer marinated pulled pork

moroccan chicken + carrot sauté/with dates

pecan studded chicken

sweet italian sausage + peppers

rosemary-sage grilled chicken

sesame chicken wrap

thai style seared salmon

turkey roulade

+ two side salads

gorgonzola, bacon + toasted walnut caesar

caribbean mango caeser salad

mexican pasta salad with corn + tomatillos

fruit salad scented with lime + mint

mâche salad with georgia peanut dressing

wild rice, apple and dried cranberry salad

coconut-almond quinoa

marinated roasted pepper + haricots verts salad

mediterranean potato + haricots verts salad

mediterranean watermelon salad

bulgar, chickpea + lentil salad

romano bean salad with bocconccini + chickpeas

shaved fennel, avocado, arugula + orange salad

spinach ensalada

thai spaghetti squash slaw

waldorf caesar salad or any of the soups on page 6

+ breads / toppings / dressings / cheese

please select bread / topping / dressing / cheese on page 10.

it's our pleasure assisting you in the design of the perfect sandwich pairings

sandwiches are cut in half and are on a bamboo platter garnished with pickles.   18pp

another sandwich selection   3pp

another salad selection   2pp

Pick and choose from any menu. We follow Mother Nature's lead and design your menu around the season.
Buffets per person based on 20 person minimum and guaranteed only with a deposit and contract. Feb 2015

Sample Catering Menu for a Sandwich and Salad Buffet

The comprehensive catering menu can be found on this book's Web site at www.wiley.com/college/cia.

APPENDIX C

PAIRINGS
palate + plate

OFF-SITE BUFFET PLANNING WORKSHEET

Client Name: _____ **Date of event:** _____

Occasion: _____ **Time:** _____

Venue: _____ **Invited:** adults ___ kids ___ **Guaranteed:** ___

Phone: home _____ cell _____ email _____

Billing address: _____

Special instructions: _____

Notes/time line: _____

_____

_____

_____

_____

Party Planner: _____ **Rental Co:** _____

Liquor/Soda/Ice Delivery (IF APPLICABLE): _____ **Valet Parking:** _____

Flowers: _____ **Entertainment:** _____

Insurance Permit: _____ **Board of Health/Fire/Police Permit:** _____

Today's date: _____ **Initials:** _____ **Contract Sent:** _____ **Initials:** _____

Deposit Received: _____ **Initials:** _____

Kitchen:
Ovens
Stovetop/Burners
Grills/Propane
Fridge/Freezer
Sink/Water
Dishwasher
Prep Tables
Utensils
Trash Disposal/Recycling
Exhaust Fan
Fire Suppression/Extinguisher
Electric
Notes/Sketch: on next page

Buffet:
How Many Buffet Lines
Stations/Buffet Tables/Risers
Dance floor/Bars
Chafers/Sterno/Electric
Lighting/Electric/Centerpieces
Tablecloths/Skirting
Platters/Serving Utensils
Dinner Tables/Chairs
Tablecloths/Napkins
China/Flatware/Glassware
S & P/Coffee Service/B & B
Tent
Other Rentals/Notes: on next page

Blank Off-Site Buffet Planning Worksheet

GLOSSARY

A

ACTIVE DRY YEAST: A dehydrated form of yeast that needs to be hydrated in warm water (105°F/41°C) before use. It contains about one-tenth the moisture of compressed yeast.

ADULTERATED FOOD: Food that has been contaminated to the point that it is considered unfit for human consumption.

AERATION: Incorporation of air by beating or whipping the ingredients together.

AIR-DRYING: Exposing meats and sausages to proper temperature and humidity conditions to change both flavor and texture for consumption or further processing. Times and temperatures vary depending upon the type of meat or sausage.

À LA CARTE: A menu from which the patron makes individual selections in various menu categories; each item is priced separately.

À LA MINUTE: French for, literally, "at the minute." A restaurant production approach in which dishes are not prepared until an order arrives in the kitchen.

AL DENTE: Italian for, literally, "to the tooth." Refers to an item, such as pasta or vegetables, cooked until it is tender but still firm, not soft.

ALLUMETTE: Vegetable cut, usually referring to potatoes cut into pieces the size and shape of matchsticks, ⅛ in/3 mm by ⅛ in/3 mm by 1 to 2 in/2.5 to 5 cm. Also called julienne.

AMUSE-BOUCHE: French for, literally, "mouth amuser." Chef's tasting: a small portion (one or two bites) of something exotic, unusual, or otherwise special, served when the guests in a restaurant are seated. The amuse-gueule is not listed on a menu and is included in the price of an entrée. Also called amuse-guele.

ANDOUILLE: A spicy pork sausage that is French in origin but is now more often associated with Cajun cooking. There are hundreds of varieties of this regional specialty.

ANGEL FOOD CAKE: A type of sponge cake made without egg yolks or other fats. Beaten egg whites give it its light and airy structure. Typically baked in a tube pan.

APPETIZER: Light food served before a meal or as the first course of a meal. May be hot or cold, plated or served as finger food.

AROMATICS: Ingredients such as herbs, spices, vegetables, citrus fruits, wines, and vinegars used to enhance the flavor and fragrance of food.

ARROWROOT: A powdered starch made from the root of a tropical plant of the same name. Used primarily as a thickener. Remains clear when cooked.

B

BACTERIA: Microscopic organisms. Some have beneficial properties; others can cause food-borne illnesses when foods contaminated with them are ingested.

BASTE: To moisten food during cooking with pan drippings, sauce, or other liquid. Basting prevents food from drying out.

BATCH COOKING: A cooking technique in which appropriately sized quantities of food are prepared several times throughout a service period so that a fresh supply of cooked items is always available.

BÂTON/BÂTONNET: French for "stick" or "small stick." Items cut into pieces somewhat larger than allumette or julienne; ¼ in/6 mm by ¼ in/6 mm by 1 to 2 in/2.5 to 5 cm.

BATTER: A mixture of flour and liquid, sometimes with the inclusion of other ingredients. Batters vary in thickness but are generally semiliquid and thinner than doughs. Used in such preparations as cakes, quick breads, pancakes, and crêpes. Also, a liquid mixture used to coat foods before deep-frying.

BENCH-PROOF: In yeast dough production, to allow dough to rise after it has been panned and just before it is baked.

BENCH REST: In yeast dough production, the stage that allows the gluten in preshaped dough to relax before the final shaping. Also known as secondary fermentation.

BINDER: An ingredient or appareil used to thicken a sauce or hold together another mixture of ingredients.

BLANCH: To cook an item briefly in boiling water or hot fat before finishing or storing it. Blanching preserves the color, lessens strong flavors, and aids in removing the peels of some fruits and vegetables.

BLOOM: To hydrate gelatin in liquid before dissolving. Also, the light gray film on the skin of apples, blueberries, grapes, and prunes. Also, streaks of white/gray fat or sugar that appear on solid, untempered chocolate.

BOUQUET GARNI: A small bundle of herbs tied with string. Used to flavor stocks, braises, and other preparations. Usually contains bay leaf, parsley, thyme, and possibly other aromatics wrapped in leek leaves.

BRAISE: A combination cooking process; to cook a food, usually meat, by searing in fat, then simmering slowly at a low temperature in a small amount of stock or another liquid (usually halfway up the meat item) in a covered vessel. The cooking liquid is then reduced and used as the base of a sauce.

BROIL: To cook food by means of a radiant heat source placed above it.

BUFFET: A traditional mode of dining where people serve themselves from a table or sideboard. Buffet foods commonly include cold meat and cheese platters, pickled fish, salads, sandwiches, and desserts but have expanded to include action stations (see page 59).

BUTTERFLY: To cut an item (usually meat or seafood) and open out the edges like a book or the wings of a butterfly.

C

CANAPÉ: An hors d'oeuvre consisting of a small piece of bread or toast, often cut in a decorative shape, garnished with a savory spread or topping.

CARAMELIZATION: The process of browning sugar in the presence of heat. The caramelization of sugar occurs between 320°/160°C and 360°F/182°C.

CARRYOVER COOKING: The heat retained in cooked foods that allows them to continue cooking even after removal from the cooking medium. Especially important to roasted foods.

CHAFING DISH: A metal dish with a heating unit (flame or electric), used to keep foods warm and to cook foods tableside or during buffet service.

CHAMPAGNE: A sparkling white wine produced in the Champagne region of France using three grape varieties: Chardonnay, Pinot Noir, and Pinot Meunier. The term is sometimes incorrectly applied to other sparkling wines.

CHIFFON: A cake made by the foaming method; contains a high percentage of eggs and sugar and relatively little, if any, fat to produce a light and airy cake.

CHIFFONADE: Fine shreds of leafy vegetables or herbs; often used as a garnish.

CHOP: To cut into pieces of roughly the same size. Also, a small cut of meat including part of the rib.

CLARIFIED BUTTER: Butter from which the milk solids and water have been removed, leaving pure butterfat. Has a higher smoke point than whole butter but less butter flavor.

COARSELY CHOP: To cut into pieces of roughly the same size. Used for items such as mirepoix, where appearance is not important.

COMMON MERINGUE: A mixture of egg whites and sugar, beaten until it reaches soft, medium, or stiff peaks. Also called French meringue.

COMPOSED SALAD: A salad in which the items are carefully arranged on a plate rather than tossed together.

COMPOTE: A dish of fresh or dried fruit cooked in syrup, flavored with spices or liqueur. Also, a type of small dish.

CORNSTARCH: A fine white powder milled from dried corn; used primarily as a thickener for sauce and occasionally as an ingredient in batters.

COULIS: A thick purée of vegetables or fruit, served hot or cold. Traditionally refers to the thickened juices of cooked meat, fish, or shellfish purée or certain thick soups.

CRÊPE: A thin pancake made with egg batter; used in sweet and savory preparations.

CROSS CONTAMINATION: The transference of disease-causing elements from one source to another through physical contact.

CRUDITÉ: Usually raw vegetables but sometimes fruit, served as an appetizer or hors d'oeuvre. Some vegetables may be blanched to improve taste and appearance.

D

DANGER ZONE: The temperature range from 41°/5°C to 135°F/57°C, the most favorable condition for rapid growth of many pathogens.

DEEP-FRY: To cook food by immersion in hot fat; deep-fried foods are often coated with bread crumbs or batter before cooking.

DEEP POACH: To cook food gently in enough simmering liquid to completely submerge the food.

DOCK: To cut the top of dough before baking to allow steam to escape to control the expansion of the dough and/or to create a decorative effect.

DREDGE: To coat food with a dry ingredient such as flour or bread crumbs prior to frying or sautéing.

DURUM: A very hard wheat typically milled into semolina, primarily used in making pasta.

E

EGG WASH: A mixture of beaten eggs (whole eggs, yolks, or whites) and a liquid, usually milk or water, used to coat baked goods to give them a sheen.

F

FABRICATION: The butchering, cutting, and trimming of meat, poultry, fish, and game (large pieces or whole) into smaller cuts to prepare them to be cooked.

FERMENTATION: The process of yeast acting to break down sugars into carbon dioxide gas and alcohol, which is essential in bread leavening and beer, wine, and spirit making. Also, the period of rising in yeast doughs.

FILET MIGNON: The expensive boneless cut of beef from the small end of the tenderloin.

FILLET/FILET: A boneless cut of meat, fish, or poultry.

FINE-MESH STRAINER: A conical sieve made from fine-mesh metal screen, used for straining and puréeing foods.

FINES HERBES: A mixture of herbs, usually parsley, chervil, tarragon, and chives. Generally added to the dish just prior to serving, as they lose their flavor quickly.

FIRST IN, FIRST OUT (FIFO): A fundamental storage principle based on stock rotation. Products are stored and used so that the oldest product is always used first.

FOND: The French term for "stock." Also, the pan drippings remaining after sautéing or roasting food, often deglazed and used as a base for sauces.

G

GARNISH: An edible decoration or accompaniment to a dish or item.

GELATIN: A protein-based substance found in animal bones and connective tissue. When dissolved in hot liquid and then cooled, it can be used as a thickener and stabilizer.

GRILL: To cook foods by means of a radiant heat source placed below the food. Also, the piece of equipment on which grilling is done; may be fueled by gas, electricity, charcoal, or wood.

H

HORS D'OEUVRE: French for, literally, "outside the work." An appetizer.

HOTEL PAN: A rectangular metal pan, available in a number of standard sizes, with a lip that allows it to rest on a storage shelf or in a steam table.

HYGIENE: Conditions and practices followed to maintain health, including sanitation and personal cleanliness.

I

INDIRECT HEAT: A method of heat transfer in which the heat is transferred to the product by the heated air instead of the heat source.

INDUCTION BURNER: A type of heating unit that relies on magnetic attraction between the cooktop and metals in the pot to generate the heat that cooks foods in the pan. Reaction time is significantly faster than with traditional burners.

INFUSION: Steeping an aromatic or other item in liquid to extract its flavor. Also, the liquid resulting from this process.

INSTANT-READ THERMOMETER: A thermometer used to measure the internal temperature of foods. The stem is inserted in the food, producing an immediate temperature readout.

ITALIAN MERINGUE: A mixture of whipped egg whites and hot sugar syrup (140°F/60°C), whipped further until shiny, fluffy, and cool.

J

JARDINIÈRE: A mixture of vegetables.

JULIENNE: Vegetables, potatoes, or other items cut into thin strips; ⅛ in/3 mm by ⅛ in/3 mm by 1 to 2 in/2.5 to 5 cm is standard. Fine julienne is 1⁄16 in/1.5 mm by 1⁄16 in/1.5 mm by 1 to 2 in/2.5 to 5 cm.

JUS: French for, literally, "juice." Refers to fruit and vegetable juices as well as juices from meats. Jus de viande is meat gravy. Meat served au jus is served with its own juice or a jus lié.

K

KNEAD: To work or mix a dough by hand to soften it to working consistency, or to stretch yeasted doughs to expand their gluten.

KOSHER: Prepared in accordance with Jewish dietary laws.

KOSHER SALT: Pure, refined salt, also known as coarse salt or pickling salt. Used for pickling because it does not contain magnesium carbonate and thus does not cloud brine solutions. Also used to kosher meats and poultry.

L

LEGUME: The seeds of certain pod plants, including beans and peas, which are eaten for their earthy flavors and high nutritional value. Also, the French word for "vegetable."

LIAISON: A mixture of egg yolks and cream used to thicken and enrich sauces. Also loosely applied to any appareil used as a thickener.

M

MAILLARD REACTION: A complex browning reaction that results in the particular flavor and color of foods that do not contain much sugar, including roasted meats. The reaction, which involves carbohydrates and amino acids, is named after the French scientist who first discovered it. There are low-temperature and high-temperature Maillard reactions; the high-temperature reaction starts at 310°F/154°C.

MANDOLINE: A slicing device of plastic or stainless steel with carbon steel blades. Most models have blades that may be adjusted to cut items into various shapes and thicknesses.

MARINADE: An appareil used before cooking to flavor and moisten foods; may be liquid or dry. Liquid marinades are usually based on an acidic ingredient such as wine or vinegar; dry marinades are usually salt based.

MARK ON A GRILL: To turn a food (without flipping it over) 90 degrees after it has been on the grill for several seconds to create the cross-hatching associated with grilled foods.

MEDALLION: A small, round scallop of meat.

MERINGUE: Egg whites beaten with sugar until they stiffen. Types include regular or common/French, Italian, and Swiss.

MIGNARDISES: An assortment of small, two-bite-size pastries.

MIREPOIX: A combination of chopped aromatic vegetables (usually two parts onion, one part carrot, and one part celery) used to flavor stocks, soups, braises, and stews.

MISE EN PLACE: French for, literally, "put in place." The preparation and assembly of ingredients, pans, utensils, and plates or serving pieces needed for a particular dish or service period.

N

NUTRIENT: A basic component of food used by the body for growth, repair, restoration, and energy. Includes carbohydrates, fats, proteins, water, vitamins, and minerals.

NUTRITION: The process by which an organism takes in and uses food.

O

OMELET: Beaten egg, cooked in butter in a specialized pan or skillet, then rolled or folded into an oval. Omelets may be filled with a variety of ingredients before or after rolling.

P

PAN FRY: To cook in fat in a skillet; generally involves more fat than sautéing or stir-frying but less than deep-frying.

PAN STEAM: To cook foods in a very small amount of liquid in a covered pan over direct heat.

PAR-BAKE: To start and then interrupt the baking process to finish it at a later time.

PARCHMENT: Heat-resistant paper used to line baking pans, enclose items to cook en papillote, and cover items during shallow poaching.

PARCOOK: To partially cook an item before storing or finishing.

PÂTE À CHOUX: Cream puff batter, made by boiling water or milk, butter, and flour, then beating in whole eggs. When baked, pâte à choux puffs to form a hollowed pastry shell that can be filled.

PÂTE À GLACIER, BLOND: Coating chocolate that is light in color.

PESTO: A thick puréed mixture of an herb, traditionally basil and oil. Used as a sauce for pasta and other foods and as a garnish for soup. Pesto may also contain grated cheese, nuts or seeds, and other seasonings.

PHYLLO DOUGH: Also spelled filo; pastry made with very thin sheets of a flour-and-water dough layered with butter and/or bread or cake crumbs; similar to strudel dough.

PRESENTATION SIDE: The side of a piece of meat, poultry, or fish that will be served facing up.

PURÉE: To process food by mashing, straining, or chopping it very finely in order to make it a smooth paste. Also, a product produced using this technique.

R

RAGOÛT: A stew of meat and/or vegetables.

REDUCE: To decrease the volume of a liquid by simmering or boiling. Used to provide a thicker consistency and/or concentrated flavors.

REDUCTION: The product that results when a liquid is reduced.

REFRESH: To plunge an item into, or run it under, cold water after blanching to prevent further cooking. Also known as shock.

ROAST: To cook by dry heat in an oven or on a spit over a fire.

ROE: Fish or shellfish eggs.

S

SACHET D'ÉPICES: French for, literally, "bag of spices." Aromatic ingredients encased in cheesecloth, used to flavor stocks and other liquids. A standard sachet contains parsley stems, cracked peppercorns, dried thyme, and a bay leaf.

SANITATION: The maintenance of a clean food preparation environment by healthy food workers in order to prevent food-borne illnesses and food contamination.

SANITIZE: To kill pathogenic organisms by chemicals and/or moist heat.

SAUTÉ: To cook quickly in a small amount of fat in a pan on the stovetop.

SAUTEUSE: A shallow skillet with sloping sides and a single long handle. Used for sautéing. Referred to generically as a sauté pan.

SAUTOIR: A shallow skillet with straight sides and a single long handle. Used for sautéing. Referred to generically as a sauté pan.

SCORE: To cut the surface of an item at regular intervals to allow it to cook evenly, allow excess fat to drain, help the food absorb marinades, or for decorative purposes.

SEAR: To brown the surface of food in fat over high heat before finishing by another method (such as braising or roasting) in order to add flavor.

SHALLOW POACH: To cook an item gently in a shallow pan, barely covered with simmering liquid. The liquid is often reduced and used as the base of a sauce.

SHELF LIFE: The amount of time in storage that a product can maintain its quality.

SMOKE POINT: The temperature at which a fat begins to break down and smoke when heated.

SOUFFLÉ: French for, literally, "puffed." A preparation made with a sauce base (usually béchamel for savory soufflés and pastry cream for sweet ones), whipped egg whites, and flavorings. The egg whites cause the soufflé to puff during cooking.

STANDARD BREADING PROCEDURE: The assembly-line procedure in which items are dredged in flour, dipped in beaten egg, then coated with crumbs before being pan-fried or deep-fried.

SWEAT: To cook an item, usually vegetable(s), in a covered pan in a small amount of fat until it softens and releases moisture but does not brown.

SWISS MERINGUE: A mixture of egg whites and sugar heated over simmering water until it reaches 140°F/60°C; it is then whipped until it reaches the desired peak and is cool.

T

TART: A shallow, straight-sided pastry crust (may be fluted or plain) filled with a savory or sweet, fresh and/or cooked filling. Also describes something very acidic or sour.

TARTLET: A small, single-serving tart.

TEMPER: To heat gently and gradually. May refer to the process of incorporating hot liquid into a liaison to gradually raise its temperature. May also refer to the proper method for melting chocolate; that is, to melt, agitate, and cool chocolate to ensure that it retains its smooth gloss, crisp "snap" feel, and creamy texture.

U

UMAMI: Describes a savory, meaty taste; often associated with monosodium glutamate (MSG) and mushrooms.

V

VEGETARIAN: An individual who has adopted a specific diet that eliminates meat and fish and products derived from meat and fish but not all animal products. Lacto-ovo-vegetarians include dairy products and eggs in their diet; ovo-vegetarians include eggs. Vegans eat no foods derived in any way from animals.

VELOUTÉ: A sauce of white stock (chicken, veal, or seafood) thickened with white roux. One of the "grand" sauces. Also, a cream soup made with a velouté sauce base and flavorings (usually puréed), usually finished with a liaison.

VINAIGRETTE: A cold sauce of oil and vinegar, usually with various flavorings. It is a temporary emulsion. The standard proportion is three parts oil to one part vinegar.

W

WAFFLE: A crisp, pancake-like batter product, cooked on a specialized griddle that gives the finished product a textured pattern, usually a grid. Also, a special vegetable cut that produces a grid or basket-weave pattern. Also known as gaufrette.

WALK-IN REFRIGERATOR: A refrigeration unit large enough to walk into. It is occasionally large enough to maintain zones of different temperatures and humidity to store a variety of foods properly. Some have reach-in doors as well. Some are large enough to accommodate rolling carts as well as many shelves of goods.

Y

YEAST: Microscopic organism whose metabolic processes are responsible for fermentation. It is used for leavening bread and in the making of beer and wine.

YOGURT: Milk cultured with bacteria to give it a slightly thick consistency and sour flavor.

Z

ZEST: The thin, brightly colored outer part of citrus rind. It contains volatile oils, making it ideal for use as a flavoring.

READINGS AND RESOURCES

BOOKS

Bastianich, Lidia Matticchio. *Lidia's Italian Table.* New York: Morrow, 1990.

Blocker, Linda, Julie Hill, and The Culinary Institute of America. *Culinary Math,* 3rd edition. Hoboken: Wiley, 2007.

Editors of *Cook's Illustrated* Magazine. *The Best Recipe.* Massachusetts: Boston Common Press, 1999.

Carucci, Linda. *Cooking School Secrets for Real World Cooks.* San Francisco: Cronicle Books, 2005

Child, Julia, Louisette Bertholle, and Simone Beck. *Mastering the Art of French Cooking.* Volume One. New York: Knopf, 1979.

Corriher, Shirley. *BakeWise: The Hows and Whys of Successful Baking with over 200 Magnificent Recipes.* New York: Morrow, 1997.

———. *CookWise: The Hows and Whys of Successful Cooking: The Secrets of Cooking Revealed.* New York: Morrow, 1997.

The Culinary Institute of America. *Baking and Pastry: Mastering the Art and Craft,* 2nd edition. Hoboken: Wiley, 2009.

———. *Garde Manger: The Art and Craft of the Cold Kitchen,* 4th edition. Hoboken: Wiley, 2012.

———. *Professional Chef,* 9th edition. Hoboken: Wiley, 2011.

———. *Remarkable Service,* 3rd edition. Hoboken: Wiley, 2014.

Fischer, John, and The Culinary Institute of America. *At Your Service: A Hands-On Guide to the Professional Dining Room.* Hoboken: Wiley, 2005.

Greenspan, Dorrie. *Baking with Julia.* New York: Morrow, 1996.

Magee, Harold. *On Food and Cooking: The Science and Lore of the Kitchen.* New York: Scribner, 2004.

Mattel, Bruce, and The Culinary Institute of America. *Catering: A Guide to Managing a Successful Business Operation.* Hoboken: Wiley, 2008.

Page, Karen, and Andrew Dornenburg. *The Flavor Bible: The Essential Guide to Culinary Creativity, Based on the Wisdom of America's Most Imaginative Chefs.* New York: Little, Brown, 2008.

Pépin, Jacques. *La Technique Fundamental Techniques of Cooking: An Illustrated Guide.* Fourth Printing. New York: NY Times Books, 1978.

Prudhomme, Paul. *Chef Paul Prudhomme's Louisiana Kitchen.* New York: Morrow, 1984.

Rosso, Julee, and Sheila Lukins. *The New Basics Cookbook.* New York: Workman, 1989.

———. *The Silver Palate Cookbook: Delicious Recipes, Menus, Tips, Lore from Manhattan's Celebrated Gourmet Food Shop.* New York: Workman, 1981.

———. *The Silver Palate Good Times Cookbook.* New York: Workman, 1985.

Shulman, Martha Rose, and The Culinary Institute of America. *Spain and the World Table.* New York: DK Publishing, 2008.

Willan, Anne. *Cooking with Wine.* New York: Harry N. Abrams, 2001.

RESOURCES

AMERICAN METALCRAFT, INC.
2074 George Street
Melrose Park, Illinois 60160-1515
800-333-9133

Your source for unique and reative food-service supplies, specializing in fine dining, catering, buffet service, and pizza supplies for restaurants, hotels, clubs, and resorts.

CAL-MIL
4079 Calle Platino
Oceanside, CA 92056-5805
800-321-9069
760-630-5100

CAL-MIL has it all: nine collections and thirty-six sections allowing food-service professionals to be inspired to create a fresh and organized display for food presentations, including beverages dispensers, action stations, chafer alternatives, ice housing, elevations, displays, and organizers.

CHICAGO METALLIC BAKEWARE
300 Knightsbridge Parkway, Suite 500
Lincolnshire, IL 60069
800-238-BAKE (2253)

Chicago Metallic has been crafting innovative equipment for professionals and serious home bakers for over 100 years. Their products are built for durability, to be depended on year after year.

CULINAIRE BY MIKON INTERNATIONAL, INC.
P.O. Box 577
Oswego, Illinois, 60543
866-830-9900

Culinaire designs and distributes unique banquet and tabletop serving and display pieces. Culinaire is recognized for quality and fresh design and is asked for by name. Culinaire also custom-designs unique pieces to meet your specific needs.

FORTESSA, INC.
22601 Davis Drive
Sterling, VA 20164
800-296-7508

Fortessa, Inc., is a leading designer, developer, and marketer of quality tableware for the high-end commercial food-service market globally, as well as for the luxury consumer market. Fortessa, Inc., offers flatware, glassware and tabletop accessories, a "total table" operation, and pioneered the concept of specialty dinnerware for the commercial food-service market with a "Cuisine Collection" of square, rectangular, and oval shapes.

FRONT OF THE HOUSE
9315 Park Drive
Miami Shores, FL 33138
305-757-7940

Front of the House is an authority on tabletop and presentation trends by designing and manufacturing smart, savvy, commercial-grade serving solutions, including all-encompassing dinnerware, buffet ware, and serve ware collections designed to be mixed and matched to create hip, streamlined style for all occasions.

LE CREUSET
877-418-5547

Visit Le Creuset, the makers of the world's finest French cookware, for cast-iron and stainless-steel cookware, bakeware, pots, pans, and kitchen and bar tools.

RIEGEL LINENS
51 Riegel Road
Johnston, SC 29832
800-845-2232

Riegel offers a complete line of quality table linen and accessories, including DiRoNA, Parnell, Beauti-Damask, Ultimate, Permalux, Premier, Monarch, and Premier-Damask. Banquet spaces come alive with conference cloth in fashion colors and table skirting in polyester and elegant designer fabrics. New products include Polyester Satin Band and RieNu, a new and exciting recycled polyester napkin. Riegel is making worry-free textiles for your dining rooms and for our earth.

SOUTHERN ALUMINUM
P.O. Box 884
Magnolia, AR 71754
800-221-0408

Maker of durable and lightweight aluminum folding tables, banquet tables, table trucks, event furniture, portable stages, laminate tables, and picnic tables.

TOP LINE APPLIANCE CENTER
576 N Avenue East
Westfield, NJ 07090
908-232-5200

Authorized New Jersey Dealer for all major kitchen appliance brands and models.

VIDACASA
1016 West Jackson Boulevard
Chicago, IL 60607
312-288-8631

The purpose of VIDACASA dining ware is to keep the food plate surface at 32°F/4°C for up to 6 hours without the use of external power. This innovative cooling feature ensures that delicate perishables like fresh seafood, Japanese raw food, cold cuts, salads, and even deserts are served freshly in all hotels, restaurants, and catering outlets.

WILLOW GROUP, LTD.
34 Clinton Street
Batavia, NY 14020
800-724-7300

Willow Group, Ltd., is the parent company of Willow Specialties, Avery Imports, and Skalny. This combination provides an extremely diversified product selection for your basket needs, packaging, floral, garden center, gift, food service, hotel and restaurant supply, home décor, and display.

EQUIPMENT REFERENCES

The photo on pages 4–5 features the following equipment: stainless-steel oval hammered bowls, stackable ornate wrought-iron chafer frames and kits, stainless-steel flame guards, brushed stainless-steel card holders by American Metalcraft, Inc. (see Resources, page 347).

The photo on pages 8–9 features the following equipment: wavy porcelain trays, stainless-steel rectangular hammered platters, black wood riser sets, brushed stainless-steel card holders, ornate wrought-iron chafer, three-tier rectangular "Step" stand, and rectangular melamine platters by American Metalcraft, Inc.; Summit portable single-zone induction cooktop with black Ceran smooth-top finish by Top Line Appliance Center (see Resources, page 347).

The photo on page 11 features the following equipment: round and rectangular metal nickel-finish stands and porcelain bowls by Willow Group, Ltd.; Mission chafer alternatives, cast-iron griddle with brackets, iron card holder, and melamine jars with hinge by CAL-MIL; Heritage covered square casserole by Le Creuset; Summit portable single-zone induction cooktop with black Ceran smooth-top finish by Top Line Appliance Center (see Resources, page 347).

The photo on page 13 features the following equipment: Elevation risers with Interlink Towers and slate serving/display stones and iron card holder by CAL-MIL (see Resources, page 347).

The photo on page 14 features the following equipment: Fiji rectangular bowl, Tela bone china dinnerware, and Schott Zwiesel glassware by Fortessa Tableware (see Resources, page 347).

The photo on page 15 features the following equipment: square glass and acrylic beverage dispensers by CAL-MIL and Schott Zwiesel champagne flutes by Fortessa Tableware (see Resources, page 347).

The photo on page 16 features the following equipment: acrylic ice housing by CAL-MIL and round porcelain bowls by Willow Group, Ltd. (see Resources, page 347).

The photo on page 28 features the following equipment: Elevation risers with Interlink Towers and slate serving/display stones by CAL-MIL (see Resources, page 347).

The photo on page 35 features the following equipment: Satin Swirl serpentine tables with tiers and spandex skirts by Southern Aluminum; brushed sign holder, metal risers, square canvas plates, knotted bamboo picks, small steel sampler footed bowl, upright stainless-steel sampler fork, Mod Ideal platter, and round footed sampler by Front of the House (see Resources, page 347).

The photo on page 36 features the following equipment: porcelain bowls, square bamboo lantern, round willow tray, oblong bamboo tray, oblong wood bowl, and aluminum leaf dish by Willow Group, Ltd. (see Resources, page 347).

The photo on page 37 features the following equipment: round metal nickel-finish stands, porcelain bowls, round granite, metal nickel-finish server stand, oval metal and porcelain server stand, oval porcelain platters, square bamboo lantern, round willow tray, oblong bamboo tray, oblong wood bowl, and aluminum leaf dish by Willow Group, Ltd. (see Resources, page 347).

The photo on page 38 features the following equipment: Fiji rectangular bowl and Schott Zwiesel glassware by Fortessa Tableware; Permalux cotton-blend Momie Weave by Riegel Linen (see Resources, page 347).

The photo on page 40 features the following equipment: rectangular wood tray on folding stand by Willow Group, Ltd. (see Resources, page 347).

The photo on page 41 features the following equipment: coppered linked bowls with inserts, copper linked risers, brushed sign holder, and Mod Ideal platters by Front of the House (see Resources, page 347).

The photo on page 42 features the following equipment: three-tier rectangular wrought-iron "Step" stand and rectangular melamine platters by American Metalcraft, Inc. (see Resources, page 347).

The photo on page 43 features the following equipment: nonstick frypan by Le Crueset; Summit portable single-zone induction cooktop with black Ceran smooth-top finish by Top Line Appliance Center (see Resources, page 347).

The photo on page 43 features the following equipment: coppered linked bowls with inserts, copper linked risers, and brushed sign holder by Front of the House (see Resources, page 347).

The photo on page 44 features the following equipment: bouillabaisse pots by Le Creuset; Mission chafer alternatives and iron card holders by CAL-MIL (see Resources, page 347).

The photo on page 44 features the following equipment: Tela bone china plate and Lucca stainless-steel serving spoon by Fortessa Tableware (see Resources, page 347).

The photo on page 45 features the following equipment: Petals plates by Fortessa Tableware (see Resources, page 347).

The photo on page 46 features the following equipment: oval, square, and rectangular cold food display systems by Vidacasa; square aluminum stands with platters and rectangular willow bottle basket by Willow Group, Ltd. (see Resources, page 347).

The photo on page 47 features the following equipment: aluminum stand and oval pewter and porcelain servers with bowls by Willow Group, Ltd.; cast-iron griddle with brackets by CAL-MIL (see Resources, page 347).

The photo on page 50 features the following equipment: ornate wrought-iron chafer by American Metalcraft, Inc. (see Resources, page 347).

The photo on page 51 features the following equipment: cold food display system by Vidacasa (see Resources, page 347).

The photo on pages 52–53 features the following equipment: oval pewter server with oval porcelain platters by Willow Group, Ltd.; bouillabaisse pots by Le Creuset; Mission chafer alternatives and iron card holders by CAL-MIL (see Resources, page 347).

The photo on page 54 features the following equipment: oblong bamboo tray, oblong wood bowl, aluminum leaf dish, and round granite and metal nickel-finish server by Willow Group, Ltd.; Satin Swirl serpentine tables with tiers by Southern Aluminum (see Resources, page 347).

The photo on page 55 features the following equipment: ornate wrought-iron chafers and brushed stainless-steel card holders by American Metalcraft, Inc.; nonstick frypan by Le Creuset; Summit portable single-zone induction cooktop with black Ceran smooth-top finish by Top Line Appliance Center (see Resources, page 347).

The photo on page 57 features the following equipment: coppered linked bowls with inserts, copper linked risers, and brushed sign holder by Front of the House; Satin Swirl serpentine table by Southern Aluminum (see Resources, page 347).

The photo on page 58 features the following equipment: wavy porcelain trays, stainless-steel oval hammered bowls, and stainless-steel flame guards by American Metalcraft, Inc. (see Resources, page 347).

The photo on page 60 features the following equipment: Ogive kettle by Le Crueset; Mission chafer alternatives and single brew stands by CAL-MIL; tableware by Fortessa Tableware (see Resources, page 347).

The photo on page 62 features the following equipment: Mission chafer alternatives and Mission induction frame by CAL-MIL; Summit portable single-zone induction cooktop with black Ceran smooth-top finish by Top Line Appliance Center; cassoulet dish and cast-iron crêpe pan by Le Crueset (see Resources, page 347).

The photo on page 63 features the following equipment: Mission chafer alternatives and Mission induction frame by CAL-MIL; Summit portable single-zone induction cooktop with black Ceran smooth-top finish by Top Line Appliance Center; cassoulet dish and cast-iron crêpe pan by Le Crueset (see Resources, page 347).

The photo on page 64 features the following equipment: acrylic ice housing by CAL-MIL and porcelain bowls by Willow Group, Ltd. (see Resources, page 347).

The photo on page 64 features the following equipment: acrylic ice housing by CAL-MIL; Schott Zwiesel glassware by Fortessa Tableware; porcelain bowls by Willow Group, Ltd. (see Resources, page 347).

The photo on page 65 features the following equipment: brushed sign holder and tiered holder with Kaleidoscope bowls by Front of the House; nonstick frypans by Le Crueset; Summit portable single-zone induction cooktop with black Ceran smooth-top finish by Top Line Appliance Center (see Resources, page 347).

The photo on page 65 features the following equipment: bouillabaisse pot by Le Crueset; Summit portable single-zone induction cooktop with black Ceran smooth-top finish by Top Line Appliance Center (see Resources, page 347).

The photo on page 68 features the following equipment: Satin Swirl buffet tables and spandex skirt by Southern Aluminum (see Resources, page 347).

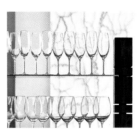

The photo on page 68 features the following equipment: three-tier full-frame riser with reclaimed wood shelf by CAL-MIL and Classico Tritan crystal Schott Zwiesel glasses by Fortessa Tableware (see Resources, page 347).

The photo on page 69 features the following equipment: RieNu recycled polyester table linen by Riegel Linen; Tela bone china dinnerware and Lucca faceted metalware by Fortessa Tableware (see Resources, page 347).

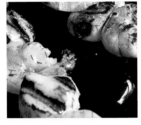

The photo on page 72 features the following equipment: Hot Rocks by Mikon International, Inc. (see Resources, page 347).

The photo on page 73 features the following equipment: nonstick frypan by Le Creuset; Mission induction frame by CAL-MIL; Summit portable single-zone induction cooktop with black Ceran smooth-top finish by Top Line Appliance Center (see Resources, page 347).

The photo on page 74 features the following equipment: stainless-steel rectangular hammered platter and stainless-steel flame guard by American Metalcraft, Inc. (see Resources, page 347).

The photo on page 75 features the following equipment: tall glass sampler by Front of the House (see Resources, page 347).

The photo on page 76 features the following equipment: looped handled tasting spoons on stainless-steel tasting spoon display by Fortessa Tableware (see Resources, page 347).

The photo on page 76 features the following equipment: Accentz stackable square pass plate and Classico Tritan crystal glass tableware by Fortessa Tableware (see Resources, page 347).

The photo on page 78 features the following equipment: brushed sign holder and tiered holder with Kaleidoscope bowls by Front of the House; nonstick frypans by Le Creuset; Summit portable single-zone induction cooktop with black Ceran smooth-top finish by Top Line Appliance Center (see Resources, page 347).

The photo on page 79 features the following equipment: oval, square, and rectangular cold food display systems by Vidacasa (see Resources, page 347).

The photo on page 82 features the following equipment: Summit portable single-zone induction cooktop with black Ceran smooth-top finish by Top Line Appliance Center; Flare Arctic bowl and Kaleidoscope slanted bowl by Front of the House; Satin Swirl buffet tables with tiers and spandex skirt by Southern Aluminum (see Resources, page 347).

The photo on page 87 features the following equipment: metal risers, square canvas plates, and upright stainless-steel sampler fork by Front of the House (see Resources, page 347).

The photo on page 88 features the following equipment: brushed sign holder, stainless-steel tasting tower, Mod Ideal platters, brushed sign holder, metal risers, square canvas plates, round footed sampler, tall glass sampler, 1.5 oz stainless-steel and porcelain mug, 3 1/2-inch tagine by Front of the House; Satin Swirl serpentine tables with tiers and spandex skirt by Southern Aluminum (see Resources, page 347).

The photo on page 94 features the following equipment: Plaza rectangular platter by Fortessa Tableware (see Resources, page 347).

The photo on page 95 features the following equipment: oval porcelain platter by Willow Group, Ltd. and Satin Swirl buffet table by Southern Aluminum (see Resources, page 347).

The photo on page 98 features the following equipment: Plaza pedestal squares by Fortessa Tableware (see Resources, page 347).

The photo on page 99 features the following equipment: Tavola Fortaluxe Superwhite platter by Fortessa Tableware and Satin Swirl buffet table by Southern Aluminum (see Resources, page 347).

The photo on page 103 features the following equipment: Mission chafer alternatives, bamboo bench riser, bamboo cube/rectangle riser, and three-tier full-frame rise with bamboo shelves by CAL-MIL; platters by Fortessa Tableware; square aluminum stand and steel spheres by Willow Group, Ltd., (see Resources, page 347).

The photo on page 108 features the following equipment: slate serving stone by CAL-MIL (see Resources, page 347).

The photo on page 111 features the following equipment: cast-iron griddle with brackets by CAL-MIL and Satin Swirl buffet table by Southern Aluminum (see Resources, page 347).

The photo on page 112 features the following equipment: Tavola plate by Fortessa Tableware (see Resources, page 347).

The photo on page 118 features the following equipment: oblong bamboo tray by Willow Group, Ltd. (see Resources, page 347).

The photo on page 121 features the following equipment: glass cone with square glass sampler by Front of the House (see Resources, page 347).

The photo on page 124 features the following equipment: double tasting spoon by Front of the House (see Resources, page 347).

The photo on page 127 features the following equipment: coppered linked bowls with inserts, copper linked risers, Mod Ideal platter, and round footed sampler by Front of the House (see Resources, page 347).

The photo on page 128 features the following equipment: Kyoto 9-square taster by Fortessa Tableware (see Resources, page 347).

The photo on page 136 features the following equipment: aluminum leaf dish by Willow Group, Ltd. (see Resources, page 347).

The photo on page 141 features the following equipment: round footed sampler by Front of the House (see Resources, page 347).

The photo on page 153 features the following equipment: Plaza deep square bowls by Fortessa Tableware (see Resources, page 347).

The photo on page 156 features the following equipment: oval porcelain platter by Willow Group, Ltd. (see Resources, page 347).

The photo on page 162 features the following equipment: oval porcelain server by Willow Group, Ltd. (see Resources, page 347).

The photo on page 167 features the following equipment: Ojo platter by Fortessa Tableware (see Resources, page 347).

The photo on page 168 features the following equipment: Temptationz Tini-Martini glasses by Fortessa Tableware (see Resources, page 347).

The photo on page 172 features the following equipment: Cielo oval b&b plates by Fortessa Tableware (see Resources, page 347).

The photo on page 175 features the following equipment: oval porcelain platter by Willow Group, Ltd. (see Resources, page 347).

The photo on page 187 features the following equipment: wavy porcelain tray by American Metalcraft, Inc. (see Resources, page 347).

The photo on page 188 features the following equipment: nonstick 6-cup giant muffin pan by Chicago Metallic Bakeware (see Resources, page 347).

The photo on page 190 features the following equipment: stainless-steel rectangular hammered platter by American Metalcraft, Inc. (see Resources, page 347).

The photo on page 197 features the following equipment: Cielo bone china plates and Schott Zwiesel glassware by Fortessa Tableware (see Resources, page 347).

The photo on page 200 features the following equipment: Plaza rectangular plate by Fortessa Tableware (see Resources, page 347).

The photo on page 203 features the following equipment: Acqua Vortex bowl by Fortessa Tableware (see Resources, page 347).

The photo on page 207 features the following equipment: mini cocottes by Le Creuset (see Resources, page 347).

The photo on page 208 features the following equipment: Cielo bone china bowl by Fortessa Tableware (see Resources, page 347).

The photo on page 212 features the following equipment: cast-iron griddle with brackets by CAL-MIL (see Resources, page 347).

The photo on page 216 includes an oval porcelain platter by Willow Group, Inc.

The photo on page 223 features the following equipment: oval porcelain platter and round nickel servers with round white porcelain bowls by Willow Group, Ltd. (see Resources, page 347).

The photo on page 224 features the following equipment: Mod Ideal platter by Front of the House (see Resources, page 347).

The photo on page 227 features the following equipment: oval porcelain platter by Willow Group, Ltd. (see Resources, page 347).

The photo on page 231 features the following equipment: Mission chafer alternatives, cast-iron griddle with brackets by CAL-MIL (see Resources, page 347).

The photo on page 232 features the following equipment: ornate wrought-iron chafers by American Metalcraft, Inc. (see Resources, page 347).

The photo on page 235 features the following equipment: 3½-inch tagine by Front of the House (see Resources, page 347).

The photo on page 236 features the following equipment: Mission chafer alternatives by CAL-MIL (see Resources, page 347).

The photo on page 239 features the following equipment: oval porcelain platter by Willow Group, Ltd. (see Resources, page 347).

The photo on page 241 features the following equipment: roasting pan by Le Creuset (see Resources, page 347).

EQUIPMENT REFERENCES

The photo on page 250 features the following equipment: Ojo platter by Fortessa Tableware (see Resources, page 347).

The photo on pages 260–261 features the following equipment: 12-cup mini popover pan by Chicago Metallic Bakeware (see Resources, page 347).

The photo on page 269 features the following equipment: nonstick large jelly-roll pan by Chicago Metallic Bakeware (see Resources, page 347).

The photo on page 275 features the following equipment: square aluminum cake stand by Willow Group, Ltd. (see Resources, page 347).

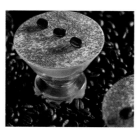

The photo on page 279 features the following equipment: Temptationz Tini-Martini glasses by Fortessa Tableware (see Resources, page 347).

The photo on page 280 features the following equipment: Tavola plates by Fortessa Tableware (see Resources, page 347).

The photo on page 285 features the following equipment: plate and bowl by Fortessa Tableware (see Resources, page 347).

The photo on page 286 features the following equipment: Kyoto 9-square taster by Fortessa Tableware (see Resources, page 347).

The photo on page 294 features the following equipment: stainless-steel oval hammered bowls by American Metalcraft, Inc. (see Resources, page 347).

The photo on page 301 features the following equipment: rectangular glass platter by Willow Group, Ltd. (see Resources, page 347).

INDEX

Numbers in *italics* indicate illustrations

P